General Sir Walter Walker, KCB, CBE, DSO, was the NATO
Commander-in-Chief Allied Forces, Northern Europe 1968-72 when he
retired from the Army after 40 years service.

His earlier appointments included being Deputy Chief of Staff in charge of
Plans, Operations and Intelligence, Headquarters Allied Forces Central
Europe and General Officer Commanding-in-Chief, Northern Command in
England.

He was awarded the KCB in January 1968, the CBE during the Malayan
Emergency in 1959, the DSO in the Burma Campaign against the Japanese
in 1945, a Bar to the DSO in 1953 when commanding his battalion against
the Communist terrorists in the Malayan Emergency, and a second Bar to
the DSO in 1965 when he was a Director of Borneo Operations, and
Commander of all British and Commonwealth forces in the four-year
campaign against Indonesian Confrontation.

Since leaving the Army, he has consistently warned of the Soviet global
military build-up and the weakness of the West's strategic position on the
flanks in Scandinavia and the Cape Route, and has travelled extensively in
Africa.

The Next Domino?

General Sir Walter Walker,
K.C.B., C.B.E., D.S.O.

*Former NATO Commander-in-Chief
Allied Forces Northern Europe*

CORGI BOOKS

A DIVISION OF TRANSWORLD PUBLISHERS LTD

THE NEXT DOMINO?

A CORGI BOOK 0 552 99020 5

Originally published in Great Britain by The Covenant Publishing Co. Ltd.

PRINTING HISTORY

Covenant edition published 1980
Corgi edition published 1982

Corgi Books are published by Transworld Publishers Ltd.,
Century House, 61-63 Uxbridge Road, Ealing, London W5 5SA

Made and printed in Great Britain by
The Guernsey Press Co. Ltd., Guernsey, Channel Islands.

For My Former Comrades in Arms

Acknowledgements

My Wife, who has borne the heat and burden of the day.
Mrs. Barbara Newman, who did all the typing and without whose dedication the book could never have been produced.

Quoted articles:
Andrew Alexander, *NOW!* Magazine, London.
Professor Ronald Hilton, Stanford University, U.S.A.
Clare Hollingworth, *The Daily Telegraph,* London.
Caroline Moorehead, *The Times,* London.
Anthony Shrimsley, *NOW!* Magazine, London.
Martin Spring's South African Newsletter, South Africa.
The Economist, London.
U.S. News & World Report, U.S.A.

Charts, maps and cartoons:
Camera Press, London.
Cincinnati Enquirer, U.S.A.
Destiny Editorial Letter Service, U.S.A.
Newsweek, The International Newsmagazine.
NOW! Magazine, London.
Pretoria News, South Africa.
St. Louis Globe-Democrat, U.S.A.
Sunday Express, London.
Sunday Times, London.
Sunday Times Business News, London.
The Argus, South Africa.
The Christian Science Monitor, U.S.A.
The Coalition For Peace Through Strength, U.S.A.
The Daily News, South Africa.
The Daily Telegraph, London.
The Times, Oman Supplement, London.
Time, The Weekly Newsmagazine, International.
U.S. News & World Report, U.S.A.
War Monthly, London.
Washington Star, U.S.A.

Contents

Acknowledgements   vii

List of charts and maps   xi

Foreword   xiii

Preface   xv

1	The Balance of power	1
2	Russia's Master Plan	11
3	The Arc of Crisis	19
4	America — No longer a 'Paper Tiger'?	27
5	Afghanistan	43
6	Pakistan, Pre — 27th December 1979	68
7	Pakistan, Post — 27th December 1979	90
8	Myth of 'Islamic Bomb'?	104
9	Iran	118
10	Oman — South Yemen	129
11	Saudi Arabia	134
12	Gulf Sheikdoms	138
13	Turkey	141
14	Indian Ocean	151
15	India	164
16	Yugoslavia	171
17	China	180
18	Zimbabwe — Rhodesia	188
19	Norway and Denmark	216
20	Unconventional War	230
21	Other Flash Points	247
22	Peace, War or Surrender?	261
23	The Solution for the Survival of the West	276

Epilogue   293

Appendices

A	How the Soviet Union Exploited Détente	338
B	The Rebellious Tribe in Russia's Path	340
C	List of Conflicts India and Pakistan	342
D	America's Abortive Operation in Iran	345
E	The 'Neutron Bomb'	348

Addendum   350

Index   356

Charts and Maps

Charts

1	The West's Jugular Vein	5
2	Russian Geo-strategic Thrusts	23
3	Monitoring Moscow's ICBM's	178
4	Blitzkrieg War	226
5	U.S. Military Inferiority	262
6	The Rival Missiles	279
7	The Global Grab	292

Maps

The Strait of Hormuz	14
Soviet advances in Afghanistan	55
U.S. present response capability	65
Afghanistan and Pakistan	79
Prize of the Gulf	135
Turkey	149
The American build-up in the Indian Ocean	158
Yugoslavia's population problem	172
Barrel to barrel — China and Russia	186
Russia's Arctic superfort at Murmansk	223
Cuba's world-wide sphere of influence	248
North and South Korea	255
East Caprivi, Southern Africa	303
Baluchistan	341

Diagrams

Explosion effects of a Standard Battlefield Atomic Weapon	348
Explosion effects of the 'Neutron Bomb'	349

Foreword

By The Rt. Hon. Julian Amery, P.C., M.P.,
Former Minister of State for Foreign and Commonwealth Affairs

During the nineteen twenties, while still a small boy, I was taken to watch a Royal procession from Victoria Station to Buckingham Palace. Standing near me in the crowd were two working men and the following dialogue ensued:

"Who's that in coach with our King?"
"Its Amanullah."
"Oh wot does 'e do?"
"Well 'e rules Arfghanistan."
"Oh, who rules the other arf?"

Vox populi, vox dei. My two neighbours may not have known it but it was, then, a major object of British policy to ensure that Great Britain's influence in Kabul was at least equal to that of Russia's. Afghanistan and Iran were, indeed, the checker-boards on which 'the great game' was played: it was the objective of Great Britain to keep these countries as barriers against Russian expansion towards the warm-waters of the Persian Gulf and the Indian Ocean.

After the British withdrawal from India, the United States took on the task and, with American support, Iran became the main bastion of the Free World in the Middle East. Meanwhile, American aid kept Soviet influence in Afghanistan in check. Then in 1978, exactly as the Shah of Iran had warned his Cento allies, a pro-Soviet *coup* brought President Tarakki to power in Kabul and turned Afghanistan from a bufferstate between East and West into virtually another Soviet republic. The Soviet invasion of the country last December only completed the process.

To be sure, the Soviets are finding the Afghan tribesmen to be a fairly indigestible meal. If the British still ruled India − or if the United States could decide how to make their influence felt − Moscow could doubtless be made to disgorge. As things are, the odds are stacked heavily against the gallant Afghan resistance.

The April 1978 Tarakki *coup* in Afghanistan was one of the major factors leading to the revolution in Iran − *a domino process.* Iran has not yet passed into the Soviet orbit; but it has already disengaged from the Western camp and seems on the verge of disintegration. The wider consequences of these developments have a geo-political significance. Coming on top of the earlier Soviet takeover of Aden and Ethiopia, the invasion of Afghanistan is drawing an ever tighter noose round the immensely rich, but largely defenceless, oilbearing states of the Gulf. The survival of these States is already in question, *and so is that of the industrial West and Japan.* Gulf oil is the lifeblood of the Free World and will be for many years to come.

But there is one piece on the checker-board that has received little attention – Pakistan. The military defeat of Pakistan, its internal political feuds and its ethnic divisions have earned the country a bad press. Yet the fact is, its geographical position, together with the martial character of its people, make it a significant factor in the gathering storm. It could follow Iran into disintegration, or it could become an invaluable partner in a Western strategy to stem the tide of Soviet Imperialism.

At the time of writing the main threat to the West centres on the oilbearing Gulf. But of course, this is only the immediate manifestation of the global threat which Soviet Imperialism presents. General Walker's military experience is global too. He served in the subcontinent as a younger officer and knows its peoples and languages well. In the mid-1960s he secured Britain's victory in the confrontation with Indonesia. He was the NATO Commander in Scandinavia and Schleswig-Holstein and has since travelled extensively in Africa and other areas of the world.

A recent visit to Pakistan set the alarm bells ringing louder than ever, in his mind. On his return, and working long hours, he set down his impressions of the immediate threat to the Gulf and the Indian Ocean. He has done so, moreover, against the broader background of the threat which Soviet Imperialism increasingly presents, not just in South Asia, but throughout the world. General Walker writes with long experience of war and high command – but also with the overpowering sense of urgency of one who really *is* ringing the alarm bell. There is nothing alarmist about this devastatingly factual book. *We shall ignore its warning, and its message, at our peril!*

Julian Amery

112 Eaton Square,
London, S.W.1.

July, 1980.

Preface

The Russian programme for global domination is on schedule and in the military sphere is moving towards the point of no return. Notwithstanding the report of "experts" to the British House of Commons on the Soviet invasion of Afghanistan, published on 5th August, 1980, which cleared the Russians of a grand strategy motive, this Soviet move represented an open declaration that the international balance of power had shifted. In fact, since the NATO meeting last December, a countdown for conflict has been in evidence – set in motion by Russia – which the West must now recognize and plan to meet with immediate resolve.

To the confounding of those who cried "peace" when they were in fact promoting appeasement, it has become evident that the Soviets are not bound by any idealistic definition of détente, despite the solemn agreements they signed with America in 1972 and 1973. They will take advantage of any faltering in the West from their present position of increasing military superiority. In a move which has potentially far reaching consequences, Russia has put forward a claim to the right of intervention in areas of a political or military "vacuum". Moscow is undoubtedly laying the groundwork for intervention in new areas such as strife-torn Iran.

We are confronted by an international situation of desperate gravity. Russia is at this moment preparing to make a bid for control of the Free World's jugular vein along the Persian Gulf and Cape supply route, with the aim of reducing Western Europe to subservience and ultimately the United States itself. It is known that President Brezhnev advised a Somalian "friend" that Russia's strategic objectives were the Gulf and the whole of Southern Africa. He described them as *"the two essential Treasure houses of the West"*. Once Russia has them, all else will automatically be added. Another factor is driving Russia towards the Persian Gulf. By about 1985 we will have reached a situation where both superpowers will depend on Middle East oil – and there will only be enough for one of them.

A decisive point is fast approaching for the West. The Soviet Union is building a military machine of such dominating force that it might, by its very threats, conquer *politically* without having to be committed to all-out action. This is where the argument of the nuclear disarmers falls flat! It is not merely the danger of nuclear war that we should fear. Even worse is the eternal humiliation of those who through fear of it, would become subject to the will of those who not only threaten but are prepared to implement a nuclear strike.

By the end of 1982, Western Europe alone will be faced with more than 1,000 Russian nuclear warheads. Human experience confirms that, when confronted with a choice between surrender and death, the majority tend to choose surrender. The Soviet leaders are clearly convinced that this kind of capitulation in Western Europe is highly probable and they may further calculate that a US administration will "freeze", when it comes to placing American cities at risk in order to defend Europe.

It is also vital for us to realize that, should the nuclear threat fail, Soviet military doctrine involves a clearly defined concept for winning a war in Europe in which "all arms" would be used and all types of weapons, nuclear, chemical and conventional, would be employed, if necessary, from the beginning of hostilities, depending on the circumstances prevailing.

Since the Soviet Union achieved virtual military superiority over the West, an entirely different doctrine and strategy has been needed by the NATO alliance to meet the Warsaw Pact's war-winning strategy, which would not necessarily lead to a strategic nuclear exchange between the Soviet Union and the United States. Accordingly, it is high time that the NATO alliance up-dated its doctrine and strategy.

In this authoritative and brilliantly written book, General Sir Walter Walker unfolds the whole geo-strategic and geo-political threat to the West, posed by Soviet Imperialism in its onward march as so powerfully evidenced by the brutal Russian assault on Afghanistan during 1980.

It is doubtful if another authority could have written with the same degree of knowledge and experience of war and high command – particularly in respect of South Asia and Africa – where the levels of conflict now being employed range from communist guerrilla insurgency to large scale Soviet operations. The author is also numbered among the very few military men, later to experience high-rank, who actually witnessed a nuclear explosion while in command, on the ground, during the atomic trials at Maralinga, South Australia in 1956.

General Walker exposes the inadequacy of Western strategic thinking and the misconception as to what is really happening around us, as it is, set into the context of what we have outlined above, coupled with the Soviet preparation of complete and overwhelming military superiority over the West. He brings us to the realization that the Western World is confronted by an unprecedented siege of its civilization. He explains in great detail what must be done – with speed and determination – to forestall disaster of an epochal order.

The author sees the 'domino' concept proven, as country after country has become engulfed by the tide of communist infiltration and inevitable revolution. He discusses the situation in many of the "domino" countries and exposes the lamentable Western response to the process which continues virtually uncontested. He identifies the pivotal strategic points upon which the conflict could be turned against the Soviets in their bid for world domination.

Beyond all doubt, the present position of the West is as serious as it possibly could be. Soviet strategists have planned for just such a "window of opportunity" which, as a result of unbelievable military and political miscalculation by the Western leadership, is now wide open. With this situation in view, General Walker's solemn *tocsin* must surely rank as one of the most imperative warnings ever given to the British nation and to the Western World. The announcement on 15th July, 1980, by the British Secretary of State for Defence, that the Trident-1 (C4) submarine-launched ballistic missile system is to be bought from the United States to replace Polaris as Britain's strategic deterrent in the mid-1990s, seemed not to take account of the perilous situation that almost certainly will arise during the first half of the 1980s.

There is no evidence in view at this time that the fortress state of Soviet Russia – *the declared enemy of the West* – is going to wait for four or five years for the United States – and much longer in the case of Britain – so that the Free World can recover a position of strategic equality. Indeed, only those incapable of informed judgment could believe that Russia will allow its present massive conventional and increasing nuclear superiority to slip from its grasp.

Since the NATO decision on 12th December, 1979, to up-date theatre nuclear weapons, Soviet productivity in the nuclear field has increased alarmingly. One new SS20, the Russian mobile missile which can cover targets anywhere in Europe, is coming into service *every five days*. The West is now rushing to bolster its European defences with Cruise missiles and Pershing 2 rockets, but these will not be in place until 1983. *It could be too late.* In any event, General Walker believes that Britain should have its own Cruise missile delivery system – and this with lightning speed. A Cruise missile air-launched system consisting of seven aircraft each carrying 20 Cruise missiles could deliver more warheads, more accurately and at about one-seventh of the cost of Trident.

With stark clarity, General Walker exposes the nonsense of NATO's whole strategy of deterrence and delivers the chilling thought that, unless the necessary degree of uncertainty is maintained in Soviet calculations – by for instance the introduction of more independent options for Britain – Kremlin imperialists can afford to gamble on the belief that the American President will back down on the defence of Western Europe in the face of nuclear blackmail or blitzkrieg assault.

With the force of argument and considered judgment of one who has the measure of the whole geo-strategic threat to the West, the author states that the period 1982–85, which we shall enter less than two years from now, will prove to be *the* most crucial phase of world history.

Individual action to alert the peoples of the West to the perilous times that face us all, must become the consuming objective of every citizen whether small or great.

"Stand in The Battle"

Throughout the long history of the Hebraic Celto-Saxon peoples, on all occasions when they ceased to honour their God and to walk in His paths, they were confronted and brought low by more powerful nations, mainly from the north. These nations, in so doing, arrayed themselves against the Kingdom of peace inaugurated by Jehovah Himself, Who used them as a punitive agency to correct His Servant people Israel, under the terms of His age-old Covenant with them. It was His proclaimed method of bringing them back into the bond of His Divine purpose – for them and for His whole human family.

In the appearance of the present great East-West confrontation, we are witnessing the outworking of the same God-prescribed principle, expanded now on a global scale. Let there be no mistake in this. Celto-Saxondom is coming under the punishment of Almighty God for its wholesale violation of their Covenants with Him which it has permitted – even encouraged – in its national life. The final breach outrages the tenants of God's Son, our Lord Jesus Christ.

Fearful though it now is, even greater menace threatens, as iniquitous practices of a God-rejecting world approach their zenith in opposition to the Divine Purpose. They are being submitted to the blows of the present day "hammer of the nations". The Soviet Union, an empire whose expanse dwarfs even that of ancient Rome, is preparing to launch itself into the pivotal decade of world history. The greatest and most evil affliction the world has known, the Marxist U.S.S.R. – *the colossus of the north* – is at this moment taking decisions which will dislocate the whole community of nations. Russia today is an embattled power in a state of advanced transition to what may well be described as the *kingdom of Satan*.

Recognizing the inevitability of events which must ensue, it seems now an inescapable probability that our Israel peoples in the West will remain transfixed, as if watching a television drama. They are, in the main, completely unaware of their duty which says that, as His Kingdom people, they are required by Almighty God to *defend* His Cause. This is nothing less than the establishment of His Kingdom on earth, in accordance with His proclaimed will.

The Divine injunction for the Christian Nations of modern Israel is to *"stand in the battle in the day of the Lord"*, discarding the pathetic pleas of the disarmers and pacifists who, although no doubt sincere, are utterly adrift when it comes to understanding the reality of the eternal struggle between good and evil in world events. They fail to see how history is unfolding itself to reveal God's Plan for His human race. It is lamentable that our spiritual leaders – who surely should have the understanding of God's purpose – seem so lacking in Gospel insight. It appears that some of them would even *desire* to see their peoples defenceless and immobile in the face of the threatening military scourge.

We affirm that we do not support this peace-at-any-price palaver. General Walker's theme strongly accords with the *Kingdom* objectives of our own Movement,* which in respect of the Defence of the Realm are stated as follows:

(a)   The Biblical principle that "when a strong man armed keepeth his house, his goods are in peace" – Our Lord's own advice;

(b)   That our national defence be brought to and kept at the highest level, in acknowledgment of the first priority – a believing and praying administration and people standing in the whole armour of God;

(c)   That universal national service in peace time with voluntary service for active duties be introduced.

We support whole-heartedly General Walker's sombre conclusion: "What is at stake is not only the whole future of the West, but civilization itself and the Christian West as we know it".

It is our main tenet that the Christian nations of the West have a special role to fulfil in upholding a Divinely-ordered civilization. We believe that the warning which the author delivers far transcends the context of party politics and that our peoples should now be impelled to a full realization of the consequences of their present God-forsaking ways.

How far the Soviet Military Machine will be allowed to roll, will, on His Holy Word be determined by the degree of abomination that we as a people and a nation continue to offer to the Lord in transgressions – *and the speed with which our peoples turn to Him in prayer and penitence.*

We need to pray *now* that Almighty God will restrain the winds of war rising in the east during the next three years and, of even greater *importance, by the power of His Spirit, move to inspire the strengthening of the spiritual and military defences of His People.*

— The Publishers in Great Britain

* Now entering our 62nd year of witness. During this crucial period in world history we have been honoured to name among our ranks a stalwart company of noble defenders of the Faith, among the highest in the lands comprising our Celto-Saxon Family of Christian Israel Nations.

CHAPTER
1

The Balance of Power

With the Soviet Union's aggression of Afghanistan, this is the third time during my life that the peace of the world is in peril as a result of *first*, the neglect by political and military leaders in the face of an obvious military threat, and *second*, the listless and suicidal indifference to which the majority of people have sunk.

Eleven years ago, when I was Commander-in-Chief of Allied Forces Northern Europe, I made the following pronouncement and have repeated it at frequent intervals, but to no avail:

"Russia's *grand design* is to outflank Europe at sea from the south as well as the north, take control of the sources of oil supply, dominate the sea routes in the Indian Ocean, South Atlantic and North Atlantic, gain dominance of Western Europe and then dictate to the West. The West fails to understand that behind the endless Arab-Israeli conflict stands a totalitarian, expansionist, powerful Russia whose relentless determination is to take over the Horn of Africa, Aden and South Yemen, which dominate the approaches to the Red Sea; spread out in the Persian Gulf from the Iraqi Naval Base at the head of the Gulf; join its substantial fleets in the Mediterranean and the Indian Ocean; dominate the whole of Africa; control the Cape Route; extend her influence into South Asia and the Far East, and totally change the whole balance of power.

"Russia, whether by blackmail, revolutionary war by proxy, or by brute force, intends to absorb the sources of oil supply and the whole of Southern Africa, and thus deprive the West of vital minerals and oil and control of Europe's lifeline round the Cape. Southern Africa and the Red Sea and Gulf States hold key bases of fundamental strategic importance to the control of the sea lanes and trade routes in the South Atlantic and Indian Oceans. The possession of these bases would give the Soviet Union overwhelming superiority in global strategy.

"What the West will suffer as a result of any Arab cutback in oil supplies is a fraction of what would happen if the Gulf or the Cape Route were to be blockaded".

Never has the world situation been so grave and dangerous since World War II. Events are showing and will continue to prove that my

1

repeated warnings about the menace of Russia's massive military might and her aggressive and expansionist intentions have been a modest understatement.

Appeasement – now known as détente – was the policy of the British and Allied Governments before the Second World War. It was a futile appeasement which led to destruction on an unimaginable scale. Hundreds of thousands of brave men and women fought heroically for a better world. They laid down their lives for justice and freedom. What is happening around us today is an insult to their memory. Until Russia's rape of Afghanistan every heart of the political leaders of the West has been faint and every head has been sick.

In her drive for world domination Russia has a carefully planned global strategy based on flexibility and keeping her options open ready to exploit every opportunity. Her short and long term intentions are governed by the following fifteen "Commandments" all of which should be indelibly imprinted in the minds of our political and military leaders, most of whom have been sleep-walking their way through one crisis after another:

1. To establish régimes sympathetic to them in strategically important theatres outside Europe, such as Vietnam, Cuba, the Caribbean, South America, Libya, the Horn of Africa, Iran, Afghanistan, Turkey, South Yemen, Saudi Arabia, the Gulf States, Angola and Southern Africa.

    South Africa and the Gulf oil States are vital bridgeheads for the Kremlin's ultimate goal, which is the United States itself and the destruction of a free capitalistic society.

2. Whenever possible to use the technique of revolutionary war by proxy forces, using mercenary hatchetmen from Cuba, Vietnam, the Warsaw Pact States – in particular East Germany – and from communist-indoctrinated trained and armed terrorist forces – as in Rhodesia – to do their dirty work for them.

3. To neutralize Western Europe, partly by denying it access to oil and critical raw materials.

4. To dominate the sea routes in the North and South Atlantic, the Mediterranean, the Indian Ocean and the Pacific.

5. To split the North Atlantic Treaty Organization (NATO).

6. To remove American forces from Europe.

7. To manipulate unilateral disarmament in the West.

8.   Then to move on to the total domination and absorption of Western Europe, first by softening us up through subversion and the disruption of ordered society before having to fire a shot in international war.

9.   To accomplish the encirclement of China.

10.   To achieve the isolation of the United States. It was Lenin who said – "We must communize the world, and encircle the United States and, if they do not surrender, we shall destroy them."

11.   Having already obtained conventional and chemical military superiority, to achieve strategic, Euro-theatre and battlefield tactical nuclear superiority, *not* parity.

12.   To reject specifically the Western doctrine that nuclear war means suicide or, in the NATO jargon "mutually assured destruction." Soviet military literature explicitly emphasizes this and Soviet forces are now structured to fight, survive and win a nuclear war.

13.   Under the umbrella of growing nuclear superiority, upper space and ocean bed technical superiority, conventional and chemical military superiority, plus gunboat diplomacy, to exert political pressure from a position of overwhelming military strength on land, on and under the oceans of the world, in the air and in the upper atmosphere.

14.   To keep immediately available and immediately useable, ready for instant take off – that is without prior reinforcement or warning – vastly superior military forces in key areas, thus giving her a crushing preponderance of conventional and nuclear superiority, thereby enabling her to speak from a position of great strength.

15.   With this big stick, which is growing bigger all the time, to threaten, intimidate and resort to political blackmail, culminating either in an ultimatum or in outright naked aggression, as in Afghanistan.

The balance of power *outside* the NATO area has already changed just as dramatically against the West, as it has *within* the NATO area, if not more so.

In the Western Pacific while the Soviet Far Eastern Fleet continues to grow, the U.S. have run down the Seventh Fleet there to a point where it no longer has the capability of protecting merchant shipping and keeping the sea lanes open. American forces in South Korea have also been run down and it is only recently that their total withdrawal has been halted.

3

In South-East Asia the Treaty Organization has been dissolved. The United States have withdrawn altogether from Vietnam and Thailand and have retained only a residual presence in the Philippines. Britain, Australia and New Zealand have left Malaysia and Singapore. Britain has even abandoned the stepping stones of Gan and Masira so that there is no longer a secure East-about route from Europe to South-East Asia. Meanwhile the Soviet Union has turned Vietnam and, through Vietnam, all Indo-China into a powerful base for Soviet Imperialism.

In the Middle East the situation is even worse. Britain has withdrawn from Aden and the Gulf. There is no longer a British nuclear capability in Cyprus. The Iranian revolution has destroyed the CENTO Alliance. All that remain to the West are the present slender facilities afforded by Diego Garcia to Britain and the U.S., and by Djibouti to France.

By contrast Iraq could replace Iran as the Gendarme of the Gulf, and Iraq of course is tied to the Soviet Union by treaty and equipped with Soviet tanks and bombers on a scale only slightly inferior to that when the Shah was the ruler of Iran. Meanwhile, to the South of the Gulf, Aden with its great harbour and airfield are in Soviet hands. So across the Red Sea is Ethiopia. Passage through the Bab el Mandeb now depends upon a Soviet "by your leave". While safe passage through the narrow Strait of Hormuz – the greatest economic choke point in the world – could be blocked by military action in a number of ways.

With Russia securely established in Afghanistan, the strategic highway to the mouth of the Gulf, is Pakistan. Russia is quite capable of striking south across the border, heading for the warmwaters of the Arabian Sea. Therefore the West's strategy must cater for this worst case and not be based on wishful thinking. The Soviet Union has long cast covetous eyes on the Pakistan ports of Karachi and Gwadar and the five hundred miles long strategically vital Baluchistan coast line.

Now that the chips are down and Pakistan has become a buffer state against communist expansion, she will no longer have to stand alone, reviled and neglected, as if of only peripheral interest to the West.

In Central Africa, the Soviets have converted Angola into a Colony and Mozambique into a Protectorate. Both territories became launching pads for terrorist operations against South West Africa and Rhodesia. The Soviet longer term objective is plainly control of South Africa and the Cape Route – yet Britain has abandoned the Royal Navy's facilities at Simonstown. To compound this act of folly Britain with the United States maintained sanctions against Rhodesia and imposed an arms embargo on South Africa, the only two countries in the area with forces capable of resisting the onward march of Soviet Imperialism.

In the Mediterranean, Algeria and Libya have been drawn increasingly into the Soviet orbit. Britain has withdrawn from Malta thus

4

THE WEST'S JUGULAR VEIN

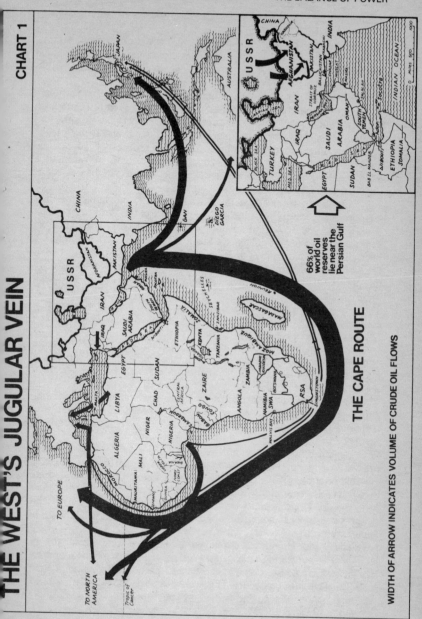

THE CAPE ROUTE

66% of world oil reserves lie near the Persian Gulf

WIDTH OF ARROW INDICATES VOLUME OF CRUDE OIL FLOWS

abandoning its harbour, airfields and strategic control of the narrow waters between Italy and Tunisia.

We have arrived at a situation where the West is, or soon will be, inferior to the Soviet Union in strategic nuclear and conventional capability both in the NATO and in other regions scarcely less vital to the survival of the Free World.

Of course the West has the technological and the economic strength to recover parity with the Soviet Bloc and even to re-establish preponderance. The West is superior in technology, wealth and manpower and thus far better placed to stand the strain. It might even help their unemployment problem. But the process of developing, producing and deploying new weapons systems and of raising the additional forces to man them must take time. And it is in the element of time that the real danger lies.

This is not to say that the Soviets will take advantage of their temporary superiority to launch a major war. But the West must expect them to take the maximum advantage of their weakness and pursue an increasingly "forward" policy. As I said earlier the Soviets will intensify their efforts to gain control of the oil of the Middle East, the minerals of Central and Southern Africa and the resources of South-East Asia. In the process they will also seek to command the sea routes by which these essential raw materials reach Western Europe, the U.S. and Japan. They may even go further and undertake local operations against a country like Yugoslavia or even against the vulnerable Northern and Southern flanks of NATO.

We are thus moving into a high-risk period. It will be all the more dangerous because of Soviet realization that their military superiority may be fairly shortlived. The temptation to press on will be very great. So will the chance of miscalculation.

Soviet forces are designed for *offensive* warfare, and their doctrine emphasizes the importance of initiative through suprise and pre-emption. The Egyptian attack in Sinai in 1973 was a classic example of Soviet tactics.

Deployed on the ground, in Western Europe, at this very moment, are vastly superior Warsaw Pact ground and air forces in key areas, capable of striking with hell-for-leather speed, with little or no warning under surprise conditions "off the march" – that is without prior con-centration of forces – under the guise of manoeuvres and exercises, and at the same time, blinding the opposition with their electronic warfare capability.

The Soviet Union has developed an air force which is capable of launching a devastating attack into Western Europe in the form of mas-sive air strikes to destroy NATO air bases – particularly those in Britain – and nuclear storage depots. This would deprive NATO of its nuclear response option and enable Soviet ground forces to advance rapidly through NATO territory.

Satellite coverage has recently revealed a newly discovered Soviet biological factory. The Soviets may well be considering the possibility of a "disabling war" in which weapons such as the neutron warhead, chemical and bacteriological weapons which could disable – not kill – people while leaving structures undamaged would achieve the Soviet's political aims at less cost to themselves and enormous gains in any post-war occupation of Europe.

The only safe prediction today is that the unexpected *must* be expected. With spies in the sky, you can photograph the enemy's capability. But you cannot photograph his intentions, particularly when his forces are deployed and pre-positioned under the guise of an exercise.

As for the maritime threat, those who argue that the powerful Soviet Fleet offers no threat, should read the lessons of history and the use of sea power.

This massive projection of sea power by a largely self-sufficient continental totalitarian state, can only have a sinister purpose. It constitutes a mortal danger to the countries for whom the seas are vital lines of communication. The purpose behind this naval build-up is to challenge the Western powers at sea and the margin of safety is wearing thin – in some places, it is wearing through. The Soviet Fleet is no longer a Fleet of defence, but an ocean Fleet with a three-dimensional challenge – air, surface and submarine.

When the Suez Canal route is fully operative, the major oil producing countries of the Middle East will be effectively ringed by the Soviet Navy. Israel's survival is the major obstacle to the Soviet domination of the Eastern Mediterranean. If we forget this, we do so at our peril.

The position of South Africa is a vital link in any defensive Western chain because its strategic location makes it the guardian of the West's oil route round the Cape and a counter weight to the Soviet naval build-up in the Indian Ocean.

Because defence is indivisible, the West cannot shut its eyes to events taking place beyond the present boundaries of NATO. In future, the Free World must be far more outward looking and realize that the defence of the Mediterranean cannot be divorced from the security of the Middle East, Africa and the Indian Ocean.

In as much as 66% of world oil reserves lie near the Persian Gulf, stability must be safeguarded in that theatre otherwise the continuing access to energy by the U.S., the NATO countries and Japan will be at grave risk. Therefore there must be joint defence of the Gulf.

It is imperative that top priority is given forthwith to the global nature of the Soviet threat and the vulnerability of the lifelines to the West and to Japan. If the Soviet Union's strategy is global, as indeed it is, then the Free World's strategy must also be global. Britain, with the United States and France in particular, must create new alliances to protect those areas outside NATO where their vital interests lie.

In the Middle East Britain needs to support America in creating what might be called a "southern tier" strategy from the Mediterranean to the Gulf and designed, with the support of friendly countries on both sides of the Red Sea, to contain and squeeze out the Soviet presence in the Horn of Africa and Aden.

In Southern Africa, Britain needs to lift the arms embargo on South Africa. That country can then acquire the means to defend itself against aggression from forces equipped, trained, financed and master-minded by the Soviets. Britain should also seek to negotiate a renewal of the facilities they once enjoyed at Simonstown so that the West collectively can take part in the defence of the Cape Route.

In the Far East Britain's diplomacy should have two main objectives. The first should be to persuade Japan to assume a much larger share of the burden of defending the area, particularly at sea. They would serve their own best interests by ensuring the safety of the shipping routes on which their economy depends. This would help the general cause by making it easier for the U.S. to deploy American ships in the Indian Ocean.

Britain's second main objective should be to contribute to the re-armament of China. Under their previous Labour Government, Britain was very cautious about the development of their relations with China and the former Prime Minister in a broadcast urged the importance of not letting the Soviet leaders feel they were being encircled by the West. He sounded very like Mr. Neville Chamberlain in the period leading up to the Munich Agreement. I doubt whether the Soviet leaders are any more concerned about the encirclement than the Nazi leaders were. *I only wish they were.* Nothing would be more likely to check their expansionist ambitions than the prospect of a major war on two fronts.

Mr. Callaghan's words reflected a widespread inability to grasp the realities of the situation which faces Britain. So did his panic reaction and that of other Western leaders to the Chinese punitive expedition against Vietnam. The Chinese are determined that Vietnam should not become a base for Soviet Imperialism in South-East Asia. To prevent this from happening they ran the calculated risk of a confrontation with Moscow. Their calculation was justified by the event. Moscow barked but was not prepared to bite. The Soviet Union was made to look a "paper bear". And the Vietnamese may now hesitate before they resume their expansionist policies in South-East Asia.

The West would do well to take a leaf out of the Chinese book. If they had stood up to the Soviet-Cuban invasion of Angola and Ethiopia by the encouragement of South African, Somali and Eritrean counter attacks, the situation in the Horn of Africa, in Central Africa and in Afghanistan would be much healthier than it is today.

As it is, the Russians are laughing all the way to Moscow at the Anglo-American policy of appeasement abroad. This has resulted in an encirclement of Marxist dictatorships having already been established

Reprinted from *U.S. News & World Report*, 14th January, 1980.
Copyright (1980) U.S. News & World Report, Inc.

through the barrel of a gun – in Angola, Mozambique, the Horn of
Africa, South Yemen, Afghanistan, Iraq, Iran, Libya, the Lebanon,
Syria, Vietnam, Cambodia, and Laos, and this is not the complete list.

If the West continues to stand idly by, impotent and paralysed the
wobbling 'dominoes' will continue to fall to the Russian Bear, whose
Red Shadow is already over Pakistan, Iran, Turkey, the Gulf, the
Arabian Peninsula, Rhodesia, South West Africa, South Africa, and the
Cape Route.

The Western Governments have stood idly by while Soviet
Imperialism has subjugated Angola, Mozambique, Ethiopia, Aden,
Afghanistan and Iran. And the heat is now on Pakistan and Turkey.
Instead of encouraging resistance to aggression and subversion the West
has sacrificed major economic and strategic interests rather than face
the risk, however, remote, of a confrontation with the Soviets. The
'domino' concept has been proven.

The Chart on the dust cover of this book and on page 23, shows how
the Russian menace in Central Asia has now reached right up to the
Durand Line and poses a direct and immediate threat to one of the most

sensitive areas of the world, Pakistan, where the internal political situation is far from stabilized. From the Khyber Pass it is only about seven hundred miles across Pakistan to the Indian Ocean where a strong Russian fleet is on patrol ready for any eventuality.

As crisis follows crisis NATO is constantly in disarray, whether it is over the "Neutron Bomb", the modernization of their Euro-theatre nuclear weapons, or the collective reaction to the Soviet outright invasion of Afghanistan. They resemble a team of boat stewards laying out chairs on the deck of the Titanic — oblivious of the impending disaster. What price crisis management!

When at long last President Carter, in his new-found leadership, tried to do the right thing and Britain supported America to the hilt, our NATO partners in Europe dithered in a blue funk, merely uttering words of condemnation or verbal outrage. The brutal nature of Soviet power politics and their imperialist aggression must be met by the West with a prohibitively high stern retribution and a willingness to bear the pain and sacrifice entailed. What did we get instead? A lack of any sense of crisis and urgency and an absence of collective will and resolution. Their attitude was one of "business as usual".

With the honourable exception of Britain, America's European allies are a fine lot indeed. They are always at the ready to accept help from America, whether political, economic or military. But when America, in crisis, asks for their help, they rush to the ramparts — ready to fight to the last adverb.

With such friends . . .

The blatant Soviet aggression in Afghanistan is a direct challenge to the democracies of the West and dramatically emphasizes the reality and closeness of the Russian threat. If, after this brutal demonstration of Soviet aggression, they do not take urgent steps to improve the military effectiveness of NATO, the future will indeed be bleak.

Russia's Master Plan

There are ten stages in Russia's Master Plan of achieving an overwhelming superiority in global strategy.

First, to control the Red Sea, namely Ethiopia, Djibouti and Somalia.

Second, to control both sides of the Gulf of Aden. South Yemen (Britain's Aden colony of old) is already a Soviet-Cuban-East German satellite. The Bab el Mandeb – which is the entrance to the Red Sea – is already under Soviet control from Aden and Massawa.

The *Third* step is to spread out in the Persian Gulf from the Iraqi naval base at the head of the Gulf.

The strategic situation on the Northern shores of the Persian Gulf and the Arabian Sea was changed dramatically for the worse in April 1978 by the Russian KGB-sponsored bloody coup in Afghanistan, to be followed by the bloody revolution and overthrow of the Shah's régime in Iran.

Soviet espionage activity in Iran through their intelligence services, the KGB and GRU, had been going on for years in close cooperation with Iran's Tudeh, their Communist party. It was too easy with a network of 100 so-called Soviet diplomats, 6,000 Soviet technicians and 500,000 Afghans working in Iran.

In fact, Iranian intelligence told the United States in November 1978 that the so-called popular demonstrators were being armed and trained by Moscow through the Palestine Liberation Organization.

The West suffered a crushing defeat – diplomatically, economically, energy-wise and militarily – by the loss of the most important pro-Western military bastion in the world's primary oil producing region.

In this power struggle the Soviet Union achieved a brilliant success by its usual tactics of siding with and supporting popular discontent, regardless of the cause which, ironically, was religious – Khomeini is merely a pawn in the Iranian Marxist plan for the establishment of a pro-Marxist state and a base for anarchists and terrorists.

Thus, long before the Soviet Union's bare faced invasion of Afghanistan in December 1979, the whole balance of power had been changed not only against the West and Israel, but also against an ally of the West's which immediately became of vital strategic importance in the most sensitive area in South Asia, namely Pakistan. Indeed, the pressure from Iran is felt both by Pakistan to the east and Turkey — a member of NATO — to the north.

The pressure from Afghanistan began to be felt by Pakistan from April 1978 when President Daoud was deposed and killed by the first Moscow protégé Nur Muhammad Tarakki. Russia has long regarded Afghanistan as the gateway to an outlet to a warmwater port on the Arabian Sea and Indian Ocean.

Well do I remember having it drummed into me as a young Lieutenant, fighting the Pathan tribesmen on the North-West Frontier in the early 1930s, that Afghanistan was the vital strategic buffer against Russian expansion southwards.

The fact is, Afghanistan became a Soviet client State in April 1978 and was soon posing a serious threat to the stability of the whole region, the immediacy of which was against Pakistan. Indeed, Pakistan was already in a precarious position. Afghanistan is only 300 miles to the north-east of the vital and vulnerable Strait of Hormuz. A hostile Iran would, of course, control and dominate the Strait.

The Soviet dominated South Yemen is only 500 miles to the southwest of Afghanistan and much closer than this to Iran. Afghanistan, tucked under the Soviet Union's southern border for 1,000 miles, projects like a wedge between Iran on the west and Pakistan to the east and south.

Afghanistan régimes from time to time since 1947, have been raising the Pakhtoonistan bogey and questioning the validity of the international frontier — the Durand Line, earlier reaffirmed twice in two treaties as the International frontier, in 1893 and 1919. When King Zahir Shah in 1973 and President Daoud later, in 1978, realized the folly of the policy of confrontation with Pakistan — which has always extended the hand of friendship to Kabul régimes — they were overthrown, because peace, stability and cooperation in the region did not suit militant marxist parties within and without the country.

Pakistan, sandwiched between India and the Soviet dominated Afghanistan, is of great strategic importance, as I shall explain at length in Chapters 5 and 7. But Pakistan is weak, literally only half of its original self with the loss eight years ago of East Pakistan, now Bangladesh. If Pakistan itself were to topple, the Soviets would certainly realize a dream dating back to the days of the Czars — a warmwater port on the Indian Ocean. Well may it be said that the "Red Shadow" is already over Pakistan.

Afghanistan is strategic for another reason. Its acquisition gives striking power to the Russian general staff in three directions. With

Afghanistan as a base, the Russian air force is within easy striking distance of Karachi, New Delhi and even more important the Saudi Arabian and Persian Gulf oilfields. With the addition of Iran as a base, the Soviet striking power would become an overwhelming threat.

To the north, Turkey has been sitting on the edge of internal chaos, and externally, is encircled by six countries – the Soviet Union, Iran, Iraq, Syria, Bulgaria and Rumania. As a member of NATO, Turkey commands the largest land army of Western Europe, but prior to the Soviet Union's invasion of Afghanistan in December 1979, it had been steering a course towards non-alignment and had already refused to allow the Americans to expand their monitoring facilities to replace the installations they lost in Afghanistan.

Furthermore, a sniffle of oil in the Aegean Sea has been worsening relations to the brink of war in the Turkish-Greek feud over Cyprus. And Greece, like France, withdrew from the military wing of NATO. Because of the insane decision by Congress to impose an arms embargo, the Turks retaliated by taking control of 26 U.S. bases. Little wonder is that Turkey moved closer to their traditional enemy, Russia. And who can say that their internal situation will not erupt as it did in Iran? Turkey, therefore, sits on the edge of a volcano.

The *Fourth* step in Russia's Master Plan is to launch the big push into the Arabian Peninsula itself by an all-out attack against the Sultanate of Oman.

Before the overthrow of the Shah, Oman shared with Iran the guardianship of a vital contemporary waterway – the rock-bound Strait of Hormuz that links the Persian Gulf with the Gulf of Oman, the Arabian Sea and the seaways of the world.

Through this sinuous channel, which at its narrowest navigable point is about 17 miles wide, super-tankers throb at the rate, on average, of 77 ships in either direction every 24 hours, carrying £45,000 million worth of oil a year to refuel the economies of more than half the globe.

There are two navigation channels through which the tankers pass, each two and a half miles wide with a separation channel in between. The northern channel used for entering the strait has a depth of at least 67 metres and the southerly exit channel is at least 88 metres deep. The strait could be closed in a number of ways. Conventional long-range guns or surface-to-surface missiles installed on either shore could dominate the channels, destroying any ship venturing into it. Mines or encapsulated torpedoes on the seabed could perform the same task. Aircraft armed with precision bombs or guided missiles could sink or halt every tanker passing through. Naval surface ships and submarines could be equally effective. International terrorists are perfectly capable of blowing up tankers and setting fire to oil slicks, thus closing the navigation channels.

Such action would make the present oil crisis look like child's play. The industries of most of Western Europe would slowly die. The

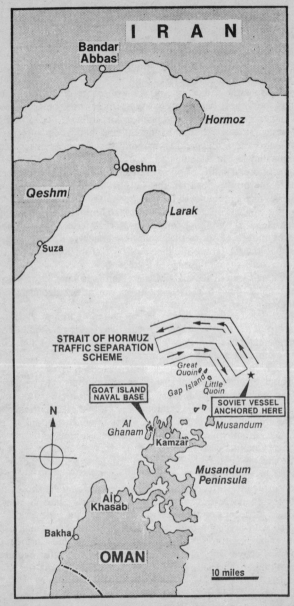

Appreciation to *The Times*, Oman Supplement, 9th May, 1980.

economy of Japan would come to a halt. The economy of the United States, which obtains an increasing percentage of its oil from the Persian Gulf would be severely damaged.

The Armed Forces of NATO would come to a grinding halt, thus allowing the Soviet and Warsaw Pact Armed Forces to over-run Western Europe without firing a shot. Whoever rules Oman, therefore, has his thumb on the Free World's jugular vein.

By mid-1979 there was a notable build-up of forces along the South Yemen's Eastern border with West Oman and East European engineers were observed preparing new fortified positions. This could be the prelude to a forthcoming invasion. What was Britain doing to guarantee the security of one of its smallest but most faithful allies? Precisely nothing, under its last Labour Government. The new Conservative Government has identified this challenge and must implement without delay an effective response, in spite of Britain's Armed Forces having already been reduced beyond the critical danger limit. The lion is mangy enough, but is not quite toothless yet.

The Soviet *Fifth* step – having subverted and subjected Oman – is to establish its long-cherished foothold on the Southern shores of the Persian Gulf; Kuwait, Bahrein, Qatar, Dubai and the Union of Arab Emirates.

The Soviet *Sixth* step is to launch the final threat into Saudi Arabia and the oil reservoirs. Saudi Arabia produces one quarter of the world's oil needs and provides one quarter of American oil imports. Furthermore, she uses her wealth to buttress anti-communism in the Middle East.

Meanwhile, the King of Saudi Arabia has every reason to fear that communists in South Yemen – Aden – supported by hundreds of Russian, East German and Cuban advisers and technicians, will sooner or later overthrow North Yemen. This must give Russia virtual control of the entrance to the Red Sea, hindered only by 3,000 odd members of the French Foreign Legion who remain in Djibouti.

The Saudi Government suffers from the fact that their vast country is virtually indefensible without outside help. At present they do not allow foreign nationals to man their weapons. It is difficult to transform an illiterate tribesman into a pilot, flying aircraft at supersonic speeds.

From what I have described so far and from what one can see on the map, the Russians are now closing in on the most vital waterways. Their aim is total encirclement of the Persian Gulf, the Gulf of Oman, the Gulf of Aden and control of the vast oil resources. *Half the world's oil reserves are in this area*. Russian oil production will decrease in 1985, while demand will be higher. What the Soviets need and what they are determined to get is control of Middle East oil. Whoever controls that oil will control the economic lifeblood of the West and Japan.

The Soviets know the value of the region that they are surrounding and do not give a damn about Afghanistan, Yemen or Ethiopia. No

15

wonder the Saudis are scared. They have what the whole world wants – *oil,* and that is a mighty powerful package. Of course, the present sad state of affairs stems from the crazy decision to abandon Aden, *for which Britain's politicians and the then Service Chiefs bear such terrible responsibility.* To leave such a vacuum was criminal negligence and gross misappreciation and underestimation of Russia's intentions and capabilities.

Having decided to quit Aden and the Gulf, Iran was the only country in the area which could possibly protect Middle Eastern oil. Had the United States persuaded the British Government to retain its presence, or had it itself taken on that responsibility, Iran would not have needed to assume a burden which probably contributed to the régime's downfall.

The Iranian revolution resulted primarily from domestic causes. But no professional strategist would deny that the Shah's opponents were greatly encouraged by the total failure of his Western allies – and after all, he was looked on as the friend of the West – to react to the Soviet takeover of Aden, Ethiopia and Afghanistan.

The timely arrival of the American Sixth Fleet in the Gulf, supported by a significant Allied multi-national naval and amphibious force, and a proper use and interpretation of intelligence, would have stopped the rot. What is now urgently required is military hardware and a framework of bases to protect the rest of the oil-bearing Gulf on which Western and Japanese industry are so dependent.

The Soviet's *Seventh* step is to secure their rear by liquidating the anti-Soviet régime in the Sudan.

The *Eighth* step is the subjection of Egypt which, by now out-flanked, would fall like a ripe orange, bridgeheads already having been established in Libya and Algeria with Tunisia and Morocco soon to follow. Morocco not only gave the Shah refuge but has given active support to anti-Soviet forces as far afield as Zaire. King Hassan is therefore a top-priority target for Moscow.

The *Ninth* step is to absorb the whole of Southern Africa, thus depriving the West of vital minerals and key bases and controlling the Free World's life-line round the Cape.

In the Indian Ocean the Soviet Union's presence is already felt in Zanzibar, Madagascar and the Seychelles. By mid-1979 Russia had a force of more than 20 ships in the Indian Ocean, almost all of them in the Arabian Sea, commanding the approaches to the Persian Gulf. This force was then more than three times the size of the American squadron in the area and included a missile cruiser, several destroyers, a submarine, probably nuclear powered, and several auxiliaries.

The Russian ships frequently visit Basra and Umm Qasr in Iraq at the head of the Persian Gulf. They have also visited the Persian Navy's principal base at Bandar Abas and have ensured that they now have the necessary facilities to base a much larger fleet in the area at short notice.

In addition to the bases at Aden and Umm Qasr, the Russians have buoys laid off the Seychelles to allow warships to carry out repairs and take on stores from auxiliaries.

The Americans are still building up a base on the British-owned island of Diego Garcia, several thousand miles to the South of the Gulf. But earlier in 1979 they closed their last mainland base in the area at Bahrein in the Gulf.

Before the Russian rampage in Afghanistan there were only four to six American warships operating in the Red Sea and Gulf, although a carrier task group detached from the Seventh Fleet in the Western Pacific cruised in the Indian Ocean every three months on average for up to a month.

The *Tenth* stage is, of course, the complete domination and absorption of Western Europe. Having achieved increasing influence and power in the eastern Mediterranean, the Middle East, the Red Sea, the Persian Gulf littoral, South Asia and Southern Africa, the Soviet Union will have set the stage for neutralization of Western Europe – partly by denying it access to oil and critical raw materials. As I have said in Chapter 1, Moscow's strategy will then be to split NATO, remove American forces from Europe and manipulate unilateral disarmament in the West.

This is why Russia, with half Europe's economic strength, continues to grind out of her people an offensive superiority which is about twice as great and grossly in excess of any conceivable legitimate defensive needs. This is why this vast Soviet expansionist Empire shuts itself off, arms itself to the teeth and indoctrinates its people for war.

The invasion of Afghanistan has advanced Russia's strategy for world domination and constitutes a major step to outflank West Europe. Indeed this latest act of aggression cannot be viewed in isolation from the Soviet offensive in South-East Asia.

East of the Strait of Malacca, a vital communication line linking the Pacific and Indian Oceans, the Soviet Union, by exploiting aid to Vietnam in its aggression against Cambodia (Kampuchea), has deployed its naval air forces from Haishenwei to the South China Sea and the Gulf of Siam near the eastern top of the Strait.

West of the Strait, the Soviet Union has built naval and air bases on the Red Sea and Bab el Mandeb Strait at its southern end. The occupation of Afghanistan will enable the Soviet Union to advance against Iran in the west and Pakistan in the south-east.

Thus, if its armed forces were to reach the warmwater ports on the Indian Ocean or the Strait of Hormuz, the Soviet Union's pincer encirclement of Saudi Arabia would be complete. This pincer drive, together with the Soviet offensive in South-East Asia, is designed to enable the ever-growing Soviet navy to dominate the Indian Ocean from the East African coasts to Australia.

If the Soviet Union were to succeed in achieving this, the sea routes

17

transporting oil from the Persian Gulf to West Europe, Japan and the United States would be controlled by the Soviet Union. Thus the Soviet Union would be able to achieve her master plan to dominate Europe and Japan and weaken and isolate the United States by controlling the sea routes which are the lifelines of these countries.

That is why, strategically speaking, the Soviet occupation of Afghanistan constitutes a major forward step of the Soviet Union to out-flank West Europe.

To summarize:

Russia intends to gain dominance of Western Europe by a four-pronged attack, keeping her options open.

The *first prong* is covert; namely, subversive warfare, the Third World War in which we are already engaged. The threat of subversion, as in Afghanistan and Iran, comes *initially* from within. It is erroneous to suppose that the threat to a country's stability comes only from external forces. But in the case of Southern Asia the stage has now been reached where the invasion of Afghanistan, following on the military occupation of Ethiopia and Aden, demonstrates that the threat has escalated from the subversive to the directly military. Hence, the United States, in con-junction with her Allies, and in collaboration with the Gulf States, must be prepared to defend the Gulf area by force.

Subversion is the war against Communist infiltration of govern-ments, trade unions, industry, law and order, the armed forces and their reduction below the safety limit thereby breaking the will of the people to resist and imperilling the safety of the home base and the military front.

Subversive warfare is now in operation and we are already engaged in the Third World War – the war against Communism – which we are losing. It is an insidious and more dangerous war than conventional, or even nuclear war, because the ordinary man in the street does not realize that we are already locked in such a war.

The *second prong* is political blackmail. Russia's control of the sources of our oil supply plus the threat of her big stick would provide a backing for blackmail. She hopes to be able to take Western Europe without firing a shot in international war. There is no military advantage in having the nuclear and conventional capability to overkill your enemy, *but the political advantages are tremendous*.

For the time being, the Soviets may not want war; but certainly they want the fruits of war. The Russian bear-hug is not a friendly gesture; it is a fatal embrace. The Russians themselves have said that "the role of the Red Army is to stand by, ready to shake the tree when the rotten fruit is ripe to fall".

The *third prong* is overt, using her military forces to threaten a blitzkrieg attack on land and the severing of our jugular vein at sea.

The *fourth prong* is to be ready to fight and survive a nuclear war if deterrents break down.

CHAPTER
3

The Arc of Crisis

A mushrooming crisis is developing in the Persian Gulf – Indian Ocean – Caribbean that threatens the very existence of the United States, Western Europe, Japan and the rest of the Free World. Its implications are so awesome that the Free World may be on the very brink of disaster.

Never in recent times has such a vast and highly strategic area of the world been threatened with such widespread political instability.

While strife-torn Iran and Soviet occupied Afghanistan are the fulcrum, the "arc of crisis" – to use the words of President Carter's National Security Adviser Zbigniew Brzezinski – extends all the way from Bangladesh, on India's right flank, to the tip of southern Africa, and as far West as the Caribbean Sea. As Brzezinski explains "An arc of crisis stretches along the shores of the Indian Ocean, with fragile social and political structures in a region of vital importance to us threatened with fragmentation. The resulting political chaos could well be filled by elements hostile to our values and sympathetic to our adversaries."

The chief adversary who stands to gain the most from the rising crescendo of chaos is the Soviet Union, the superpower which is positioned geographically beyond key elements of the arc of crisis. The work of Soviet agents, coupled with a relentless chorus of propaganda from Radio Moscow, is stimulating and exploiting instability in this vast area.

The Kremlin, moreover, knows what it is after.

Without oil from the Persian Gulf, wheels and factories of the vast industrial free world – from Japan through Europe to the United States – soon would grind to a halt. Moreover, nearly half the non-communist world's total supply of oil moves through the world's most critical "choke point" – the narrow Strait of Hormuz, separating Iran from the Arabian peninsula.

Long before the Soviet Union's outright invasion of Afghanistan in December 1979, the former U.S. Energy Secretary, James Schlesinger, had underscored the West's vulnerability to political chaos in the Middle

East when he stated that "there must be clear and unequivocable evidence. to other nations in the Gulf area of the firmness and steadfastness of American support and American presence."

By "other nations" he meant Saudi Arabia, Kuwait, Qatar, and the oil-producing sheikdoms grouped in the United Arab Emirates (UAE).

However, the United States failed to display the "firmness and steadfastness" necessary to thwart Soviet inroads into the Area. Just the opposite prevailed. It was precisely U.S. indecision, vacillation and outright weakness which compounded the gravity of the situation.

Washington wavered back and forth on how long to give public support to the Shah of Iran. Part of this was due to the fact that American intelligence had fallen down in giving President Carter an accurate portrayal of how badly the Shah's fortunes had been slipping. The President subsequently criticized the ineffectiveness of the Central Intelligence Agency – without mentioning that his and previous Administrations were largely responsible for crippling the agency's intelligence-gathering apparatus.

The worst example of U.S. vacillation, however, came shortly before the Shah was forced into exile in mid-January.

As a last-ditch show of support for the beleagured monarch, Mr. Carter ordered a U.S. carrier task force to steam from the Philippines to the Persian Gulf. Three days later, however, on the advice of his foreign policy aides and State Department officials (not the military), the President changed his mind and ordered the ships to remain on station in the South China Sea.

This unprecedented start-stop action typified the limits of American power and the then lack of a strong policy under the Carter Administration. An American political columnist described the whole exercise as "the first example of no-gunboat diplomacy; we showed a naked flagpole".

America's allies were mystified about U.S. indecisiveness over Iran and the entire crisis arc. Saudi Arabia's Ambassador to the U.S., Ali Abdallah Alireza, stated: "Our friends (the Americans) do not seem to realize that a crisis of historic magnitude is close at hand for the Western world and for those who share its values in our entire area." His sombre warning was echoed by Pakistan's Ambassador to the U.S.: "I fear that historians will look back at 1978 as a watershed year when the balance of power shifted against the Western World."

The Saudi envoy went on to lament the fact that "no one in the Carter Administration seems to be listening to his government's warning about the Russians." This should really come as no surprise. Three years ago, President Carter, in an address at Notre Dame University, said that a maturing America had finally shed its "inordinate fear of Communism."

Events proved that shed along with that fear was an awareness of Soviet aims and strategies. Pro-Western nations came to regard the

American administration as being less concerned about Soviet expansionism than any administration since World War II.

It was precisely the crumbling image of the United States in this strategic region (as well as in Africa) that has emboldened the Soviet Union to take advantage of one crisis after another.

Former U.S. Secretary of State, Henry Kissinger, made clear the all-important factor on the world scene — U.S. weakness — in January 1979, when he stated: "During the post war period, the countries bordering the Indian Ocean believed the United States was strategically predominant in that area and that, therefore, friendship with the United States assured their security . . . The Soviet march through Africa, with Cuban troops, from Angola to Ethiopia, and the Soviet moves through Afghanistan and South Yemen . . . altered that perception; that inevitably decreased the importance of friendship with the United States."

Even staunchly anti-communist Saudi Arabia was considering diplomatic relations with the Soviet Union in order to "hedge its bets" with the U.S.

Asked what more we could expect in the way of Soviet inroads in the arc region, Kissinger again replied it was all up to the actions taken by Washington; "The more that the United States looks out of control of events, the more it appears as if our friends are going down without effective American support or even effective American understanding of what is occuring, the more this process will accelerate . . . A problem avoided turns into a crisis and the crisis not mastered turns into a cataclysm further down the road."

The former Secretary of State then reserved special condemnation for America's failure to thwart the Soviet Union's use of Cuban proxy forces in Africa. "I simply cannot believe that it can be beyond the capacity of the United States to stop Cuban expeditionary forces thousands of miles from home. It just cannot be. To claim that it is, is in itself a symptom of such weakness that it will accelerate the geo-political decline of which we have been speaking."

Watching some of the wobbling 'dominoes' that Moscow intends shall fall as a result of the Iranian disaster and the savage invasion of Afghanistan, it is crystal clear that the Kremlin's aim is to destablize politically and economically neighbouring Turkey and Pakistan, by instigating confrontation of Leftist elements against the religious Rightists, leaving a political void on the huge Soviet land frontier with the Middle East. It was the stopping of U.S. aid to these two countries that played straight into the Soviet Union's hands and helped them to achieve their objective of the destabilization of this region.

It was obvious that Moscow was intent on absorbing South Yemen and Afghanistan and stepping up her relationships with Syria and Iraq, while the Cuban forces in Ethiopia were to crush the last resistance in

Eritrea — thus tightening the ring of Soviet influence around the oil States.

The deteriorating political climate in the arc of crisis is made to order for radical disruptions, aggravated by Soviet mischief-making, jeopardizing the economic structure of the entire world.

None of this would have happened had not Great Britain and the United States fallen so precipitously from pinnacles of political and military power.

Postwar British governments succeeded — if that is the word — in shrinking their once globe-girdling navy virtually back to the Thames estuary itself.

British naval bases throughout the Mediterranean and Persian Gulf were abandoned, leaving a gaping power vacuum. The once-powerful British bastion at Aden is now encompassed within a Communist "republic". It is also a base used by East Germans and Cubans for training terrorists and subversives world-wide.

Britain no longer protects the oil-rich sheikdoms of the Persian Gulf nor ensures that the Strait of Hormuz "seagate" remains open. Now Iran will no longer play that role.

The Soviet navy looms ominously throughout the Mediterranean, once a British "lake". Under the prow of Red naval vessels passes 25,000 million barrels of oil in the Mediterranean at any given time on 300 plus tankers.

At the southern tip of Africa the British abandoned the strategic Simonstown naval base, guardian post for 24,000 ships — many of them oil tankers — which round the Cape of Good Hope every year.

After Britain's fall of power, America's high-prestige role continued to ensure the pre-eminence of the West in the tide against Communist encroachment — *until Vietnam.*

In South-East Asia the price of America's power was shattered beyond repair. Since that time, the Soviets, utilizing their Cuban legionaries, have won virtually uncontested victories in Angola and Ethiopia. Thousands of Cubans are positioned in the radical states of Africa and elsewhere.

The timorousness of U.S. foreign policy caused key nations throughout the Persian Gulf — Indian Ocean region seriously to question America's resolve, and also the inevitability of communism.

Against this background there developed a deteriorating situation and perilous drift towards anti-Western, pro-Soviet sentiment among nations in the Indian Ocean — Persian Gulf regions.

In July 1979 — five months before the Soviet Union's onslaught against Afghanistan — I wrote these words before my departure from Pakistan:

"Time is indeed short as zero hour approaches. Complete economic collapse of the Western World may be just over the horizon, unless the deteriorating events in the arc of crisis are arrested.

RUSSIAN GEO-STRATEGIC THRUSTS

CHART 2

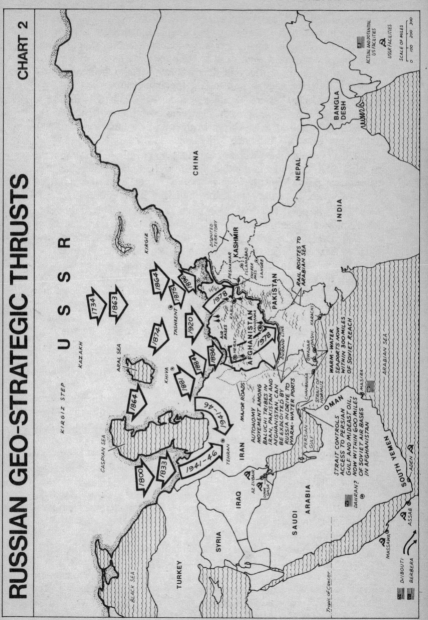

"Standing alone, – except when the chips are down – is Pakistan, over which the Soviet shadow now hovers menacingly. Western Europe and the U.S.A. have remained placid and blind to this serious threat which has developed in what must now be regarded as one of the most sensitive areas in the world. Pakistan has now become the "meat in the sandwich" between Afghanistan and the Indian Ocean.

"Against this Western negative attitude, Pakistan's only insurance has been her friendly contact with China and the existence of the strategically important Karakorum Highway which links Pakistan with China's most westerly Province – Sinkiang."

The wishful thinkers will argue that it is not accurate to say that the invasion of Afghanistan is the first time that the Soviet Union has used its military power directly and massively in an unprovoked attack against a sovereign country not belonging to the Soviet Bloc.

They will point to Chart 2 on page 23 and say that Afghanistan has traditionally been an area in which Russia has exerted influence or actively intervened over a period of time and that she has always regarded Afghanistan as being very much in her sphere of influence.

They will say that the failure of the West to react to the overthrow of President Daoud and its passive acceptance of Afghanistan's transformation into a satellite state, can only have confirmed Russia's belief that Afghanistan was treated by the West as being in the Soviet Bloc. Therefore, they will maintain that the invasion of Afghanistan cannot be regarded as a new and dangerous escalation in Russian international aggression.

This school of thought will state that Moscow's primary purpose in invading Afghanistan was to tighten its control of that rebellious country. They will point out that the tide of Islamic fervour, which had already shaken Iran, was now threatening Afghanistan. Unless it were checked, might it not also spread across the border into the Soviet Central Asian Republics and stir unrest among their substantial Islamic populations? Thus the Soviet leaders felt that they had only two options: One, to allow a Moscow-leaning socialist state on their border to dissolve into chaos and possibly pass into the hands of Muslim fanatics. Or two, to move in strength to take control of the country.

In view of the Soviets avowed long and short term aims I have no doubt that the above was their secondary and not their primary purpose. The invasion was an integral part of their long-range strategy to dominate Pakistan, Iran and the Gulf nations.

The Soviets have a vested interest in influencing events in Iran. The reward in political, economic and military terms would be enormous. It would enable them to stop the supply of oil to Western consumers almost at will when the oil shortage really starts to bite later in the 1980s.

The Soviets would be well poised to seize control of the Gulf's oil at a time when their own domestic output falls short of their own internal requirements.

What has not so far been observed is that the strategic foundations now crumbling under the weight of Russia's military might were laid by the Duke of Wellington and his colleagues, notably Ellenborough, 150 years ago.

It was the Duke of Wellington as Prime Minister who gave the signal for the opening of "the great game". The strategy was to keep the Russians out of the Indian subcontinent (and out of Iran) by slowing up their advance in Central Asia and excluding them above all from Afghanistan. (Secret Committee to Governor of Bengal, 12th January, 1830).

What is happening now brings nearer the fruition of a Russian imperial hope. For centuries Russian strategists have had their eyes on the warmwater ports of the south. Now that they have large numbers of troops in the positions which Wellington and his successors recognized as the most threatening of all to the security of the Indian subcontinent. Today the Russians have reached Herat at least. One can only look into the 1980s with deep foreboding about the future of India, Pakistan and Iran.

The writer of the Foreword to this book has been a Service Minister, Army, Air and Aviation. He also wrote the Foreword to my previous book "The Bear at the Back Door". On the 1st February this year the following letter appeared in that prestigious newspaper *The Daily Telegraph* under the title "Warnings should not be heeded too late":

"However late, it has now, after the Afghan invasion, become even more appropriate to comment on Mr. Julian Amery's articles, which you had the foresight to print (26th and 27th November 1979).

Although well before the Afghan occupation, Mr. Amery illustrated clearly Soviet intentions, their propensity to extend the Empire and called for urgent and effective deterrent moves as the only restraining factor to prevent a fatal encroachment of the West's vital interests.

Many of his critics now profess surprise and dismay that his views consistently expressed over some 20 years have been so completely vindicated by events.

The warnings he has given, against withdrawal from the Gulf, abandonment of Aden and the geo-political upset of the whole region, are presently seen as historically sound strategic foresight, beneficial to all, including the oil States.

It is evident that, had Mr. Amery's advice been followed, not only would the upheavals in that area have been better contained, but there would be now a more peaceful world situation.

Past neglect propels us into great dangers – which we have unavoidably to face to prevent graver ones – as the now indispensable deterrent will have to be that more forceful to have any effect at all.

Why then have Mr. Amery's warnings been derided by snide, uninformed, smug comments; why was he misnamed a "Romantic," "Right wing" and so on? To counteract views unpalatable in some quarters?

Warnings have been disliked throughout history, from the biblical prophets on to ancient times when messengers of bad tidings were executed.

A more recent example of a far-sighted statesman being branded a "Romantic" is

25

Winston Churchill in the 1930s, who turned out to be the supreme realist. His correct assessments and cries for preventive medicine were disliked by both the Establishment of the day and the Left – but were also fought by his country's enemies.

For the peace-minded people at large it was easier to face the shadows than the glare of prospective dangers. It was also more convenient.

The Daily Telegraph has – honourably – not shirked unpleasant present issues.

Will Mr. Amery's realistic prognosis and prescription be now heeded – late or too late?"

The two articles referred to dealt with the threat to the Middle East. In the first article entitled "The Russians are the real threat to the Middle East", Mr. Amery discussed Egypt's role after the Camp David agreement. In the second article he dealt with the Kremlin's grip under the title "Countering the attraction of Moscow's puppet theatre", in which he compared Communist Power with an Israeli – Egyptian – U.S. entente.

It is now time for me to look at the situation at the Western extremity of the arc of crisis – the Caribbean Sea.

While the Soviets gather troops and tanks in Afghanistan to invade Iran from the west when the time is ripe to seize the Iranian oil fields, they are also establishing bases around the Caribbean Sea from which to stop supplies of oil and basic strategic minerals to the United States. The Soviets continue to hold their troops, missiles and attack aircraft in Cuba. They already have allied Communist forces in Panama, Nicaragua and on most of the Windward and Leeway Islands encircling the eastern edge of the Caribbean Sea. Also, they have Communist allies in most countries in South and Central America, including Mexico. With Castro's aid from Cuba, the Soviets can establish military and naval bases that will encircle the Caribbean and thus cut off vital shipping to the United States.

Even before the Soviets seize sources of oil in the Middle East, they plan to prevent the United States from receiving oil tankers from Venezuela, Mexico and large shipments from overseas. Super-tankers sailing from the Persian Gulf around Africa cannot dock directly in U.S. Atlantic or Gulf ports. They must transfer their cargoes at the Virgin Islands, Trinidad or Curacao into standard-size tankers which can then sail to the eastern and southern seaboards of the United States. This can all be cut off if the Soviets are able to control the Caribbean.

By withholding supplies needed to defend Nicaragua, the Carter Administration, in effect, aided the Communists in taking over the country. The Administration then strongly urged President Somoza to end his authoritarian government and give up Nicaragua. What has been the result? The country is now occupied by a totalitarian government under the Marxist Sandinistas and the Carter Administration now contemplates giving them $75 million in aid.

Senator Jesse Helms, the Republican Senator, has stated he had information that there were 1,500 Sandinista troops from Nicaragua fighting in neighbouring El Salvador and 4,000 of their Marxist troops in Guatemala.

America — No longer a 'Paper Tiger'?

The Soviet Union did to Afghanistan what it had done to Latvia, Estonia, Poland, East Germany, Rumania, Bulgaria, Hungary and Czechoslovakia, and helped proxies to do to South Vietnam, Cambodia, Laos, Angola, Ethiopia, South Yemen, Iran and Rhodesia.

The rape of Afghanistan was a demonstration of the clockwork speed and precision of Russia's military might. She knew she had nothing to fear because of the crumbling of America's willingness to exercise its power.

The United States had stood helplessly as frenzied mobs stormed its embassy in Iran, capturing its citizens as hostages. One month before that, President Carter had capitulated to the Soviet Union over the stationing of Russian troops in Cuba.

Why has the greatest power the world has ever known been so weak and ineffectual and treated by the Soviet Union with such utter contempt? The answer boils down to one of a complete lack of respect.

Because the U.S. enjoyed so little respect and its world-wide prestige was so low, Khomeini's mobs were able to get away with storming the American embassy with no fear of reprisal. As former Secretary of Defence James Schlesinger said: "An image of weakness is going to elicit this kind of behaviour. Wild as the Ayatollah seems to be, he would not dare to touch the Soviet embassy."

Schlesinger's words seemed almost prophetic. Shortly afterwards, another U.S. embassy was stormed, this time in Islamabad, capital of Pakistan.

Former Secretary of State Henry Kissinger, alarmed at the shocking episode unfolding in Iran, said that America "must not elevate impotence" on the international scene "into a political principle . . . We must not turn a sense of our limits into a doctrine of abdication, for without our commitment, there can be no world security . . . Without faith in us, our friends will despair, and without respect for our strength, our adversaries will be emboldened."

The most ringing denunciation of American foreign policy was delivered by the American syndicated columnist George F. Will. He wrote: "Enduring the contempt of the contemptible is just one severity that life has in store for a declining nation.

"A nation that loses a war (in Vietnam) that it could have won by confidently employing its conventional military assets had better get used to humiliation ... A nation that has no serious response when three ambassadors are murdered (in Cyprus, Sudan and Afghanistan) had better get used to spittle on its cheeks ... A nation that collaborates in throwing to the wolves an ally like the Shah should not expect respect from the wolves ..."

The grim Iranian affair amounted to the second slap in the face for Uncle Sam within the space of a month. In early October, President Carter acquiesced to the Soviets over the presence in Cuba of their 3,000 man armed brigade. The President had initially said he would not accept the "status quo" in Cuba, but ended up doing precisely that. Mr. Brezhnev, in a much stronger position than his predecessor in a previous Cuban crisis (Nikita Khruschev in 1962) would not budge an inch.

Now the Russians have been allowed to get away with stationing a permanent armed force in the Western Hemisphere, 90 miles from the U.S. shores, and are upgrading facilities at the Cienfuegos naval base for use by their naval vessels, including submarines.

Former U.S. Secretary of State Cyrus Vance even admitted that one building the Soviets were erecting was of the same type they normally use for storage and repair of nuclear missiles. In 1970 the Soviets tried to sneak into Cienfuegos – but President Nixon put his foot down.

How has the United States come to find itself in such a dilemma? A brief review of current history provides the answers.

In 1945 America emerged from World War II as the strongest military and economic power in the world. Never had there been a nation of such pre-eminence.

Because of its unchallenged position, the U.S. was thrust into the role of leader of the Free World. It helped put defeated enemies, Japan and Germany, as well as the rest of war-torn Europe, back on their feet. It thereby prevented these strategic areas from falling under the world's newest threat to freedom – communism.

Washington subsequently proceeded to construct a global system of alliances to contain the advances of communism. For a while it succeeded. But slowly America's resolve began to erode. Communist aggression was thwarted but not defeated in 1953 in Korea. U.S. leadership spurned the advice of General Douglas MacArthur, who told both Houses of Congress that there could be "no substitute for victory."

The United States failed to respond to an opportunity caused by relative Soviet weakness in 1956. A popular uprising overthrew the Communist régime in Hungary. Freedom lasted for about a week while Moscow waited to see if Washington would step in with more than mere words to seal the pro-West victory. When Washington did nothing, Red Army tanks rolled in.

When a similar event threatened to occur in Czechoslovakia in 1968, the Kremlin knew it didn't even have to wait for an American response. It would not be forthcoming.

The folly of fighting a "limited" war in the style of the Korea stalemate was doomed to be repeated later – in Vietnam – with far more devasting consequences. After an expenditure of $300 billion and 55,000 American lives, Vietnam was lost.

Quickly, in domino fashion (again, proving the theory was correct after all), went Cambodia and Laos. The appalling horror of Cambodia today – with the gruesome prospect of the starvation of three million people (the ruthless Pol Pot régime having already killed off another three million previously) could have been prevented had the United States fought to win in Vietnam.

Furthermore, the experience in South-East Asia shattered American confidence. The pride of America's power was broken.

Shortly after the Vietnam debacle in 1975, the pace of aggression and opportunism around the world picked up. Washington was in no mood to react. Angola was lost to the West – with victory in sight – in 1975, and Ethiopia in 1978.

The fall of Ethiopia was very crucial indeed, because another Communist government had already established itself across the southern tip of the Red Sea in the former British protectorate of Aden, the strategic "seagate" abandoned by Britain. The new People's Democratic Republic of Yemen – supplied with money from Moscow and radical Libya – now trains Leftist terrorists from all over the world in the art of guerrilla warfare.

While the challenge of communism and radical "liberation" movements grew all the more severe, the most remarkable change of all occurred in Washington. The Carter Administration which took over on 20th January, 1977, unilaterally declared that the Cold War was over!

In a major speech at Notre Dame University in the Spring of 1977, President Carter exclaimed that the American public was ready to shed its previous "inordinate fear of communism." Thus, with a whiff of rhetoric, the global struggle for power in existence since the end of World War II was magically whisked away. Better yet, *wished away*.

According to this new approach, world problems should henceforth be viewed in the light of supposedly commonly shared "human issues" instead of concentrating further on "political confrontations."

The man who became Mr. Carter's National Security Adviser, Zbigniew Brzezinski, had earlier outlined this new approach when he wrote in a 1970 book, *Between Two Ages:* "Today the old framework of international politics ... with spheres of influence, military alliances between nation states, the fiction of sovereignty, doctrinal conflicts arising from 19th century crisis — is clearly no longer compatible with reality."

Did the Soviet Union share this new "reality"? Obviously not. But, according to Brzezinski, that was only because of the "delayed development" of Soviet Society. It would surely "mature" to see things from this new "global perspective" rather than from traditional national self-interest.

This erroneous belief that there exists a common fundamental approach to world problems colours everything the Administration does with regard to the Kremlin. It surfaced during the recent Cuban crisis. Mr. Carter decided not to press the issue of the Soviet troops so as not to endanger the SALT II treaty. The entire issue, he claimed, was "certainly no reason for a return to the cold war . . . The greatest danger to all the nations of the world is a breakdown of a common effort to preserve the peace . . ."

As Brzezinski had declared: "Where once upon a time an American President might have sent Marines to assure the protection of American strategic interests, there is no room for force in this world of progress and self-determination."

America, its citizens were told officially, was "powerless" to influence deteriorating events in Iran that ultimately led to the downfall of an American ally in one of the most strategic areas of the world. As soon as the Shah got into trouble, the U.S. backed off.

The result? According to Dr. Kissinger, the collapse of the government of Iran and the exile of the Shah resulted in "the biggest foreign policy debacle of the United States in a generation." He said the ousting of the Shah "shifted the balance of power in the Middle East to radical forces."

America's fickleness towards the Shah was evident in that only a year earlier he had been praised by Mr. Carter on a visit to Tehran for his wise, "enlightened" rule over a nation called at that time an "island of stability" in a volatile part of the world.

A similar situation occurred later in the year in Nicaragua, when Soviet and Cuban-backed guerrillas representing themselves as the "forces of democracy" launched an all-out campaign against the government of Anastasio Somoza. The American response — to shrink back from a government (however imperfect) it had earlier supported — was the same. Now the Sandinista revolutionaries are purging non-radical "counter-revolutionaries" from their ranks.

In nearly every case, Washington has over-estimated the power of the "moderates" and "democrats" in the opposition movement and under-estimated the strength of the well-organized Marxists or other radicals (the ones who eventually come to the fore and who have adopted a position hostile to the U.S.).

America's loss of direction will change world-power relationships as never before. Her allies — Western Europe and Japan primarily — will soon be forced to make their own arrangements for survival.

During the ill-fated Cuban crisis, West Germany's *Frankfurter Allgemeine Zeitung* said, for example, that "Mr. Carter has to do something, otherwise America stands before the world as a paper tiger. The Europeans await deeds from their strongest ally for their destiny and that of the Americans cannot be separated." The United States could have bases and ships all over the Middle East and be no better off if it remained paralysingly reluctant to use its military assets in any way.

At the very beginning of the Iranian crisis an ultimatum should have been sent saying that unless every single member of the embassy staff were, within 48 hours, handed over unharmed to representatives of the U.S. Government at some place outside Iran, bombing and other measures would be taken on selected targets. If Iran had not complied, or had responded by killing the hostages, the U.S. should have taken the following action:

* Immediately expelled Iranian diplomats instead of waiting 39 days before they did so.
* Jammed all radio and television transmissions in and from Iran, thus cutting off the country from the outside world and putting paid to their propaganda and psychological warfare campaign.
* Imposed an immediate blockade, keeping food out and oil in.
* Bombed the Abadan kerosene refinery, leaving the whole population to shiver in the winter dark.
* Bombed the tunnels and bridges of the mountainous railway.
* Cut the pipeline that supplies natural gas to the Soviet Union.
* Occupied the three islands off Iran's coast that the Shah seized in order to settle a sovereignty dispute.
* Immediately flown an air task force to Britain's former air base on Oman's island of Masira.
* Assembled a formidable naval task force, including two or more aircraft carriers, in the Arabian Sea.
* Mined the entrance and exit to the Strait of Hormuz.
* Cut the subsidy to the U.N.'s budget for the failure of that organization to condemn Iran.

Such action as the above would have recovered the nation's morale and élan of a great-power. No doubt it would have brought forth howls of protest from the timid West and the Third World, but this would not have lasted for long against the magnitude of the *fait accompli*. The lives of 50 employees of Government cannot count more than those of 50 soldiers or sailors in another war situation.

It took the outright invasion of Afghanistan to awaken President Carter and to neutralize the pitiful, helpless giant syndrome induced by the Tehran kidnap. At long last he seemed determined to restore the credibility of the United States as a force to be reckoned with by the Soviet Union.

As President Carter suddenly saw it, the Afghan invasion was

'NEGOTIATIONS ARE IN A VERY DELICATE STAGE . . .'

Appreciation to *St. Louis Globe-Democrat*, U.S.A.

Moscow's first step *en route* to the sea lanes and oil fields of the Persian Gulf. Britain agreed but other Europeans found such talk melodramatic. To them Afghanistan was a preventive strike to defend a rebellion on the southern border.

President Carter admitted that the Soviet invasion had caused him to change his opinion "more dramatically in one week than in the previous two and a half years about the Kremlin's ultimate goals." It is almost beyond belief that the leader of the most powerful nation on earth could have been so ill-informed and so badly advised that he was in any doubt about the Kremlin's ultimate goals. His admission was as disturbing as it was frank.

"This is the most serious threat to world peace during my Administration", he said. "It's even more serious than Hungary or Czechoslovakia." He called the Afghanistan invasion a "callous violation of international law and the United Nations Charter", and "a deliberate effort of a powerful atheistic government to subjugate an independent Islamic people." He sounded the alarm bells against Soviet designs on Iran, Pakistan and the Persian Gulf as a "stepping stone to possible control over much of the world's oil supplies." He announced, "The world simply cannot stand by and permit the Soviet Union to commit this act of impunity."

The Iranian and Afghanistan crises had finally triggered a new realization in President Carter that the survival of the West will ultimately depend on who controls this region.

Included in the tough set of economic and political reprisals that he ordered were the following:

* He recalled the U.S. Ambassador from Moscow.
* He took the case against the Afghanistan invasion to the U.N.
* He shelved SALT II.
* He consulted Peking on counter-measures.
* He urged Pakistan to accept military aid.
* He barred the supply of high technology and strategic items to the Soviet Union.
* He imposed a stiff cutback on grain supplies.
* He stopped the fishing rights of Russian trawlers in American waters.
* He boycotted the 1980 Summer Olympics in Moscow.
* He cancelled new cultural exchanges between the two countries.
* He postponed the opening of a new Soviet consulate in New York and a U.S. consulate in Kiev.

The President decided to draw up a "Carter Doctrine", a new long-term strategy to contain Russian expansionism in the Middle East and Southern Asia. In view of the vital importance of Middle East oil supplies to the industrial world, the President was now attaching virtually the same importance to the defence of the Middle East as to Western Europe.

The U.S. sent its biggest warship, the nuclear-powered *Nimitz* to join its carrier force off the Strait of Hormuz, and Britain despatched four small vessels to the Mediterranean to free units of the U.S. 6th Fleet.

Unquestionably the U.S. would have blockaded the Gulf, and sowed enough mines to bottle up the Iranian navy and any Soviet ships using their Iraqi ports. But beyond that, Carter's options were limited. Without the use of Portugal's Azores airstrips, heavy armour would have to come from the States with several in-flight refuellings and even then might have nowhere to land.

Efforts to open up new "facilities" ran into opposition, as in Somalia, Kenya and Saudi Arabia, or hesitation, as in Oman. Britain's Diego Garcia base, though being made available to the Americans, is far away. And the Rapid Deployment Force will take several years to prepare.

President Carter, seeking to promote a regional defence system in the Middle East and South-West Asia offered Egypt £444 million in new credits to modernize its armed forces. The defence system is aimed at resisting further Russian expansion in the region. Britain, the NATO allies and Japan, all of whom have a vital stake in the Gulf oil supplies would be expected to make contributions to a joint "Framework for Regional Co-operation." A key feature would be that the nations in the area – including Sudan and Somalia – should themselves take a lead in developing mutual defence supported by the West.

At the end of January, President Carter announced a new record defence budget. This would provide:

* Seventeen new Navy ships to be built and two converted. They would include:

>The ninth Trident nuclear strategic missile submarine.
>
>An additional SSN 688 class nuclear attack submarine.
>
>A third and fourth CG47 class Aegis cruiser.
>
>Four additional FFG 7 patrol frigates.
>
>Five anti-submarine warships.
>
>An amphibious landing ship.
>
>A rescue and salvage ship.
>
>Two maritime prepositioning ships, to provide combat unit equipment and supplies for specially organized marine amphibious brigades.
>
>These floating depot vessels will enable combat supplies to be kept near the Gulf or other threatened areas. In some small measure these vessels will compensate for the loss of former RAF and naval facilities in Aden, Masira, Bahrain and the Gulf States.

* A new long-distance troop transport aircraft, the HCK, for rapid deployment of combat forces.
* Improvements to the Minute-man strategic nuclear missile.
* The MX mobile strategic nuclear missile. This is to be America's main shield against a possible Soviet missile attack.
* Full-scale production of the air-launched Cruise missile – including adaption of the B52 aircraft to carry and launch them.

* Stepping up production of the F-16 and F-18 fighter aircraft.
* For the Army, production of the new main battle tank, the XM-1, to replace the M-60, will be stepped up.
* High-flying reconnaissance planes, and new air tankers.
* Last, but not least, a 100,000-man rapid-deployment force for far-flung trouble spots.

These overdue measures, including the reintroduction of registration for call-up, put some muscle on Mr. Carter's pronouncement of his readiness to use force to defend the Gulf. They also put America even further ahead of her foot-dragging and reluctant European allies. The reason why I refer to the measures as overdue is because for the past decade the Soviet Union has been increasing its real spending on defence by 4-5 per cent a year and allotting some 11-13 per cent of its gross national product to the same purpose, even though its economic growth was slowing and its people suffering increasing shortages. Put that together with the build-up of tanks and new nuclear missiles in the European theatre, the massive submarine programme, the extent of Soviet military aid to third world countries, the use of Cuban troops in Africa, and now the massive invasion of Afghanistan, and Mr. Carter's response was certainly not excessive but merely adequate. He could not have done less.

Within one month of the announcement of his 1981 defence budget of more than £75,000 million General David Jones, Chairman of the American Joint Chiefs of Staff, informed the Senate that the budget would have to be increased if new programmes were to be put into effect in response to the Afghan crisis. For instance, extra money would be needed if military supply ships were to be stationed in the gulf on permanent standby ready to support the Rapid Deployment Force of at least 100,000 men.

America's deed must be made to match her leader's solemn pledge. At present the truth is the United States just does not have enough "conventional" military strength in the region, either deployed or immediately deployable, to carry out the Carter promise that "an assault ... will be repelled by the use of any means necessary." The American carrier fleet in the Indian Ocean provides only part of a credible deterrent. The more important missing part is the 100,000-man emergency strike force which America is raising. Until recently there was talk of a two-year gap before it could be made fully operational. That gap must be closed to make the President's commitment wholly credible.

The next essential is that, now America has given the strong lead which was called for, her friends and allies must move to help her carry this heavy burden. Full emergency facilities must be provided along the African and Arabian route for the huge air bridge which is now being built. Moreover, whether within the formal framework of NATO or out-

35

side it, her alliance partners must come forward with all the concrete assistance they can.

Unfortunately in the West, the uproar was registered in some positive measure but largely in throttled noises. The Olympic boycott was the issue that refused to catch fire, partly because of French resistance to it, partly because of lack of popular support outside the United States, partly because the world sports establishment considers the Olympics more important than what happens up the Khyber Pass.

The French alone made any tough concerted policy by the West virtually impossible. They banned discussion of the Olympics from the formal session of the February Rome meeting of the E.E.C. Foreign Ministers and they pulled the rug from under Mr. Vance's bungled attempt to convene a conference of his leading European peers. Only on 22nd April, 1980, did the E.E.C. governments agree to impose full-scale trade and economic sanctions on Iran.

That apart, some Western European leaders were more sceptical than Mrs. Thatcher over the meaningfulness of declarations made in the United States during an election year in which a weak president is fighting for a new term.

If one examines the speech of Mr. Harold Brown, the former U.S. Defence Secretary, dated 11th February, 1980, several points emerge: he does not envisage the creation of a new Indian Ocean fleet and he believes the present level of naval deployment will be reduced once the Tehran hostages are released; he is not considering selling arms to China or making it part of an anti-Soviet alliance; and he is set on going ahead with the ratification of SALT II once the "immediate problems" created by Afghanistan are out of the way.

The history of resistance to both Nazi and Soviet aggression teaches one plain lesson. Guarantees without muscle are not merely useless. They can actually be dangerous by provoking blows which the aggressor knows cannot be warded off.

It will be several years before there is an American force capable of fast action to stem an Afghanistan-type invasion by conventional means. It is the immediate as well as the long-term dangers which have to be met.

Let us have a look at some of America's present readiness shortcomings.

* For her NATO role the U.S. is supposed to have 90 days' worth of war stocks in Europe but has less than 30 days' worth.
* In 1979 the Services had their worst recruiting year with a shortage of 24,000.
* The most critical shortages were 2,400 Air Force pilots, 45,000 Army non-commissioned officers and 20,000 senior Navy petty officers.
* The manning of Navy ships and aircraft squadrons was significantly below combat readiness.

* In February this year there were two completed and two partially built destroyers that Iran was going to buy. They should have been at sea under the U.S. flag. But the U.S. Navy lacked the skilled personnel to man them.
* The fewer the ships that the U.S. Navy can rotate the worse does its retention problems of key personnel become.
* U.S. reserves are alarmingly weak. By contrast the Soviet Union has 20 million trained reservists.

No wonder conscription became an issue. Of course, it immediately stimulated university campus rebels whose lives had become frustratingly barren of things to rebel about.

The U.S. recruiting shortfall of 24,000 would, in fact, touch only 12 of every 1,000 18 year-old males. The choice in America is therefore between an all-volunteer and an almost all-volunteer force.

The pros and cons of conscription are too numerous to discuss here, but its great asset is two-fold. First, it provides the reserves essential for sustained combat. Second, it demonstrates a nation's seriousness of purpose.

Of course, if political leaders – and this applies to Britain, also – would lead a revival of respect for military careers and would express society's respect through pay commensurate with that for comparable private-sector employment, there would be no shortage of manpower, nor the problem of the retention of key personnel in the Services.

Within a week of throwing down the gauntlet to the Russians, President Carter admitted that to defend the Gulf area would not be easy. His exact words were: "I don't think it would be accurate for me to claim that at this time or in the future we expect to have enough military strength and enough military presence there to defend the region unilaterally." Therefore if the Carter Doctrine is to have any teeth, the U.S. must be able to count on practical help from its NATO allies as well as from the key countries in the region itself.

By virtue of oil, position and population, Iran is the most important state in the Middle East. Rebuilding relations can now only begin once the hostages are released. Relations will have to be developed with caution and sensitivity if the country is not to become fertile ground for a Left-wing takeover that would place it within the Soviet Union's "Commonwealth."

The Soviet Union has the largest – and by far the best-equipped – Army in the world. In strategic weapons, it is at least the equal of the United States and continuing to advance. The Russian Navy, once weak and limited to coastal defence, now is able to challenge America in the world's oceans. And the Soviets are far ahead of the U.S. in civil defence.

Yet barely two decades ago the Soviet Union lagged far behind the U.S. in military power – forced to back down when President Kennedy in 1962 called its nuclear-weapons bluff in Cuba.

How has the Soviet Union grown so strong? Russia is outspending and outbuilding the United States year after year to buy the guns, tanks, aircraft, ships and nuclear missiles needed to challenge America as the world's No. 1 military power.

In 1964, the U.S. had a 4-to-1 lead over Russia in intercontinental ballistic missiles (ICBMs); it had 10 times as many submarine-launched ballistic missiles, over seven times as many long-range bombers and an overwhelming 17 times as many nuclear warheads.

Today, Russia has taken the lead in ICBMs and submarine-launched ballistic missiles. America's lead has been narrowed to a mere 340 to 156 in long-range bombers and only 9,200 to 6,000 in total warheads.

In conventional-military strength, Russia is far ahead of the United States. Since 1970, while the U.S. armed forces have been shrinking by a million — from 3.1 million to 2.1. million — the Soviet forces have expanded by more than 400,000 to an estimated 4.4 million. That's more than twice the American level.

In tanks, guns and planes, the picture is similar. And Russia is steadily building up its advantage. From 1977 to 1979, Russia outbuilt the U.S. by a yearly margin of 2,000 to 650 in tanks, 500 to 275 in combat planes, 350 to 150 in helicopters, six to three in attack submarines and 5,000 to 1,000 in other combat vehicles. Only in big surface ships is the U.S. holding even at 10 per year.

On 29th January, 1980, Defence Secretary Harold Brown, in a report to Congress, gave the following picture of how the Soviet Union has built up its conventional forces since 1964:

* Tanks — up from 30,000 in 1964 to 45,000 in 1980, an increase of 15,000.
* Divisions — up from 145 to 170, adding 25 divisions.
* Artillery pieces and rocket launchers — up from 11,000 to 20,000, almost doubling in number.
* Fighter attack aircraft — up from 3,500 to 4,500.
* Total military manpower — up from 3.4 million in 1964 to an estimated 4.4 million now, an increase of 1 million.

The U.S. by comparison, has 12,100 tanks, 19 divisions and 5,018 tactical airplanes.

In naval strength, the expansion in the past decade has been enormous. Between 1970 and 1975, the Soviets were launching 40 surface warships and seven submarines annually, while the U.S. output was averaging a little over seven surface ships and less than one submarine each year.

According to Defence Secretary Brown, between 1964 and 1980, the Soviets increased their number of major surface combatants and amphibious ships from 260 to 360 and their total naval tonnage from 2 million to 2.8 million.

Today's naval comparison is: the United States has 13 aircraft carriers to two for the Soviet Union, 234 other surface combatant and amphibious ships to Russia's 360 and 75 nuclear-powered attack submarines to Russia's 86.

Impressive, too, is the build-up over the past decade of Russia's capacity to project military power into almost any part of the world. The Kremlin has the naval and aerial transport that it once lacked.

All this has been accomplished at enormous cost to and sacrifice by the Russian People. While defence spending by the U.S. trended downwards for most of the 1970s, Russia's military spending has soared steadily. According to a study by the Central Intelligence Agency, Soviet military spending from 1970 to 1979 exceeded the U.S. total by 30 per cent. In 1979 alone, the Soviet total of 165 billion dollars was approximately 50 per cent higher than the 108 billion spent by the United States.

Such spending is a crushing burden on a Soviet economy with a gross national product that is only about 60 per cent that of the U.S. The Pentagon estimates that the Russians spent 11 to 14 per cent of their GNP on military activities throughout the last decade. By contrast, defence spending by the U.S. accounted for approximately eight per cent of the national GNP in 1970 – a Vietnam War year – and only five per cent in 1979.

One can take no comfort in the nuclear field. Within three years the Soviets will have the capability of destroying most American *land* based missiles in a surprise attack, together with many of their missile submarines and nuclear bombers, without inflicting massive destruction on the American *civilian* population. Dr. Kissinger has suggested 1982 as the likely date; that is less than two years off. Other analysts have argued that it may even be sooner. In any case, the Americans will not be able, in the same time scale, either to strike with sufficient accuracy at the Soviet intercontinental ballistic missile force or to develop means of protecting their own. The Soviets will thus have achieved *strategic* nuclear superiority.

Of course, it would still be open to the U.S. to retaliate against Soviet *cities* with their surviving submarine based missiles and bombers but since this would lead to Soviet strikes against American *cities*, would any American president feel justified in taking this decision? He would after all be taking an almost suicidal step, *not* in retaliation against a massive attack on the American *people*, but to avenge a crippling strike against the American nuclear triad – land based missiles, missile submarines and nuclear bombers.

Western superiority in shorter-range tactical or battlefield nuclear weapons is being rapidly overtaken. At present there is no Western response to the Soviet deployment of their *theatre* medium range nuclear missiles, namely the SS20 and the Backfire bomber.

For the next three-four years Europe will have no effective anti-ballistic missile defence nor deterrent against this latest Soviet intermediate-range nuclear missile, the mobile SS20. This is the world's most advanced intermediate range ballistic missile.

Each missile carries three independently targetted nuclear warheads with a range of more than 2,200 miles, which means they can hit any target in Western Europe from Gibraltar to the North Cape.

Although the SS20 could destroy much of the war capability of Western Europe it is not included in the SALT II negotiations – the *Strategic* Arms Limitation Treaty. Thus, these new "Eurostrategic" weapons not only neutralize America's intercontinental nuclear weapons, but also make a nonsense of NATO's whole strategy of deterrence. *No American president would now put Washington at risk in order to avenge London!*

We have thus to face the fact that in *conventional* capability, *tactical* nuclear capability, *theatre* nuclear capability, and *strategic* nuclear capability the U.S. and NATO are now or soon will be inferior to those of the Soviet Union. And it must be several years before the West can hope to close the gap.

This vulnerability of Western Europe has been confirmed by the NATO decision to introduce *theatre* medium range nuclear missiles for deployment in Europe. But the stark reality of the situation is that Western Europe over the next three-four years, before the new weapons are on the ground, will be in supreme danger.

We have seen how the combined effect of Iran and Afghanistan was to shake the Americans out of the passivity that characterized their approach to international affairs after Vietnam. Their new determination had important implications for the presidential election. The immediate effect of the crises was to rally opinion behind the President. But for how long would foreign affairs drive other issues off the political agenda? Once the hostages were released, would foreign policy become any more important than other principal issues – although more important than it had been previously?

The Americans negotiated deals for air and naval facilities in the vicinity of the Gulf of Aden and the Persian Gulf, but once the election was over and the hostages released would American public opinion support a forward policy which had no tangible support from their allies?

America's allies were doing a lot less than pulling their weight when it came to backing up the U.S. over the Tehran hostages or facing up to the Russians over Afghanistan. The French turned up their noses at the notion of boycotting the Moscow Olympics. The Germans murmured nervously about the need to adhere to their *Ostpolitik*. "Détente is indivisible" was how Hans Dietrich Genscher, Bonn's Foreign Minister, put it to German reporters in Washington after seeing Mr. Carter.

While the West Germans agree that the Soviet Union must be deterred from more Afghanistan-style annexations, they are not prepared to sacrifice their détente policy whatever the provocation. Their

Left and Right—just an armband apart!

"pussy footing" and appeasement policies are due to the fact that they have the most to fear from war in Europe and the most to gain from détente. Berlin is nearer than Kabul and they dread a return to the cold war. What they forget is that Moscow's long term plans to seize control of the West's supplies of raw materials will not merely wipe out millions of jobs *but bring them and their allies to their knees*.

As far as oil is concerned the West Europeans, Japanese and the so-called Third World have a great deal more to lose than America if the Russians were finally to get a strangle-hold on the Persian Gulf. Indeed, America would be well advised to pay much closer attention to Alaska, Athabaska and Mexico for their alternative sources of energy supplies. The oilfields, tar sands, shale and natural gas deposits have already been tapped in the Western hemisphere. The Athabaska tar sands in Alberta, which spill over into Montana, alone have immense potential. There exist enormous reserves of oil – not to mention hundreds of years' supplies of coal – in the Americas, perhaps as much as in Arabia, if not so easy to extract.

There is really no need for America, therefore, to let itself be at the mercy of any crazy bunch of Islamic zealots who want to turn time back to the Middle Ages, nor yet to militant Reds or other envious or plain greedy pests.

It might hurt a bit, of course. Some readjustment might be

necessary to life-styles, but it is really no more, basically, than a question of prices, for at some point Middle East oil could get too expensive to bother with. American ingenuity should be able to develop alternatives. After all, it is barely a century since they struck oil in Pennsylvania, which is what sparked off the petroleum age.

The Americans could, at a pinch, and without bleeding too much, retire into their continent and let the rest of us go to blazes. Those Britons of us who are old enough will, of course, recognize the symptoms. We remember how it was when we were the guardians of the seas. Nobody thanked us, either.

CHAPTER
5

Afghanistan

The key dates in Afghanistan's bloody past include:

329-27 BC	Alexander the Great conquered Afghanistan, part of the ancient Persian Empire.
9th Century AD	The country converted to Islam.
1400	Conquered by Timur.
1504-1738	Part of Mongol Empire.
1747	Became independent under Ahmed Khan.
1838-42	First British-Afghan War, to deflect growing Russian influence. Epic Retreat from Kabul left one white survivor.
1878-80	Second British-Afghan War. Kabul occupied. Many Afghans hanged. Lord Roberts, later C-in-C India, makes reputation at Relief of Kanghar. Gladstone calls it "most frivolous war ever waged."
1885	Russians occupy Penjdeh, just north of Afghan Frontier. British Stationery Office prints declaration of war but this was never issued.
1894	Sir Mortimer Durand defines "Durand Line" – present Afghan-Pakistan frontier – dividing the warring Pathan tribes.
1897	Heavy fighting round Wakhan salient, as British secure southern flank and Russians the north.
1902	Curzon, Viceroy of India, dissuaded from annexing Afghanistan.
1907	Britain and Russia effectively partition Persia and agree status quo in Kabul.
1919	Third Afghan War. Britain briefly opposes independence (making first use of air power to strafe villages) but then grants it under Treaty of Rawalpindi.

1945-55	Heavy U.S. aid, abruptly cut off with rise to power of the so-called "Red Prince" Daoud.
1973	After steady growth of Soviet influence, monarchy replaced by republic as Daoud seizes full control in military coup.
1978	Daoud deposed and killed by first Moscow protégé Muhammad Tarakki.
September 1979	Tarakki killed in palace shoot-out, replaced by Hafizullah Amin.
Christmas 1979	Amin executed in Moscow-backed *coup* to install Babrak Karmal.
	Full-scale naked invasion by Russia.

To understand the seriousness of the present situation it is necessary to go back into history. Hence the importance of the above key dates and the following quotations.

In 1885 this statement appeared in the Moscow newspaper *Novosti* — "Herat must be taken and so pierce a window looking south-eastwards, a convenient halting place for a still further advance towards the Indian Ocean in fulfilment of Russia's historic destiny."

This picture, published in 1896 by Lieut. C. A. L. Totten places the Russian Bear's paw over Afghanistan and Persia (Iran) with head and right paw menacing Turkey.
Destiny Editorial Letter Service, U.S.A.

It was Tzar Nicholas II (1894-1919) who stated "All we have to do to paralyse British foreign policy is to send a telegram mobilizing our forces in Turkestan."

Lord Curzon, Viceroy of India, advocating the pre-emptive annexation of Afghanistan in 1902, announced — "Russia is steadily swallowing the Persian artichoke leaf by leaf."

By the 1860s the great Russian drive into Central Asia was well under way. The Tsar and his Generals saw in Central Asian conquests not only prospects of Russian aggrandisement but the opportunity to threaten Britain through the back door of her Indian Empire.

Once the Russian drive had begun it was not too difficult to maintain the momentum. Traders and settlers pushed farther afield and came into contact with other Central Asian tribes. There were problems of raiding and disputes which called for Russian intervention. Thus the army advance continued. In this way, one after the other, the Khanates of Central Asia collapsed like so many cards before the Russian advance.

Chart 2 on page 23 shows this only too clearly and illustrates how the Russian menace turned the whole area into a corridor of invasion. The encroachment has now reached right up to the Durand Line, thereby posing a direct and immediate threat to Pakistan. This means that the Tarakki *coup* of April 1978 has resulted in bringing the Russian threat to the Khyber Pass itself. Thus Afghanistan's role as the 'buffer' state, which the British had designed, has now disappeared.

The Soviet Union's aim to control the major energy resources of the capitalist world is nothing new. It is a long standing aim as can be proved by documents in the archives of the German Foreign Office, at present in the State Department in Washington, which tell that, after the non-aggression Pact between the Nazis and the Russians was signed in 1939, Russia demanded that: "the area south of Batum and Baku in the general direction of the Persian Gulf be recognized as the centre of the aspirations of the Soviet Union."

Those of us who have served in that part of the world and have the background experience and knowledge know perfectly well that if the Soviet hold on Afghanistan can be consolidated, Moscow's next move will be to extend subversion into Pakistan by supporting Baluchi and Pathan separatism and Afghan irredentism. For Russia securely established in Afghanistan, the road to the Gulf is Pakistan, just as in the past the road to India lay through the Punjab.

From what I have written so far it should be perfectly obvious that there is absolutely no excuse for Washington and London to have been unprepared for Moscow's takeover. The basic preparations had been in train for 32 years, namely when Britain's departure from India in 1947 removed the traditional counter-poise to Russia's centuries-old policy of Asiatic expansion. Then in 1955 America abruptly cancelled their aid programme in protest at the radical policies of "Red Prince" Daoud.

Twelve years ago in 1967, travellers observed the large-scale engineering extensions at the Oxus river port of Termez, where the Russian T-54 and T-62 tanks and their self-propelled artillery units were shipped across for the Christmas invasion last year.

Despite denials by Afghanistan's leaders, the leftist military government which seized power in April 1978, in a bloody revolution, turned the country into a virtual Soviet satellite. Head of that remote but strategically important Moslem nation of about 14 million was Moscow's protégé, President Nur Muhammad Tarakki, secretary-general of the ruling People's Democratic Party.

Tarakki was a father figure, a poet and writer. His life story was taught in schools, just as Mao's was in China.

In an attempt to assuage conservative Moslems, Tarakki declined to call his government Marxist (though few doubted that was its true orientation) and officially claimed to be non-aligned.

The facts, however, spoke for themselves. On 5th December, 1978, Afghanistan and Moscow signed a 20 year "peace and friendship" pact, with military aspects, further tightening links between the two countries which share a 1,000 mile border. At the time of my visit to Pakistan in June-July 1979, the current number of Soviet advisers in Afghanistan was assessed to be about 5,000 – more than double what it was before the *coup*. Moreover, since April 1978 the Kremlin had supplied plenty of T-62 tanks, MiG fighters and MI-24 helicopters – the latter being used in a helicopter gunship role against the guerrillas.

Tarakki and the Khalq (or People's Party) took over the government of the country in a short bloody *coup* that ended the near feudal rule – and the life – of President Daoud.

Afghanistan was then used by the Soviets as a base to foster and promote trouble among ethnic minorities in neighbouring Iran and Pakistan, especially the Baluchis who are inhabitants of the sparsely populated southern coast and the southern area of Pakistan, and the adjacent southern coastal area of Iran north of the Gulf of Oman. This, coupled with the inciting of the ethnic minorities of Khuzestan, Kurdistan, and Azerbaijan in Iran, is designed to open the way to the warm, oil-rich ports of the Persian and Oman Gulfs and the ports of southern Pakistan. If these three countries were forced into the Soviet inspired Asian Collective Security System, Russia would achieve a multi-dimensional strategic thrust whose tremors would be felt all the way from Japan to Western Europe.

The threat to the Baluchistan Province of Pakistan could be as great, if not greater, than it is to Pakistan's North West Frontier Province.

The depth of opposition to the Tarakki régime was due to the belief that the government's radical modernization programmes threatened Afghanistan's Islamic traditions. There was also a deep-seated hatred of the 5,000 Soviet advisers aiding the régime.

While I was in Pakistan, in mid-1979, the guerrilla movement in the Afghan countryside and the erosion of public support throughout Afghanistan's Muslim society was threatening to topple the country's Soviet-backed Marxist government.

The ability of President Nur Muhammad Tarakki's government to maintain law and order had deteriorated despite massive backing of Soviet arms and advisers. It was obvious to me that whether the Tarakki régime would survive or fall would be decided by their Soviet masters — unless, of course, Tarakki himself were to fall to the assassin's bullet. The régime was entirely dependent upon the Soviet Union.

The situation was being watched anxiously by Pakistan on account of the foothold that the Russians had obtained in the region, which is a strategic highway both to the Indian subcontinent and to the mouth of the Gulf.

Communications in this remote, mountainous country are poor, and foreigners were restricted in travels outside Kabul and in contacts with Afghan citizens, so it was difficult to assess the political situation outside the capital. However, it was probably true to say that the government controlled only about half of the country, with major areas of eastern, western and central Afghanistan then under control of the guerrillas. Fighting between Tarakki's armed forces and a variety of guerrilla groups was taking place in most areas. The only regions reported quiet were the southern provinces of Kandahar and Helmand.

The guerrilla movement was mainly spontaneous, with local tribesmen fighting predominantly under their own leaders within their own regions. Although there were signs emerging of organization among tribal groups, it remained a splintered but effective movement with little central direction, planning, control or outside support. In fact, the major source of new weapons for the guerrillas appeared to be Soviet arms surrendered or abandoned by Afghan army units.

It was one of the few purely spontaneous revolts going on in the world. Whatever they lacked in organization was made up in religious fervour and Soviet xenophobia. There were all kinds of groups fighting against the government, but there was no "they" holding them together. There was only "it" — Islam. With central control, training in the techniques of modern guerrilla warfare and armed with hand-held anti-tank and anti-aircraft missile firing weapons, they would have been, and will still be, a force to be reckoned with.

The Russians, of course, were fully aware of the difficulties that the guerrillas would experience unless they were able to operate from the safe sanctuary of a neighbouring country. Hence the embarrassing situation in which Pakistan found itself. At that time — July 1979 — there were about 100,000 refugees in tribal areas in Baluchistan and the North West Frontier Province.

This gave the Soviet Union, through the medium of psychological warfare, an ideal opportunity to exploit the situation by accusing

Pakistan of arming and training the refugees and launching them into Afghanistan to bolster the guerrilla forces. Pakistan, in fact, was doing no such thing and was being very careful not to exacerbate the delicate situation. Furthermore, the 100,000 or so refugees were a strain on Pakistan's economy.

Well may it be said that Pakistan was walking a tight-rope and already had a more sensitive refugee problem than that posed by the Vietnam "boat people" to the countries of South-East Asia and to the West as a whole.

The Afghan regular army had been purged and there were political "commissars" attached to each unit who acted as the "eyes and ears" of the Government. In addition, there were Russian "advisers" right down to sub-unit level.

The Afghan infantry as a whole was not considered to be reliable and for the most part were deployed in a static role. The real offensive fighting was being undertaken by the four battalions of Afghan Commandos, supported by Russian tanks, aircraft and helicopter gunships. The latter were the main anti-guerrilla offensive weapons and were a real battle-winner. They were taking off at first light on sorties against rebels and their villages, and at night searchlights scanned the hills.

The size of the country and the vast barren areas was affording ideal opportunities to the guerrillas to be able to cut regularly the major arterial roads and to hold them for several hours at a time before they were dislodged by tanks and Russian piloted heligunships and aircraft. The land-locked country's main link with the outside world, east over the Khyber Pass to Pakistan, was particularly vulnerable.

There are two main routes to Afghanistan: the Khyber–Kabul road which carries 70 per cent of the country's imports and exports, and the Kabul–Russia road which accounts for the remaining 30 per cent.

At the time of my stay in Pakistan the government still controlled all the large urban centres in the country and major arterial roads most of the time, although considerable effort was needed to keep them open. The Kabul road east to the Khyber Pass and Pakistan, for example, was heavily patrolled and vehicles were stopped and searched at numerous checkpoints. At some locations tanks guarded the road.

Guerrilla groups were able to capture and hold for a number of hours small urban communities in many parts of the country. In the rugged eastern border areas, several towns remained under siege, with government forces able to relieve them only by air or by armoured tank column. As the government ruthlessly suppressed opposition to its modernization programme, its popular support continued to erode, and the overwhelming majority of the population appeared opposed to it.

With the aid of an 11 p.m. to 4 a.m. curfew, the government controlled the capital of Kabul, although even here some fighting had taken place. Troops were guarding major installations, and Russian advisers, once a common sight in the city's shopping areas, were conspicuous by their absence.

Remote Afghanistan tribes have traditionally resisted control by governments in Kabul, and many Afghan leaders have ruled for long periods controlling little more than what the Tarakki government controlled then. But the depth of anti-Soviet feeling and the fear that the country's Islamic traditions were under attack had generated a convulsive uprising and it was obvious to me that it could eventually engulf Kabul and other cities.

Khalqis (members of the ruling Khalq or People's Party) were going out to remote villages trying to redistribute land and bring girls into schools. The villagers became perturbed and afraid whereupon the mullahs and landowners stirred up these fears. It was then that all hell broke loose.

In urban areas, the Tarakki government was rounding up large numbers of civilians suspected of opposing its rule. There were also reports that the government was conducting a systematic campaign of executions to remove opposition. One report that I read said: "The level of executions going on here makes what is happening in Iran look like child's play. The problem here is they don't bother with show trials, so it is hard to keep the score."

By Western standards, the Khalq reforms would appear to have been long overdue. They included basic land reform, an end to usury and the custom of bride-price (where the husband must purchase his wife) and encouraging education of women.

But the Khalqis, who draw their support mainly from the country's thin band of intellectuals, teachers and advanced-level students, seriously misjudged the depth of Islamic roots and traditions among the country's largely illiterate, rural population. The Khalqis showed no sensitivity to the values of the country. They tried to do too much too soon and after realizing their mistakes, did too little too late to correct them.

The rise of staunch Islamic governments in neighbouring Iran and Pakistan had added more spiritual resolve to the rebels to "fight godless Communism".

As pressure on the Tarakki government mounted, its fate hinged on two key factors: how long the armed forces were willing or able to continue their distasteful task of killing their fellow countrymen in the face of heavy losses and increased unpopularity; and how long the Russians would continue to support Tarakki.

What the Russians would do was the 64 thousand dollar question. There were two alternatives: continue as they were then doing but with more Soviet "advisers" and more tanks, aircraft and helicopters; or engineer a *coup* to remove Tarakki and intervene militarily with troops.

If the Russians were to wait too long, a revolt within the country's hard-pressed armed forces would take the decision out of their hands.

Indian journalists who accompanied Mr. Desai, Prime Minister, on his visit to Moscow in June 1979, reported that Mr. Kosygin, the now late Soviet Prime Minister, told them that the Kremlin would protect the Kabul government "whatever happens". And, at a dinner in honour of Mr. Desai, President Brezhnev, according to the Indian journalists, said: "We will not leave our friend (Afghanistan) in need."

Despite defections during an uprising in the western city of Herat in March 1979, a subsequent mutiny of an army garrison in Jalalabad in April, and unconfirmed reports of unit defections, the military had so far stuck grimly to its task of maintaining law and order against rising resistance.

But a series of purges and liquidations of officers coupled with heavy casualties and desertions of both officers and the rank and file had created a manpower crisis for the military.

One source estimated that only a quarter of the army's 8,000 officers at the time of the Tarakki Marxist *coup* on 27th April, 1978, were still alive. Morale within the conscript army was reportedly flagging. To fill up the junior ranks, the government was drafting its own Khalqi cadre, students and day labourers.

If the Tarakki Government was overthrown there was bound to be a bloodbath. It was widely believed in Kabul that dissidents had already prepared lists of Khalqis for execution. To an Afghan, revenge is a cornerstone of life. Those who had suffered under his régime wanted their revenge first, then they would think about what kind of government to set up.

In mid-July I had a long meeting and lunch at Government House, Peshawar, with Lieutenant-General Fazale Haq, the Governor of the North West Frontier Province (NWFP). He is also the Corps Commander. Present at the meeting were the Commissioner of the NWFP, Mr. Jamshed Burki, the Chief Secretary and the Home Secretary. This meeting is described in Chapter 6 on Pakistan.

The following day, accompanied by the Commissioner of the NWFP and two of his political Agents, I was motored in the Corps Commander's air-conditioned Mercedes, from Peshawar through the Khyber Pass — which I know so well — to Tor Kham, right on the frontier with Afghanistan — the Durand Line.

I soon discovered that Mr. Burki's father and I had served together in the same Division in Burma in World War II. The Division was the 7th Indian Division (The Golden Arrow Division), and Burki's father was the Assistant Director of Medical Services, with the rank of Brigadier. Throughout our journey Burki proved to be an excellent companion, very knowledgeable and answered all my questions. A great deal of what I have written so far in this chapter was gleaned from him.

All was peaceful on the drive from Peshawar and little had changed since my last visit there 45 years ago. We stopped at Jamrud Fort and had refreshments with the Commanding Officer of the 27th Punjab

Regiment and met some of his officers and his Subedar Major – the latter every inch an outstanding figure of the old Indian Army type. Then on to Fort Maude (named after General Maude, a former Commander-in-Chief of the pre-partition Indian Army), and now called Shaghai Fort, garrisoned by the Khyber Rifles.

The next stop was Landi Kotal, the Headquarters of the Khyber Rifles, and also garrisoned by a regular Infantry Battalion. It is here that the famous railway ends – one of the marvels of the world, built by my kinsman, Sir Cussack Walton, between 1920-25. Residing on the mantlepiece of our dining room today is a section of the carved pillar – Gandhara – of a temple, 200 BC – AD 200, unearthed by Cussack Walton and presented to him by the Indian Government.

At Tor Kham I inspected the Guard of the Khyber Rifles and had refreshments with the local tribal leaders and elders. Through Burki, acting as interpreter, I spoke to the Afghan sentry on duty at the frontier and shook hands with him. A short distance in the background was the small frontier post with the Red flag flying from the tower. All the notices at the frontier on the Afghanistan side are painted in red. This, and the flying of the Red flag was, I was told by Burki, introduced in October 1978 – Afghanistan's National Day.

It was interesting to observe with my own eyes once again how the Durand Line, the international frontier reaffirmed as such by Afghan régimes in two treaties of 1894 and 1919, follows the tactical features favouring Pakistan.

The defences built during World War II were intact, but in need of a good deal of restoration. It was easy to see how the whole area could be outflanked and overflown from the air by surprise attack using parachutists and helicopter-borne troops.

Although all was quiet on the Pakistan side of the border, the number of tourists had fallen from a daily 300–400 before the Tarakki *coup* in April last year to only 20-25 each day at the time of my visit.

On the return journey we stopped at Landi Kotal, had refreshments in the Officers Mess of the Headquarters of the Khyber Rifles, where I was led on a conducted tour. Then we had lunch in the official residence of the Political Agent. After lunch his father joined us and I discovered that not only were we about the same age but that he had been one of the Pathan tribesmen who had spent his time sniping at my soldiers during operations in Warizistan in 1939-41! He recounted several experiences and remarked how high in their esteem they had held and respected Gurkha soldiers in particular. He also described how he and a party of tribesmen had all but wiped out a piquet held by a recently arrived British Battalion, not yet acclimatised to and sufficiently highly trained in frontier warfare techniques.

To revert to the situation that existed in Afghanistan at the time of my visit to Pakistan, in June-July 1979.

From the display of banners and slogans all over Kabul, Afghan loyalty to the government could scarcely be questioned. Yet the activities in the hours after the U.S. Ambassador, Adolph "Spike" Dubs, was assassinated on the 14th February, 1979, painted a different picture.

The assassination convinced many Afghans that the counter-revolution had started. Down came the red bunting from many buildings. Off came the Khalq Party's red star insignia from army caps and uniforms and the plastic badges from suits and dresses signifying party membership.

Mr. Tarakki professed that he personally decried the practice of putting up red cloths printed with his portrait in shops all over the city. His denial of any personality cult, despite constant references to him as a "great leader of the revolution" or occasionally as a "genius writer" for his poetry, lacked the ring of total conviction.

The Khalq Party had rushed through land reform with more speed than preparation. Since the new year (1979), about 700,000 acres had been distributed to 180,00 families and twice as much land would be handed out if the authorities were to be believed.

The Russians were said to be willing to pay the bill for the party's speed, which apparently had been forced upon them in order to win popular backing in the face of growing insurgency in the countryside. Neither seeds nor fertilizer were provided and no adequate land ownership surveys were completed so that some recipients had been returning their deeds.

Many farmers refused to plant crops that winter once they knew land reform was coming. Combined with a bad drought and a shaky administration and further weakened by constant purges, it was assessed that the failure could cause a deficit of about 500,000 tons of wheat that year. There was the possibility that some areas, notably in the east and north-west, could face famine conditions late that year or early this year. And as Eastern Europe shows, the bitterest legacy of such tough tactics is peasant suspicions for decades.

In any case, insecurity in much of the countryside and ham-handed reforms had combined to make major development schemes impractical for the time being.

It was during my visit to Pakistan that Afghanistan sent their Deputy Foreign Minister to Islamabad. He was the first Afghan Minister to visit Pakistan since the Tarakki coup. General Zia suggested the visit as the start of a dialogue to end the feuding between the two countries and to pave the way for a possible summit meeting between him and President Tarakki. The hope was that General Zia would be able to convince the Afghan Minister that Pakistan was not training or equipping the refugees and would gladly see their early departure.

The role of neighbouring India to the events in Afghanistan seemed to me to be very dubious. While the traditional buffer was being overrun by Soviet advisers and military hardware, India was keeping the hate-fires against Pakistan and China burning and adding to her arsenal of tanks, guns and aircraft. Brigadier Noor Husain said to me: "Does she see in this situation her chance of the century as she did against East Pakistan in 1971, or is India so completely overawed by Russian might and 1971 favours, that she had accepted in principle the Russian-inspired Asian Collective Security System? Is this the 'Little Game' – the Indian version of the historical 'Great Game?' "

By now it should be abundantly obvious to the reader that the brutal blow from the Soviet Union's steel fist should certainly not have come as such a surprise to Washington and London. As usual it was a sad chronicle of wishful thinking, complacency, surprises and mis-calculations.

Over the past fifteen years or so the assessment of Soviet intentions by the so-called professionals employed in the White House, the U.S. State Department and the British Foreign Office could not have been more inaccurate. As for the majority of NATO leaders, they could not or would not look beyond the confines of the Alliance's present boundaries; the Tropic of Cancer being the most southerly.

The Press, television and radio wield an immensely powerful weapon in their power to influence public opinion. But with one or two honourable exceptions the Western Press has largely mis-led its readers for the past thirty years on the Russian and Warsaw Pact military build-up. They did the same before World War II when they were responsible for promoting the merit of the status quo with Hitler's Germany which resulted in appeasement, whereas all along the Nazis were intent on sheer domination unless resisted.

The fashionable French word of the 1970s, *détente*, is equivalent to appeasement, the equally fashionable word of the 1930s. The late 1970s can be compared to the late 1930s, but this time with Russia supplanting Germany as the main threat. The jackboot is still there, so is the goose-step – the cartoon on page 41 is most apt.

During World War II there was a Ministry of Information whose job it was positively to inform. Today we have a hamstrung public relations whose responsibility is almost to conceal. It is as if there was a conspiracy of silence.

As long ago as September 1978 President Mohammed Zia ul-Haq warned that a Marxist government in Kabul, supported by the Soviets, had gravely upset the balance of power in the region. He gave notice that "the Russians are now at the Khyber Pass". But that was certainly a message of warning that neither Washington nor London wanted to hear.

Two months after I departed from Pakistan, on 16th September, 1979, Tarakki was overthrown and killed by Hafizullah Amin, his Prime Minister. As former Prime Minister as well as Defence Minister and head of the secret police he had earned a reputation for ruthlessness. He played the role of Robespierre, ordering waves of purges and was the architect of the Tarakki government's most repressive measures, including atrocities, the execution of at least 2,000 political prisoners and the imprisonment of 30,000 others. By this time the Muslim tribesmen controlled twenty-two of the country's twenty-eight provinces. Therefore, if Amin's government was to survive it had to win quick success on the battlefield or come to terms with some of the tribal groups. But few people had any confidence in Amin's ability to restore peace to their embattled country.

Said one state trading company executive in Kabul: "Amin's much worse than Tarakki. If he is not killed within two months, I'm afraid we'll see fighting for another ten years." Amin's future was assessed in the words of an old Afghan folk expression, "Barre Duroz Shah": King for two days. Meanwhile the Soviet "advisers" had been trampling on Islamic sensibilities like a clumsy bear.

On 21st October, with the help of the 3,000 Soviet "military advisers" and pilots then in the country, Amin opened a full scale offensive against the guerrillas. Helicopter gunships went in and started strafing villages. Napalm bombing was used with devastating effect. Refugees, who until then had only been trickling into Pakistan, started to flood over the border.

But the guerrillas' determination seemed to increase in the face of this assault and it was clear that in Moscow it was realized that Mr. Amin was so universally unpopular and incompetent that he would have to be removed before long and replaced by a Muslim inspired régime — so the Soviet decision to move into Afghanistan was taken.

In a ruthless *coup* Amin was overthrown and executed, and in his place was installed the Soviet protégé, Babrak Karmal, who had been kept on ice by the Russians until he was needed. Karmal, the well-born son of a General, is a dyed-in-the-wool Communist. It is unlikely that he has the agility necessary to reconcile the tribal, religious and ideological disputes that divide his volatile country. But Moscow will ensure that he responds as a puppet should when its strings are jerked.

By the time the Russian Army struck brutally and decisively they had already endured a number of provocations, including the shooting, public torture to death, even flaying alive, of hundreds of Soviet "advisers" and citizens and the decapitation of thirty-five advisers with the parading of their heads on spikes by torchlight. On top of this was the danger of a Marxist régime, on the very doorstep of the U.S.S.R., falling victim to a wave of Muslim fanaticism.

The desk warriors of the West had continued to wallow in their sleeping sickness. Even the visit of two very senior Russian envoys did not cause the alarm bells to be tinkled. These two VIPs were none other than the Commander-in-Chief of the Soviet ground forces, General Pavlovsky, and the Red Army's chief commissar, Alexei Shepilov. The latter was heavily involved in crushing Czechoslovakia in August 1968.

The final refinements in the Soviet plan were being worked out before Amin seized power on 16th September, 1979. The week between

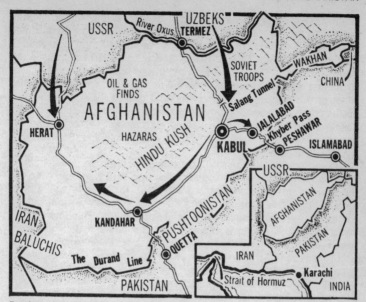

Brezhnev, tribesman and the battleground: arrows on map show Soviet advances.
Appreciation to *Sunday Times*, London, 6th January, 1980.

Christmas and the New Year was not chosen merely because the West would be in a festive mood and more somnolent that usual, with their seats of power, military headquarters and units at skeleton strength. Not only were the Americans preoccupied with events in Iran, but militarily the over-riding factor was the necessity to secure in strength all the main roads and key towns before the oncome of the heavy snows, and to ensure that the Red Army's garrisons were self-sufficient in supplies and manpower without the need of constant replenishment and reinforcement before the Spring. This was one of the reasons why the Soviet forces were deployed in such strength in this rugged and vastly inhospitable country. They then proceeded to dig-in for the Winter.

Like Prague in 1968, Kabul was a lightning, highly organized take over. Russia's assertion that they were invited in to help the country against outside aggression was manifestly false, for the person Brezhnev claimed had invited them to come into the country was President Amin, whom the Russians killed immediately after they staged their *coup*. The Russians made no attempt to disguise the fact that their airlift began two days before the *coup*. Furthermore, the first radio address was beamed to Afghanistan from a station inside Russia, and President Karmal did not put in an appearance in Afghanistan until four days after the *coup*.

The strength, speed, efficiency and smoothness of the Russian blitzkrieg in crashing across the Afghan border with at least five divisions

55

(80-85,000 men) in 10 days, is proof enough that it was a carefully stage-managed operation, whose Trojan horse beginning took almost everyone by surprise. It was a textbook-in-miniature for conventional warfare in the 1980s. First, Russian "Saboteurs" disarmed unsuspecting Afghan soldiers. Next, Soviet airborne troops seized the capital, Kabul. Then fast-moving motorized rifle divisions swept across the border. Most of the soldiers were reservists who proved their adaptability to such a combined operation involving armour, infantry, supporting arms, airborne and air-delivered troops and air support. The command and control system was exceptionally good and flexible and the leadership, dynamic and daring.

The Soviet swoop was quickly turned, not into an invasion, but a full-scale occupation of the country. The iron fist behind the *coup* and the lightning invasion and ruthless seizure of the country was a demonstration to Pakistan, Iran, Rumania and Hungary — and, indeed, Yugoslavia — of what happens to unruly neighbours. The Soviet Union could repeat the Afghan scenario — on a far larger scale — anywhere from Western Europe to the Persian Gulf to the Chinese frontier.

It was not worth going to war for Hungary, or Czechoslovakia; nobody is going to war with Russia over Afghanistan. They know it, we know it. *The Russians will remain*. The U.S. do not have a trump card that will force the Soviets out of Afghanistan.

The country has been annexed. Having imposed military domination the Soviets proceeded to take over the administration with a view to the long-term occupation of Afghanistan. Civilian advisers arrived in the country to take up positions in the top tiers of government. These new administrators speak fluent Farsi, the official language, and are well-tutored in local customs. Each one of the Russians in his department has been expertly trained for the job. The result is the virtual colonization of Afghanistan.

The Soviets are now sitting pretty for a strike into Iran if the Khomeini régime were to disintegrate. They would have the eastern half of Iran before the U.S. could react. There is nothing to stop them. The only impediment would be one inferior Iranian division at Mashad.

Pakistan is equally vulnerable and this is discussed later. From Afghanistan both Baluchistan and Iran can be subverted. Therefore the U.S.S.R. are preparing for a long stay.

It is important that the military lessons are not forgotten. The Soviet forces quickly controlled the five main population centres in Afghanistan, the three big airfields at Bagrum, Shindand and Kandahar, and all the important intersections of the motorway network linking Kabul and other main Afghan cities. As the map on page 55 shows, the Russian-built road system offers perfect access to reach the main centres of population from Soviet territory and from there to move into Iran or Pakistan.

The Red Army divisions were of three types — armoured,

motorized rifle and airborne. Each division has its own full complement of chemical, biological and radiological decontamination units as an integral part of the division, which is an indication of the Army's Chemical Warfare (CW) capability and the importance they pay to it.

Within 10 days Moscow's Army of occupation was substantially larger than Afghanistan's own military conscript forces, once more than 100,000 strong and soon reduced to 65,000 by defections.

Appreciation to *Sunday Express*, 24th February, 1980.

A few weeks before, Mr. Brezhnev with a great fanfare withdrew tanks and troops from East Germany. *We now know why he did so.*

The Soviet forces have five main tasks in Afghanistan:

1 Garrison the main towns.
2 Control the main airfields and military bases.
3 Keep the main highways open.
4 Seal the frontiers.
5 Impose military domination over a wild and mountainous nation larger than France, against the tough, fanatical Mujahideen. The Russians will find themselves so alien that even the animals will hate them.

Rudyard Kipling's words will come true once again:

"When you are wounded and left on Afghanistan's plains,
And the women come out to cut up what remains,
Just roll to your rifle and blow out your brains,
And go to your God like a soldier."

Having become a *de facto* Soviet satellite two years ago, Soviet occupied Afghanistan is now in danger of becoming the *de facto* 16th republic of the U.S.S.R. But the Kremlin did miscalculate some aspects of world reaction; also it undoubtedly miscalculated the reaction of the Afghan population.

An army of 70,000 soldiers was not even sufficient to carry out an internal security role in a handful of hostile cities and main towns, all seething with hatred. To control the main towns and roads would require a further 50,000 soldiers.

To crush the tribesmen in the mountains and break their stubborn spirit might well require 300,000-400,000 more soldiers, particularly if the freedom fighters are properly commanded, controlled, organized, trained and equipped to fight a guerrilla war against a first class modern army.

However, to redress any given military situation, it should not be forgotten that the Russians would not think twice about resorting to the use of chemical weapons. Their military doctrine regards the tactical use of chemical weapons as a normal form of warfare and in this field they are better militarily equipped and psychologically prepared than any other country in the world.

Rebel opposition to Amin was generally along traditional clan and tribal lines, although six different groupings had started to emerge. With the arrival of the Soviet troops all the old tribal differences were swept under the carpet. The fighting Mujahideen – Muslim "holy warriors" – may still retain their old loyalties. But they are totally united in their determination to throw the last Russian out of their country.

At first, during the severe winter conditions, the Russians conducted the war with cautious restraint, with the tribesmen wary of taking on armoured gunships with .303 rifles. Initially their action was sporadic and confined to hit-and-run ambushes.

These tactics disrupted communications to a considerable extent, but there was no evidence that the Soviet troops had ever been in real difficulty in securing a road or town if they wanted to – despite a U.S. State Department disclosure on 17th April, that 8,000 Soviet troops had been killed or wounded since Russia occupied Afghanistan almost four months previously.

In fact, they were able to rely on the Afghan Army to do most of the real fighting for them. This was because these soldiers were deliberately based in a different area to the one where they had their ethnic roots.

Where the Mujahideen were most successful was in the remote and mountainous areas, and that means most of the country. But these are areas which have never really been effectively controlled from Kabul.

The real state of the fighting was almost impossible to assess. The different groups make wildly exaggerated claims of their victories to impress each other.

It would be foolish to take comfort in the supposition that the Soviets have trapped themselves into a "new Vietnam". True the Afghans are probably the toughest, bravest and most ruthless fighters in the world. Also true is that the soaring mountains (anything under 7,000 feet is officially a hill), heavy timbered, broken country, and cave-dotted gorges provide the ideal terrain for agile, sure-footed tribesmen. But without centralized control and a properly organized cohesive guerrilla force armed with modern hand-held heat-seeking anti-aircraft and anti-tank weapons, and equipped with efficient and rugged radio communications, they will be no match against the military might of the highly trained Red Army and Air Force equipped with the most modern weapons of devastating destruction and used with utter ruthlessness.

It was interesting to read in letters to the press and in newspaper articles the past bitter experience of the British and Indian Armies in Afghanistan and their unsuccessful efforts to subdue the tribesmen of the North West Frontier – a branch of the Pushtu-speaking Afghan tribes across the border.

One such letter contained the following highly out-dated view which is a typical example of today's underestimation and ignorance of the military might of Russia's modern massive military machine:-

> "As one who has had considerable personal experience of engaging in military operations against the hill men of those regions I know exactly what the Russian Army is up against. I firmly believe that the Russians have bitten off a lot more than they can chew. Let them stew in their own juice, and go on wasting a lot of military effort to no purpose."

I, too, have had considerable personal experience of fighting these hill tribesmen, followed by many years of counter-insurgency, anti-terrorist and guerrilla-type operations elsewhere. And, as a former NATO Commander-in-Chief, and prior to that a NATO Staff Officer in charge of Intelligence, I have had to know all about my Russian enemy.

The experience of the British Army and the former Indian Army of fighting these tribesmen bear no relation to what the Russians are doing and will be experiencing in Aghanistan in 1980, and thereafter.

The outcome of Afghanistan's ruthless occupation by the Russians will be as successful as their occupation of Hungary in 1956, and the tribesmen will be treated in a far more brutal manner with precision weapons of lethal devastation than were the Hungarian Freedom Fighters.

The Soviet equipment includes:

* The capability to parachute armour and guns into the mountains.
* Truck-mounted BM-21 rocket launchers with 40 tubes each of 122mm rockets.
* Amphibious BMP-Is, the world's most effective armoured personnel carrier (APC). This APC is so advanced that a description of it is included later.
* Although the majority of the tanks may have been reported as being 17-year old T-55s, the Soviet Army will obviously take the opportunity to put its latest tank, the T-72, through its paces under the extreme conditions of climate and terrain.
* The 25-year old MiG-19s, a smaller number of MiG-21s, with the ultra sophisticated MiG-25s held in reserve, so far, in Russia but having been spotted overflying combat zones.

The Russians are constructing six new airfields inside Afghanistan.

* The Topolev troop-carrier aircraft.
* MI-24 helicopter gunships, virtual flying tanks. Their ability to operate in tribal mountainous country will, of course, be limited because their effective operation height is reported to be about 1,500 feet.
* Napalm — a devastating weapon when dropped by aircraft on mountain villages.
* Nerve gas or some form of chemical weapon or poisonous gas. This could flush tribesmen out of their mountain hide-outs.
* Self-propelled artillery.
* Self-propelled anti-aircraft guns.
* Self-propelled anti-tank missile firing guns.
* Armoured snowploughs.
* Armoured earth-moving equipment.
* Pontoon bridges.
* Mess tents.
* Field hospitals.
* Huge balloon-like fuel depots.
* Electric generators and building materials — tell-tale fixtures of an army digging in for a long stay.

One of their deadliest armoured vehicles is the BMD, a combination of a light tank and an armoured personnel carrier, with which Soviet airborne divisions are equipped. This versatile 8-ton vehicle is armed with a 73mm gun, three machine guns and an anti-tank missile launcher, and carries a crew of five. Like all Soviet armoured vehicles – including the similar but slightly larger BMP which has also been deployed in Afghanistan – the airtight BMD can crunch its way through clouds of nerve gas and is impervious to biological, chemical and radiological warfare.

Out-gunned and out of date, the forces of Mujahideen had to rely on their locally manufactured weapons and captured Soviet weapons and deserters from the Afghan army, plus automatic rifles and other light arms – but probably nothing heavier than mortars or light artillery pieces – provided by the Chinese.

It does not require a military expert to see what will be necessary in the way of modern armaments – particularly anti-tank and anti-aircraft missiles – communications equipment, training, organization and unified command and control, if the tribesmen – freedom fighters – are to wage a successful and modern guerrilla-type war against such a highly sophisticated, equipped and organized Red Army of occupation, whose troops will expect no quarter and give no quarter, either to men, women or children, as valuable combat experience is gained.

The Russian soldier is subjected to harsh, iron discipline, drilled relentlessly in obedience and vigorously trained using live ammunition and often diluted poison gas. But he has almost no postwar combat experience because Hungary in 1956 and Czechoslovakia in 1968 were mounted essentially against civilian populations.

In tightening their grip on this country the Soviets are prepared to pay a high price in blood. The tribesmen will attack their bivouacs, ambush their convoys, torment Soviet patrols with sniper fire, launch hit-and-run raids into the more vulnerable Soviet-held towns, blow up pylons supporting the main power lines, destroy telephone lines, demolish bridges, fire at water towers, maraud and mine highways, and engage in large-scale skirmishes. With training and modern weapons their targets will be able to include aircraft, airfields, tanks, supply depots, etc.

Against this form of guerrilla-type fighting the Russians will be ruthless, relentless and remorseless. They will hit hard, hit quick and keep on hitting under a devastating umbrella of helicopter gunships and fixed wing aircraft. They will pour in troops until the job is done and all political opponents killed. The types of Soviet equipment already described is proof enough that for all their courage, hardiness and profound Islamic faith, the Mujahideen will not emerge from this ordeal without suffering terrible casualties. However, the Yom-Kippur War showed how single men using modern hand-held weapons of devasting power – firing heat-seeking anti-aircraft and anti-tank missiles – can

61

Appreciation to *The Daily Telegraph*, 3rd January, 1980.

inflict incredible losses against tanks and aircraft. The Mujahideen must be trained in the use of and armed with such weapons.

This Soviet invasion of Afghanistan is no version of America's Vietnam. Not for them a "Bay of Pigs" or the shambles in Saigon. The problems facing Soviet troops fighting in a country just across the Soviet border bear no resemblance to those that confronted American troops embattled 10,000 miles from the U.S. Furthermore, Afghanistan and the U.S.S.R. share a long border; at the drop of a hat the Soviets can send in whatever is needed to reduce the Afghan insurgency to tolerable limits. The Soviet supply lines to Afghanistan are short and the local population relatively small: 14 million to 18 million. The tribesmen have no organized government of their own nor will they receive billions in arms comparable to the aid that the Vietnamese received from the Soviet Union.

Most important of all, there is no Afghan Ho Chi Minh – no magnetic leader, at present.

In America television coverage of the Vietnam war was largely responsible for sapping the moral fibre of the American people. With friends like U.S. television commentators the U.S. military had little need of enemies. The Soviets will use television – if they use it at all – in precisely the opposite way; to bolster the morale of their people and to glorify the deeds of their soldiers on the battlefield. Soviet citizens have no professional verbalizers at home to tell them nightly on television of the atrocities their troops are committing out there in a war they do not understand.

While the Soviet soldiers were digging in for the Winter, Moscow was planning the concept of "Pushtoonistan" — an independent or autonomous Pathan state — and an autonomous "United Baluchistan", which would create a Pathan state stretching virtually the whole 1,200-mile length of the present Afghan-Pakistan frontier, from Peshawar, adjacent to the Khyber Pass, down to the Makran coast on the Gulf of Oman. By inflaming Pathan ambitions, Pakistan would be faced with infiltration and subversion along one of the least-defensible borders imaginable.

The more immediate threat, however, springs from Moscow's aim to create an autonomous United Baluchistan, linking all the Baluchi tribes that spread across the coastal plain at present divided between Pakistan, Afghanistan and Iran. By exploiting the unrest and the strong separatists movements which exist on both sides of the Iran-Pakistan border that divides nearly three million Baluchi tribesmen, the Kremlin aims to give the Baluchis their long-fought-for national independence. Russian agents are working on the Baluchi tribes to inspire them to revolt against the Government in Islamabad and Teheran and establish the new state of Baluchistan.

To acquire this new satellite, Moscow's aim is to carve a 50-mile wide corridor from the Afghan border down to the Gulf of Oman, reaching the sea at Gwadar. The homeland of the disaffected Baluchi tribes lies astride that corridor. Attaining access to the warmwaters of the Indian Ocean would complete a Russian foreign policy programme first laid down by Peter the Great.

The Russians would construct naval and air bases at Gwadar or Pasni on the Makran coast, within 350 miles of the vital Strait of Hormuz which controls all sea and oil tanker traffic leaving the Persian Gulf. This would mean one more Soviet stronghold on the oil route and an added menace to the lifeline of the U.S.A., Western Europe and Japan.

Russia, now poised in Afghanistan, with short internal lines of communication, will be able to launch a surprise, lightning attack in massive strength against Iran or Pakistan at extremely short notice. What is to stop them? Where is the deterrence? Time is not on our side. Will Russia give us the breathing space we require?

Without landbases, airfields and a naval presence — all close at hand — how can America forestall this threat and fulfil President Carter's promise to defend the Gulf? The map on page 65 shows the United States' present response capability in terms of time and military reinforcements. It is hopelessly inadequate.

Therefore, in the case of Pakistan, she must be given massive military aid in the form of modern weapons and modern aircraft. And would not a Chinese military presence on Pakistan soil act as a deterrent, particularly as she is a nuclear power?

As for Iran, she was still in utter confusion at a time when her internal and external security were of such vital importance to the West. The Russians could invade to-morrow with impunity.

Meanwhile all Moslem countries must bind themselves together in an Islamic Alliance to resist aggression and be armed and equipped by the West to do so. A guerrilla Islamic Alliance for the liberation of Afghanistan is merely one bite at the cherry.

Western policy should now be clear: no wheat, no butter, sugar or meat mountains to Russia on give-away terms, no SALT II, no technology, no Olympics, no détente (appeasement), no mercenary hatchet-men – and no lack of an army, air and naval presence in the Middle East and elsewhere.

Strategically, nothing in the region can compensate for the loss of Britain's air, naval and land base at Aden to the Russians. But the air base on the island of Masira, off the coast of Oman, must be reactivated, together with bases offered by friendly Arab States. Obviously there are problems here – sensitivity to the desire for independence and internal political troubles. Foreign troops on national soil are objectionable to the peoples of a sovereign country. Israel, Egypt and Turkey offered military facilities on their soil. Turkey, of course, is a member of NATO. But to accept Egypt's offer would cause Arab outrage against President Sadat. And to accept Israel's offer would stir up the whole Muslim world.

It was in late February 1980, that the world began to hear of Russia's Kabul massacre. This was a bloody reminder of the Kremlin's determination to crush all resistance however inhuman the methods employed might be and regardless of the resulting slaughter. The up-welling of rage by the non-Soviet controlled world was conspicuous by its absence. The supply of oil, self-interest and subservient détente take a higher priority than compassion for the victims.

If the resistance of Afghanistan's fiercely independent tribesmen is proven to be as determined as present indications suggest, the inhuman slaughter will be incomparably greater, as improved weather conditions will allow Russian forces to bring their huge superiority in weapons and technology to bear. The Russians will not shrink from genocide, as Stalin showed, and the Cambodian tragedy confirmed more recently.

It would be wishful thinking to expect concrete results from the proposal mooted by Britain and adopted by the European Community of neutralizing Afghanistan on the Austrian pattern in return for a Soviet military withdrawal. Mr. Brezhnev's reaction was to repeat what he had been saying, mainly for Third World consumption, ever since his ruthless seizure of Afghanistan, namely that Russia had only given her "fraternal assistance" to Afghanistan to help that country defend itself against aggression from America, Britain, Pakistan and the rest.

Mr. Brezhnev used similar words about the invasion of Czechoslovakia 12 years ago; his troops are still there!

Mr. Brezhnev has added that the need for Soviet military assistance would cease if the United States, "Together with the neighbours of Afghanistan", were to guarantee that "all forms of outside interference . . . are fully terminated".

There is not one shred of official evidence that the one word, "guarantee", implies that the Soviet Union is prepared to have Afghanistan clinically removed from the East-West power game, as Austria was a generation ago.

Even if the Kremlin was to respond favourably to the neutrality proposal they would win a great psychology warfare victory. Why? *Because to clobber Afghanistan by brute force and then have your aggression sanctified by a cloak of neutrality is no mean achievement.* Both the clobbering and the so-called neutrality might one day be extended to Pakistan, Iran, Turkey, Somalia or Oman.

The Russians regard negotiations, such as the neutrality proposal, as a weapon, just like a submarine in the Atlantic, or a strategic missile. If Brezhnev cares a damn about Western proposals, which is unlikely, it is only to entangle the democracies in a propaganda battle, counting on the television cameras and squeamish, gullible and frightened public opinion to keep perhaps a shoe, rather than a jack-boot, on the Afghan's neck.

Can one really imagine Russia willing to withdraw and leave a neutral Afghanistan free to choose its own Government – which would certainly not be communist? If, which is doubtful, the Red Army ever

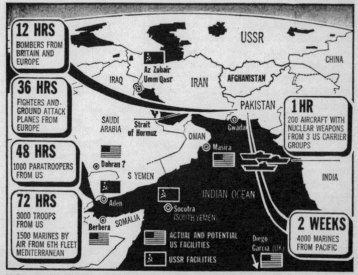

U.S. present response capability.
Appreciation to *Sunday Times*, London, 3rd February, 1980.

leaves Afghanistan, it will only do so when the armed forces, the security and compliancy services and the key ministries of that country are all firmly under control of its nominees or its own specialists left behind "on loan". Moreover, should its divisions – withdrawn just across the border – ever want to intervene again, they have a pretext – this time enshrined in international law – of acting to redress the "abuses of Afghanistan's neutral status".

If, as part of any Afghan neutrality deal, the Russians want to clear the United States fleet out of the Indian Ocean and dictate what sort of arms should be supplied to Pakistan, the protection of Afghanistan will have gone beyond recall, while the original aggressor still sits only one mountain pass away.

Afghanistan — Postscript

By June 1980, an important development had taken place in that the resistance fighters had been supplied with large numbers of the SAM-7 Soviet-built anti-aircraft missile, which is particularly effective against slow-flying propeller-driven planes and especially the helicopter gunships which have been wiping out entire villages. Earlier in this Chapter I mentioned the need of this weapon by the resistance fighters and in fact, it was the Commissioner of the North West Frontier Province in Pakistan who emphasized this to me June-July 1979 – six months *before* Russia's brutal invasion of Afghanistan. The missiles were probably acquired from Libya, Algeria and Syria, although they are easily obtainable on the international market.

The Soviet military pattern had been to concentrate on punitive and pre-emptive strikes and murderous strafing of villages, guerrilla bases and mountain passes in the vicinity of urban areas and highways. The technique involved the obliteration of whole villages by rocket fire from MI–24 helicopter gunships and MiG–21 strike aircraft. The Russians also used MI–18 transport helicopters, converted with rocket pods and machine guns.

Although the Red Army turned Kabul, Kandahar, Herat and Jalalabad into fortress towns, they were increasingly subjected to sniping and ambush by an unrelenting population, while the Mujahideen resistance fighters ambushed Russian tanks and armoured personnel carriers on the roads and controlled large areas of mountainous country. Far from being beaten back by the Soviet Army's Spring offensive, the Mujahideen once again took on their almost mystical power when confronted by an infinitely superior conventional military force.

With the collapse in morale of the Afghan Army – whom the Russians had mistakenly thought they could reinforce rather than replace – the Russians found themselves faced with a serious guerrilla warfare campaign requiring an enormous military effort. To make matters worse, Afghanistan's domestic front became riven by internal disputes. In mid-June Mr. Babrak Karmal's Government was confronted with a power struggle as the rival Parcham and Khalq cliques within the ruling People's Party wrestled for influence. On 15th June, Mr. Karmal, leader of the Parcham movement, executed three ministers – all were Khalq members who served in the government of his predecessor, Hafizullah Amin. The situation was such that the Soviet Army had to airlift reinforcements of tanks and artillery into Kabul.

Meanwhile, the numbers of Afghan refugees in Pakistan had reached 800,000 and obviously it would not be long before the figure reached the one million mark. The strain on Pakistan's economy amounted to £100 million when in June, the World Bank stepped in with £50 million for refugee relief as part of an aid package to Pakistan. For Pakistan there were difficulties enough when they were suddenly faced with infiltrators from Afghanistan who began a spate of bombings, aimed at creating enmity between the local people and the swelling community of Afghan refugees. The bombings caused a tension that did not exist before between the mainly Pushtu-speaking Pathans of Afghanistan and Pakistan.

In addition to the refugee problem, jets and helicopters were being flown into the frontier area of Pakistan from bases in Afghanistan, in pursuit or search of, the Mujahideen fighting Afghan and Soviet troops. There were also cases of shelling across the border. Such incidents were part of the war of nerves designed to cause fear among the local people of the fighting or "hot pursuit" spilling over the border.

The Russians now appear to be learning a few military lessons in Afghanistan. The "Search-and-Destroy" missions followed by a return to base, are useless, because the ground is immediately reoccupied by the tribesmen. The proper technique in guerrilla warfare is "Clear-Hold-and-Dominate". This of course would require twice as many troops as they have in Afghanistan at present, who are now merely "holding the ring" – the main towns, roads and airfields. In my view, the Russians have every intention of settling in for the long kill. The possession by the Mujahideen resistance fighters of hand-held anti-aircraft and anti-tank missiles will make the struggle longer and bloodier still.

As we past the middle of the year, it became clear that Russia had realized she would either have to pull out or go the whole hog and commit everything. Having no intention of adopting the former course, and in order to bring the Mujahideen to heel and garrison the country, the Soviets embarked on a big build-up of armour, material and men, who, it was reported, were more suited to the mountainous conflict. Preparations for an all out assault with "no holds barred" are being made and the most likely date will be later in the year when the memory of the Olympic Games has faded.

CHAPTER
6

Pakistan Pre-27th December, 1979

During my month's visit to Pakistan as a privileged guest I travelled extensively and met a large cross section of people holding positions of high responsibility. The exchange of views was frank and uninhibited. In addition to official engagements I also had the opportunity to talk to individuals at all levels during purely informal social occasions.

I had the additional advantage of knowing the country and people well for I had served there in the old Indian Army on and off for fourteen years and I understand their language, their religion, customs and traditions. I value the friendships that I made in those days and the new ones I made during my visit.

I returned to England with old ties strengthened, but perturbed by the sound of the alarm bells ringing throughout Asia, from the Gulf to Peking. I had felt the stinking hot breath of the Russian bear breathing down the neck of Pakistan.

I was convinced that the situation, and that in the Gulf as a whole, posed a crisis for the West — as well as for Australia, New Zealand, Japan and the ASEAN nations (Association of South-East Asian Nations) — of even greater significance than the confrontations between China and Vietnam and China and Russia.

What concerned me and my hosts was the fact that America and Western Governments in Europe had not yet woken up to this potentially mortal danger.

I was also concerned by the failure of America and the West to appreciate that Russia has a *global* strategy. In Pakistan I found a school of thought that regards Africa as a secondary theatre and believes that the intrusion of Russo-Cuban military penetration into that continent, whether in Angola, Ethiopia and Rhodesia, has been merely a diversionary tactic designed to distract the attention of the Western Governments from the real focal point of Soviet expansionist ambitions. This school of thought maintains that the Russians have always worked along interior lines except in Cuba. They argue that the Russians regard Africa as expendable, but not Eastern Europe and certainly not the oil rich areas of the Middle East. I agree with the latter but not with the former.

What this school of thought overlooks is that the Russian bear has gone to sea. As Admiral Sergei Gorshkov, Commander-in-Chief of the Soviet Navy, has stated: "For the first time in our history our Navy has become a long range armed force in the full meaning of the word."

The Soviets massive naval building plans and their naval deployment show that they regard their navy as a *global* instrument of world power. The Soviet Union can now use its fleet to lie astride the traditional sea routes. In other words, through sea power they are now able to operate along exterior lines.

In his book entitled *Sea Power of the State* Admiral Gorshkov makes the following key claims:

* "Today's Soviet Navy has the capacity of isolating outlying islands and territories in case of war.
* "The Soviet Fleet can flag down and cripple the flow of oil and other strategic materials to the U.S. and Western Europe (The U.S., remember, depends on imports for 87 of its 93 strategic materials).
* "In preparation for possible war, the U.S.S.R. is now engaged in placing naval task forces on strategic locations throughout the world's oceans and constructing elaborate overseas bases in friendly countries to support them.
* "The Soviet Navy is being expanded as rapidly as possible as a major instrument in the Kremlin Plan to communize other nations. It is planned to have a critical role in eliminating imperialist attempts to control the world's oceans."
* Gorshkov concludes "our seapower will determine the success of future political measures and the accomplishment of strategic missions."

Thus, through seapower, combined with its integral air and amphibious components, the Soviet Union now has the capability of conducting offensive operations on a global scale using exterior sealines. This was evident as long ago as 1971, and again in 1975 when they conducted their "OCEAN I" and "OCEAN II" naval and air exercises, in which the Soviet TU 95 (20) "Bear" aircraft overflew the frontline countries of Turkey, Iran and Pakistan from the northern to the southern hemisphere, completely unchallenged.

It is, therefore, wrong for the school of thought I have mentioned to maintain that Soviet and Cuban penetration into Africa is merely a diversionary tactic. The essence of the Soviets global strategy is flexibility and the ability to keep their options open. They use every opportunity to move in to increase their influence wherever they see an opening which they can exploit without excessive risk.

They were ready to move into Angola when the opening was there and they moved into Ethiopia for the same reason. Obviously the Horn of Africa featured high in the Soviet's global strategy because of its proximity to the Middle East. Now, with the serious situation in Iran and the Soviets strong foothold in the Horn of Africa, South Yemen and Afghanistan, combined with Russia's relentless determination to improve relations with Turkey – the underbelly of NATO – it is crystal clear that the pressure is being brought to bear on Pakistan in no uncertain way.

In the precarious position in which Pakistan found itself at the time of my visit, the burning question was: what will be the reaction of the U.S.A. to its ally of long standing? Would the U.S.A. continue to sit paralysed as they did on *three* previous occasions elsewhere?

The *first* was when reinforcements left Cuba by sea and air for Angola beneath their very noses. The *second,* was when the Soviet Union launched their bare-faced aggression in the Horn of Africa. The *third* – but this was not mentioned by my hosts – was when the U.S. abandoned the Shah of Iran to his fate and the country to anarchy, bloody revolution and a reign of terror. In the process Iran was dragged back into the Middle Ages and the Shah's once-proud army of 400,000 men, with sophisticated weaponry and its crack Imperial Guard, surrendered to the Islamic revolution.

I warned my hosts that the then weak administration in the U.S.A. was far too preoccupied with four considerations: (1) the trauma of the Vietnam defeat and a determination not to get embroiled in any new foreign military adventures – in spite of all their military pacts; (2) a successful SALT II at almost any cost; (3) a solution to the Arab-Israeli problem; (4) the then sagging image of President Carter at a time when the Presidential Election was looming on the horizon.

By failing to come to the aid of her allies, the United States had by then become discredited in the eyes of those countries threatened by instability or external threats. United States guarantees of maintaining internal and regional stability were being greeted with cynical derision, whereas similar pronouncements by the Soviet Union were treated by the world with respect and fear.

Wherever I went every civilian and military Pakistani uttered similar words of condemnation, namely that it was high time that America and Western Governments in Europe woke up to what was potentially a mortal danger.

Before leaving Pakistan in July, I wrote: "It is up to Britain to give the lead, for her historic association with the subcontinent has special importance. I am convinced that the time is short because the threat to the stability of the whole of this part of the world from Soviet expansionist policies is imminent. Britain has not the global power and the military strength of the Imperial era, but she still has diplomatic skill and standing which is appreciated in many parts of the world to a far greater extent than most people in Britain realize.

"Events in Afghanistan must have brought home to the Indian Government," I said, "that it is powerfully in the interest of India that there should be a friendly and stable régime in Pakistan." I said that I agreed with Lord Alport (Deputy Speaker, House of Lords, with vast experience of the British Commonwealth) that it was most important from a military, economic, political and psychological point of view, as a contribution to stability in Pakistan, that there should be reconciliation between Pakistan and India.

I wrote: "Lord Alport believes – and again I agree with him – that if the Government of India could show to its smaller Moslem neighbours the desire for reconciliation, it would receive an immediate response from Pakistan. As Lord Alport explained in the House of Lords if, for instance, the Government of India were to sponsor an invitation to Pakistan to renew its membership of the Commonwealth – which President Zia has publicly said he wishes, providing the terms are honourable – it would have a more far-ranging effect than the realities of renewed membership imply. That reconciliation between India and Pakistan would enable logistical, military and economic aid to be provided to Pakistan by the friends of both India and Pakistan without creating suspicion and fear on the part of India.

"Surely, it is only through reconciliation that a solution to the problem of Kashmir is likely to be found? Does not long-standing friendship between Britain, India and Pakistan place a special obligation on Britain actively to promote the process of reconciliation following the initiative which General Zia has already taken? Pakistan in particular, as a result of the grievous errors of the Bhutto régime, such as Pakistan's withdrawal from the Commonwealth, must be rescued from the isolation from which it now suffers.

"Time is not on our side now that the 'Red Shadow' is over Pakistan.

"A glance at the map *(on page 79)* shows that despite the small size of the country, Pakistan's location in the central land mass of Asia sandwiched between India and the Soviet Union, is of the utmost strategic importance. Therefore, with Russia now striving to consolidate its hold on Afghanistan, it stands to reason that Pakistan – at present without an international guarantee for its security – has a vital role to play in the region and must be supported to the hilt. Has the U.S.A. forgotten that had it not been for Pakistan, America's relationship with the People's Republic of China would not have been re-established?"

The government was worried over the shift of neighbouring Afghanistan into the Soviet camp and Washington's apathetic ho-hum reaction to it. America's new pro-India tilt had served further to aggravate U.S.–Pakistani relations. Sensing which way the wind was blowing, Pakistan re-assigned its Ambassador to the U.S. and sent him to Moscow with an eye towards securing better relations with the Kremlin.

The hostile attitude of the outside world towards Pakistan continued to revolve around the execution of deposed Prime Minister Zulfikar Ali Bhutto who lost his appeal to the Supreme Court against the death sentence for charges including murder.

The world's media and, indeed, former President of Pakistan, Chaudhary, had voiced serious portents if Bhutto was executed. In the event the tensions did not explode into the predicted massive violence. General Zia maintained that he had proved by this one action of his that the rule of law exists for everybody – high and low. He stated categorically that he could not allow Mr. Bhutto, who had appointed him Army Chief of Staff over seven other more senior Officers, to get away with murder just because he happened to be a former Prime Minister.

Furthermore, according to General Zia the country by now had become aware that Bhutto had prostituted all the institutions in the country, including the legislature, judiciary, police, administration and bureaucracy. But he had been unable to shake the Army which remains the only solid and united institution that Pakistan has today. General Zia is determined that the Army will have the constitutional power to act in an emergency to save any given situation.

General Shahid Hamid, the Minister for Information and Broadcasting, had stated to me in his letter of May 1979, inviting me to Pakistan, that it was the sincere desire of the military government in power, under the President and Chief Martial Law Administrator, General Zia ul-Haq, to hold a General Election in November 1979 in an impartial, peaceful and orderly manner, and that within the country every effort was being made to create conditions conducive to that end.

Power was to be transferred to a civilian Government, *providing it would bring about a party or a group of parties capable of governing the country for a specified period of time*. This was the proviso and in the opinion of General Zia this stipulation was not met. Hence the elections were not held.

Sitting in my house in England after my private trip to Pakistan, whose soldiers for almost two centuries fought side by side with us in Asia, Africa and Europe, in World War I and World War II, and in numerous other wars and campaigns, manning outposts from Hong Kong in the east to France and Italy in the west; whose sons, fathers, brothers and relatives lie buried alongside British soldiers in our War Graves Commission's cemeteries in almost all parts of the strategic world, what indelible impressions did I bring back?

Fitting the pieces together

According to the Director General of Pakistan's Institute of Strategic Studies – Brigadier Noor Husain – the political and military traumatic experience of 1971 – the war in East and West Pakistan – was the product of a conspiracy in which Mr. Bhutto and a few megalomaniac politicians of the country were involved with Mrs. Gandhi, Prime Minister of India. It not only shook the entire Pakistan nation, but also made it sit up and ask many questions to fit the jigsaw-puzzle together. Brigadier Noor Husain informed me that with full freedom to the insiders, writers, scholars, credible and balanced journalists, many books, articles and research papers have appeared during the last two years inside and outside the country, giving an objective, unbiased and analytical account of what happened in 1971, and in 1965 – the war in Kashmir and West Pakistan – and even earlier.

The Brigadier and I had a number of meetings, including one whole day when we travelled together by car from Islamabad to Abbotabad and back to see the Karakoram Highway, linking Pakistan with China. Since I cannot put all that he told me in such a short space, I shall condense the highlights.

The Brigadier said that according to the late Mr. Bhutto, leader of the PPP, there were three parties in the country in 1970 to 1971 – the Awami League, the Pakistan People's Party and the Armed Forces.

Brigadier Noor said there was little doubt that the separation of East Pakistan, now Bangladesh, was connived at by Mr. Bhutto and a small gang of politicians with the dual purpose of firstly, eliminating the overall majority party (the Awami League) from the political scene of Pakistan, through a confrontation with the Armed Forces, and secondly, in the process bringing the military régime down and into disrepute, by accusing it of exaggerated atrocities.

The Brigadier stated that after the first phase of this "grand strategy" had been manoeuvred i.e. confrontation of the Armed Forces with the Awami Leagie, and had failed, because the Armed Forces had regained control and restored normalcy in East Pakistan, the second phase was implemented, i.e. connivance with Mrs. Gandhi and certain Indian politicians for military intervention under the pretext of solving the "refugee problem".

The Brigadier told me that a Pakistan Army Officer taken prisoner from East Pakistan as early as April 1971, and evacuated to India, saw hectic activity of the preparation of Prisoners of War cages, and on enquiry was told "Don't you understand that this is for Pakistan Army units, expected here by the end of the year?"

The Brigadier who was commanding a Brigade in Bangladesh at the time then proceeded to give me the following description of the course of events.

Having satisfied themselves that Pakistan Army units operating in

73

East Pakistan under adverse terrain, climatic, and logistic conditions for over a period of 8 months, and against India infiltrators and saboteurs, constantly cutting communications, mining roads and bridges and laying ambushes, had reached the end of their stamina and endurance, the Indian Army was launched in a multi-dimensional thrust in overwhelming strength in numbers, fire power and air superiority and at a time of the year when the North Himalayan Passes had closed (1962 syndrome).

The Brigadier said it was to the credit of the brave, simple, frugal, undemanding Pakistani soldier and his leadership that, in spite of such adverse conditions, no infantry battalion locality was over-run or captured. Noor maintained that although the superior mobility of India's Land and Air Forces enabled them to outflank Pakistan's forces, yet battalions had to be launched to capture Pakistan army platoon localities; brigades to capture company localities, and in the process Indian Army units suffered heavy casualties. This, he said, was borne out from an objective study of the war accounts of both sides, and was as true of the war in East Pakistan as in West Pakistan; and as true of the 1971 Indo-Pakistan War as of the 1965 Indo-Pakistan War.

At the time it was noteworthy, he said, that in both the 1965 and 1971 wars, the offensive operations by the Pakistan Army, though restricted in time and space due to limitations of manpower, supporting arms and air support, were highly successful at brigade and divisional levels. An example of this was the capture in 1965 of the strongly held territory of Chamb in Kashmir, in spite of the loss of surprise and deception.

In Noor's opinion the Pakistani soldier is probably superior in offensive operations to his Indian counterpart and whenever he was launched with adequate preparations, support and determined leadership, he attained his objective, regardless of casualties. The Islamic concept of "Ghazi" (fighter for righteouness) and "Shaheed" (death in the cause of Allah), whereby in life or death he is a winner, gives the Muslim soldier an unparalled motivation to do or die.

Noor said that the strong revulsion left in the minds of Pakistan's senior officers was that while a ceasefire of the 1971 war could have been arranged by the U.N. resolution, Mr. Bhutto, the leader of the Pakistani delegation to the U.N., tore up the ceasefire resolution, walked out, feigned illness, and did not attend the debate, because he was determined to destroy the image of the Pakistan Army through surrender — which indeed, came about.

Noor said that another unsavoury feature was the obvious reluctance on the part of Pakistan's power-hungry politicians to have their prisoners of war repatriated, because these angry young men would have held them responsible for the break up of their country. When they were eventually repatriated two years later, the majority, he said, were physically and mentally broken, unfit to bear arms or make a normal living. He explained that almost every family and village in Pakistan had its share of these unfortunate youths, victims of political intrigue in the struggle for power. But Noor was in no doubt that soldiering is still a very popular, honourable and sought after profession in the country, and that the desire for revenge is strong.

So much for the 1971 pieces of the Pakistan jigsaw-puzzle. What about the 1965 War? What, said Noor, prompted Pakistan to challenge her much bigger neighbour, India, and "bring its Army to a grinding halt, when it crossed the international borders, in stealth, under cover of darkness, without a formal declaration of war?"

According to Noor, the picture was not very different from that of the war, including certain common actors and the same political power struggle, directed at bringing down President Ayub Khan (in 1971 it was President Yahya Khan), "by getting him involved in a war with neighbouring India through deliberate misrepresentation of facts, intrigues and machinations, using at that time, the corridors of the Foreign Office. In a book about the 1965 war entitled, *The First Round*, written by the former Commander-in-Chief of the Pakistan Air Force (PAF), Air Marshal Asghar Khan, and published in London, Mr. Altaf Gauhar, in the Foreword, makes some interesting revelations on how Pakistan became involved in the war.

Noor described how by 1965, President Ayub Khan has been at the helm of affairs for seven years, that the country had witnessed a decade of development, peace and progress, and was lauded by international agencies as a model of growth. Noor said his main fault was his ex-army background, irksome to some power-hungry politicians, and the only way to unseat him was to get him involved in a war with neighbouring India. *Casus belli?* The unresolved Kashmir dispute over which the Pakistan and Indian armes had fought an inconclusive war from 1947 to 1949. According to Pakistan published accounts, the then Foreign Minister – Mr. Bhutto – and the local military commander in Kashmir, known for his political and military ambitions, the late Major-General Malik, got together and convinced President Ayub Khan that the valley could be captured by commando infiltrators, and that India would be a helpless spectator due to weak political leadership displayed in the Rann of Kutch conflict earlier in 1965.

Noor explained that in spite of bitter opposition on the part of the Pakistan Army's General Staff, the plan was hatched and executed in July-August 1965. What was its aim? If it succeeded, the two architects of the plan – (known as "Operation Gibraltar") would be national heroes, rightful successors to Ayub Khan; if it failed or misfired, it would bring President Ayub Khan, as the Head of State, into disrepute, leading to his decline and possible exit, thus clearing the room at the top. Noor remarked: "The same murky political struggle and intrigues as was witnessed later in 1971."

According to Noor the events of 1965 are a landmark in Pakistan's history, in that the situation was retrieved by the steadfastness of the Armed Forces, and India's four to one superiority was halted in its tracks, with India suggesting a ceasefire.

It also saw the exit, he said, not of President Ayub Khan, but of the Foreign Minister, Mr. Bhutto. Noor remarked bitterly that if the nation had seen through the 'game' then, the traumatic experience of 1971, and the suffering that the nation underwent from 1971 to the present day would have been avoided.

Noor went on to say that since its creation in 1947, this young, dynamic and strategically located nation has thrice been forced into conflict with a much bigger neighbour, a record surpassed only by the Arabs and Israel. Noor's version is that from 1947 to 1949, when the Central Government administration and the Armed Forces were still in the process of formation, the country was dragged into a conflict after neighbouring, strategically vital, Kashmir was attacked by Indian Armed Forces to save the local unpopular ruler from a popular revolt. The Indian Army, he said, was brought to a halt at what today is the line of control. Fighting as newly raised units and formations without adequate ammunition, clothing, reserves, and no air support, Pakistan's young army managed to safeguard the integrity and sovereignty of the country. The conflicts of 1965 and 1971, he said, are more recent history.

Noor's account of the course of events which I have described above were corroborated by two Generals, one Brigadier, one Lieutenant-Colonel, one Major and two civil servants. The civil servants were loud in their praise of the military régime. They told me they were given clear instructions, were expected to carry them out without delay, that maximum efficiency was demanded and corruption was conspicuous by its absence.

It was obvious that the strong impression they all wished that I would take back with me was this. While wishing to live in peace, and goodwill with its neighbours, this nation is resolved as in the past, to defend its sovereignty and freedom and determined to extract a heavy price from any aggressors – irrespective of their size. Pakistan has had a fair share of teething troubles but let no one doubt, they emphasized, the patience, resolve, fortitude and determination of its God-fearing, simple, resilient, brave, frugal, hardy and above all martial people to survive and live as one nation.

The bitter hatred that the Armed Forces have for Bhutto knows no bounds.

I asked Noor to write out for me a list of conflicts between India and Pakistan from 1947-1979, with a brief description of the fighting. This he did and it is reproduced as Appendix C. Having paid four visits to India to stay with my old Gurkha Regiment, and once as a personal guest of my old friend Field Marshal Sam Manekshaw, I know that their official account of their conflicts with Pakistan would be somewhat different to the above! But I have a great affection and admiration for the soldiers, sailors and airmen of both nations and it is tragic that they should be in conflict.

Instead they should be in close alliance facing the common enemy – Russia.

To Peshawar and Baluchistan

In August 1979, I received a letter from Noor, in which he wrote: "Two days after your departure I received a directive from General Zia asking me to prepare a panel of names of likely authors for a history of the Pakistan Army from 1947 to 1979 to cover the three years, two insurgencies, and their role in aid to the Civil Power and Martial Law.

"Obviously a challenging task, which is engulfing me. I wonder if you, Sir Walter, would like to be on this panel, especially with your background, experience in the subcontinent and your recent four week exposure to Pakistan? It involves at least three to six months of collection of all material by this Institute; at least three months of study, research and writing by the author or authors in Pakistan, backed by this Institute, typists/stenos, draughtsmen, war diaries and archives. I will ensure that Akbar *(my civil servant guide and mentor from the Ministry of Information)* is exiled from Pindi for the period! In any case it would be mostly a Services back up support, and planned in execution down to the smallest detail."

I had to tell Noor that such a mission was impossible, due to the problems that they appeared to be encountering over the publication of the book which I had already written.

One month later, Noor wrote to say: "Off and on the panic button has been pressed and I have been summoned. I am hopelessly confused but I am equally keen that the project should go through."

Noor had exercised a great deal of effort on my behalf, particularly in obtaining photographs of the Karakoram Highway, the Khyber Pass and the weapons and equipment of Pakistan's Armed Forces. He had previously published in his journal, "Strategic Studies", part of Chart 2 illustrated on page 23. His version of the chart had excluded the more recent arrows showing Russia's geo-strategic thrusts, but it was enough for the Soviet Embassy to ask for a meeting with him. Their envoy got no change from Noor, who in reply to his protest remarked: "I have listened to what you have to say, but can you deny the truth?" The Soviet diplomat replied that this was not the point. To portray past history in such an aggressive way was regarded as an unfriendly act. Noor did not relent.

Noor and his wife come from high aristocratic stock, and her father was the first Pakistani Governor of the North West Frontier Province. At dinner in their house one night I met Noor's son who had been badly wounded as a very young officer in the Bangladesh war of November

1971. He had then been kept as a prisoner of war for two years in India after the cease fire. He had returned as a physical and mental wreck and was still in hospital in Rawalpindi undergoing psychiatric treatment.

Little wonder is it, therefore, that Noor had expressed himself so vehemently to me about the past India and Pakistan wars and the part played by Bhutto throughout. He is held in high esteem by senior and junior officers and is obviously close to President Zia.

When he took me to Abbotabad to see the Karakoram Highway it was fascinating listening to him recounting past and present events both military and political. At Abbotabad we lunched in the Officers Mess of the Depot of the Frontier Force – the famous "Piffer" Regiment. The trophies, medals and pictures from the days of the British Raj have been faithfully preserved and expertly displayed and I was shown them with great pride and admiration. The Commandant presented me with their Piffer tie and made me an honorary member of their Officers Mess. Also at Abbotabad is the Depot of the Baluch Regiment. The eyes of every officer to whom I talked flashed with anger and hatred whenever anyone raised the subject of the retention by India, with Bhutto's connivance, of 90,000 Pakistani prisoners of war for no less than two long years after the cease fire had been signed.

I mentioned in Chapter 5, on Afghanistan, that I had a long meeting and lunch at Government House, Peshawar, with Lieutenant-General Fazale Haq, the local Corps Commander who is also Governor of the North West Frontier Province. We had a lot in common as he had commanded their 7th Division for two years – the "Golden Arrow" Division – in which I served during the war in Burma against the Japanese. He is a Pathan and ex-Guides Cavalry. As Corps Commander he is responsible for the defence of the Afghan border in the North West Frontier Province. I found him a great talker, even more than me! There was no disagreement between us on the imminence of the Soviet threat to Afghanistan and Pakistan and Moscow's overall global strategy. But unfortunately for General Fazala Haq, his Corps then consisted of only two infantry divisions plus the Khyber Rifles; highly professional, tough, disciplined troops but they lacked modern arms and radar. Four-fifths of Pakistan's Armed Forces are deployed along the eastern border with its now historic enemy, India.

I got the impression that the General knows only too well that until he is reinforced on the ground and in the air, re-equipped with modern weapons and the vital roads are made wide enough for modern tanks, the Russians, once having consolidated in Afghanistan, could strike in massive strength across the border with impunity, on land and in the air.

The General told me that he was walking a tight-rope in that it would be only too easy for the Russians to fabricate a pretext through a border incident, or the alleged training and arming of the Afghan refugees.

However, I also got the impression that the General's appreciation

Appreciation to *The Daily Telegraph*, 8th January, 1980.

of the situation was that the Russians might well go for the soft under-belly of Pakistan in Baluchistan and head straight for the warmwaters of the Persian Gulf. So off I went to Baluchistan – my old stamping ground.

Before I describe my visit to Baluchistan, I must mention that on my return journey from Peshawar I stopped short of Rawalpindi and climbed the long, steep steps leading to the towering Column overlooking the plains of the Punjab. This is the inscription that I found engraved on a plaque:

"This Column is erected by friends, BRITISH AND NATIVE, to The Memory of Brigadier-General John Nicholson, CB who, after taking a hero's part in the four great wars for the defence of British India:

79

Kabul	1840
1st Sikh War	1845
2nd Sikh War	1848
Sepoy Mutiny	1857

And being as renowned for his Civil Rule in the Punjab, as for his share in its Conquest, fell mortally wounded on 14th September, in leading to victory the main column of assault, at the Great Siege of Delhi, and died 23rd September, 1857.

Aged 34
Mourned by the two Races with equal grief."

They certainly bred Generals young in those days.

Having soldiered for many years in Baluchistan, I soon found myself standing in the Khojak Pass. I travelled through the excellent tank country on both sides of the Pass, motoring along the strategic highway that starts in Afghanistan at Kushka, thence to Herat, Kandahar and so into Pakistan via Chaman, Pishin and Quetta. I stayed at the Staff College, Quetta, as their guest for four days. As an "old boy" both as a student and as a member of the Directing Staff 35 years ago, I could not have been made to feel more welcome and at home. The Commandant, Major-General Mohammed Iqbal, gave up a great deal of his time and appointed one of his Instructors, Lieutenant-Colonel Ali Kuli Khan Khattack, to be my conducting officer throughout my stay. The Colonel proved to be a great companion and corroborated so much of what I had been told by General Shahid Hamid and Brigadier Noor Husain.

A most impressive and distinguished figure was the Deputy Commandant, Brigadier Mohammed Jafar Khan, late of the Guides Cavalry. He was another who had spent two years as a Prisoner of War after the Bangladesh War. He is Shahid Hamid's son-in-law and, unless I am mistaken, is destined to reach the highest positions in their Army. He is a real professional armoured corps expert and one who has been blooded in a number of tank battles with the Indian Army. He shows no traces — physical or mental – of having been a POW.

I was able to discover the site of the bachelor's quarters where I was sleeping at the time of the devastating Quetta Earthquake in 1935. The band-stand of our Officers Mess was still there and being used as such. I also found the bungalow where my wife and I had lived when I was a student, and the concrete earthquake-proof bungalow which we occupied when I was an Instructor. Then after some searching, my Colonel conducting officer and I found the "hut" where my wife and our twin sons — who were born in Quetta in 1942 – lived for three years while I was away fighting in Burma. With much pride I was shown their Staff College Museum which is housed in the quarter which Field Marshal Montgomery occupied when he was an Instructor there in the early 1930s.

On our way to the Khojak Pass, the Colonel and I stopped for refreshments at the Rest House at Pishin where my wife and I had spent a weekend forty-one years before. There the Political Agent came to call on me and we discussed at length the Russian threat via Baluchistan and his current problems with the Afghan refugees.

At the end of a somewhat nostalgic and impressive visit, the Commandant presented me with a handsome pair of cuff links and a photograph album. I reciprocated with a copy of my biography *Fighting General*[1] by Tom Pocock, and my book *The Bear at the Back Door*.[2]

Meeting with the high-rank

On 21st April, 1980, General Iqbal Khan took over as chairman of the Joint Chiefs of Staff Committee. At the time of my visit he was the Army's Deputy Chief of Staff, General Iqbal told me that the Indian Army possessed as many as 30,000 tanks. Why, he said, did they require so many? He emphasized that they could not be used in the Himalayas against another Chinese invasion, but on the other hand they could be used against Pakistan. During our meeting in his office, the General made a number of caustic and strongly worded criticisms of the blatant ignorance being displayed about the state of affairs in Pakistan, even by people such as former British comrades in arms. He said he had recently been in England where he had attended a Regimental Reunion. The remarks made to him by some of the senior retired British Officers of his Regiment were pathetic, unfriendly and merely showed that they had been taken in by a hostile mass media. These people, he complained, were men of the world and should know better.

He was particularly critical of the attitude of a certain Commandant of Britain's Royal College of Defence Studies, who had visited Pakistan with a party of senior officers and senior civil servants and others of similar ilk. The General said that after a very careful and thorough briefing based on facts, figures and the truth, the Commandant had turned round and stated bluntly: "I do not believe that there is any threat to Pakistan from India." In the General's view this was a typical example of a desk-warrior coming to Pakistan with pre-conceived ideas and having no intention of even entering into intelligent discussion and examination of another person's point of view.

I sympathised with the General and said that was the very reason why I had accepted General Hamid's invitation to come out immediately and see the situation for myself and write a book. I said the West invariably underestimated the situation, constantly indulged in wishful thinking and were always caught with their trousers down.

The General looks every inch a soldier's soldier, has a strong personality and speaks fluently and emphatically about the situation in South Asia and the capabilities and intentions of the Soviet Union.

---

[1] Out of print.

[2] Available from Covenant Books, London and Destiny Publishers, U.S.A.

On my visit to Lahore, I lunched at Government House with Lieutenant-General Sawar Khan, the then Corps Commander who was also Governor of the Punjab. His divisional commanders were present – an impressive team, friendly and in no two minds about the imminent threat from Russia through Afghanistan. The date was then 17th July, 1979.

We had a long session after lunch. I had no hesitation in describing the performance of Britain's Labour Government in slashing Defence expenditure by £10,000 million within five years and, by deliberate design, cutting so deep through the flesh and muscle right down into the bone that our military capability had reached such an all-time low that the safety of the Realm was now imperilled. This deplorable situation, I said, had been condemned by myself in a succession of letters published in *The Daily Telegraph* over the past six years, so I had no qualms about speaking my mind when outside my own country. General Sawar Khan remarked that their Army had suffered an even more bitter experience at the hands of Bhutto who had set out to destroy them in collaboration with India.

Lieutenant-General Sawar Khan has since been promoted to full General and has succeeded General Iqbal Khan as Deputy Chief of Staff of the Army.

I met most of the other high-ranking officers at a buffet supper hosted by the Minister for Information and Broadcasting, General Shahid Hamid and his wife at their house. At one stage I was hauled away by my host to sit next to the Minister of Finance. The General told him: "Here is the person who will be able to tell you about the Soviets present nuclear capability in the strategic and tactical field, and their overall conventional superiority and what they intend to do with it." For about thirty minutes I gave him my views, including the balance of power, the arc of crisis, Moscow's Master Plan and her short and long term intentions. One did not have to convince him, for he was obviously well briefed and knowledgeable. Before we parted he said – "You have corroborated my worst fears."

I came across only one tiresome officer – the Army Director of Military Training, who posed as an expert on NATO! Later I asked Noor about him and he said: "He is too clever by half but, in fact, has never heard a shot fired in anger. He is small fry and of no consequence."

Finally, I came to my audience with the President the day before I left. Shahid Hamid asked me to outline briefly to General Zia what my views and findings were on the Soviet global threat, with particular reference to Pakistan's sphere of influence. I enjoyed our discussion and found General Zia highly intelligent, a good listener, very friendly and not at all the ogre that he had been painted by the mass media. Indeed, I remarked to Shahid that if I had been President and Martial Law Administrator some of the people who were then preaching sedition, such as General Tika Khan – the "Butcher of Bangladesh" – would have faced a firing squad long ago.

I did not hesitate to give the President my opinion on the biased views perpetrated by areas of the communications network in Britain, but said that the British public was not unaware of the fact and had made a pungent adaption of *one* corporate name.

Present at the meeting was the Minister for Foreign Affairs and also General Shahid Hamid. The new British Ambassador was due to present his credentials after I had left the President, so I was able to see the panoply that is laid on for such occasions – mounted escort, open carriage and so on.

As I was climbing into Shahid Hamid's official Mercedes car one of General Zia's senior Aides approached me and said that the President had asked him to put in the boot of the car a present for me. On returning to Shahid's house we opened a long roll done up in white silk and inside found a very handsome carpet.

The following day I was seen off from the VIP building at the airport by Shahid's charming and striking looking wife, Tahira. In her heyday she must have been one of Pakistan Society's beauties. Because my old slow-coach of a bear-leader – Akbar – was once again forty minutes late in fetching me from the hotel, I found a somewhat agitated Tahira pacing the verandah of the VIP lounge when I arrived. I had already given Akbar and his protocol officer a couple of broadsides for their slackness and bad manners, so I hastened to make my apologies to Tahira. She remarked that she had warned Shahid before I even arrived in Pakistan that Akbar was a bad choice, but Shahid was not to be put off.

In the event, the aircraft was an hour late in taking off, so Akbar had the last laugh! The first class compartment was chockfull and I was amused to see that my Pakistani fellow travellers could hardly wait for the drinks to be served. They did full justice to the champagne and wine, and who can blame them?

July to December 1979

What were the highlights of events in Pakistan between my departure in July and the occupation of Afghanistan by the Soviet Union at the end of December?

In September an official Soviet commentator, Ivan Lavrov, made the following statement of facts: "The situation in Afghanistan is that the rebel elements who oppose the Government of Afghanistan and its reforms in the interest of the working masses are making use of Pakistani territory and some of its material resources. During the riots in Kabul, Jalalabad and other places saboteurs from Pakistan became directly involved in anti-Government disorders".

This was the first time that Moscow had fully and officially

83

incriminated Pakistan in the uprising in Afghanistan. The significance of it should *not* have been underestimated. All the more so because Lavrov went on to warn of the likely "dangerous consequences for Pakistan", adding that if Pakistan continued to "promote its own objectives" in Afghanistan, it might become necessary "to replace that outdated and archaic régime". He did not say who would do the replacing. Lavrov also roundly condemned "the reactionary quarters in Pakistan", who were "openly interfering in the internal affairs of a sovereign state".

However, even if Lavrov did not say who would act to replace the "outdated archiac régime", he suggested who *should* be preparing for it. He formally backed those "people of Pakistan" who were no longer prepared "to act in the interests of the imperialists, who can't reconcile themselves to the fact that a progressive government is now in power in Afghanistan". These people of Pakistan, he said, should take decisive action. Only an idiot would fail to realize that this was a call for a *coup* in Pakistan, made by an official Soviet spokesman.

What was needed in Pakistan, he said, was a government prepared to recognize the reality of the Afghanistan revolution and to pursue "a peaceful and good-neighbourly policy towards that country".

What was happening, according to Lavrov, was that the "United States and Chinese intelligence services" were being allowed to operate freely in Pakistan, directing a dangerous conspiracy against Afghanistan. The startling fact, Lavrov explained, was that the regional headquarters of the CIA had been moved from Iran to Pakistan – needless to say, totally against the wishes of the Pakistani people. This meant that the "reactionary quarters in Pakistan" were co-operating with the CIA and the "Chinese intelligence service" to bring about a "counter-revolution" in Afghanistan, and in the process trampling underfoot the legitimate interests of the Pakistani people.

This almost sounded like a replay of the record explaining the "counter-revolution" in Czechoslovakia on the eve of the "rescue" operation by the Warsaw Pact forces in 1968. The circumstances were, of course, entirely different, but what seemed evident was that the ground was being prepared for some form of direct meddling in Pakistan, once more ostensibly in support of the "people".

What was significant was that Peking suddenly showed a lively interest in the Soviet allegations and started warning Moscow not to overstep the line. *Hsinhua,* the Official Chinese agency, stated bluntly: "The root cause of this turbulent situation lies in the Soviet Union's ruthless intervention in the internal affairs of Afghanistan which Moscow is trying to cover up by throwing the blame on Afghanistan's neighbours as well as other countries."

As for the accusations against Pakistan, Peking warned that this could be seen only in the context of the Soviet drive "to turn Afghanistan into a bridgehead and then to continue expanding southwards towards the Indian Ocean". In order to accomplish this,

Peking pointed out, it would become necessary for the Soviet Union to extend its grip over Afghanistan's southern neighbours, Pakistan in the first place but certainly also Iran in due course.

What Peking was saying was that the struggle going on in Afghanistan concerned much more than just control of Afghanistan itself. China also made the allegation (which cannot be confirmed but is probably true) that during 1979 the Soviet Union had forced the Tarakki Government in Kabul to conclude more than 40 separate treaties with Moscow committing Afghanistan totally to further the Soviet drive southwards, namely into Pakistan and Iran, if the Soviet Union could succeed in keeping Tarakki and his crowd in power.

In short, China was taking the struggle in Afghanistan, and the overt threat to Pakistan, much more seriously than the West was doing.

China's strategic interests were, of course, more immediately affected by what was happening than those of the West, but then the West usually wakes up only *after* it has suffered a strategic loss, when it is too late to do anything about it.

China also warned that it would be folly to think of the uprising as some sort of counter-revolution. "The guerrillas are now operating in all 26 provinces", Peking stated and pointed out that Afghanistan was just not the kind of country where a co-ordinated counter-revolution could be staged on such a scale.

Peking was well-informed about what was going on. Even so far as the tactics were concerned the military authorities in Peking were able to assert that the Afghan guerrillas had given top priority to the need to cut the vital highway running north from Kabul to the Soviet border, thus interfering with the flow of Soviet military supplies. Peking was equally well-informed about the quantities of weapons, and the types, then reaching the insurgents, while at the same time professing ignorance about where the weapons were coming from.

The question of whether China would accept a confrontation with the Soviet Union if Pakistan was threatened remained, however. A possible answer, only hinted at in Peking was that a great deal would depend upon whether China would receive Western support in stemming the tide, the argument being that Western interests were involved there and that China would need at least moral support internationally.

It was, however, most unlikely that the West had even thought that far yet.

Meanwhile the political situation in Pakistan by mid-October was that General Zia had declared that unless he was confident that elected politicians could form a stable government, he would not transfer power. He ruled that foreign-funded parties and those advocating lawlessness, or preaching hatred against the judiciary and the armed forces, would be banned.

This was obviously aimed at Mr. Bhutto's Pakistan People's Party (PPP), led by his widow. The PPP remained widely popular and Zia realized it would sweep the board in any free election. Bhutto, as political martyr was being praised as seldom he was when he held office and his régime ended in yet another débâcle of parliamentary democracy, with himself the first civilian Chief Martial Law Administrator.

General Zia announced that the election date of 17th November was not sacrosanct and that the Koran had not stipulated that his pledge to hold elections must be redeemed. The leader of the Tehriki Instiklal Party (Movement for Solidarity), the retired Air Marshal Asghar Khan, former C-in-C of the Pakistan Air Force, asked Zia to let him know where it was stated in the Koran he could tell lies.

Towards the end of October, Zia renewed public flogging for a wide range of offences. Amongst the first 200 victims were corrupt officials, black marketeers, hoarders and vice racketeers. General Zia said his Government had four priorities: maintenance of peaceful conditions; keeping prices at a reasonable level; ending bribery; and the availability of quick and inexpensive justice for the people.

It would not be out of place to mention here that a little medicine like this, but of a milder kind, is what is required in Britain to put an end to vandalism and street and other violence. Such crimes should carry a public stigma, the culprits being made publicly ashamed of what they have done by putting them in the stocks.

Addressing newspaper editors in late October, Zia said: "I want to introduce Islam in Pakistan, in the true sense.

"Our present political edifice is based on the secular democratic system of the West which has no place in Islam," he said of the legal, political and economic system developed by the British Raj during its 200 years of rule over the Indian subcontinent.

Most of the political parties had been demanding the continuation of Westminster-style parliamentary democracy, as well as Islamization of those British Laws which offend Islamic beliefs.

But a number of military leaders who came to power in the past 32 years preferred an American-style presidential system, with most powers vested in the Head of State.

Asked what safeguards he would adopt for the enforcement of the new Islamic order since the constitution – providing for a Western-style democracy – was still in existence, General Zia said that he would seek a mandate from the people, which could be done through a referendum.

"In Pakistan neither anarchy nor Westernism will work" he said. "This country was created in the name of Islam, and in Islam there is no provision for Western-type elections. Even the good points of Western democracy have been derived from Islam," he said.

He told the editors that censorship imposed on all Pakistani newspapers and magazines (foreign newspapers and despatches for foreign news media were not censored) would soon be lifted from "the responsible and patriotic newspapers."

He said he regretted that he had to resort to such harsh measures, adding: "It was inevitable because too much rubbish was being poured out in the name of journalism."

After the U.S. Embassy in Tehran was seized, Washington ordered its embassies throughout the world to review their security. The embassy in Islamabad had finally concluded on 21st November that it was totally dependent on the Pakistani government for protection. The very next day that prediction proved to be only too true.

Angered by false radio reports and rumours that the Americans and Israelis were responsible for the assault on and seige of the Great Sacred Mosque in Mecca, some 10,000 Pakistanis attacked the U.S. embassy in Islamabad and set it ablaze. The assault started at 1 p.m. and not until 2 p.m. did the police arrive. Finding themselves outnumbered they left, and it was not until 4 p.m. that Pakistani soldiers arrived when they proceeded to give a demonstration of masterly inactivity – so did the fire brigade.

The first group of about 40 Americans, women and children, fled to safety a few hours after the rioting began. A second group of more than 100 Americans and local employees were rescued when troops arrived. The last to emerge were the marine guards, carrying the body of a dead marine. Also killed were a U.S. warrant officer, two Pakistani employees and two rioters.

Although Pakistan radio reported that President Carter had expressed appreciation to General Zia by telephone for subduing the mob, a number of pertinent questions remain unanswered.

* Why did an American ally's army take several hours in a captial under strict martial law, to disperse the attackers and put out the fire?
* Why was Zia's response so little as well as being so late?
* Why was the Pakistani Government, which had been warned already by the State Department to expect trouble, so completely taken by surprise by the mob?
* Who started the rumours about American involvement in the take-over of Mecca's Grand Mosque?

There were also large demonstrations and violence in Karachi, and the American cultural centres in Lahore and Rawalpindi were burned and gutted. The British Council library in Rawalpindi was also burned.

There is no doubt that the military régime of General Zia lost the initiative against religious frenzy and failed to maintain order. The prestige of President Zia and the Pakistan Army undoubtedly suffered a serious blow. Moreover, there were longer-term implications in all this for the unpopular two-and-a-half-year-old régime.

Its opponents must have seen what damage could be inflicted on the régime by street violence organized by small, highly motivated

87

groups. The assault on the Embassy and violence elsewhere laid bare the striking limitations of the Army's power.

I had warned both General Shahid Hamid and Brigadier Noor Husain in July that their Army did not possess up to date anti-riot equipment, and I even went so far as to tell them from where to get it. I have read reports that state that the military régime connived at the violence in an effort to deflect domestic resentment on to the Americans. But it is clear to me that incompetence also played a considerable role. In Islamabad, for instance, the woeful state of the Army's communications equipment was obvious.

President Zia is a realist and knows on which side his bread is buttered. At that moment in time he was an advocate of the conventional minded military requirement for friendly relations with the United States, which was needed in any case to ensure imports of vital commodities such as wheat and cooking oils. And unlike India, he had interceded with Ayatollah Khomeini to release the Tehran hostages.

Among ordinary Pakistanis there were no signs of xenophobia: they continued to be personally friendly towards foreigners and helpful as usual. But the Iranian revolution posed a major challenge for Pakistan. Pakistan has to maintain good relations with Tehran. It realizes that any break-up of that country by ethnic groups threatens Pakistan as well. Islamabad has to work to acquire credit in Tehran and the right-wing régime is basically in sympathy with the Ayatollah's Islamic revivalism.

That is why a régime with little popular standing can only proceed cautiously when events like the seizure of the Ka'aba in Mecca puts mass support behind tiny, militant groups. "When people hear of their religion being attacked they don't listen to the Government or the police or anyone," said a Rawalpindi shopkeeper. He had watched the crowds pour on to the streets on 21st November when special one-page editions of the newspapers and Pakistan radio finally gave the news.

But the writing is on the wall. No one can be sure that if the régime were faced once again between protecting the diplomatic community and tolerating Islamic mob frenzy it would choose the former. Watching events like hawks were – and are – of course, the Russian KGB and GRU representatives in Pakistan, the GRU being the military intelligence members of the network.

In addition to the import and export trade between the two countries I was told that there were several thousand Russian technicians working in a steel mill and elsewhere. There is certainly ample scope and cover for covert action and intelligence-gathering by the KGB and GRU. I made it my business to find out the names of those employed in the Soviet Embassy at the time of my visit. Having checked the names with my knowledge of KGB and GRU officials, I discovered that the Soviet Consul-General and one of the vice Consuls were KGB officers and that the deputy chief of the Soviet trade mission was a major in the GRU. I knew that up to 1972 there had been twelve KGB officers engaged in clandestine activities in Pakistan:

1957	Served in Pakistan
1957-58	Served in Pakistan
1958-61	Served in Pakistan
1960-61	Served in Pakistan
1961	Expelled from Pakistan
1961-64	Expelled from Pakistan in 1964
1963-66	A GRU* officer who was later expelled from Great Britain in 1971.
1966	Previously expelled from Norway in 1963
1966-70	Served in Pakistan
1966-71	Previously expelled from Ghana in 1966
1970	Served in Pakistan
1971-72	Served in Pakistan

In addition, General Ivan Ivanovich Agayants, the first director of the KGB's Department "D" (Disinformation: Poisoning Public Opinion) slipped into Pakistan in 1965.

Pakistan will have to build up its hopelessly inadequate counter-intelligence and surveillance if it is to be able to deal with Russia's covert actions and intelligence-gathering activities.

It was on 20th February, 1980, that the man who might have been President of Iran if the mullahs had their way, said that conditions in Pakistan were just right for an Iranian-style revolution.

Dr. Seyed Hassan Ayet, a senior member of the Islamic Republican party, the largest in the country, reflected a desire felt by many influential Iranians to export their revolution, when he said: "There is no other country so ripe for revolution as is Pakistan. God willing, there will soon be an Islamic revolution in that country." Dr. Ayet would probably have been the official presidential candidate of the Islamic Republic party had the poll been postponed. "Since the creation of Pakistan, a majority of its rulers have been working for imperialist forces and never really cared for the welfare of Pakistanis," he said.

---

* The GRU, or Chief Intelligence Directorate, is a division of the Soviet General Staff. Administratively it is independent of the KGB, or Committee for State Security in Russia.

On 17th June, 1974, I had the honour of being Chairman of the launching in London of John Barron's book, "KGB – The Secret Work of Soviet Secret Agents."

By virtue of my NATO appointment, I was already well acquainted with this subject, but it was a great experience to meet and talk to John Barron, having taken great pains to go through his brilliant book with a tooth-comb. It was extremely difficult to foot-fault him.

CHAPTER
7

Pakistan, Post 27th December, 1979

Three days after the massive Soviet armed intervention in Afghanistan on 27th December, the American Government publicly reaffirmed its binding commitment to Pakistan under a 1959 defence agreement.

The strategically situated country of Pakistan, which not only borders Afghanistan but also Iran and fronts on to the Arabian Sea, is the country most directly involved, after Afghanistan itself, in the Russians' arrival on the Khyber Pass. In fact, as I have already explained, the next Russian target could be Baluchistan, a province that has been in a state of constant near-revolt against Islamabad.

With the neighbouring provinces of Iran also in turmoil and susceptible to provocation to rise against the Tehran régime, the American fear was that Pakistan and Iran might eventually disintegrate and the Russians would then reach the Indian Ocean.

The United States therefore decided to reassert that they would take every step, including the use of armed force, to preserve Pakistan's independence.

The text of the relevant clause of the 1959 defence agreement states:

"In case of aggression against Pakistan, the Government of the United States in accordance with its constitutional procedures, will take such appropriate action, including the use of armed force, as may be mutually agreed and is envisaged in the joint resolution, to protect peace and stability in the Middle East, and in order to assist the Government of Pakistan, at its request."

The resolution that the agreement mentions is a joint resolution of the American Congress, affirming the Eisenhower Doctrine, which states America's determination to resist communist aggression in the Middle East. The defence agreement is not a treaty, but is equally binding upon both parties.

The U.S. had ruled, over Pakistan's protests, that the agreement did not apply to its wars with India. Relations had been particularly cold since the 1971 war with India over Bangladesh. Subsequently, all American military aid to Pakistan was suspended by act of Congress because of the issue of Pakistan's nuclear potential.

At one time the U.S. and Pakistan had such close ties that many Pakistanis referred to their country as the 51st state. The burning down of the American Embassy in November 1979, in an excess of anti-American feeling, shows how wide the rift between the two countries had become. America's concern about the doctrine of non-proliferation, which is also dear to the heart of President Carter, was now being over-whelmed by the threat to the future of Pakistan and the subcontinent.

It became clear at the very beginning of January that Pakistan would not accept the offer of supplies of arms from America until she knew their quantity and type, and the conditions that the United States had in mind governing their use. No strings must be attached. As far as Pakistan was concerned she had to be able to defend herself against aggression from any quarter. It was made clear to America, by Pakistan, that clarification was required on what would be done to guarantee a completely reliable supply of arms and to circumvent the Symington Amendment which stopped aid and arms in April 1979.

Pakistan also had to keep in mind her relations with the Moslem world, particularly Iran. With the Russians having turned the region's historic buffer state of Afghanistan into a Soviet satellite – the first Soviet invasion of a Muslim country – Pakistan either had to obtain high quality modern defence equipment to defend its sovereignty or be sub-verted by the Soviet Union.

This is what Iran had to be made to appreciate if the Islamic brotherhood was not to be impaired.

The outcry by India was ironic indeed with that country's own sub-stantial dependence on Soviet arms and defence assistance, and at a time when she had recently taken a decision to acquire a regiment of Soviet T72 tanks and the Anglo-French Jaguar aircraft. Delhi was more angered at the prospect of American arms supplies to Pakistan than by the invasion of Afghanistan by Soviet troops.

No wonder Pakistan had to exercise much care and diplomatic skill before taking any momentous decision. Zia could not be seen to be crawling before Washington for help. Not only would it damage his already unpopular régime internally but would certainly create problems with some of Pakistan's friends in the non-aligned and Islamic blocs.

In mid-January we heard that President Carter intended to ask Congress to approve $400 million (£178 million) in economic and military assistance – roughly half of it for "defensive" weapons. This was not enough to satisfy General Zia who wanted more concrete reassurance than of "one-shot" assistance. He made it clear that he was looking for more than military aid from the United States. He wanted to see a long-term commitment to help his country, not only in re-equipping the outmoded armed forces, but in helping to put the Pakistan economy on a firm footing. The last balance-of-payments deficit was $1,200 million. In 1979 Pakistan relied on $1,000 million in international aid, two-thirds of it from the West. Therefore Zia desperately needed help, both economic and military. But he was determined, to make the most of his country's suddenly enhanced international role. Furthermore, he himself, assailed only a short while ago as a ruthless dictator, was suddenly emerging as plucky and courageous General Zia, the man who would keep the Russians at bay. The West, and most of the Islamic countries, shared his consternation of having 1,200 miles of his country's border with the Soviet Union. Consequently the self interested race to help was now on, after thirty years during which Pakistan had so often been ignored. Would the help come from the United States, China, the Islamic countries – or even the Soviet Union? The correct decision would decide whether the Soviet Union would ultimately obtain access to more oil and a port on the Indian Ocean.

Zia described President Carter's offer of $400 million aid as "peanuts". In a week when the U.S. had given Egypt $2,000 million, who could fail to agree with him? Although Zia's 400,000 strong army is well trained, most of its equipment dates back to the Fifties or even earlier. To defend itself Pakistan requires a wide range of modern equipment, including communications systems, SAM anti-aircraft missiles, anti-tank weapons and aircraft.

The problem facing the Carter Administration was plainly that General Zia was head of a shaky régime – more shaky many of them believed, than that of the deposed Shah of Iran. In the wake of the Iran fiasco could he be seen to be bolstering a fragile régime? Furthermore, President Carter risked running foul of Mrs. Gandhi's India and pushing it nearer to the Kremlin.

At the beginning of February, President Carter pulled out all the diplomatic stops to convince Pakistan that its future and that of South-West Asia, lay in a close security relationship with America. He sent Mr. Zbigniew Brzezinski, National Security Adviser, and Mr. Warren Christopher, Deputy Secretary of State, to lead a mission for detailed discussions with President Zia in Islamabad. The task of the Brzezinski mission was to try to persuade General Zia that a $400 million (£178 million) American aid offer would provide a solid base for a new and lasting security arrangement, and that it was not "peanuts", as he had said it was. The American team would also try to put some flesh on the bones of President Carter's declaration that there should be a regional security framework in the area, with American backing.

The talks hit more snags than were anticipated, one theory being that Washington's concern over Pakistan's alleged venture into the nuclear field had led to a brittle exchange. My personal view is that if the Western powers had not meddled with Pakistan's nuclear programme that country might now have a nuclear weapon and the Russians would have thought twice before invading Afghanistan.

One chilling suggestion is that the situation the U.S. was facing in Iran could arise in Pakistan. But Zia had strongly endorsed the revolutionary régime in Iran. Co-operation with Ayatollah Khomeini's arch enemy – Washington – would not be a popular move among many Pakistani Muslims. Thus the Zia government had to be careful about how close it was seen to be co-operating with America. The solution to this is the proposed consortium of aid-giving nations, so that Zia will not be put in the position of accepting handouts direct from the U.S.

'Just going down to the beaches. Why do you ask?'

LePelley in *The Christian Science Monitor*, U.S.A.
Copyright 1980 TCSPS.

Can we expect some of the aid to find its way into the hands of the Afghan freedom fighters? The Soviets will obviously play *this* propaganda card. Already in mid-January, an article in *Pravda* charged that the tribesmen were being trained by American, Chinese and Pakistani officers and that money and weapons were flowing in "an endless stream from the United States, China and a number of other countries." Certainly the Western allies should not become involved in smuggling arms to the Afghan tribesmen. That task should be left to China and to the sympathetic Islamic states that condemned Soviet actions at the Islamabad Foreign Ministers' conference in early February.

The aim of providing Pakistan with modern weapons should be to give Pakistan the capability of dealing with minor Soviet border incursions and to control its own ethnic separatists against Moscow's attempts to foment rebellions among the minorities. No matter how much military equipment they have, the Pakistanis could not on their own, defend themselves against an all-out Soviet attack without American military intervention.

As for Mrs. Gandhi's contention that the renewal of military aid to Pakistan would constitute a threat to India – as was shown by the three wars during the past thirty-three years in which Pakistan used American arms – the U.S. Special Envoy, Clark Clifford, promised her that Washington would carefully monitor the uses to which Pakistan put any weapons supplied. Furthermore, to allay India's fears, America did not intend to provide Pakistan with highly sophisticated weapons. India, of course, has not had a similar embargo imposed against her!

In what may prove to be a watershed in Moscow's dealings with the Third World, foreign ministers representing the thirty-five members of the Islamic Conference met in Islamabad in early February and condemned the Soviet invasion of Afghanistan as a "flagrant violation of international war". The delegates, who represented such traditional friends of Moscow as Algeria, Libya and the Palestine Liberation Organization, also demanded "the immediate and unconditional withdrawal of all Soviet troops stationed on Afghan territory" and suspended Afghanistan's membership in the international Islamic organization.

The resolution was a far more stinging rebuff to the Soviet Union than the U.N. General Assembly's mildly worded statement, a fortnight earlier, calling for a Soviet withdrawal from Afghanistan. In addition, the Islamic summit, to which the Afghanistan government was invited but failed to attend, also managed to get the feuding Afghan rebel groups to form an *ad hoc* united front: the Islamic Alliance for the Liberation of Afghanistan. The front's spokesman, Burhanuddin Rabbani, former head of the faculty of Islamic law at Kabul University, told the conference that although Soviet troops controlled the main Afghan cities, roads and airports, the rest of the country was largely in the hands of the guerrillas.

In addition to the host, Pakistan's President Zia, the most influential voice at the conference was that of Saudi Arabia's Foreign Minister, Prince Saud al Faisal. Arriving in Islamabad, Saud emphasized that the conference must take a strong line on the Soviet occupation of Afghanistan, which he said "threatened the independence of Muslim countries". He urged Islamic states to break diplomatic ties with Kabul, boycott the Moscow Olympics and provide assistance to the refugees. In the end, those points were included in the resolution, though only as recommendations. The final vote of the foreign ministers on the anti-Soviet measure was not known but, as one Pakistani diplomat said, "There was no dissenting voice on this issue." The strong language of the resolution, he added, was "commensurate with the outrage." The U.S. by comparison, was given only a tap on the wrist. In surprisingly moderate language, the foreign ministers registered their disapproval of the Camp David accords and called on Iran and the U.S. to resolve their differences peacefully.

The Soviets were plainly shocked by the resolutions. *Tass* denounced the declaration calling for removal of Soviet troops from Afghanistan as "gross interference in the internal affairs" of that country. Casting about for an explanation of this massive Muslim repudiation of Soviet policies, *Tass* declared that the vote was the result of "arm twisting" by the U.S., which was seeking to distract attention from the "threat posed by the forces of imperialism and Zionism."

On 4th January, 1980, President Zia gave an interview during which he stated his forthright views on many of the problems now facing Pakistan as the result of Soviet forces being on his country's very doorstep. The interview was reported in full in the United States, but not elsewhere, which is a pity as it gives an interesting insight into how his mind was working. His statements were also very much in line with what I had been told by his inner circle.

When asked what he thought the Soviet Union was trying to achieve in Afghanistan, he replied that it certainly could not be motivated by a desire to acquire new resources because Afghanistan did not have any. Although very poor, with 15 million to 17 million people and no oil, it was strategically very important. With an abundance of oil in Iran, Afghanistan and Pakistan constituted the back door to the Gulf, and direct access to the Indian Ocean. He said he had been trying to warn Washington about this ever since the first Marxist *coup* in Kabul in April 1978, but without much success. He emphasized that the linch-pin was Pakistan. This did not mean that they were scared. In fact, they were quite confident. But given the new power equation in the world, self-reliance would be the key to their survival as a nation. Pakistan was now an island of stability and they intended to keep it that way.

He was asked why he thought the Russians invaded when they did, thus jeopardising détente with the United States in general and SALT II in particular. He stated that the Soviets made a very careful assessment of potential gains and losses. The Soviets were not impulsive. It was a carefully calculated decision. So there was only one conclusion. Their assessment was that the timing was perfect. America was tied up with the hostages in Iran and with an early start to its presidential campaign. But the Russians action was, nevertheless, fraught with grave dangers for the entire region. Any country that tried to change the balance of power through military action was setting a dangerous precedent, especially when such a move went unchallenged.

He said he saw Moscow's long-term objective as being the neutralization of Western Europe by the acquisition of strategic control in the areas upon which the West depends for its survival. That much was clear. But he was at a loss to understand the interplay of super-power politics. Was Russia doing this on its own or in tacit collusion with the other superpower, or again were we presently witnessing an osmotic process that would lead to the partition of the Gulf between the two superpowers? He did not know. But he considered the question to be pertinent. Soviet forces were on his border, close to his capital. How did this new power equation affect his own thinking? Did it militate in favour of a position equidistant between the two superpowers or in favour of a rapprochement with the United States? He replied, on the contrary it was in favour of a third option. The cornerstone was their relationship with China. They had given Pakistan tremendous moral and material strength. They had received almost $2 billion worth of aid from China since 1966. They had taught them self-reliance and for that they would always be grateful. But the Soviet invasion of Afghanistan had drastically altered the power equation. Soviet power was indeed on their doorstep. So geography dictated accommodation with what was their superpower neighbour. So also was it with Iran and India.

Soviet power was now predominant in the region and the United States ineffective, either *intentionally* or unintentionally. But Pakistan had to view this realistically. "If you have to live in the sea, says an old proverb, you have to learn to live with the whales." They would, of course, dearly love to see a more active participation by the United States. But history had taught them not to harbour any illusions on that score. Was America still the leader of the Free World and in what respect? He hoped the U.S.A. would soon restore its countervailing role, abandoned after Vietnam. There were signs that it was waking up. But so far he believed it was mostly words.

Asked what his reaction was to America's reaffirmation of its 1959 bilateral treaty commitment to safeguard the integrity of Pakistan, General Zia said that he had been delighted to hear Dr. Brzezinski's announcement. But he had asked Washington some very hard questions and he would appreciate some very blunt and honest answers. He said they did not want any U.S. troops, but they did want to know how serious the United States was about being the leader of the Free World — its real aims and objectives.

It was too late for platitudes. Was the nuclear issue now out of the way? What was to happen to the Symington amendment (which bans most U.S. aid to countries that appear to be involved in nuclear development outside international controls?) Would it be rescinded by congressional act or suspended by executive order? Was America going to restore its role and its credibility through words or with practical steps?

Relations between Pakistan and the United States had been very shaky since the beginning of the Carter Administration, primarily due to the controversy over Pakistan's nuclear development programme. Was it his impression that the United States now wanted to wipe the slate clean?

General Zia replied that he wished it were so, but he feared not, at least not on the basis of everything they had been through. They had never made any progress with the United States in two-and-a-half years of trying. Warren Christopher (Deputy U.S. Secretary of State), Lucy Benson (Under-secretary for security assistance), David Newson (Under-secretary for political affairs), etc., had all come to see him. He hoped that he was wrong, but his impression was that the United States had lost interest in that region. Soviet actions were totally different. They had seen (the United States) acquiesce in other major power plays, so they were trying it again.

Asked if he could put a figure on Pakistan's military hardware requirements, General Zia replied that it was hard to be precise in such matters, but the $100 million figure that was being discussed in press reports – which would be cash sales even though they knew they did not have the cash – was ludicrous. That did not even buy a squadron of modern jet fighters. But if the United States was serious he would like to emphasize two things. They needed a major qualitative improvement in their defensive capability – not offensive weaponry. At the mere mention of U.S. military assistance to Pakistan, India started yelling. India should *want* to see a strong and stable Pakistan.

Secondly, they could not separate the military from the economic. Pakistan would like to see the United States assist, as China had done in improving (Pakistan's) economic stability; they did not wish to be burdened with new debts. They were still hurting and had never really recovered from the cut off of U.S. military aid after the 1965 war with India. So what they really needed was U.S. assistance for their own defence industry, as Russia was doing in India on a huge scale.

General Zia was asked how he saw events in Iran? He explained that Iran had gone through an ideological revolution – a return to the fundamental teachings of Islam. And Imam (Ruhollah) Khomeini had acquired a reputation as a very prominent leader – a sort of combined emperor and ruler, the *Imam* in the literal sense. They had always been good neighbours. And since the Shah's departure, relations were still reasonably good and they wanted to go on improving them.

Zia was then asked if he approved of the U.S. plan to apply selec-

97

tive economic sanctions against Iran as a means to get the hostages released? He replied that he was against economic sanctions or military reprisals because that was precisely what the Marxists would like the United States to do. They knew it would play into their hands and help them to channel the revolution to a Marxist takeover. This was certainly what would happen if Khomeini failed. If he thought economic sanctions would work he would say go ahead and try it. But they have never worked in the past and in this case they would backfire badly and achieve exactly the opposite of what U.S. officials intended.

America was now virtually helpless and it didn't suddenly happen that way. There had been a long series of unmet geo-political challenges since Vietnam that had led to America's present predicament. By way of contrast, the Soviets seemed to know what they were doing. The United States could not suddenly correct the situation by taking action against Iran. He was not suggesting that the United States should have turned the Shah back. But he was saying that given the United States' present weakness, it had no alternative but to try to dialogue with the Imam.

Finally, Zia was asked if Pakistan was trying to develop *a nuclear bomb?* He replied "Absolutely not". That canard, he said, was invented by Israeli propaganda, which said they were being financed by Libya to make a bomb for Colonel Gadhafi, the Libyan leader, and Yasser Arafat, the Palestine Liberation Organization leader. It was pure fiction. They did not want to make a bomb. They were not in competition with India and did not want to engage in a nuclear race. If India had one, it did not mean they must have one too. They must go on living as good neighbours. But Pakistan must become self-reliant for energy in the future. Their oil bill had just gone over $1 billion a year, which was over half their total export earnings. By the end of this decade they must have nuclear energy.

General Zia visited Baluchistan in early February to stress to local government officials and tribal elders the need for national unity. Since Pakistan became independent, Baluchistan has risen in open revolt on several occasions. The Province is ripe for agitation and contains the nearest equivalent to organized Communism. General Zia's fear is that Marxist "Moles" might already have been planted to work among students and dissidents. This is exactly the type of movement the Russians would try to foster. One theory is that the true danger to Pakistan from the Russian occupation of Afghanistan might not be a full-blooded invasion but subversion in the form of money and practical aid sent across the border to insurgents. *(see Appendix B)*

Baluchi Leftists were openly saying that they would welcome union with Moscow and one public figure, a former diplomat, had already stated: "We Baluchis would not mind if the Russians came here from Afghanistan. We have no love for Pakistan and have never been given a fair deal, although we voted for Pakistan in 1947.

"We have been dubbed traitors, the Army has been used against us and we are dominated by the Punjab. The Baluchi people felt they were 'just a colony' of the Punjab, as they had been of the British."

Much of the Baluchis' bitterness is traceable to 1970, when the then President, Yahya Khan, held what they regarded as the first and only fair elections in the province. Mr. Bhutto's People's Party did not win a single seat, while the old Left-wing National Awami party triumphed and formed a provincial administration.

Mr. Bhutto, however, exercised his considerable political skills and, by a variety of manoeuvres, threats and favours, soon gained control of the provincial Legislature.

Unrest and demonstration followed. The army was sent in with helicopter support, and many tribesmen took to the mountains or crossed over into Afghanistan. There was small-scale sabotage and some guerrilla activity, which continued until Bhutto was overthrown on 5th July, 1977 by military *coup* and subsequently executed on 4th April, 1979.

With such a background it is hardly surprising that Baluchistan is seen by General Zia as something of a soft underbelly to Pakistan and his warning about the need for national unity was more than mere rhetoric.

The fear of this danger was shared by Lieutenant-General Fazale-Haq, the Corps Commander and the Governor of the North West Frontier Province. His view was that once the campaigning season had started later in the Spring, Russia could easily have invoked the right of "hot pursuit" against the Afghan tribesmen if it had wanted an excuse to invade Pakistan. The Russians could leapfrog the Khyber Pass; they would drop their armour by parachute around Peshawar, or strike deep inside Pakistan through the desert plain of Baluchistan leading to the warmwaters of the Gulf. He thought the latter was the most likely course of action, leaving the Iranian pot to boil; leaving it until it boiled over.

The General's fear was that he himself might be forced into giving the Russians the pretext they wanted. The Russians, he said: "could sit 25 miles away and shell the refugee camps which they say are being used as bases by the guerrillas. Then the refugees would look to me to help them. And we would have to hit back because otherwise there would be a danger of the government's authority being eroded."

Pakistan had, up to now, firmly denied that its territory was being used as a base for Afghan guerrillas. But Kabul insisted that raids were being made from Pakistan, and in February a thinly veiled warning, with an implied threat of Russian military action, was made by Mr. Gromyko, Soviet Foreign Minister. He claimed at a banquet in New Delhi that Pakistan was "interfering in other countries' affairs" and said that if it continued to do so its independent status "would be gravely undermined."

At an emergency session of the U.N. General Assembly in mid-

January, the Bulgarian representative, speaking in support of the Soviet Union, asserted: "It has been well-established that Pakistan, with the help of the United States and China has allowed the territory along its border with Afghanistan to become a stronghold for training supplying with weaponry and sending back into Afghanistan anti-Government troops."

The refugees in Pakistan are certainly going to be a potent factor in the wider confrontation between the West and the Russians over Afghanistan. Meanwhile Pakistan was already the unwilling host of hundreds of thousands of refugees and will be faced with the largest single refugee problem in the world. Without massive international aid the strain of feeding so many extra mouths would cause economic havoc.

It was at this juncture that General Zia turned down a passionate appeal by tribal leaders of the North West Frontier Province to be allowed to wage *Jihad* (holy war) against Soviet troops in Afghanistan. It was, he told them a time for restraint.

The President visited Peshawar and was welcomed by Shahzada Khan, headman of the fierce Afridi tribe, which traditionally controls the Khyber Pass. A former Indian Army major who fought in the Second World War, he is today one of the most respected leaders in the tribal lands and was chosen by the other elders of the three million tribesmen in the Province to tell the President they wanted to wage *Jihad*.

The chiefs argued that it was right to declare *Jihad* against the Russians because they did not believe in a god, Shahzada Khan argued this point vehemently to the President, but as a trained soldier he accepted the President's refusal.

The President showed he was aware that feelings were running high and that the tribes might not listen to appeals for restraint. "This martial spirit is the hallmark of our tribal culture," he said. "It was because of this martial spirit that even big powers could not succeed in their efforts to absorb the tribal areas."

He denied once again Soviet allegations that Pakistan was being used to train Afghan guerrillas. The point was, he said, to consider why 421,000 people had been compelled to leave their homes; they had come to Pakistan because their life, honour and property were in danger and an attempt was being made to force on them an ideology opposed to their own.

It was, he said, "a cruel joke" that, while Pakistan was spending about £75,000 a day on providing humanitarian aid to the refugees, "those who have pushed them across the border into our country are accusing Pakistan of giving military aid." He repudiated the "unfounded and mischievous charge" which appeared to be "part of a sinister design".

Should this "sinister design" include a Soviet invasion of Pakistan, it was clear from his courtesy to them that the President was relying on the tribesmen as a formidable first line of defence.

It also seemed he felt he could do no more than turn a blind eye if the tribesmen did start fighting in Afghanistan. "I am confident that, as long as tyranny and oppression last, our Afghan brothers will continue to receive your traditional hospitality", he said. Continuing, he revealed, that in practice there was nothing Pakistan could do to control order sufficiently to prevent guerrillas coming in and out.

An underlying theme of the President's speech was an appeal for national unity, and it was increasingly clear that he was being able to use the Afghan crisis as a way of keeping firm control of the country. The national unity he appealed for was, he considered, the best answer to Soviet aggression in Afghanistan. "It is not the planes or the tanks or the guns which will defend our country. What matters is our resolution, which by the grace of God we have."

While 80% of Pakistan's military forces are deployed to the east facing 13 Indian Army divisions, the 800 mile border of the North West Frontier Province with Afghanistan is very lightly guarded. NWFP Tribal Territory, a belt 30 to 50 miles wide which runs along the Durand Line, is not even occupied by Pakistan Army units. The NWFP Tribal Territory is chiefly patrolled and pacified by Pakistani paramilitary forces totalling 18,000 men, including such famed units as the Tochi Scouts, Waziri Scouts and Khyber Rifles.

At present, defence of the Khyber Pass rests with the 1,800 strong Khyber Rifles, with headquarters at Ford Jamrud and a garrison at Landi Kotal. General Fazale-Haq's XI Army Corps, consisting of two divisions of about 20,000 men, with Korean war vintage weapons, has the task of rendering immediate support to the defence of the Khyber Pass. Meanwhile, covert KGB agents are maintaining surveillance on weapons manufacturing for Afghan guerrillas now taking place in the Kohat Pass, 25 miles south of Peshawar near the Khyber Pass.

In early March, Pakistan rejected the $400 million (£178 million) aid package proposed by Washington which was meant to stem the tide of the Soviet aggression in the region. The American package consisted of $200 million of military equipment on credit and $200 million of economic aid spread over a period of 18 months. This was accompanied by an offer to fortify the security commitment in the 1959 pact.

The Foreign Affairs Adviser to President Zia said that Pakistan had to depend primarily for its security on its national unity and strength; and, in the second place, to rely upon political, moral and material support from the Islamic and non-aligned worlds, as well as the time-tested friendship of China.

Pakistan informed the United States that the proposed American aid package was not acceptable because it was wrapped up in onerous conditions which would detract from, rather than enhance, Pakistan's security.

The President's Foreign Affairs Adviser said: "We could not ignore the fact that the United States' sensitivity to Indian reactions appeared to be determining the size and nature of the aid package, denuding it of revelance to our defensive capacity."

He said there was also a suggestion that the acceptance of the aid package would affect Pakistan's nuclear research programme.

Pakistan's rejection of Washington's offers of aid was another severe blow to American foreign policy. The President seemed to have concluded that his best hope for survival was to be conciliatory towards his enemies to the north and to the east – the Soviet Union and India.

On 17th March, 1980, President Zia acknowledged for the first time that his Government had crushed a plot against him. Pakistan officials originally described reports of an aborted *coup* on 11th March as "absurd and malicious fabrication".

But President Zia, in response to a local reporter's question on the reports acknowledged that the plot had been broken up and the ringleader arrested. "I have the very firm conviction that this could not have taken place unless there was a foreign hand", he said, without singling out the country.

Retired Major-General Tajmal Hussain Malik was arrested for allegedly engineering the conspiracy against the President, who himself seized power by a military *coup* less than 3 years previously. Without mentioning General Malik by name, President Zia said: "An individual person has subjected himself to the mischief of the law. We will deal with him according to the law."

President Zia announced changes in his martial law Government. He relieved four provincial military governors and two Cabinet ministers of holding commands in the 6th Army Corps. The move, which took effect immediately, was made to "enable the governors to devote themselves to their civilian duties."

If dissension existed within the Pakistani armed forces it would stem from deepening fears among junior and senior officers that the President was playing into the hands of the Russians by rejecting American aid.

There was some confusion between the arrest of General Malik and the reported jailing of 16 junior officers described as "Leftists". The General is no Leftist, and was dismissed from the Army previously for plotting against Mr. Bhutto.

The arrest of the 16 junior officers, if true, was seen by most as potentially more intriguing, as was the name of one of the other alleged conspirators in the plot to depose General Zia. He was Major-General Saghir Hussain, commanding officer of the important armoured base at Kharian. General Saghir is regarded by most as potentially the focus of any plot to remove President Zia. In the crucial days before Mr. Bhutto was hanged, General Saghir was known to have voiced strong opposition to the execution, and to have won the favour of younger officers.

To close this Chapter; in a nutshell, what is the conclusion to be drawn from the whole catalogue of events in Afghanistan?

For obvious reasons the over-riding need is to guarantee the territorial integrity of Pakistan. The question whether the West should be embracing a régime like that of President Zia becomes secondary. Political parties have been banned and martial law looks like being in force for a long time. The paradoxical result of the invasion of Afghanistan is that it has turned President Zia into an ally, to be supported as a bastion of the Free World.

THE NEXT DOMINO?

Appreciation to Borgman and *Cincinnati Enquirer*, U.S.A.

CHAPTER
8

Myth of 'Islamic Bomb'?

In view of the fact that in June 1979, President Zia ul-Haq had categorically denied that Pakistan was making the nuclear bomb, I can do no better than to give Pakistan's explanation – as made available to me – of their activities in the nuclear field. Hence the liberal use of quotations in the account that follows.

In June 1979, when briefing journalists on a report which appeared in the London Weekly *8 Days-Middle East International* on Pakistan's peaceful nuclear research programme, the Foreign Affairs Adviser, Mr. Agha Shahi, debunked the idea of an 'Islamic Bomb', he described the report as "false and baseless".

The Chairman of the Pakistan Atomic Energy Commission (PAEC), Mr. Munir Ahmad Khan, was also present.

The title of the article was "How Pakistan Fooled the World and Got the Bomb". According to this article, Pakistan's General Zia intended to explode a nuclear device in the Autumn of 1979.

The caption went on to say that: "Behind this shock news lies a story of international intrigue and deception. For five years – ever since India exploded its atom bomb in 1974 – Pakistan fooled the nuclear powers into believing that it had neither the scientists, the materials nor the know-how to make a bomb. All the while, using a series of 'Front' companies, bogus purchasing orders, shadow intermediaries, and foreign trained scientists, Pakistan got all it needed to out-trump the world and build a hydrogen bomb. These resources came from the very Western countries who were trying to stop them joining the Nuclear Club. *8 Days* special investigators went to Germany, Holland and France to discover exactly how Pakistan fooled the world, and got the bomb."

Describing the article as "an attempt at a fiction thriller", Pakistan's Foreign Affairs Adviser cited it as "a prime example of the sensational and carefully orchestrated propaganda campaign launched against Pakistan's peaceful nuclear programme in the Western capitals."

He proceeded to give the following "glaring examples of the false and tendentious reporting in the article under question:"

1.   "The article stated that Pakistan reacted to the Indian nuclear explosion of May 1974 by embarking on a crash programme to acquire nuclear weapons capability. The fact of the matter was that Pakistan reacted by undertaking a campaign to intensify in international forums its efforts to strengthen its security against the threat of nuclear attack or blackmail, through nuclear guarantees to non-nuclear States by nuclear weapon or would be nuclear weapon powers.

2.   "To this end the former Foreign Minister visited Washington and London and the Adviser himself went to Peking. Later in 1974, Pakistan proposed to the United Nations General Assembly the establishment of a nuclear weapon-free zone in South Asia. This proposal entailed the total renunciation of nuclear weapons by the countries of South Asia and international inspection of their nuclear facilities and a corresponding obligation on the part of nuclear weapon Powers not to threaten the countries of the Zone with nuclear weapons.

3.   "The allegation of Libyan or Arab money being received by Pakistan to manufacture an 'Islamic Bomb' was an utter falsehood. Pakistan was not in any financial collaboration with any other country and was pursuing its peaceful nuclear programme on a basis of self-reliance.

4.   "The article made the wild and reckless charges that Pakistan was producing a hydrogen bomb. Even a few moments sober reflection should convince an informed person that this would be impossible for Pakistan. Even the superpowers had to spend years on research and development to master the fusion technology. Pakistan was only a developing country.

5.   "No Pakistani had ever worked at the Almelo plant, nor had access to it. This had been confirmed by the Dutch-British-German Consortium itself, by the name of URENCO. Furthermore, the Almelo plant produced low grade enriched uranium whereas Pakistan was being charged with wanting to produce weapons grade uranium.

6.   "The allegations that the hydrogen bomb was being fabricated at Nelore was a pure figment of imagination run wild; no work on fusion technology was being conducted at the Pakistan Institute of Nuclear Science and Technology (PINSTECH). There was a small research reactor there which was being operated under International Atomic Energy Authorities (IAEA) safeguards since 1963 and its regular inspection.

7.   "No banned item of equipment had been purchased by Pakistan in foreign countries. This had been confirmed by several Western European Governments after inquiries at the request of the United States.

8.   "The report that a site near Multan, or according to Tass in Chitral, had been chosen for a nuclear test, was utterly false as also was the statement that the explosion was scheduled to be carried out in the autumn of this year" (1979).

Here I would interject an observation made to me by Brigadier Noor Husain. Were "the Russians and their Indian allies busy inventing a *casus belli* for the November 1979 Elections? The strategic area being adjacent to the disputed State of Jumu and Kashmir and the Karakoram Highway?"

9.   The Adviser went on to state "a fear psychosis was being whipped up, with the active co-operation of biased journalists, by those suffering from a crusades syndrome. The 'Islamic Bomb' was a bogey and a figment of the imagination."

10.   Continuing, the Adviser said that "Pakistan could not but take a very serious view of the tendentious article published in the *8 Days* magazine. It had been noted that the journal was owned by the Ambassador of the United Arab Emirates (UAE) to the U.K. The UAE was a country friendly to Pakistan and therefore it was shocking that a publication owned by the Ambassador should lend itself to a smear campaign against Pakistan to bring about its political isolation at the behest of circles which were openly instigating aggression and implicating Arab countries. A strong protest would be lodged with the UAE Government against publication of the article."

11.   The Adviser "reiterated Pakistan's commitment to the peaceful uses of nuclear energy and the unassailable right of all States for equal access to peaceful nuclear technology. The massive and malicious propaganda campaign was aimed to tarnish Pakistan's image as a peace-loving country, to depict it as the villain and transgressor and thereby to stop it from exercising a sovereign right. Why was it that not a word was being said or printed about other countries which were carrying out far more advanced nuclear research? In the case of Pakistan, certain quarters and news media had gone to the extent of inciting aggression against Pakistan by suggesting that a pre-emptive attack could eliminate its nuclear facilities within fourteen minutes. Such statements were instigatory and irresponsible and would fail to achieve their criminal purpose."

Replying to a question from the BBC correspondent regarding the supply of enriched uranium to PINSTECH. The AEC Chairman said that "the small research reactor there was operating under IAEA safeguards and that its fuel supply was being maintained through the IAEA."

The BBC correspondent then asked about "the nature and purpose of the Special Works Organization." The Adviser replied that "it was unfair and misconceived to put tendentious questions of this nature. Would he put such questions in regard to nuclear research and development being carried on by any other government or even the British Government?" The correspondent replied that he had been "allowed to enter the nuclear plant at Windscale." The Adviser asked if he had been given access to the other nuclear facilities in the U.K. concerned with research and development. Pakistan could no more let him inspect their nuclear facilities than their Ordnance factories at Wah.

The BBC correspondent admitted that journalists had considerable freedom and access to information in Pakistan and that "the purpose of this question was to arrive at the truth in order to dispel the confusion that had been created." The Adviser replied that "Pakistan had nothing to hide and would gladly throw open its research facilities as long as this could be ensured on a non-discriminatory basis. It was unfair and discriminatory to single out Pakistan and to put it under pressure to throw open its research centres; why was it that such demands were not being made on South Africa and Israel?"

The Adviser asked: "Why has no interest being shown in the hijacking of a consignment of uranium some years ago? Why were the findings of investigation being suppressed? Why was no notice being taken of the unsafeguarded reprocessing of plutonium in Israel and the method of enrichment of uranium perfected by South Africa?

"On the other hand," said the Adviser, "Pakistan which had neither the technology to manufacture a nuclear weapon nor had conducted a nuclear test was suspect, not taken at its word and subjected to pressure." The BBC correspondent evaded answers by saying that "as they were in Pakistan, their interest was in finding out what exactly Pakistan was doing." The Adviser replied that "there were limits to their right to gather news. It could not be extended to allowing them to create tension between Pakistan and the Soviet Union as in the case of reports filed on Afghan refugee camps, or to claiming the right of access to nuclear research and development. You may not approve of our peaceful nuclear programme but you cannot proceed from there to make wild accusations against us," the Adviser concluded.

Another foreign correspondent interjected that "the clandestine and devious manner in which hardware was purchased in the West and the inappropriateness of certain of these items for Pakistan's development needs suggested ulterior motives." The Chairman of PAEC replied that "all countries were obliged to make purchases abroad for their research programmes and that Pakistan had done the same in a very straight-forward manner. There was nothing clandestine or ominous about their purchases. Orders had been placed with foreign firms for items on which there were no local export restrictions."

The correspondent asked "whether when placing the order for inverters, it was stated they were required for the textile industry?" The Chairman PAEC rejoined that "the inverters were accepted by everyone as multi-purpose and with a wide range of applications."

Replying to another question from the same correspondent, the Chairman of PAEC said that "the supersonic wind tunnel was a basic facility required for a wide range of research. Such tunnels were commonly found in U.S. universities. They were a basic research tool, like a computer."

Only a few days before this Press Conference, President Zia had categorically stated in a BBC interview broadcast in London that "it was totally wrong to say that Pakistan was making the nuclear bomb." The President "had made it abundantly clear that Pakistan was trying to acquire the technology for peaceful purposes only." The President stated that "Pakistan had tried to obtain a nuclear reprocessing plant·from France but had failed to do so, principally as a result of the pressure brought to bear by the United States."

Since then India's Foreign Minister, on his return from a visit to Algeria and France, announced that "the French President, Mr. Giscard d'Estaing, had told him that France would not provide any assistance to Pakistan that would enable her to make the atom bomb. Ironically, he added that France appreciated India's decision to use nuclear energy only for peaceful purposes." India, of course, has already tested the bomb!

A few days later, on 5th July, 1979, the *Washington Star* published, under a three column headline, a letter from the Pakistan Embassy in which many of the above rebuttals were reiterated. The letter included a significant 'sting in the tail': "We recognize today that the major powers between themselves possess nuclear weapons with over fourteen billion tons of explosive power, i.e., three tons for every man, women and child on earth. We do not have the capability or the intention to add to that awesome arsenal of destruction."

Then came the statement of the then U.S. Secretary of State, Cyrus Vance, on Pakistan's alleged nuclear programme which was regarded by Pakistan as being the latest tirade in the relentless smear campaign being jointly pursued by American Government officials and a section of the Western media. What irked Pakistan was that in the manner of similar statements in the past by others U.S. Government officials, Mr. Vance's observations on the subject were devoid of substance and were based only on suppositions, fiction and myths that had been woven round Pakistan's peaceful nuclear project by openly biased and hostile Western newsmen.

"The American Secretary of State did not accuse Pakistan of anything worse than 'thinking of developing nuclear weapons' and yet", in the eyes of Pakistan, "he showed himself concerned more with persuading Pakistan not to develop a nuclear capability than with doing something about those countries who," Pakistan complained, "are known to have acquired the nuclear know how, who openly defy all international covenants on the issue and who also have a history of naked aggression against neighbours. The American Government's concern over the dangers of nuclear proliferation is understandable" to Pakistan, "but what they fail to understand is why the U.S. should concentrate its concern only on Pakistan which has time and again declared itself committed to the development of nuclear energy for peaceful purposes alone and has an unblemished record in the matter.

"Why", Pakistan argued, "does the U.S. leave out of account South Africa, Israel and even India to whom it continues to make vital nuclear supplies despite their having exploded a nuclear device." Pakistan feels that "the discrimination is too obvious to be missed and is an indication that U.S. policy has other considerations than those of nuclear security." Pakistan maintained that "if the unmistakable slant in American Government statements," before Russia's putsch in Afghanistan, "is any guide, the basic aim is none other than to slander Pakistan, create a climate of opinion hostile to the country and reduce its position in the comity of nations."

Pakistan pointed out that "the U.S. Government stopped economic aid to Pakistan on the basis of reports that Pakistan was developing an offensive nuclear capability." They emphasized that "the U.S. Secretary of State said that his Government would use its influence with Pakistan to persuade them not to develop nuclear weapons because the latter may be contemplating such a step." In the eyes of Pakistan "it is unbelievable that the U.S. Government does not possess the capability to ascertain the truth. America has many sources to do so. Therefore," said Pakistan, "if the U.S. decides to make accusations on the basis of unconfirmed journalistic kite-flying and groundless assumptions then the only conclusion that they can draw is that Pakistan is the victim of a conspiracy whose roots can be traced to those controlling the levers of the American political system as well as those international forces who are for ever seeking to harm Pakistan."

Pakistan felt strongly that "as part of this anti-Pakistan axis, a particular section of the Western Press has carried on a sustained vilification campaign calculated to project an image of Pakistan as a nuclear-weapons-mad country posing a grave threat to world peace." Pakistan asserted that "nothing could be farther from the truth and yet stories have been regularly concocted regarding the clandestine purchase of nuclear material in world markets, choice of a site for an explosion and even a date. The term 'Islamic Bomb' used by the Western media is a clear indication," said Pakistan, "of the way their mind works." They

109

pointed out that "it cannot be said that the prejudice is due to the fact that the Pakistan Government has withheld from foreign journalists facilities to work in and report on Pakistan." Indeed, they maintained that "no other country has a more generous attitude in the matter than Pakistan — a fact which is acknowledged by foreign journalists themselves. They are free to go anywhere and talk to anybody they like, and yet when they file their stories they are based not on what they see and hear but on their own preconceived notions. There are," said Pakistan, "numerous examples of such misuse of facilities, even to the extent of going beyond minor infringement of the law of the land, of which the Government has continued to take a lenient view. Foreign journalists have indulged in activities which Pakistan views as bordering on espionage, as illustrated by the case of BBC correspondent, Mr. Christopher Sherwell, the correspondent of the BBC and *Financial Times,* London. Trespassing into security areas is no part of a foreign journalist's professional duties but," according to the Pakistan authorities, "he did so with the transparent aim of making a sensational story out of the episode, as part of the campaign to cast doubts on Pakistan's intentions. Foreign journalists are known to have been sent packing by other Governments for much milder offences."

"If Pakistan has so far taken a soft line towards them despite their numerous transgressions, it does not mean," they warned, "that it will not act where its vital security interests are concerned. There is always a point where a line has to be drawn and Pakistan intends to safeguard its sovereign rights whether it be undue interference by foreign Governments or tendentious reporting by foreign correspondents.

"Instinctive feeling that nuclear energy and nuclear bombs are essentially the same phenomenon cautioned the industrial nations to transfer slowly nuclear technology to the less developed countries. Then came India's 1974 nuclear explosion that shook the foundations of the 'Atom for Peace' programmes.

"It used to be a standard American and Canadian policy to promote nuclear energy for countries considered allies or potential allies of the Western World. The Indian nuclear explosion was the primary force that reversed the American and Canadian thinking in providing nuclear aid to the less developed countries. Canadians who had a genuine concern for the nuclear proliferation retracted most of their nuclear assistance programmes from the less developed countries.

"American strategists saw India's nuclear test as befitting their game of 'Regional Powers' in South Asia. Thus the United States continued to provide not only economic and military aid but also supplies of enriched uranium to India. However, at the same time, America also needed to reaffirm its position in the international community on such matters as nuclear arms proliferation by less developed countries. Therefore, the issues of the nuclear arms proliferation systematically propagated by the American government and flared by its news media, became the major arguments for further denying the nuclear technology to the poorer nations.

"It is interesting to note that India, Egypt and Israel, all three non-signatories to the NPT (Nuclear Proliferation Treaty), have been the prime recipients of American nuclear aid. Unfortunately, Pakistan did not fit into any American foreign policy grand designs. Thus Pakistan became the testing point for the Carter Administration's efforts to demonstrate its concern for nuclear proliferation. Pakistan, not India, was selected for punishment and this for a crime uncommitted.

"Now, after the Three Mile Island nuclear Plant accident near Harrisburg, Pennsylvania, a new dramatized crusade by the news media is leading the American public to believe that the nuclear power generation is both dreadful and dangerous. This new battle against nuclear energy may catch fire in the other industrial nations. Thus, concerns about nuclear plant safety, waste disposal and environmental effects will provide additional excuses to the more fortunate nations to deprive the less fortunate nations of the blessing of the 'Atom for Peace'.

"Nearly forty per cent of Pakistan's total energy needs are met by imports, whereas, India imports only sixteen per cent of its total energy needs. The major source for the production of energy in Pakistan (nearly 76%) is natural gas. The natural gas reserves are expected to last for almost sixty more years. Despite such a heavy contribution by natural gas to meet its energy needs, Pakistan is heavily dependent upon imported oil." Their "domestic production of petroleum is nearly half a million tons annually and the estimated consumption is almost ten-fold, i.e. 5 million tons a year.

"In fact", says Pakistan, "the importation of petroleum is the single largest annual drain on our already depleted foreign exchange. We have but little choice to turn to nuclear power for our 'energy independence' ".

The above quotations represent a fair cross-section of the denials that reached me from Pakistani sources in July 1979 that Pakistan was developing a nuclear weapon. My own personal view was that in her then state of isolation she would be well advised to possess the weapon, both as a deterrent and as a bargaining counter. But would it not be far cheaper to buy it from *China?*

Now that Afghanistan is a Russian satellite, perhaps the Soviet Union would be deterred from its aggressive drive southwards were Pakistan to possess an 'Islamic Bomb' or a 'nuclear *Jihad.*'

According to Zalmay Khalilzad who is Assistant Professor at Columbia University, New York, the exact 'state of the game' regarding Pakistan and the bomb is as described below.

Bhutto had urged his country long ago to keep up with the Indians in the nuclear field. In 1966 for example Bhutto, then Foreign Minister, said that if India produced a nuclear bomb, Pakistan would follow suit, even if the population had to 'eat grass' to do so. In an interview with the London *Financial Times,* Bhutto revealed that during this time he pressed President Ayub Khan to have Pakistan undertake development of a nuclear device.

The Indian nuclear explosion in May 1974 brought a forceful response from Pakistan. The then Prime Minister Bhutto called the Indian explosion a 'fateful development' and a 'threat' to Pakistan's security, and said that 'a more grave and serious event . . . has not taken place in the history of Pakistan. The explosion has introduced a qualitative change in the situation between the two countries.' Bhutto said that his country would not succumb to 'nuclear blackmail', would not accept Indian domination of the subcontinent, and would not compromise its position on the Kashmir issue.

After the Indian nuclear explosion, the late Prime Minister Bhutto sought to persuade the United States to lift its arms embargo (originally imposed after the 1965 Indo-Pakistan War); he threatened that if Pakistan did not receive a 'sufficient conventional deterrent' she would explode a nuclear device; he increased efforts to acquire a reprocessing plant; he changed his stand on leaving the Central Treaty Organization (CENTO); he pushed for the strengthening of the alliance, and participated in the alliance's largest exercise, called the Midlink, which originated in Karachi, in 1974. Bhutto also sought American guarantees against nuclear attack.

While the United States agreed to lift the embargo, she remained reluctant to provide Pakistan with heavy weapons, such as aircraft, and decided on 100 million dollars as the upper limit for the sale of arms to Pakistan. The limit was imposed to placate Pakistan without antagonizing India. Besides the limited lifting of the embargo, little else was done to increase Pakistan's sense of security; the CENTO pact was not strengthened and a guarantee against nuclear attack was not offered.

Pakistan's security, psychological concerns about the Indian nuclear explosion and the Western (especially U.S.) response to Pakistan's demands, further increased her incentives for the acquisition of a nuclear weapons capability. When an agreement was signed with France in 1976 for a plutonium separating facility, Pakistan's relations with Canada and the U.S. were seriously strained. Canada discontinued nuclear assistance to Pakistan. Mr. Bhutto, still then Prime Minister, said in February 1977 that Canada's conditions for continued nuclear co-operation – no reprocessing and no nuclear explosions whether peaceful or otherwise – were not in the interest of Pakistan and violated the country's sovereignty.

In 1976 the United States threatened Pakistan with the withdrawal of economic and military aid if she insisted on carrying out the construction of a reprocessing facility. For a few months in 1978, the United States reportedly halted all economic aid. American rejection of the Pakistani request for 110 Vought A-7 attack aircraft was another consequence of the reprocessing controversy. According to Bhutto, in August 1976, the United States Secretary of State, Henry Kissinger, threatened that, unless Pakistan cancelled its reprocessing plans, America would make 'a horrible example' of him. Bhutto had charged that the U.S. lived up to this promise and actively encouraged the post-1977 election turmoil in Pakistan through channelling 'large amounts of funds' to his opponents in order to topple his government. He also accused the United States of following an unfair and hypocritical policy towards Pakistan:

"India is reported to have plans to carry out a series of nuclear explosions, having already conducted one on our doorstep. Her nuclear capability was built on the materials and technology she derived from an unsafeguarded reactor and heavy water supplied by Canada and the United States respectively. Can it be claimed that there is not some discrimination involved here."

This accusation has not been confirmed by the policies of the post-coup d'état government in Pakistan, which have generally followed Bhutto's policies on reprocessing. For a variety of reasons, including U.S. pressure, the agreement among suppliers and the relatively small size of the Pakistan market for reactors, France changed her mind on the export of a reprocessing plant to Pakistan and asked Pakistan to accept a co-processing plant, but this offer was not accepted.

The French decision not to export the reprocessing facility would have made it difficult, if not impossible, for Pakistan to acquire nuclear weapons capability in the immediate future, if Pakistan had not also been trying to construct an enrichment plant. It appears that in 1977, in order to construct a centrifuge enrichment facility, Pakistan set up a number of front organizations around the world for the purchase of centrifuge plant components. German companies such as the Team Industries, and a Dutch firm called Weargate were used to buy inverters and martensite steel from a number of countries including Great Britain, the Netherlands, Switzerland, West Germany and the United States.

The ostensible destination of these purchases was a textile mill in Pakistan. Inverters are used for heightening electric frequencies to speed the centrifuge process for separating the fissionable uranium (U-235) from natural uranium. Martensite steel is a hard ferrous material used to make critical components of jet aircraft, gas turbines and centrifuge plants. The surreptitious Pakistani attempt to build an enrichment plant in Kahota, near Rawalpindi involved the technical services of Abdul Qadir Khan, a Pakistani scientist who worked at the Dutch enrichment plant at Almelo. Public estimates of a possible Pakistani nuclear explosion vary from a few months to five years.

Based on public data it is very difficult to judge the accuracy of these estimates. It is not clear whether Pakistan has obtained enough components to construct even a small centrifuge enrichment plant. The construction of this plant is a fairly sophisticated technological undertaking and even with the training and assistance that Pakistan has received, she may still need to expend a considerable amount of effort to construct it in a reasonable amount of time. However, in the next decade, it is likely that Pakistan will have the capability to produce at least a few nuclear weapons. She may by then have overcome the difficulties and have a small centrifuge plant operational. In addition, she might obtain a reprocessing plant from the People's Republic of China, or indigenously produce such a plant, and may obtain a co-processing plant from France, which from a proliferation standpoint is virtually as bad as a reprocessing plant.

Based on Pakistan's nuclear power programme, it is possible to make some estimates of the number of nuclear weapons she could have by the late 1980s. Pakistan has two reactors in operation, one research reactor and one power reactor. The pool-type 5 MW research reactor has been in operation since 1965, the KANUPP power reactor (137 MW PHWR) since October 1972. The research reactor does not produce any significant amounts of plutonium. The power reactor produces approximately 74 kg of separable fissile plutonium each year. By the end of 1978, the power reactor will have produced a total of about 144 kg of separable fissile plutonium; this figure is likely to reach 285 by 1985, assuming that the reactor can be kept operating at a reasonable capacity factor.

Present Pakistani nuclear plans predict the installation of a 600 MW reactor which, if constructed, will provide Pakistan with an additional 30 bombs' worth of plutonium annually. As far as enriched uranium is concerned, the amount of material available to Pakistan would depend on the capacity of the centrifuge enrichment facility under construction.

Even if Pakistan acquires access to sufficient quantities of weapons grade plutonium or uranium, decisions about producing nuclear weapons will not be easy. The most important factor is likely to become the Indian nuclear programme. If India 'weaponizes' its 1974 explosion, Pakistan is likely to follow suit, but the likelihood of this development in India is difficult to estimate. Although former Indian Prime Minister Morarji Desai indicated that his country would not explode another device, several other parties, including part of the Congress Party, have expressed support for the acquisition of nuclear weapons by their country. Of course, Indian decisions will also be affected by what Pakistan does. If Pakistan explodes a device, India is all the more likely to opt for production of nuclear weapons.

The acquisition of even a few nuclear weapons in the late 1980s could provide Pakistan with considerable countervalue capability, and is likely to make other countries more cautious in threatening Pakistan and to increase its international prestige, especially among the Middle Eastern countries. Once a member of the nuclear club, Pakistan could provide nuclear assistance to other nations, including some Arab countries. The Arab countries, especially Libya, Iraq and Syria have for some time assumed that Israel possessed nuclear weapons and saw such an Israeli capability as a threat to their security.

In recent years Libya has been seeking a nuclear capability of its own. She has reportedly attempted to purchase a nuclear device from China and has also reportedly financed Pakistan's efforts to acquire a reprocessing plant and an enrichment facility. If these reports are correct, it is possible that Pakistan may provide Libya with some bombs as a form of repayment when she acquires these weapons herself. However, as in the case of other nuclear weapon states, once Pakistan acquires nuclear weapons, she might very well be reluctant to supply other countries with nuclear devices.

Besides the military and political benefits, Pakistan's acquisition of nuclear weapons would also involve serious risks. It would increase the incentives of regional rivals for a similar capability and would provide India with the rationale for an overt and more extensive programme. The nuclearization of two major south Asian protagonists would not only lead to a catastrophic increase in likely damage should a war occur, it would also deteriorate relations with conventional arms suppliers, increase the possibility of threats of use of nuclear weapons in domestic conflict and add to the regional instability.

Based on the experience of the Soviet Union and the United States, a number of authors, such as Pierre Gallois, have argued that the acquisition of nuclear weapons by regional adversaries tends to bring about automatic deterrence. However, there is a substantial difference between producing a few nuclear weapons and possessing a deterrent force. A country can be said to have a nuclear deterrent force if it can achieve the following: survive a nuclear attack from an adversary; if it can make and communicate decisions for a nuclear response, even after an attack has taken place; if it has the delivery systems capable of reaching the target areas and overcoming the enemy's defences; and finally, if it is able to inflict large destruction against the enemy, despite preventive measures that it might have taken.

Both India and Pakistan are unlikely to have nuclear forces meeting these standards in the immediate future. Both are likely to have vulnerable forces. A few nuclear weapons delivered by aircraft, would be vulnerable to non-nuclear as well as nuclear attack. In a crisis, such as a conventional war each side might expect the other to initiate a nuclear attack because of the vulnerability of their nuclear forces. That is likely to increase the incentive for a pre-emptive strike against the adversary's dual-capable aircraft and/or nuclear installations. The tendency to preempt will be based on the calculation that whoever strikes first might strike last.

An article by Caroline Moorehead was published in *The Times*, London, on 8th March, 1980, in which evidence is produced which indicates that Pakistan may be, or was, indeed intent of joining the nuclear club. The article entitled "Pakistanis rejected aid to protect nuclear programme" is reproduced overleaf.

THE NEXT DOMINO?

"Pakistan turned down the American offer of $400 million (£180 million) in military and economic aid in order to protect its nuclear development programme, Mr. Agha Shahi, Pakistan's foreign affairs adviser disclosed in early March.

Speaking in Islamabad, Mr. Shahi said that unless the American offer was 'substantially modified', it would detract from, rather than enhance, the country's security.

'There was also the suggestion', Mr. Shahi said, 'that the acceptance of the package could affect the pursuit of our nuclear research and development programme.'

Mr. Shahi's words come not long after a high-level military source in Islamabad let it be known Pakistan was hoping to test a thermonuclear (H-bomb) device sometime this Spring (1980) despite the efforts of America and other nuclear powers to prevent more countries from acquiring the weapon.

This week's statement can only add to international alarm at the prospect that Pakistan may indeed be intent on joining the 'nuclear club'. It will also lend weight to the forty or so questions that Mr. Tam Dalyell, Labour MP for West Lothian, has been hammering out in the House of Commons day after day for the last couple of months on the subject of Pakistan, security breaches and nuclear proliferation.

Mr. Dalyell has described the work of Dr. Abel Qadar Khan as a prelude to a 'possible world holocaust'.

Dr. Khan, a Pakistani, worked as a metallurgist in 1972 with the Joint Centrifuge Project at Almelo in The Netherlands, a high-security research establishment set up jointly by Britain, West Germany and Holland for enriching uranium.

During his three years there Dr. Khan was briefly seconded to the centrifuge project as a translator where, by some unexplained breach of security, he had access to the most sensitive material.

In 1975 Dr. Khan returned to Pakistan, bearing with him, so the story goes, a blueprint of the enrichment plant – in other words, the design, technology and list of parts necessary to create an advanced pilot centrifuge in Pakistan.

Since then observers inside Pakistan have reported evidence of the building of an enrichment plant at Kahota, near Rawalpindi.

Pakistan embarked on 'nuclear technology for peaceful purposes', in the 1950s when it sent a string of promising young scientists to study in the United States, Canada, West Germany and the Soviet Union, so that by 1972, according to its own figures, it had 550 qualified scientists and engineers.

During this period Pakistan signed a nuclear co-operation agreement with the United States, and bought a five megawat (thermal) swimming-pool type reactor.

By March, 1976, it was in the throes of signing an agreement with France for the purchase of a nuclear processing facility when, because of growing international doubts about whether Pakistan's nuclear plans were peaceful and the relatively small size of the Pakistan market, France cancelled the deal.

This might have been a severe blow for any nuclear weapons policy, had Pakistan not already been well ahead with an alternative plan. For by 1976 Dr. Khan was back at Kahota and Pakistan, using a number of front organizations, was busy buying components for a centrifuge plant on the world market.

In the summer of 1978, for instance, Pakistan bought thirty-one high-frequency 'inverters' from the Emerson factory in Swindon, escaping a Department of Trade ban.

Other vital components, like valves, welding equipment, gauges and radiation-proof glass were bought from Switzerland, West Germany, Holland and the United States under the guise of materials intended for a new textile mill.

Separately, these items have for many years been sold for a variety of industrial uses; it is only when combined with a known goal of producing enriched uranium that their sale has been restricted.

Dr. Khan had brought home the knowledge, and shopping around produced the parts. Now all that was needed was the uranium. Weapons-grade uranium U-235 could, assuming a large enough amount could be acquired, have been extracted from uranium ore, but the process is expensive and long.

Instead, it appears, a lorry containing twenty tons of uranium concentrate left Arlit in northern Nigeria for its eventual destination in France last September, and vanished.

The empty lorry was finally discovered, not along its route to Cotonou, the West African port, but inland, 100 miles from the Libyan border.

Intense investigation led to the conclusion that the uranium concentrate, had made its way across Libya, and from there to Pakistan. It is now thought probably that earlier lorryloads, which also disappeared, have ended up at Kahota.

Today experts say Pakistan's centrifuge plant is probably capable of producing enough weapons-grade uranium U-235 in any one year to cause one thermonuclear explosion. By 1985 Pakistan could have 605 kilograms of separable fissile plutonium – enough for sixty bombs.

The question no longer seems to be whether it can join the 'nuclear club', but whether it wishes to."

On 16th June the title of the BBC programme *Panorama* was 'Project 706 – The Islamic Bomb'. This film was very detailed and unfolded a story in which for the first time details of Libyan involvement in Pakistan's so-called 'Islamic Bomb' were exposed. From the remote Central Saharan State of Niger, vast open-cast mining operations were shown busily producing "yellowcake," a uranium bearing ore which is passed on to Colonel Gadaffi's Libya and thence to Pakistan. There were interviews with former aides of the late Mr. Bhutto who let it be known that he intended to get the bomb even if the population had to eat grass. The film portrayed Pakistan as being well advanced along a two-way path to the bomb. They will use plutonium if they can get it, enriched uranium if they can't, and Libyan money either way. It was claimed that Colonel Gadaffi had invested a total of $500 million in the project and fully expected a *quid pro quo* from Pakistan in the form of nuclear skill. The thought of Colonel Gadaffi's finger on the nuclear trigger is pretty grim indeed.

Although General Zia has denied any intention to build a nuclear bomb, nevertheless BBC reporter, Philip Tibenham, revealed that he had unearthed the evidence of a massive Pakistan purchasing effort for the bomb's programme, organized from the Pakistan Embassy in Paris. *Panorama* showed that the French had known since 1975 that Pakistan intended to build a bomb yet still permitted the purchasing operation to be run from their capital. Among those interviewed were engineering firms in Italy, France and elsewhere, who supply equipment of various kinds and who are only too pleased to take Pakistan's money and ask no questions. The film was not so much a criticism of Pakistan itself, but of Western nations who had made the equipment available and will have made it possible for Pakistan to be ready to test its first nuclear bomb by the end of 1981.

CHAPTER
9

Iran

What happens in Iran is of critical importance to the West for a number of reasons. As the world's second largest exporter of oil after Saudi Arabia, Iran has supplied some eight per cent of U.S. import needs and a far greater percentage to the economies of Japan, Western Europe and previously also to Israel and South Africa.

Equally important is Iran's geographical position. To the North it shares a 1,500-mile border with the Soviet Union. To the South Iran, under the Shah, acted as a "policeman" of the vital sea-lanes over which most Iranian, Persian Gulf and Saudi Arabia oil flows to the West. After Great Britain withdrew her military forces east of Suez in the late 1960s, the Shah stepped into the vacuum to become the "gendarme" of the Persian Gulf on behalf of the West – the Khomeini faction however, has stressed that Iran will not play this role, but will pursue an independent course in foreign policy.

In the light of these obvious strategic considerations it is not difficult to detect a Soviet hand, to one degree or another, behind Iran's turmoil. The well-organized strikes by oil field-workers could not have been carried off without Communist direction, or at least heavy involvement. Whichever faction wins in the end in Iran, it is strictly a no-win situation for the Western World. And for that very reason the U.S.S.R. stands to gain a victory.

Russia's border with Iran on the Caspian Sea provides Moscow with its nearest point to the warmwaters of the Persian Gulf and in turn an outlet to the Indian Ocean. The Soviets like the Czars, are extremely anxious to acquire a warmwater port on this ocean which they regard currently as "no man's water".

The overthrow of the Shah combined with the disintegration of the defence forces and nation-wide disturbances and civil unrest can only benefit the Russians in the long term.

The seizure of the American and British Embassies in Teheran, together with the taking of American hostages, by mobs of "students" on 4th November, 1979, had been provoked, if not actually authorized, by the Ayatollah Khomeini's anti-Western hysteria. It was the sign of disintegration in Iran. Verbal attacks against a foreign enemy is one of the oldest tricks of the political game. But when the tirades overspilt into physical violence, the situation became infinitely more serious, especially when foreign diplomats were being held hostage.

It was all the more dangerous with Iran in a state of chaos, spinning out of control. Despite 600 executions, 2,000 political prisoners held, 22 newspapers and magazines closed and the total repression of human rights, the country was in a state, not of order, but of anarchy. The "Government" of Dr. Bazargan made little pretence that its writ ran. The Prime Minister had responsibility without power. His authority was continually undermined by the vicious blood lusting Khomeini who had power but refused to control the situation. The Khomeini régime had both destroyed Iran's economy and installed not revolution but general disorder. The holding of Americans in the U.S. Embassy as hostages against the return of the seriously ill Shah was sickening evidence of the extent to which Khomeini's "revolution" had failed. *A failed revolution needs scapegoats*. The burning of American flags and the public humiliation of American officials provided Khomeini and his mullahs with a distraction to wave in front of the people.

The longer Khomeini remains in power the stronger will the Communists become. The Shah was at least an enlightened despot, who wanted to push his country into the Twentieth Century. The Ayatollah, on the other hand, is a twisted fanatic, who is bent on pushing Iran back into the Middle Ages. Those who forecast that the Shah's downfall would be followed by something much worse have been proved only too right. The West is now having its face rubbed in the result of its general spinelessness and lack of muscle.

The only hope for Iran is that this revolution, like so many others, will devour its leaders, and that a strong, sane man will emerge to bring order and stability.

It was typical of Khomeini's followers that they gave as the reason for attacking the British Embassy that Britain was "sheltering" Mr. Bakhtiar, the last Prime Minister before the Shah's exile, when in fact Mr. Bakhtiar was living in Paris, France of course, also "sheltered" Khomeini before his return. That cunning ploy did France no good at all. It certainly did Iran immense harm.

The handful of Iranian students not only grabbed the world by the scruff of its neck but shook it and scared it. In the frightened eyes of the world there was the prospect of a direct confrontation between America and a country which borders directly with Russia. The Soviet Union, with powerful forces stationed permanently in the Caucasus along a common border with Iran, had the power to intervene, but at that precise moment the Kremlin was otherwise engaged — preparing for the ruthless seizure of Afghanistan.

The Russians would infinitely prefer Iran to slide gradually into the vortex, thus giving their protégés time to station themselves to grab what

119

THE NEXT DOMINO?

`WHATEVER YOU SAY, IMAM — I GUESS YOU KNOW WHAT YOU'RE DOING...`

Appreciation to Oliphant in *The Washington Star* and Universal Press Syndicate.

is left. Whether in the short or long term, the Russians are the only people to gain from further collapse in Teheran. The tragedy is that neither the blinkered ayatollahs nor their bloodthirsty mobs seemed to realize this, or care. In the celebrated words of Khruschev: "Iran is like a ripe apple. All we have to do is wait and it will fall into our hands."

In his capacity as Secretary-General of the Islamic Press Union, London, Mr. Muazzam Ali wrote a letter at the end of November 1979 to *The Times,* asking to know what the difference was between the ex-Shah and Nazi criminals. He received the following tart reply:-

"The problem here arises out of certain *similarities* between excesses committed under the Shah and those of the hysterical bigot who now rules Iran.

Some of the highest ranking Nazi criminals were allowed a *tu quoque* defence at Nuremburg on certain charges. They were also given a real trial — not delivered into the hands of gibbering and screeching lynch mobs, or subjected to the tender mercies of a ranting liar whose falsehoods have caused the death of innocent people outside his own frontiers.

One Moslem voice (Iraq) has stated that Khomeini is worse than the Shah. I leave that to Moslems to judge, but I do find it sickening that any Moslem should seek to justify behaviour — criminal by any civilized standard — which has disgraced his faith."

Professor Ronald Hilton of Stanford University who is Executive Director of the California Institute of International Studies and Editor of its quarterly *World Affairs Report,* has written an account of how Khomeini sold Islam to the Kremlin. He shows Khomeini to be the most important of five top Soviet agents in Iran. I now reproduce Professor Hilton's report:

120

American intelligence on Iran was incredibly bad. Just· before the Shah fell, the CIA had reported to President Carter that there was no danger of his overthrow. Since then, television has provided *ad nauseam* pictures of the frenzied (programmed?) mobs outside the American Embassy in Teheran: the uninformed comments by the courageous reporters who accepted the assignment in Iran simply strengthened the visual impression that we were confronted with a case of collective Islamic madness.

In fact, there is method in this madness. The Paris student riots of 1968 which nearly overthrew de Gaulle revealed starkly how student mobs can be manipulated for political purposes and the tactic is being employed all around the world. There is convincing evidence that behind the mob scenes and seeming chaos in Iran there is a master plan involving "student" terrorists around the world, financed largely by Libya (or, in the case of the IRA by Irish-Americans) and tied to Moscow, that uses détente as a cover for these destabilising activities and which the Kremlin propaganda machine loudly attributes to fascists, Right-wingers and U.S. agents. The network includes the Baader-Meinhof gang in Germany, the Japanese Red Army, Puerto Rican terrorists and the IRA Provisionals.

The tie-in between the Iranian students and the network is evident. On 16th July, 1978, a suspected West German woman terrorist was arrested when she and three companions tried to cross the American-Canadian border by a little-used road in Vermont. She was carrying a false Iranian passport and was believed to belong to the Baader-Meinhof gang. The passport was one of several stolen by radical Iranian students when they occupied the Iranian Consulate in Geneva in June, 1976. Two of her companions when she entered the United States turned out afterwards to be wanted in West Germany for terrorist activities.

It is probable that the well-known Venezuelan terrorist "Carlos" was involved in the take-over of the American Embassy in Teheran. *Le Monde* (17th December, 1979) translated an interview he gave the Paris Arab-language newspaper *Al-Watan Al Arabi*. In it he described his role in terrorist activities, including the planning of the attack on the French Embassy in The Hague on 3rd April, 1974, by the Japanese Red Army and of the seizure of the OPEC Ministers in Vienna on 21st December, 1975. He boasted that he could inflict a mortal blow to 'American Imperialism' by blowing up all the oilfields in the Persian Gulf and said Marxism was the religion to which he had devoted all his life.

Behind this terrorist network stands Moscow. The American Embassy was seized, Sunday 4th November, 1979. Dr. John Clark, of Harvard said the act had been long planned: It certainly was not accidental or spontaneous. On Tuesday 6th November, at a meeting of the National Security Council, President Carter was informed that foreign intelligence had identified some of the "students" as KGB agents. He decided not to make the information public since he planned to pursue quiet diplomacy to negotiate for the release of the hostages. Teheran University is the focal point of Moscow-line Communism, embodied in the Tudeh party. There are lesser Marxist groups associated with it in a confused way: such as Islamic Students In Line with Khomeini; the Islamic Nationalist Mujahedden-E-Khali (People's Strugglers) and the militant Cherikaye Fadaye Khalg (People's Sacrifice Guerrillas).

Khomeini did not oppose the student take-over. A former Polish espionage Chief, Colonel Michael Goleniewski, who defected to the West in 1960, told the CIA that Khomeini was the most important of five top Soviet agents in Iran and that he reported to a high Iraqi official who in turn passed the information to the KGB through its agents in Warsaw, where Goleniewski was stationed.

Some have questioned this story, but there is other evidence of Khomeini's ties with the Soviet apparatus, L'Express of Paris, (5th December, 1979) devoted a feature article to these ties. Jean-Francois Revel and Branko Lazitch discussed a Tudeh declaration of 30th April, 1979, laying down the strategy to be followed, obviously with the approval of the Kremlin.

Raymond Aron said the Tudeh party would follow the normal Soviet method and use Khomeini while it was preparing a Marxist republic.

Khomeini was torn inwardly between his Moslem fanaticism and his Marxist ties and outwardly between his desire to assert himself as the supreme commander of Iran and his fear that he would lose control of the students. At first, he tried to act tough: he banned the Tudeh paper *Mardon* and criticized Russia. Then, obviously, a deal was made: *Mardon* was allowed to reappear, Khomeini stopped criticizing Russia and turned all his invective on America and President Carter. He approved the take-over of the Embassy. Baptist, God-fearing Carter was called an agent of the devil, while Soviet atheism became a non-subject.

In all this, Russia was, as usual, playing a double game. The long-range aim of the Bear has always been to gain access to the Indian Ocean and to deprive the West of Iranian oil. Following the Communist tactic of accommodating itself to reality, it co-operated with the Shah, who was never criticized in the Soviet Press. The Soviets' deals with his régime are seldom mentioned and never attacked in the Iranian Press: admittedly, they were mostly useful to the Iranian economy, like the Isfahan steel mill.

As soon as the Shah fell, the Moscow propaganda machine gleefully depicted his régime as rotten and an American tool, encouraging the students in the takeover of the Embassy, using a radio station, "The Voice of Iran", at Baku, close to the Iranian border. At the same time, it increased its already large Embassy in Teheran: many of the more than 300 staff were thought to be KGB agents. The Embassy building is being expanded and remodelled into a ten storey building. The KGB had penetrated the Iranian armed forces: Deputy Army Chief

Major General Ahmad Mogharrabi spied for Moscow for 11 years before he was caught.

In the United Nations Security Council debate about censuring Iran, the Soviet delegate could not vote against the measure but his speech was ambiguous, unlike most of the other members of the council. Meanwhile, Soviet broadcasts continued to encourage the students. When both President Carter and Mr. Vance, the former Secretary of State, protested, Moscow went through the motions of asking the students to release the hostages, but then it resumed its old tactics. The Iranian students were satisfied that Moscow was backing them: and when they were told that America might ask the United Nations to impose sanctions, they scoffed that the Soviet delegate would veto them.

Meanwhile, Khomeini was under two-fold pressure from Moscow. The Moscow-line students in the University could be counted on to keep him in order, but if that were not sufficient, pressure could be applied by promoting the secessionist movements in Azerbaijan and Kurdistan. Soviet comments backing the insurgents and calling on Khomeini to meet their demands showed that the Kremlin was using them. Strangely, it has been operating in this area and in Indo-China through Bulgaria and the nearest thing to an admission that it was involved was a denial that Bulgaria was supplying the anti-Khomeini rebels with weapons!

The idea of the spy "trial" of the American Embassy staff probably originated in Moscow, with the trial of Pol Pot and Ieng Sary in Cambodia as a model. They were condemned to death *in absentia* before a crowd which included a number of foreign lawyers, mostly pro-Soviet, as well as representatives of Moscow-front organizations: the World Peace Council, the Afro-Asian People's Solidarity Organization, and the International Association of Democratic Lawyers.

Mr. Shubin, Deputy Chairman of the Russian Federation of Soviet Socialist Republics, who attended the trial, wrote a highly favourable report on its *modus operandi*. The curious thing is, the trial was held in August (1979). But Shubin's report did not appear until 30th September in *Pravda*. It seems a reasonable conclusion that a show trial was part of the original plan for the take-over of the American Embassy in Teheran. It would be a humiliation for America and a triumph for Soviet propaganda.

Two basic aims of Soviet policy are to promote race war in America by turning blacks against whites as part of a broad plan to incite the "Third World" against "U.S. Imperialism". Khomeini's release of the black staff members of the Embassy, and his insistence that blacks should be among the American clergy allowed to visit the Embassy for Christmas services, was a sign to American blacks that the Khomeini régime supports them in their struggle against their white American "oppressors".

Within the "Third World" a special target has been the Islamic countries, whose historic and even rabid, dislike of the West was a tinderbox just awaiting a spark. The attack on the Mosque in Mecca was carried out by agents from Moscow-orientated by South Yemen. A story that it was the work of CIA agents, spread by the Soviet propaganda machine, was widely believed in Islamic countries while the sharp denials by the American and Saudi Governments, as usual, never caught up with the rumours.

What of the future? Even if Russia were, for appearances sake, to go along with American demands that the Security Council impose sanctions, this would not prevent it from supplying Iran across the extensive common boundary. After all, it has had little difficulty supplying distant Indo-China.

While sanctions proved ineffective in the cases of Rhodesia and South Africa, the main use of the United Nations is as a sounding board for Soviet propaganda to the "Third World". A blockade? It might be no more successful than what Moscow calls the American "blockade" of Cuba. Some kind of American military action? The radical network in American universities and the Iranian students there would organize protests like those which hamstrung the war effort in Vietnam.

Iran may fall into utter chaos; Khomeini would be thrown away like a squeezed orange and the Tudeh party, with Soviet support, would pick up the power lying in the streets, as Lenin put it.

The Soviet occupation of Afghanistan following the assassinations of Tarakki and Amin, both of whom assumed they had the total support of the Kremlin, jolted even the most loyal Kremlin henchmen in Teheran. It suddenly dawned on them that the same fate might be awaiting them and that they might be replaced by someone like Babrak Karmal, even more loyal to the Kremlin and more ruthless. The other horn of the dilemma was that Iran was counting on the Soviet Union to veto sanctions in the United Nations. The Revolutionary Council released the contents of a note to the Soviet Embassy charging that the Soviet invasion of Afghanistan was a hostile act and repugnant throughout the world. This was an implied threat that Iran could redirect Muslim animosity from the United States to the Soviet Union and Iran could become to Afghanistan what Egypt is to Libya. The oriental poker game continues.

The abortive U.S. rescue mission has greatly increased the crisis of authority for the Western superpower. A question mark is set against Carter's ability to use great power for the maintenance of peace. Immediate action in the early days of the hostage crisis – outlined in Chapter 4 – could have prevented what may now become a wider conflict in the days ahead. One thing is certain; if America fails to meet this challenge, there will be only *one* superpower left!

The bloody spectacle in Iran was only a misleading facade, which hides the true reasons of the fall of this state into the hands of the Soviets, with all the serious consequences we can imagine for the Free World. *The real responsibility for the fall of Iran has to be attributed to the United States.* It was Washington that pressured the Shah into "liberalizing" his régime. When he yielded to the pressure, and accorded democratic reforms, the Moslem communist groups took advantage of the newly granted freedoms, in order to provoke serious disturbances. They were not interested in democracy, but in the overthrow of the Shah. When the Shah, logically, tried to protect himself with the intervention of the army, he heard nothing but criticism from President Carter, who demanded he continue in those reforms which were bringing all these disturbances. At the same time, Ayatollah Khomeini, from his comfortable residence near Paris, continued to encourage the riots with his inflamatory proclamations, and made the application of the reforms totally impossible. Faced with the situation, the American government was deaf and dumb to his activity, while continuing to condemn the "repressive" policies of the Shah.

After pushing the Shah into liberalizing his government, with heinous consequences, the American government withdrew its support from the Shah, exactly when he needed it the most, and expected it, since Iran was tied to the United States by a regular treaty. By applying his "human rights" policy in the wrong way, President Carter had pushed the Shah into an impossible situation, and when he tried to protect himself and his country against the communist horde, he abandoned him. He began the withdrawal of American citizens from Iran, and this gave the signal to continue the offensive, as the days of the Shah were numbered. When the tension reached the highest point, President Carter advised the Shah to abandon the throne, in order to bring peace to the country. Cornered by the unleashed mob, and by an unfaithful ally, the Shah decided to make the sacrifice, in order to spare the country much bloodshed.

He left in charge of the country a government of which the Americans approved, a government that was to restore order to the country. The Shah, the main reason of all these disturbances, was no longer in power. It would have been logical then that, once the cause was removed, the effect would also disappear and the people would return to the daily routine. But it did not happen. The new government was attacked with the same fury by the Moslem leadership, and ordered to hand the power to Ayatollah Khomeini, who had returned from Paris with the permission of the current government, and immediately busied himself with the preparations for the last attack. The function of this government has been exactly that of the Kerenski government in Russia, that of eliminating the last obstacle from a revolutionary take-over. This government did a priceless favour to the Moslem revolutionaries, when it ordered the army to "fraternize" with the people. The Moslems then attacked all the ammunitions depots, armed themselves, and took over the major cities of the country.

Within a short time of their invasion of Afghanistan Soviet troops were only thirty kilometres (eighteen miles) from the Iranian frontier.

Obviously they now pose a serious threat to Iran's south-eastern province of Sistan and Baluchistan.

In Azerbaijan the Russian KGB had recruited agents who were busy operating in Tabriz and other Iranian cities to stir up anti-Khomeini demonstrations and commit acts of violence.

One of the Russian aims of stirring up this kind of internal unrest is to enable them to fabricate an excuse to invoke its treaty of 1921 with Iran, whereby Moscow has the right to intervene militarily if threats in Iran threaten its own security. In November 1979 the provisional Government of Iran revoked the treaty, *but the Soviet Union did not respond*.

No wonder that these events, coming on top of the Kremlin's advances into Ethiopia and the Horn of Africa, created an impression everywhere that the Western position was crumbling while that of the Soviets inexorably was improving in the Gulf region as a whole, which supplies 60 per cent of Europe's, 25 per cent of North America's and 90 per cent of Japan's oil.

As each 'domino' topples in this vital area, how can one fail to become incensed at the supreme folly, stupidity and short-sightedness of Britain's flaccid politicians and intimidated Service Chiefs in their abandonment of the Gulf. Far from hanging their heads in shame they are relishing the comfortable existence and perks that is their reward for long service and good conduct. We could have stayed in the Gulf. We *should* have stayed, at least while our Gulf friends wanted us to do so. If we had done so, the Shah would not have over-liberalized Iran, thereby hastening his downfall, and America and Britain would not now be looking for the military facilities and political allies they now need to reinforce the position of the West and its friends throughout Arabia and the Western Indian Ocean.

By far the most important prize is Iran because once it is won it is only a matter of time before the rest of the dominoes in the Gulf will follow. In one year, Iran has gone a long way towards anarchy and disintegration. The Iranian revolution has been a revolution of madness, motivated by hatred and a spirit of destruction. Economic life is paralysed. The fate of the American hostages is dwarfed by that of the millions of other hostages to revolution – the Iranians and the ethnic minorities of Azerbaijan, Kurdistan, Khuzestan (Arabs), Baluchistan and the Turkomans. All or any of these could join a winning counter revolutionary combination. All are increasingly exploitable. The Tudeh party and other communists are already active within all these mentioned areas.

What is the West's response and strategy to all this? There are able people, such as Dr. Shahpour Bakhtiar available and there is the middle class movement of Matine-Daftary (National Democratic Front) which would undoubtedly give intellectual support and leadership to any Western-orientated change. The West must unite the many Iranians who sooner or later will try to liberate their country. But we are giving them little help or encouragement when the very fact of this would draw hesitant Iranians to the banner. More than most they like to be on the winning side.

The election of Mr. Abolhassan Bani-Sadr as President of Iran, and the overwhelming majority of votes that he received, soon turned to dust when the mullahs began to see him as a growing threat to their fanatical hold on power in Iran. He is a radical economist and there is little doubt as to what he would do if restored to power – restriction of oil output, nationalization of foreign-owned companies, the rallying of opinion in Islamic countries against Western economic influence – being not to the West's interest, nor Iran's for that matter. But Mr. Bani-Sadr is said to be firmly anti-communist and was showing signs of being fully aware of the threat to Iran from the Soviet Union. However, it would be naïve to consider him a moderate, for he had stated quite clearly that Iran still required an official American apology for Washington's complicity in the Shah's crimes.

Mr. Bani-Sadr made it clear that he was opposed to the existence of parallel power centres such as the militants holding the hostages in the American Embassy. He accused the Islamic students of behaving in a tyrannical manner and of creating a state within a state. Obviously he wanted a quick end to the hostage deadlock so that he could consolidate his power and get on with the job of returning Iran to a semblance of normality. Khomeini strengthened Bani-Sadr's grip by appointing him Commander-in-Chief of Iran's armed forces and chairman of the Revolutionary Council. But Khomeini then proceeded to clip his wings by deferring a decision on the hostages and declaring through Ayatollah Mohammed Beheshti, the since assassinated secretary-general of Iran's Revolutionary Council, that it might take even until late 1980 before Iran's new Parliament could decide on the release of the hostages. Obviously Khomeini was going to use the hostages as tools in domestic politics.

At the same time trouble arose over the mandate of the five-nation United Nations Commission charged in dubious terms with conducting some kind of enquiry into Iranian charges against the Shah and the former U.S. Secretary of State, Cyrus Vance, said firmly that the Commission's mission was twofold: to hear the grievances of the Iranians and also to bring about the speedy release of the hostages and thus end the crisis. But Iran just as firmly insisted that there had been no such gentlemen's agreement. Thereupon the Commission proceeded to assemble evidence of "crimes" committed by the Shah.

Intent on putting the United States in the dock, the president of Iran's Association of Human Rights, described the CIA role in the 1953 *coup* that toppled Prime Minister Mohammed Mossadegh, and restored the Shah to Iran's Peacock Throne. He accused the U.S. of helping the Shah to transform a constitutional monarchy into a dictatorship, complete with a one-party system, press censorship, and its own secret police.

The U.N. commissioners were then led on a conducted tour of the Shah's gaudy palace, the grim slums of south Teheran, SAVAK's torture prison and attended a rally of maimed survivors.

It looked as if Khomeini had succeeded in taking the U.S. and the U.N. for a ride. The lesson is that the continued humiliation of the hostages' imprisonment is the penalty that America has to pay for letting down their defences so far. The U.S. now has to decide whether Iran or Russia is the immediate threat!

I believe that Russia is virtually already in possession of the future of Iran. What is left of the old Iranian State is a conglomeration of ideas, political parties, and men, on top of which Ayatollah Khomeini moves like a puppet. Soon, very soon, the Communist party will put "order" among all this confusion, and it will be directed by the revolutionary experts of Moscow. *It is a dangerous illusion to believe that Moslem fanaticism can dominate Communist fanaticism,* and form a nation free from foreign domination. The unforgiving fury with which Khomeini supported the massacre of the civilian and military personnel of the old régime, demonstrates clearly that he is under the influence of Moscow. According to this plan, the State will remain unprotected, after the extermination of the old leading class, and can be easily taken over by the Bolsheviks. How can Khomeini possibly restore the authority of the State, when he has liquidated the army, the only instrument capable of restoring order to a mob which has been ensnared in the whirlpool of anarchy? In the situation he has created himself, if he will try to resist the pro-communist radicals, he will be himself eliminated, in the same callous way as he has eliminated the other statesmen, whose assassination he has supported with a bizarre lack of principles.

With the departure of the Shah, another free country had fallen under the direct influence of Moscow. Can the Moslem movement separate itself and its cause from that of international Communism? Is it now only a matter of time, perhaps just a few months, to when the hammer and sickle will rule in Teheran? I believe the process has begun and cannot be stopped. Another 'domino' will fall.

CHAPTER 10

Oman — South Yemen

Strategically, Oman, on the eastern corner of the Arabian Peninsula, is now one of the most important countries in the world. Nowhere is the Russian threat to Oman more apparent than in the South Yemen capital of Aden where the Russians have completely taken over. It is a Russian base bristling with weaponry.

To the north there is the continuous movement of enormous oil tankers coming down the Persian Gulf and passing through the narrow and vulnerable Strait of Hormuz, carrying 60% of the Free World's oil. Because it is so vital to the West, any attempt by the Russians to interfere with free passage would be a *casus belli*. They must know that it is too important to be interfered with for short-term advantage.

The lesser dangers of hi-jacking or sinking a tanker seem to the naval officers on the spot less alarming than might be supposed. If a tanker was put out of action, it would not block the waterway. As for hi-jacking one of these monsters, it is hard to see what object that would achieve.

Possibly the most serious threat to the waterway comes from mines being dropped onto the sea bed. The latest development in mines detonated by noise, magnetism or pressure waves, makes them far more lethal and harder to neutralize. Oman, however, has no mine-sweepers.

Under the Shah, Iranian forces kept constant watch from the shore and the Iranian navy checked all vessels in the area, but since the Revolution in Iran, the Gulf has lost its policeman. Other countries in the area are unwilling or unable to take on the task. Only Oman tries to monitor what is going on, but with only six patrol boats is hard pressed to maintain any form of surveillance in the Gulf.

The Iranian shoreline is empty — how long it will remain so is anyone's guess. Soviet forces could cross Iran to the Straits *within one week*.

With only two missile boats and four gunboats, even the southern coast of the Strait of Hormuz can hardly be said to be controlled. And yet through these Straits must pass all tankers, day and night, carrying crude oil to Europe or Japan. Something much more will be required to ensure that nothing upsets their freedom of passage. If Oman is to safeguard the Western World's oil supplies at this choke point the Sultan must be given the weapons and equipment with which to do the job, and this will include not only modern mine-sweepers, but radar and sonic detectors, also aircraft, including helicopters, to survey the coastline and waterway 24 hours a day.

The situation has grown more alarming over the past few months because of the rapid build-up of Soviet forces in Aden together with the massive stores depot at Khormaksar, 4 miles from Aden. In this area, the Russians have:

* A joint army, navy and air force staff Headquarters, at work with Cuban and East German personnel, which is virtually running the country.
* This joint staff Headquarters also controls all pro-Russian forces in Ethiopia. It also contains the offices of the Russian KGB secret police whose operations stretch far wider than the Oman and the Yemen.
* A cruiser and five Krivak class destroyers.
* Nuclear submarines.
* Mine-sweepers, frigates and "elint" ships — trawlers fitted with radar to monitor movement of the American task forces in the Arabian Sea.
* 300 Russian tanks (Oman has no tanks at all), deployed to the East of Aden and posing a constant threat to Oman and the Strait of Hormuz. The Sultan urgently needs more anti-tank weapons.
* MiG-17s flown by Cubans, MiG-21s flown by Russian pilots — and now, the advanced MiG-23, which the Soviets are said to have based at Aden.
* Ilyushin light bombers.
* A security service, run by East Germans, in a ruthless way that allows for no dissent. Ten concentration camps have been set up for those who try to oppose the régime.

South Yemen's neighbour, North Yemen, has suffered civil war, the assassination of two presidents and the Moscow-backed invasion from South Yemen itself in February 1979. With this Soviet threat on its door-step, Saudi Arabia appealed to the United States who responded by providing arms to North Yemen, paid for by Saudi Arabia to the tune of about £200 million. There can be no doubt that the Soviet Union intends to absorb North Yemen either by direct military assault by South Yemen, or by internal subversion, or through a combination of both.

The People's Democratic Republic of Yemen (South Yemen), is mostly barren desert and has a population of less than 2 million. Nevertheless, it threatens to become as malignant for the Middle East as Cuba has proved to be for the Caribbean, Central America and Africa. This potential malignancy stems from two factors:

1.   A fanatical Marxist-Leninist régime is in power, and
2.   The Soviet Union is using South Yemen in its quest for world supremacy.

The Soviet Union has signed a 20-year friendship and co-operation pact with South Yemen with terms more sweeping than those of any other Soviet alliance outside the Warsaw Pact area. The Russians have committed themselves under this treaty to support and defend South Yemen under all circumstances. This applies even if the threat should come from a "world power", an obvious reference to the United States.

The treaty has given the Russians power to station up to 18,000 troops in South Yemen. A Russian general will command the strategic Perim Island in the Bab el Mandeb Strait leading into the Red Sea, and the pact provides for five Soviet warships to be permanently based on Aden.

Cuban officers are training the gendarmerie force, while 116 East German insurgency experts man three camps, at Mukullah, Hauf and El Gheida, where international terrorists are sent for training.

Last year, those attending the courses included members of the Popular Front for the Liberation of Palestine, the most extreme of all the radical Palestinian groups; the Italian Red Brigades; the rump of the German Baader-Meinhof gang; the Japanese Red Army; and five members of the Provisional IRA.

The Soviet Union is providing both massive military and economic aid to South Yemen. At present the South Yemeni army is small and has only about 25,000 soldiers, however it is probably the most effective fighting force in Arabia. The Russians have promised to double the size of this army during the next three years and to arm it with the latest weapons including ground to ground missiles.

South Yemen has been promised $750 million a year in Soviet aid with help for the setting up of economic enterprises, plus a guaranteed supply of oil. An extensive drilling programme to prospect for oil around the coast is also to be carried out.

South Yemen provides obvious military advantages for the Soviet Union. Fifteen thousand Russians and Cubans were installed there by the end of 1979. The Russians are rapidly developing bases which could serve as a launching pad for Russian troops. Already they control the huge airfield near Aden and a second giant airbase is under construction in the Hadramaut. These are located within easy reach of Saudi Arabia and the vital Strait of Hormuz and the Bab el Mandeb.

The Soviet Union has been preparing a special task force for emergency use in the Middle East. It consists of 7 divisions including paratroops, light armour and artillery. A significant part of it could be transported by air to any Middle East target area within 48 hours. At present this force is based in Bulgaria, and the advantages given by the bases in South Yemen are obvious.

No wonder the Sandhurst-trained ruler of Oman takes a rueful satisfaction at being proved right in all his so-called "alarmist" predictions of Russia's drive for world domination. Since the invasion of Afghanistan the Sultan of Oman – who views the takeover as a threat close to his own part of the world – has asked for increased arms, training and military support from the West.

"There is no doubt that the Soviet Union followed a policy of expansionism and used every opportunity, whether through lack of resolve by the West or the West being caught napping," the Omani Minister of State for Foreign Affairs, stated on 11th January, 1980. Furthermore, he said, "they have and will continue to take military action to intervene whenever the possibilities and opportunities arise. We feel they will not be content to remain in Afghanistan, if they are allowed to move further south to warmwaters, into the Gulf of Oman."

The threat nearest to Oman is South Yemen – the Omanis are continually anxious about the future. More widely, there is an obvious risk to the interests of the Western World as a whole in the narrow channel for oil tankers passing through the Strait of Hormuz.

The Omanis, whose army is trained and led by about 500 British officers, are not seeking a Western military presence, still less the arrival of the American fleet. "We want to defend ourselves," said the Omani Minister of State for Foreign Affairs. "What we want is for the West to help us defend ourselves. But if the Russians intervened in the area, then we would expect a response by the Americans to redress the balance."

Fortunately, events in Afghanistan have had the effect of halting any tendency there was to reduce the British commitment to Oman. It will be maintained and where practicable be strengthened. The only limiting factor is likely to be the Omani military's capacity to take over responsibility.

There has been a renewal of the anti-Oman propaganda by Omani dissidents based in Aden. Oman fears this may be the prelude to attempts at stirring up more trouble in the Dhofar region of Oman which borders South Yemen. A Marxist-led rebellion there was crushed only two years ago with the help of British and Iranian forces.

The Sultan is confident his small but efficient army, air force and navy, stiffened with British seconded and contract officers, can compete with any attempt at infiltration from South Yemen, but not with anything greater.

Oman is the only Arab State with a ruler supported by a British military presence. The 39-year-old ruler, Sultan Qaboos bin Said, is the only one in the area who stands up to be counted and makes no secret of his lone crusade to stem the tide of Communism. He fully appreciates how the fatal bear hug could squeeze the life out of his country.

In the Gulf is Oman's next-door neighbour, the United Arab Emirates. There, as a result of uncontrolled immigration, are Palestinian Liberation terrorists prepared for guerrilla warfare.

The strength of Oman's armed forces is no more than about 17,500 supported by about 500 trained British military personnel on contract to the Sultan's forces and 142 seconded to them. Not only are anti-tank guns a priority requirement, they need 155mm guns and missiles which can fly "blind" to strike targets by night or day. The air force of about 12 Hunters, a dozen Jaguars and eight Strikemasters must be increased by at least a squadron of Jaguars.

There is no doubt where Oman stands. The Sultan himself is resolutely identified with the West, yet, either by choice or diplomatic hamhandedness, the country, in the past, has more or less been excluded from the councils of the pan-Arab world.

The Sultan has agreed that refuelling, storage and other military facilities may be used by Britain and the United States at the former Royal Air Force station on the island of Masira. But he has insisted that a new base should not be developed there. He is the only ruler in the Gulf area to make such an offer. Other rulers are apprehensive about the effects such a gesture might have on the population.

Omani relations are already somewhat strained with the Arab world beyond the Gulf. And in the Gulf itself, the Omani attempt to mobilize an international effort to patrol and protect the waterway was handled so clumsily that it failed before it started.

What is at stake is *oil!* Cut off the oil and the West will starve. NATO would be crippled. Japan would grind to a halt within three months – one month in Winter – and the USA would be in dire trouble. Oman must therefore be included as another 'domino' in this vital strategic area.

CHAPTER
11

Saudi Arabia

Saudi Arabia is an expansive country as large as Western Europe, including Britain and Ireland, but for all its size its has a population of only nine million (1976 estimate) and of this total one million are temporary foreign workers.

Even before the fall of the Shah and the Soviet takeover in Afghanistan, Saudi Arabia was a key area of the Middle East. Its huge oil reserves and its dominant position on the Gulf makes its security of vital importance for the industrialized and developing world alike.

Unfortunately the country is in a far weaker position than its huge oil reserves and bulging dollar-gold stockpile would indicate. It has been referred to as an oil giant with feet of clay. For the following twelve reasons I would call it a sitting duck for Russia:

* The disintegration of Iran has seriously endangered Saudi Arabia, whose ruling autocracy is extremely vulnerable to Islamic Marxism of the type practised by Colonel Gaddafi in Libya.
* The stunning display of brutal force by the Soviet Armed Forces in their invasion of Afghanistan has 'shaken the Saudis rigid'.
* The seizure of the Grand Mosque in Mecca in November 1979, by terrorists, some of whom were religious fanatics, weakened the prestige of the royal family, who are regarded as the custodians of the holy places. It also showed that the Government, like that of many other Muslim countries, is vulnerable to disruption.
* The ruling royal family is wracked with rivalries and split over modernization versus traditional Moslem ways of life. When King Khalid dies, the successor to the throne will probably be the present Crown Prince Fahd and that should be a smooth succession. But rivalry and challenge over the selection of a new Crown Prince could trigger off an upheaval.
* There is no constitution; nor are there political parties or elections. The system is archaic and the 'government' knows it – the

government being largely the private domain of the ruling Saudi family. There is, therefore, a strong potential for unrest and subversion. The introduction in January 1980 of a consultative council, a nominated body to share in decision-taking, is certainly a step in the right direction.

* The Saudis now see themselves surrounded by radical states and menaced by the rapid build-up of Soviet Bloc forces in the region.
* Russia from its expanding presence in both North and South Yemen is ideally deployed to wage a war of subversion in Saudi Arabia.
* At least half of the workers are foreigners, with Egyptians and Palestinians holding most of the professional and clerical jobs. These conditions make the Saudis highly vulnerable to outside pressures.
* The subversive groupings include the Moslem Brotherhood, the Palestinian Organizations and Ayatollah Khomeini's agents, who have been active among the Shia community in the eastern provinces.
* The granting of overflight rights to Soviet aircraft *en route* to South Yemen.
* The opposition to military facilities for America in their country.
* The small size of their military forces which are rift with division.

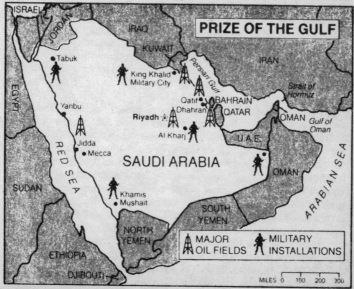

Appreciation to *Newsweek*, 3rd March, 1980.

Cynthia Z. Rachlin—NEWSWEEK

So much for the reasons why I consider Saudi Arabia to be the prize target in Russia's intrusion into the peninsula.

Saudi Arabia is not another Iran. It does not have the same seeds for discontent, the same urban poor, it is less industrialized, less populated, and most of its people are of a different sect to the Muslims who hold the American hostages in Teheran.

The breakout of internal dissent expressed in Mecca is rooted in the same anti-materialist feeling which swept Iran, and that, in the prolific oil producing country in the world, is a grim thought.

Saudi Arabia is producing nine and a half million barrels (a barrel is 35 gallons) a day, almost a fifth of world consumption, equal to more than the total of the imports into the United States, six times the production from the North Sea and three times the output from Iran.

Prolonged disruption of those supplies in the event of unrest would bring the West to its knees. No wonder the revolt in the Mosque at Mecca sent a shiver of warning through the oil consuming world. Unrest in Saudi Arabia is the oil companies' waking nightmare.

There was unrest also in other parts of the country which could be a foretaste of what is to come. Demonstrations turned to violence in several towns of the Eastern Province which is the nearest to Iran and the area most heavily populated by Shia Moslems who migrated across the Gulf. It is estimated that about 125,000 people living in the Eastern Province belong to the Shia sect of Islam.

One of the most disquieting features of the incidents for the Saudi authorities was the evidence revealed of large-scale armaments being held in the country. The attackers in Mecca had many modern weapons and huge amounts of ammunition. Towards the end of December 1979 Israel was reported to be worried that the Saudi royal family might be unable to withstand international revolutionary pressure, and that with disturbances such as the attack on Mecca, its days as rulers could be numbered.

It seemed that Israel felt the United States might be placing too much reliance on the Saudi royal family and the concern was that American arms, being requested by the desert kingdom would end up in unreliable hands, as happened in Iran.

On 2nd January 1980, new commanders of the Saudi Arabian armed forces were announced after the biggest shake-up in the kingdom's military and public services since the assassination of King Faisal in 1975. The appointments were made after the dismissal of the Governor of Mecca, a half-brother of King Khalid, and the forced resignations of the Chief of Staff, two other senior military commanders, and many public officials. All these changes stemmed from the attack on the Grand Mosque by some 500 Moslem fanatics, these included Yemenis, Kuwaitis and Egyptians, as well as Saudis. The raid had the sort of precision timing entailing detailed staff work, and a similar attack at Medina, was beaten off only by chance.

The fundamental changes made, underlined ideas that there were political as well as religious motives for the events in Mecca and Medina. A power struggle between leaders of the 5,000 strong Saudi royal family had been going on, and the new appointments indicated that the pro-American group had won.

This is made up basically of the "Seven Sudeiris", sons of King Abdel Aziz ibn Saud, founder of the kingdom. The main indication of the scope of the purge, was the dismissal of the Emir Fawaz, Governor of Mecca, a son of King Abdel Aziz. He had held the post for 10 years. The risk inherent in such a dismissal with all the possibilities there had been of building up a personal following showed something much more than a raid by religious fanatics was involved at Mecca.

A new crisis could shake the Saudi royal house at any time and in the process the whole stability of Saudi Arabia would be undermined. From their forward base in South Yemen the Russians could not be better placed to increase their subversive activities.

The crucial question is, will an American and, I hope, an *Allied* military presence "just over the horizon" be a sufficient deterrent to prevent Russian incursion into the Arabian peninsula and seizing control of the oil tap? Or will Saudi Arabia prove to be *yet another* 'domino'?

CHAPTER
12

Gulf Sheikdoms

The tiny Persian Gulf sheikdoms are Kuwait, Bahrain, Qater and the United Arab Emirates. The region is now *highly* combustible. The question is, where will the fire start? If it does start it will be difficult to extinguish.

The outward calm of lagoons, water-sports and the luxury hotels all conceal fearful problems – an excess of money, tiny populations, tribal differences, religious conflict and superpower rivalry. Above all, there hangs a sense of threat – the product of the Iranian revolution.

The strategic position of the Sheikdoms makes them a prime target for foreign intervention, and they have virtually no capability to defend themselves. Bahrain's ruling family has governed the 33 islands, that make up the archipelago, since 1783. Today, Bahrain is the business and financial centre of the Gulf. Though oil production has dwindled to 50,000 barrels a day, the sheikdom's superb communications system has helped lure more than 50 offshore banks to Bahrain and twenty major firms enjoy tax-exempt status.

A majority of Bahrain's 370,000 people are Shi'ite Muslims – whose spiritual leader is Iran's Ayatollah Khomeini – while the ruling family belongs to the Sunni sect. So far, pro-Iranian demonstrations have failed to gather much support, however, the writing is on the wall.

Kuwait is also sharing in the wealth. Oil revenues of more than $15 billion last year and overseas investments worth more than $30 billion have helped sustain a comprehensive welfare state that provides benefits ranging from health care and education to free local telephone calls. Despite such outpourings of official funds, Kuwait's ruler could face problems sparked by other Mideast confrontations. Nearly one-quarter of the population is Palestinian while almost 20 per cent are Shi'ite Muslims. In the past three months, the Kuwaiti Government has expelled nearly 20,000 people, many of them Iranians.

Until recently, the seven sheikdoms that comprise the United Arab Emirates (UAE) had little in common except a name. Abu Dhabi controls the Emirates' major oil wealth, producing more than 600 million barrels a year, while Dubai (which has only a 100 million-barrel output) has concentrated on becoming the country's business centre; the disparities between the sheikdoms – and the ego trips of their rulers – have resulted in competing airports, competing industrial schemes and competing attitudes over how the emirates should be run. In 1979, the UAE came close to dissolution until Abu Dhabi's Sheik Zaid bin Sultan al Nahyan and Dubai's Sheik Rashid bin Said al Maktum decided to settle their differences. Sheik Zaid remained President of the federation, and Sheik Rashid took over day-to-day operations as Prime Minister.

All the Gulf States look to Saudi Arabia as the leading economic and military power in the area. But they are concerned, especially after the attack on the Grand Mosque in Mecca, that the Saudi rulers may be losing their grip. "The royal family has got out of touch with the people," said one Gulf leader. "Political institutions do not exist, and there are great disparities of wealth – horrible poverty along with conspicuous consumption." Though the Gulf States are determined to maintain their independence, they fear the fervent Islamic revolution that struck the Muslim world with such force last year. "Any of these worries – Iran, Afghanistan or Mecca – can give you a nightmare," said one UAE leader. For the sheiks who control the Gulf States, it is the kind of bad dream that is unlikely to go away.

The rulers maintain that the U.S. treated the Shah's Iran without regard to the Iranians. It treated the country "only as a market" for its own exports. The basic flaw in U.S. policy was to accept the Shah's despotism, and not to persuade him to democratize. "If the Americans had bargained as strongly for democracy in Iran as they bargained for arms sales, they would have succeeded and the Shah would not have been overthrown."

What shocked the rulers of the region was the ease with which the Americans cut out the Shah. As they saw it, he had been an umbrella for them, the ultimate defence, a symbol of strength, the policeman of the area. Yet as they now see it, the Americans just dumped him, leaving these rulers with a sense of having been betrayed. They believe the Americans would be ready to ditch *anyone* for the sake of compromise. Thus today the rulers feel unsure of the ground they stand on. Their general thinking is that America does not really protect anybody, that she has certain interests but no friends, and will sacrifice anybody.

One of the rulers has described their predicament in these terms: "The Americans have taken us for granted for a long time. They even took Saudi Arabia for granted, and if they do that, then they can throw us in the wastepaper basket very easily. We are now between fire and ice, scorched by Khomeini's strength and frozen by America's weakness. We don't need Western advice to recognize Russia as our enemy. We know our enemy. *But do we know our friends?*"

It should be apparent from all this and from the two preceding chapters on Oman and Saudi Arabia, that over the past decade the West has lost not only control over oil production and prices as a result of the neutralization of the oil companies, but strategic control over the region as well. For this loss Britain bears a heavy responsibility, through her abandonment of Aden and her withdrawal from the Gulf in 1971. Had we only tried harder and waited longer, it should have been possible at the time to have converted Britain's political and military position into a defensive alliance between the resolute Sultanate of Oman and the United Arab Emirates, an alliance that would have afforded some protection today to Western nationals in the region, as well as to Western oil interests. The opportunity was not taken, with the melancholy consequences that we now see around us.

I agree with J. B. Kelly, the author of *"Arabia, the Gulf and the West"*, that if the West is to recover strategic control over the Gulf, it will have to steel itself to take some hard decisions. The threats now posed to our interests there by Islamic militancy can be overcome only by resolution, steadfastness and the skilful use of the numerous political, economic and military resources at our disposal. They will not be averted by a humiliating display of pusillanimity such as that with which Western Europe reacted to the Arab oil offensive in 1973. Rather than attempting to placate a resurgent Islam that is utterly implacable, the West should reassert the naval supremacy in Arabian and Persian waters it held for four-and-a-half centuries after Vasco da Gama first rounded the Cape.

Command of the sea is the prerequisite of power in the Gulf, and the West should make it plain to the littoral states, and to the Soviet Union, that it is prepared to exert that command to protect its very great interests in the region and the lives of its own nationals.

Such a declaration of intent, backed by a demonstration of naval strength and air power, would go a good way towards calming the feverish speculation about Western resolve now agitating the Gulf states, and restore a measure of stability to the region as a whole.

CHAPTER
13

Turkey

Turkey, having a direct border with Russia, acts as a buffer not only between Russia and Southern Europe, but also between Russia and the Middle East and is therefore of crucial strategic importance to the defence of NATO's southern flank.

With nearly half a million men under arms and the "eyes and ears" of the Western Alliance on its territory, Turkey is the southern bastion of NATO, where the eastern tip of NATO and the western end of Islam overlap.

The American listening posts in Turkey are vital to NATO and so is Turkish airspace for U-2 reconnaissance aircraft. To sign the SALT II agreement would be one thing: to verify its compliance would be quite another.

Unfortunately it is only *after* the events in Afghanistan and Iran that Turkey has at last been recognized by the wretched short-sighted politicians of the West as being of vital strategic importance.

In the grip of disastrous economic and social problems, Turkey has become a battleground for revolutionary factions. Now, belatedly, the West is pouring aid into the country which is rife for Soviet exploitation. But why only now is the aid forthcoming? It is not as if the writing had not been on the wall ever since 1975 when America took the disastrous decision to impose an arms embargo on this NATO ally.

We must go back to 1975 and trace the course of events. Turkey maintains some 465,000 men under arms – the largest NATO standing army outside that of the U.S. – and has long been regarded by NATO's military hierarchy as one of the alliance's most strategically vital countries. The 1975 American arms embargo – promoted by Turkey's invasion and occupation of 40 per cent of Cyprus – raised serious doubts in Turkey about how genuine Washington's friendship really was. Unfortunately the arms embargo coincided with a period of growing religious unrest and social instability in Turkey.

Despite the fact that the embargo was finally lifted in August 1978, its effects lingered. While pledging to remain loyal to NATO, Turkey let it be known that it could no longer rely on a "single source" (the U.S.)

for its military supplies. NATO officials were gravely concerned. They were keenly aware that Turkey is a soft spot in the alliance's strategic underbelly.

Turkey's historic suspicion of its Russian neighbour no longer ruled out any serious alliance with the Soviets. Indeed there were many indications that Ankara intended at least to hedge its bets by pursuing closer ties with its northern neighbours. Under a trade agreement signed at the end of 1978, Ankara and the Kremlin agreed to raise the volume of their trade by 50 per cent (to $1,275,000,000) over the next three years. The Russians were also building an oil refinery and a steel plant at Iskenderun near the Syrian border — and significantly, Soviet naval vessels were permitted to anchor at Istanbul in November 1978, the first time in 40 years.

Although the ill-conceived arms embargo was lifted, irreparable damage had been caused to NATO because Turkey had lost confidence in her allies.

In December 1978, serious rioting in Turkey between leftist Alawite Moslems and rightist Sunni Moslems forced the former Prime Minister, Bulent Ecevit, to declare martial law in 13 of the country's 67 provinces in what was the most difficult period in the 57 year history of the Turkish republic. Ecevit labelled the sectarian clashes as a serious threat to Turkey's national unity. The wave of terror was comparable to the left-right clashes throughout Turkey that led to more than two years of martial law in some provinces in 1971.

In June 1979, Robert Moss, Britain's well-informed journalist, gave an interesting account in an article in *The Daily Telegraph* of the PLO's deepening involvement in Turkey's current political upheaval. According to Moss, reliable sources in Beirut stated that about 20 members of Turkey's revolutionary underground — most of them belonging to the Kurdish minority — arrived in Lebanon at the beginning of June 1979, in order to receive guerrilla training in PLO camps.

Several groups of Turks (with the Kurds again preponderant) were already undergoing military instructions at Fatah camps in Syria. This was the latest evidence of the PLO's deepening involvement in Turkey's political upheavals. For several months the PLO had been providing important propaganda back-up for the outlawed Turkish Communist Party.

The PLO's radio station in Lebanon was putting out regular Turkish-language broadcasts in the name of "The Voice of the Communist Party in Turkey."

The main flow of arms to the ultra-Leftist terrorist groups in Turkey was across the Syrian border. The weapons were carried into Turkey by professional smugglers and by Turkish revolutionaries returning from training in the Fatah camps. But the PLO had been acting as the main supplier. In the course of the clashes in Turkish Kurdistan in 1979, the security forces discovered large caches of arms from these sources in the towns of Diyar Bakir, Erzincan, Elazig and Agri. A number of Iraqi Kurds were captured and they confessed, under interrogation, to having infiltrated Turkish Kurdistan under PLO direction in order to fan the revolt there.

The Kurds had again been used as pawns in the struggle for power in the Middle East. The Kurds are one of the oldest-established and most numerous peoples in the region. Estimates of the total Kurdish population in the region range from 8 million to more than 16 million.

The broad band of uncertainty results from the fact that the local governments refuse to publish reliable census data on the ethnic breakdown of their countries' populations and deliberately understate the size of their Kurdish communities when given an opportunity.

The area that Kurdish nationalists think of as "Kurdistan" is divided by the borders of the Soviet Union, Turkey, Iran, Iraq and Syria. About half of the Kurdish people live in Turkey – between four million (on the lowest estimate) and eight million (according to the probably inflated figures put out by the Kurds themselves).

The next highest concentration is in Iran (between two million and five million), followed by Iraq (1.5 million – 2.5 million), with smaller Kurdish communities in Syria (400,000 – 600,000), the Soviet Union (100,000 – 300,000), and Lebanon (50,000 – 70,000). Most of the Kurds are Sunni Moslems.

While none of the governments involved have been prepared to make a significant accommodation with the claims of Kurdish nationalism inside their own borders, some of them have been far from reluctant to stir up trouble among Kurdish communities in neighbouring countries as an instrument of political pressure. Ayatollah Khomeini's régime in Iran has accused the Iraqis of meddling both in Iranian Kurdistan and in the Arab community of Khuzestan, the scene of serious fighting.

The Turks have long sought to blur the separate identity of their own Kurdish minority. Turkish governments have preferred to describe the Kurds as "mountain Turks". But Turkey's Kurdish leaders have refused to be assimilated. The revolt in the eastern provinces was the single most challenging security problem in the country, and in addition to that, it was notable that Kurds were playing a leading role in Marxist-Leninist groups that were ideologically, rather than ethnically, based.

How does the PLO fit into the picture? It has long been a PLO objective to open an office in Ankara and win Turkish backing for the Palestinian cause. The map on page 149 is enough to recall that Turkey is one of the three important non-Arab states on the borders of the Arab world – the others are Iran and Ethiopia – that were able, in the past, to adopt a position of neutrality in the Middle East dispute.

But Ethiopia and Iran were, and are today, under the heel of revolutionary (if unstable) régimes. Only Turkey had so far escaped revolution, although its institutions had been seriously undermined by

143

economic chaos and the rising wave of terrorism. As Robert Moss concluded, Turkey's importance to NATO and the United States made it an attractive target to the PLO's Soviet patrons, who were not above channelling covert support to revolutionary groups at the same moment that they were openly wooing the former Prime Minister, Mr. Bulent Ecevit.

Ecevit had to contend with bloody sectarian civil strife, severe food shortages, rising inflation, unemployment, increased tension with Turkey's NATO neighbour, Greece, increased suspicion of her eastern neighbour, Iran, an almost disintegrating government in Ankara, and a widespread feeling among his people that had changed from frustration to disillusionment to fear and to hatred. The hope was that the badly needed aid package that Ecevit had then received would prevent the country from sliding into greater anarchy and a take over by the army — the largest in NATO.

The poor performance of Ecevit's government, both on law and order and on the economy, led to a spectacular swing in the October 1979 elections to the main opposition group, the Justice Party (JP). The JP leader, Mr. Süleyman Demirel, became Prime Minister (for the sixth time in 14 years) one month before Soviet tanks rolled into Afghanistan. Turkey's commitment to the West was clearly spelled out, first to NATO ambassadors in Ankara and then at a NATO ministerial meeting in Brussels. The new Premier hoped that a firmer political commitment to the West would enhance Turkey's role in NATO and speed up the economic aid the West had promised. An inflation-ridden economy had brought the country to the verge of bankruptcy. As for law and order, political violence was claiming 10 lives a day.

On 2nd January, 1980, Turkey's military leaders issued a stiff warning to the politicians to stop their "sterile bickering" and unite to cope with the "anarchy and separatism" threatening the country with a general uprising.

"The developments in our region could turn into a flagrant conflict at any time," the armed forces commanders said in one of their sternest statements in years. The warning, in a letter signed by General Kenan Evren, Chief of the General Staff, and the four commanders-in-Chief of the Army, Navy, Air Force and Gendarmerie, was handed to President Koruktuk during General Evren's routine weekly visit.

President Koruturk summoned Mr. Demirel, the Prime Minister, and Mr. Ecevit, Opposition Leader, and read them the letter. Prime Minister Demirel, clearly distressed after discussing the statement with President Fahri Koruturk, said: "We are now in a serious situation. But my Government has been in power for only 30 days, so obviously we cannot take responsibility for the problem."

Turkey has been living with political terrorism and political killings for the last five years. More than 5,200 people have been killed in the last two years — 2,300 of them since Mr. Demirel took office at the end of last year, despite martial law being in force in 19 of the 67

Provinces. In a separate note to the President, General Evren said the warning letter represented the unanimous view of generals and admirals, which they had expressed to him.

The armed forces were known to be most reluctant to take over the country. But the military intervened twice before in the last two decades – in 1960, and again in 1971, when they toppled Mr. Demirel's elected Government by a communique without dissolving the parliament.

A reliable military source described the warning as a "safety valve" in the face of pressures from within the armed forces on their commanders. The generals said in their letter that "instead of our national anthem, the Communist international is being sung". They complained about terrorism and the Kurdish separatist movements, and attacked "those who advocate the imposition of Islamic law and others who would institute fascism in place of democracy". They asked for the close co-operation of political parties in the face of these dangers. "Anarchists and separatists are rehearsing for a general uprising all over the country," the letter said.

The reference in the statement to anarchists meant the right and left-wing extremists who carry out vendetta street killings. The term, separatists, was the strongest reference to date to the Kurdish movement in eastern Turkey. There are at least 8 million Kurds in Turkey. Although it is 99 per cent Muslim, Turkey has been a secular state for more than 50 years. The generals also expressed concern about recent developments in the Middle East, which they said could turn into a war.

A military source commented: "Thousands of young officers are restless and worried about the country. They want their commanders, as members of the National Security Council, to speak up to show their concern, and shake-up the politicians, who are only fighting with each other in Parliament. They even failed to reach an agreement on measures against terrorism."

The generals' letter said that many decisions taken in the National Security Council were not implemented because of the political parties. Although the military warning was unusual, the two main political party leaders did not express fear of military intervention.

Mr. Ecevit said he had no worries about the good intentions of the armed forces, "because they are sensitive to our democratic régime." Sources close to the military leadership said that commanders were fully aware of Turkey's economic difficulties and other problems. How could they not be aware when the country had no money to pay for oil imports, most homes were without heating or hot water and cities were without light for up to nine hours a day. Many basic goods were unavailable.

The threat that the Kurds may seize on the turmoil in the whole region to attempt secession poses a direct challenge. In their memorandum to President Koruturk, the generals put the main emphasis on this. It is important to repeat again what they wrote: "The

145

danger is that while developments in our area could easily turn into a hot war at any moment, anarchists and secessionists at home are rehearsing for a general uprising." Because the Turkish army, historically, is highly sensitive to separatists movements, the Kurdish activists have moved with circumspection. Instead of agitating openly for autonomy, they use the cover of Marxist groups.

The Turkish army would be tempted to apply a military solution to this problem, but successive governments, concerned about the country's image, have used their restraining influence. This restraint, however, has emboldened some Kurdish groups to set up autonomous pockets in some inaccessible mountain areas of eastern Anatolia, where only the Kurdish flag flies, Kurdish is spoken and even Turkish travellers are required to produce their passports.

What alarms the Turkish military is that, whereas in the recent past the Kurds of Iraq, Syria and Iran were mostly controlled by U.S. agencies as pawns in the Middle East power game, the Kurdish militants today are mainly under Moscow's direct tutelage and receive arms from the Soviet Union and its allies.

If the Soviet aim is, indeed, at some point to create a satellite Kurdistan, this will not only be a direct threat to Turkey's territorial integrity, but, even more, to her geo-political role as the main buffer between Soviet expansionist ambitions and the world's largest oil reservoir.

Mr. Demirel once said that he would co-operate with the former Prime Minister, Mr. Ecevit (the Republican People's Party of the centre-left) only in time of war. The problems Turkey now faces are as serious as any that war could pose. If there was ever a moment in a nation's history when country should be put before party, it is now. That, is seems, was the sense of the message addressed to the politicians by the armed forces. A threat of military intervention may or may not be implied. It should not, in any case, be needed.

On 9th January, 1980, America signed four agreements with Turkey covering military and economic aid, and in turn the Ankara Government granted permission for the United States to continue operating its air base and two vital intelligence-gathering stations in Turkey. The installations are the air base at Incirlik, near Adana, the listening station at Sinop, on the Black Sea, and the radar installation at Pirincilik, near Diyarbakir. The radar and listening posts, which monitor Russian rocket test-firings, are vital since the loss of similar facilities in Iran.

Between 4,000 and 5,000 American Servicemen are stationed in Turkey, and the number is expected to rise slightly when America sends training teams to help Turkey set up its defence industries.

America also committed itself to a five-year programme of economic aid to Turkey. Turkey had asked for $2,500 million (£1,116 million) in aid for a five-year plan, and more than $450 million (£200 million) will be given for the next financial year. A joint Turkish-American Commission will be formed to study the country's needs, while the aid will be approved each year by Congress. Obviously the Russian invasion of Afghanistan had precipitated agreements, so had the warnings from the Turkish generals that they might act if the country's politicians did not stop squabbling.

At a NATO meeting in Brussels on 10th January, 1980, Turkey undertook to take part in any measures against Russia. This was an indication of the Ankara Government's deep committment to NATO. Obviously Turkey will have to be strengthened if the country is to fulfil its NATO role and also be able to stand up to any internal stresses caused by a disintegration of Iran, or the installation of a Communist régime there.

At present the Turkish army would be unable to cope with the defence of the country's borders, the internal terrorist problem and revolt by possible breakaway groups in the East. The Prime Minister blamed the gravity of the struggle against terrorism on the amnesty introduced by Mr. Ecevit's government in 1974 and, implicitly at least, on the Army intervention which forced his own government out of office in 1971.

Turkey intends to apply before the end of 1980 for full membership of the European Community. This may not be welcome by the Commission because of Turkey's great problems. Her finances are in such bad shape that she is having to borrow this year roughly the same amount of foreign currency as she hopes to earn from exports, and some two thirds of that is being spent on servicing outstanding debt. She has devalued her currency by 50 per cent, but some economic experts doubt whether even the new parity is anything like realistic when it comes to comparing the cost of industrial investment per unit produced.

On top of all this, many West Europeans would question whether Turkey fulfils the most basic of all conditions for membership of the Community – that of being a European state.

But Turkey is not just a Mediterranean country. She is and has been by conscious decision, ever since 1923, a Western country. She was accepted as such implicitly by President Truman when he proclaimed his doctrine in 1947. She subsequently became a member of the Council of Europe and of NATO. Indeed, Turkey forms the corner-post of Europe, facing both the Soviet Union and the Muslim, oil-bearing Middle East. *The defence of the West has everything to gain by binding Turkey more securely to the Western democratic system.*

Towards the end of February two more provinces had to be placed under martial law, including the Aegean province of Izmir where troops and left-wing militants had clashed. The city of Izmir had been the scene of political violence for more than a month. The Cabinet, acting on the recommendation of the National Security Council, the country's highest advisory body, also placed under martial law the southern Hatay province on the Syrian border, where there had been political killings and other acts of violence for the past two months.

While the West was still debating its response to the Soviet invasion of Afghanistan, West Germany was already working on its main contribution – massive financial and military aid to strengthen its most vulnerable NATO partner, Turkey.

Herr Hans Matthöfer, the Finance Minister, organized a huge international financial rescue operation for the bankrupt Turkish economy, with West Germany raising the lion's share. Bonn was also expected to provide weapons, in particular modern German-built tanks, and other material for the badly equipped Turkish army.

With this help for their long-time friends, the Germans were putting into practice their principle of division of labour in the Western reaction to Afghanistan. Unenthusiastic about punitive measures such as sanctions, they believed each country should play a role which suited it best and not take actions which would harm itself as much as the Soviet Union. In particular they did not want to endanger the achievements of their détente policy.

To criticisms in foreign newspapers that the West German attitude was feeble, officials retorted that when it came to signing cheques their financial contribution to the West's response would probably be greater than that of any other country.

How much this would be had not yet been decided. But since the Turks felt they needed some $1,500 million (£650 million) just to get the economy moving again and much more in medium-term aid, and since the government expected West Germany to shoulder even more than the 40 per cent it contributed in the last rescue operation, the sum would clearly be enormous.

The key element in Herr Matthöfer's efforts was speed. If the aid was to be effective it had to be available at once. The Turks needed ready money, in particular to buy oil to get their factories going again. Turkish industry was working at only about one third of its capacity.

The Germans believed that the first aid would be of little lasting use if it was not followed up by medium-term help over the next few years. Herr Matthöfer was also seeking means of helping Turkey to postpone paying foreign debts and to prolong credits from private banks. He expected to raise the money from the International Monetary Fund, the World Bank, private banks, the Organization for European Co-operation and Development (OECD), countries and other governments, including Saudi Arabia.

The Germans conceded that Turkey would have needed assistance even under normal circumstances, but the Afghanistan crisis had made its plight particularly serious and urgent for the rest of the Western alliance. They feared severe inflation would bring political and social instability.

Turkey's strategic position on NATO's south-west flank near the

area made insecure by the Afghanistan invasion, and its vulnerability to Islamic religious unrest, made it essential that the country was put back on a sound economic basis and securely linked to the West. One glance at the map is enough to show what a hole would be made in the stability of the region if Turkey were to become "the next domino".

What was the reaction of the Soviet Union to all this, particularly the new defence agreement between Turkey and America? The Soviet Union made its strongest appeal yet direct to the Turkish people to take whatever action was needed to prevent the ratification of the new defence agreements between Ankara and Washington negotiated in January. The appeal was reinforced with the ominous warning: "American Presidents come and go, but Turkey's proximity with the Soviet Union remains".

If the agreements, which provide for the reactivation of former U.S. bases in Turkey were ratified, the Turkish people were told by Radio Moscow that there could be no further détente between the Soviet Union and Turkey.

The bases, said Moscow, were needed by the U.S. following the "popular revolution in Iran" and the Soviet response to "the request of the Afghan people for aid" in order to further the American "new plans for aggression in the Near and Middle East".

According to Moscow "the Afghan people have risen in defence of the gains of their revolution against the evil intentions of the U.S. and its Chinese cohorts", and the Turkish people were urged to take similar action.

The negotiated agreement had no validity in international law, the Turkish people were told, because they had been negotiated under severe pressure and threats from the U.S. Government.

"It is the will of Allah", claimed Moscow, that peace and goodwill should exist between the Soviet Union and the devout people of Turkey, and by concluding the agreements with the U.S. the Demirel Government had flouted the will of Allah. That, coming from Moscow, may be considered by some to border on the blasphemous, but the message was, of course, directed at the revolutionary hotheads who had already brought their country to the brink of ruin.

As for Afghanistan and its consequences, there was also an easy explanation. The U.S. was using the Soviet demonstration of "good neighbourliness and co-operation within Afghanistan" as an excuse for a war of aggression against Islamic countries, and the U.S. was determined "to involve Turkey in these plans".

It must be asked if such crude attempts at subversion were likely to impress anybody. The answer must be that they were addressed to a volatile people verging on anarchy right then, that Demirel's Government was a minority government, and that it was going to be touch and go whether Demirel would succeed in rescuing his country from the abyss which otherwise awaited it.

The Moscow broadcasts, in Turkish, came from radio stations on Turkey's borders and competed directly with the local radio stations. In other words, these were not 'foreign' broadcasts, or appeals coming from a distant "foreign" country. Their impact was therefore immense.

Turkey – Postscript

An unprecedented deterioration of the situation in Turkey developed at the beginning of September 1980. The politicians having refused to listen to the repeated attempts of General Kenan Evren, Chief of the General Staff, to warn them of the dangers Turkey had to face, were suddenly overtaken by events.

At dawn, on 12th September, the military seized power in the third bloodless *coup* in 20 years. General Evren, who led the takeover, is one of the most respected military figures in the country, with a reputation of having wanted to keep the army out of politics. His previous warnings to politicians were paternal in tone rather than threatening.

Parliament and the Government were suspended, the immunity of Members of Parliament revoked and martial law imposed throughout the country. By this action, General Evren and the National Security Council, prevented an imminent civil war and the collapse of a key NATO member – the last remaining bastion in the Balkans and the Middle East against Soviet domination of virtually the entire region. As a top priority 'domino', Russia undoubtedly will seek to keep the anarchy and chaos going in the country. Thankfully however, in the Turkish military there is a formidable counteracting force.

CHAPTER
14

Indian Ocean

The strategic importance of the Indian Ocean, and the vital Cape Route that passes through it, must now be examined with perspectives in the wake of the Russian rape of Afghanistan and the serious upheaval in Iran.

The term Indian Ocean is a misnomer for it washes the coast lines of three continents – Africa, Asia and Australia.

Twenty-four nations form the basin that is filled by the Indian Ocean (10 others if the basins of the Red Sea and the Persian Gulf are included). The United Nations also recognizes the interest in the Indian Ocean of countries that do not have seaboards – a 1979 UN-sponsored meeting of littoral and hinterland states of the Indian Ocean drew 44 participants. Afghanistan was one of these. South Africa, South West Africa and Zimbabwe were not present, nor was Angola.

Co-operation amongst the Indian Ocean countries is complicated by the great diversity in their ideological outlook – ranging from the staunch anti-Communism of South Africa to the strident Marxism of Madagascar, from the monarchial government in Saudi Arabia to the military dictatorship of Pakistan, from the moderate one party state of Kenya to the Communist client status of South Yemen.

The difficulty of effecting co-operation amongst these countries is compounded by the fact that ports of call are geographically remote from one another (unlike the situation in the far larger Atlantic and Pacific Oceans), complicating logistics planning for effective operations in the area.

The 1970s were marked by an intensive build-up of Soviet influence in the littoral and hinterland countries and of her naval presence in the waters of the Indian Ocean. The Indian Ocean theatre threatened to become a major arena for Big Power rivalry.

Following a call by the Non-Aligned Summit in Lusaka in September 1970, the United Nations General Assembly passed a resolution on 16th December, 1971 which read *inter alia:*

1. Solemnly declares that the Indian Ocean, within limits to be

determined, together with the air space above and ocean floor subjacent thereto, is hereby designated for all time as a zone of peace.

2. Calls upon the great Powers in conformity with this Declaration, to enter into immediate consultations with the littoral States of the Indian Ocean with a view to:

(a)   Halting the further escalation and expansion of their military presence in the Indian Ocean;

(b)   Eliminating from the Indian Ocean all bases, military installations and logistical supply facilities, the disposition of nuclear weapons and weapons of mass destruction and any manifestation of great Power military presence in the Indian Ocean, conceived in the context of great Power rivalry.

The resolution called for the banishment from the Indian Ocean of warships and military aircraft that might represent a threat or be used against "the sovereignty, territorial integrity and independence of any littoral or hinterland State of the Indian Ocean in contravention of the purposes and principles of the Charter of the United Nations".

In 1972 the United Nations established an Ad Hoc Committee to monitor the growing military build-up in the Indian Ocean and has repeatedly expressed concern at the arms race in this Ocean. Despite the British decision to withdraw east of Suez in 1968 and the declared intention of the Carter administration in the United States in 1977 to "demilitarize" the Indian Ocean, the build-up of military power has increased, and bilateral talks between the United States and Russia on this issue were later suspended.

When considering arms control measures in the Indian Ocean and the establishment of a so-called "zone of peace", it is imperative to remember that the Indian Ocean is only one of three jugular veins and cannot be viewed in isolation from the Pacific, the Mediterranean and the Atlantic. In all these oceans the swimming Russian Bear has gone to sea, on and under the water and on the sea bed.

Thus, the Soviet Union has a global strategy, whereas the West and the Free World are far too inward looking, with the consequence that they find themselves having to react to events and are forced to dance to the Russian tune.

At the end of World War II, the Soviet Union had hardly any naval capacity worth speaking of, but since has built up a massive naval strength, possessing over 2,400 warships of all types, and over 430 submarines.

Often overlooked is the fact that the Soviet Union has the largest merchant maritime fleet in the world today, 2,500 ships.

On any day in the year, 2,800 merchant ships are alongside in the ports of NATO Europe while 800 are loading or discharging on the East Coast of North America. Moving to and from these ports are some

3,350 merchant ships, while a further 750 are underway in the Mediterranean. Nearly 60 per cent of the huge volume of shipping rounding the Cape of Good Hope belongs to NATO and on the same day, 200 Western tankers are at sea in the Indian Ocean.

These are the ships, unseen and unknown to the vast majority of our citizens, upon whom every one of us depends for his or her life and livelihood. It is the thought of how vulnerable these trade routes are to any nation opposed to us which should shock the reader.

No shots need be fired. If the Soviet Union sees us weak and unprepared the mere presence of large numbers of powerful and operational ships could so easily disrupt our communications and bring the Free World to a halt.

Russia's merchant ships, like their warships, are under one central control in Moscow. The merchant navy is now able to establish a global maritime presence corresponding to their naval strategy of control of the seas. The Russians regard their merchant navy as a fourth arm of defence and its ships are used in a reconnaissance and surveillance role, an example being the electronically-weighed-down "fishing trawlers" that shadow NATO ships and submarines in the North Sea and Atlantic.

The merchant navy also provides a follow-up lift of a significant number of combat divisions to their amphibious forces. Officers and ratings of the Soviet navy serve in their merchant ships which visit ports all round the world every week. It is not difficult to imagine the scale of espionage that is being carried out all the time and it could well outweigh that posed by communist bloc diplomats.

The Soviet Union also has over 460 tankers, which is a significant feature, as oil for the Warsaw Pact front would be transported by land in time of war, as Russia at present is self-sufficient in oil, and does not need ocean-going tankers for its own defensive purposes.

The Soviet merchant fleet is available to supply arms to client states at short notice, and to back up any Soviet-instigated intervention, such as Cuban expeditionary adventures into Angola and Ethiopia. In short, unlike that of other nations, the Soviet merchant marine is not primarily influenced by purely commercial considerations: it exists largely to further the declared Soviet policy, as enunciated by Admiral Sergei Gorshkov, chief of the Soviet Navy.

The Soviets have steadily increased their naval strength in the Indian Ocean for five main reasons:

a.   To dominate and cut the sea lines of supply through the Indian Ocean, thus severing a vital life line to Japan, Australia, Western Europe and the United States.

b.   To exploit the unstable political and military situations in South Asia, and in the Middle East and Gulf areas which hold the major oil reserves of the world.

c.   To use the Soviet navy as a major instrument in the

Kremlin plan to communize other nations by stirring up local conflicts and tensions in the littoral and hinterland States of the Indian Ocean.

"The goal of Soviet sea power is to effectively utilize the world oceans in the interests of building Communism".

(Admiral Sergei Gorshkov, 1975).

d.   To deploy task forces in preparation for possible war and acquire bases to support them.

The Soviet Union has already obtained ports, airfields, repair facilities and ammunition and fuel resupply from Hodeida and Aden in the West to the island of Socotra, the Iraqi harbour of Umm Qasr at the head of the Gulf, and the naval base of Visakapatnam on the East coast of India.

e.   To blockade ports and isolate outlying islands and territories in the event of war.

Western military strategists have every reason to view with concern the Soviet Union's new move to boost its naval and air activity in the Indian Ocean and adjacent land areas.

In April 1979, the 40,000-ton Soviet aircraft carrier *Minsk* entered the Indian Ocean. What was particularly significant was that the *Minsk* was accompanied by the new 13,000-ton amphibious assault ship, *Ivan Rogov,* which is designed to carry at least a battalion of marines with supporting armour and to put them ashore by helicopter and landing craft.

The two ships were escorted by two missile cruisers. This task-group increased the number of Russian warships in the Indian Ocean to 24 – the largest force yet deployed in that area.

The *Minsk* is the sister-ship of the *Kiev,* the second Soviet aircraft carrier, used for helicopters and the Forger vertical take-off and landing fighter aircraft.

The other activity has been the Soviet TU-16 bombers making regular surveillance missions out of Aden, covering the approaches from the Arabian Sea to the Strait of Hormuz and the Persian Gulf.

The reasons for this increased Soviet activity in the area were the serious situations in Iran and Afghanistan and the political situation in Pakistan. It is crucial from the Soviet viewpoint, to control the area with bombers, surface ships, submarines and extensive mining in the event of a crisis.

The major cause for concern about the stability of the Indian Ocean has been the Russian presence that has intensified since the early 1970s. As far back as 1940, in the secret protocols resulting from the Ribbentrop-Molotov consultations, Russia signalled her intentions on the Indian Ocean: "The Soviet Union declares that her territorial aspirations centre South of the National territory of the Soviet Union in the direction of the Indian Ocean".

In 1967, Admiral Sergei Gorshkov said: "In the past our ships and naval aviation units have operated primarily near our coasts, concerned mainly with operations and tactical co-ordination with ground troops. Now we must be prepared for broad offensive operations against sea and ground troops of the imperialists on any point of the world's territories".

Russian politico-military gains in the littoral states of the India Ocean since the announcement in 1968 of the British withdrawal east of Suez include:

*   Aden, once a major British port of great strategic importance, has become the *principal* port of call in the Indian Ocean for the Russian Navy.
*   Massawa, in Ethiopia, once an important port of call for the United States, no longer permits the entry of American vessels but is now Russian-controlled.
*   Maputo, once a normal turnover port for incoming and outgoing U.S. units joining and leaving the Middle East force, no longer plays host to American ships but is a regular Russian port of call.
*   Likewise, Indian ports, once favoured by U.S. Middle East force units, are today seldom so favoured but are visited more frequently by Russian vessels.
*   The Russian Navy now has forward operating facilities in Vietnam that were previously under Western control. The implications of this are discussed below.
*   Russia has an air base on Dahlak Islands, near Massawa, built to offset the loss of the base she built and used in Berbera, Somalia, before being expelled from that country in 1977.
*   In addition to the above, the Russian Navy has anchorages at several strategically vital points including Madagascar, the Seychelles, Socotra Island and Angola. The latter was the scene in early 1979 of a Soviet show of force with the visit of units of the Russian Navy, including, as I have already described, the 40,000-ton *Minsk* which then went on to the Indian Ocean, the first Russian aircraft carrier to enter this Ocean.

In the above list I have, of course, included Vietnam. The gains in this area include the strategic Vietnamese port of Da Nang. Haiphong, being modernized by the Russians, is also said to be virtually in the hands of the Soviet Union and the predictions are that Cambodia's (Kampuchea) key port, Kompong Som, in southern Cambodia under Vietnamese occupation, will also soon be under Soviet control.

Russian warships are using facilities at Cam Ranh Bay, the former American logistical base on the south-east Vietnamese coast.

The presence of the Russian Navy in Cam Ranh waters — considered one of the world's finest natural harbours — calls for major strategic reassessments thoughout the Western World. It will have immediate and vast implications for the key United States naval facility at Subic Bay, in the Philippines.

A Russian base at Cam Ranh is in an ideal location to interdict Japan's oil supply line from the Middle East, and would clearly enhance Soviet Indian Ocean naval strength which in the past has operated out of the eastern Russian port of Vladivostok.

Cam Ranh Bay is a sprawling port area with huge land storage facilities and an airport capable of taking almost any size of military aircraft. It is the strategic equivalent to America's Subic Bay and its availability to the Soviet Navy, amounts to a fundamental switch in the balance of big-power naval strength throughout the region. The movement of the Russian navy to Cam Ranh coincides with the largest concentration of Russian warships on the South-East Asian seaboard for the past 20 years.

These developments are not only threatening the Indian ocean area but also the western Pacific. The danger became evident when the Soviet Pacific fleet sailed in early 1979 from the base of Vladivostok to the Gulf of Siam via Vietnamese waters, threatening the sea routes of the U.S., Japan and Western Europe.

The U.S. response to these Soviet threats was the sending of its aircraft carrier *Midway* and the frigate *Downes* to the Indian Ocean in mid-April 1979 through the Straits of Malacca. Earlier it had sent the aircraft carrier *Constellation* to cruise in the Indian Ocean. Although the U.S. had only 14 vessels in the Indian Ocean as against the Soviet Union's 24, this was the first time that the U.S. had concentrated two aircraft carriers simultaneously in the area.

It was also the first time that the Russian Navy had deployed two carrier task groups far outside home waters. When the *Minsk* arrived in the Indian Ocean, in the Spring of 1979, the *Kiev* was operating in the North Atlantic with some 20 other warships.

The departure of the *Minsk* for distant waters so soon after her completion is regarded as something of an achievement by Western naval experts. It shows great confidence in her design and capabilities, as most new Western warships are usually operated reasonably close to home ports until both the crew have gained experience in operating the ship and it is reasonably certain that no major snags are likely to develop.

Normally, the Russians have between seven and nine "combatants" and five to seven "support" ships in the Indian Ocean although their numbers have on occasion reached 25 and even 30. Moreover, as I have already said, the military arm of the Russian Navy is strengthened by the presence of its merchant fleet, fishing fleet and oceanographic research fleet which are all geared to augmenting the Navy if and where required. The United States, in contrast, maintains the Middle East Force composed of a flagship and two to four destroyers, with visits by units of varying size of the Seventh (Pacific) Fleet. Some U.S. naval strategists are urging the establishment of a separate Indian Ocean Fleet, but the U.S. Navy is down to 455 ships, its smallest fleet in 40 years and there is no assurance when it will bottom out.

The Soviet penetration of the Indian Ocean is one component of the global expansionism of Communism in the 1970s, the sum total of which presents a frightening picture to the West. Senator Gordon J. Humphrey of New Hampshire told the Institute for Foreign Policy Analysis in Washington in July 1979:

"In the past decade we have witnessed a massive armament effort by our principal adversary, the Soviet Union, that exceeds by far that of the United States. In spite of the efforts of successive administrations to promote an improved relationship with Moscow, the Soviet Union has exploited to its advantage the numerous crises that have erupted in remote corners of the globe – in South-East Asia, in the Persian Gulf and the Middle East. We have seen the establishment of Soviet-supported client states in Vietnam and in Afghanistan, as well as the massive Soviet effort to extend Moscow's influence in Africa. . . . The Soviet Union has extended its influence into regions vitally important to the survival of the United States and its allies. This is the meaning of the growing Soviet encirclement of the world's leading oil-producing region – the Persian Gulf."

If the Soviet Union can succeed in dominating the Indian Ocean and its north-west entrance, it will have outflanked NATO to the West, China to the East and Japan, backed by the U.S., in the Far East.

To meet this Russian naval threat an American carrier naval task force, with a Western component – British, French, Dutch and German – should be deployed in the Indian Ocean. Surely the presence of two superpowers is preferable to the unchallenged pre-eminence of one? Such a task force, equipped with nuclear weapons, would fill the gap between the existing U.S. Sixth Fleet in the Mediterranean and the Seventh Fleet in the Atlantic.

It is imperative to complete as a matter of urgency the construction into a forward naval base of the strategically important British Island of Diego Garcia in the geographic centre of the Indian Ocean, 1,000 miles South of Sri Lanka. The work has involved building an airfield with a 12,000 ft. runway at which a squadron of P13 Orion maritime patrol aircraft have been for some time. A mile-long jetty, in which an estimated seven miles of concrete-filled steel piles are being laid, will allow a carrier task group to be based in the lagoon. Other tasks have included building 17 miles of roads, warehouses, a radio station, eight large fuel tanks, an air-conditioned barracks for 600 men, a club for naval ratings, sports grounds and a swimming pool.

Diego Garcia lies 2,600 miles from Bahrain in the Gulf; 2,100 miles from Aden at the entrance to the Red Sea, and 2,000 miles from the Malacca Straits, the main eastern entrance for shipping to the Indian

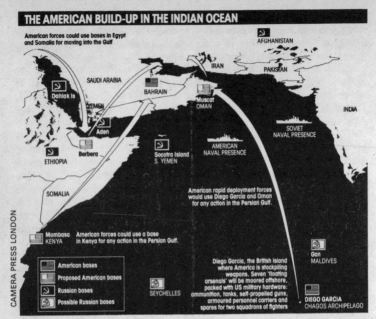

THE AMERICAN BUILD-UP IN THE INDIAN OCEAN

American forces could use bases in Egypt and Somalia for moving into the Gulf

AFGHANISTAN

SAUDI ARABIA

IRAN

PAKISTAN

Dahlak Is

BAHRAIN

YEMEN

Muscat
OMAN

INDIA

Aden

SOVIET
NAVAL PRESENCE

Socotra Island
S. YEMEN

AMERICAN
NAVAL PRESENCE

ETHIOPIA

Berbera

SOMALIA

American rapid deployment forces would use Diego Garcia and Oman for any action in the Persian Gulf.

Mombasa
KENYA   American forces could use a base in Kenya for any action in the Persian Gulf.

Gan
MALDIVES

Diego Garcia, the British island where America is stockpiling weapons. Seven 'floating arsenals' will be moored offshore, packed with US military hardware: ammunition, tanks, self-propelled guns, armoured personnel carriers and spares for two squadrons of fighters

American bases

Proposed American bases

Russian bases

Possible Russian bases

SEYCHELLES

DIEGO GARCIA
CHAGOS ARCHIPELAGO

CAMERA PRESS LONDON

Appreciation to *NOW!* Magazine, 6th–12th June, 1980.

Ocean. When the base is completed it will go some way to offsetting the Russians plans to build up a base at the Umm Qasr in Iraq at the head of the Gulf. Although the Russians would be closer to bring pressure on the Arab oil states, the confined waters of the Gulf make it unsuitable for operating large aircraft carriers.

The importance of Diego Garcia is that it would enable the Americans to keep a carrier task group off the Gulf for long periods. At present a task group has to be supplied from Subic Bay, 6,000 miles away in the Philippines. The presence of Marines and troop-carrying helicopters, with close air support provided by Harriers lends weight to President Carter's announcement that America is prepared to intervene militarily to protect gulf oil supplies.

Diego Garcia will also permit a more potent American presence without provoking Arab nations, like Saudi Arabia, which are keen enough to get help when they feel threatened but sensitive about granting long term facilities or a military presence.

Another advantage is that it will quicken reactions in emergencies. For example, when President Carter ordered the carrier *Constellation* (85,000 tons) and her escorts to go from Subic Bay in the Philippines to Arabian waters during the 1979 Yemeni flare-up, it took them 10 days to make the passage. The fact that Mr. Carter had ordered *Constellation* to the Indian Ocean during the Iranian crisis that led to the Shah's downfall, and then thought better of it made American power less credible.

It is significant that the Diego Garcia facilities are genuinely opposed by only four countries; India, Iraq, Ethiopia and South Yemen. These four countries are either aligned with, beholden to or already a Soviet client state.

It is difficult to equate the sincerity of India's "zone of peace" exhortations with the fact that she herself is engaged on a growing naval build-up in the area and the establishment of island bases. For instance, in the strategically located Nicobar Islands in the Bay of Bengal, near the Straits of Malacca, India plans to build a so-called export processing zone. This is an interesting revelation, for the Nicobar Islands are considered to be unsuitable for economic development. A strategic appreciation of this plan leads one to the inevitable conclusion that the real purpose is to construct an airfield and a naval infrastructure as a base for military operations. Thus, India will have two fleets — Eastern and Western.

The importance of the Indian Ocean is mirrored in the intensified naval activity that occurs wherever conflict situations arise in littoral and hinterland states. For example, the U.S. Seventh Fleet responded to the Indian-Pakistani war of 1971; to the South Yemen attempt at about the same time to seal the entrance to the Red Sea and to the Russian involvement in Ethiopia in 1978. The instability factor resulting from this Big Power rivalry in the Indian Ocean is, in turn, mirrored in the concern of littoral and hinterland states about their security. A meeting of the latter at United Nations headquarters on 13th July, 1979, noted:

"Despite the expressed wishes of the littoral and hinterland States of the Indian Ocean and that of the General Assembly, the military presence of the great Powers in the Indian Ocean conceived in the context of great Power rivalry has intensified and that there has been a deterioration of peace and security in the Indian Ocean area. The escalation of the great Power military presence, as well as other military preparations, continues to threaten the peace and stability of this area . . . "

This followed a December 1978 appeal by the United Nations General Assembly to the United States and Russia to resume talks on their respective military postures in the Indian Ocean. But the jolt to the United States and her Western allies came only with the Soviet Union's invasion of Afghanistan following close on the heels of the crisis in Iran.

December 1979 saw the largest American task force in the Indian Ocean: 21 ships including the attack carriers *Kitty Hawk* and *Midway* with 160 aircraft. In January 1980, the Carter Administration negotiated for base facilities in Saudi Arabia, Oman, Kenya and Somalia, despatched the missile cruiser *Long Beach* and six troop-landing ships with 1,650 marines and tanks to augment a force of about

25 warships in the volatile northern Indian Ocean, and ordered the expediting and expansion of construction at the giant Diego Garcia naval base originally scheduled for completion in 1981.

In London, Lord Carrington, Britain's Foreign Secretary, said the British Government would consider a new presence east of Suez.

France, always more conscious than her allies of the strategic importance of the Indian Ocean where she has been maintaining a fleet larger than America's and the Soviet Union's but not as powerful, reinforced her naval presence immediately after the onset of the Iranian crisis.

In West Germany, Government concern about Communist intentions in respect of the Cape Route was voiced in a report published in *Die Welt*.

Among the findings of the West German report were that the Russians, in their active involvement in Southern Africa since 1960, aimed to gain control of the raw materials of the subcontinent and the lines of communication along which they pass and, in particular, to threaten the Cape Route as a means of bringing political pressure to bear on the West.

Shortly before this came a warning from the authoritative *Jane's Fighting Ships:* "If ever political dogmatism and subsequent indecision have put a strategic issue at risk it is on the oil route around South Africa. This sea lane is vital to the Western nations and irrespective of Mexican, North Sea and possibly Moroccan oil supplies it will remain so for many years. The Western countries have neither a base nor a safe haven on the African coast in the same area."

The latter assessment serves to underline the supreme folly of the British and American decision to ignore the South African facilities at Simonstown, the only permanent modern naval base, supported by a modern industrialized society and a stable government – backed by one of the world's most sophisticated communications tracking networks – in the vast stretch of ocean between Australia and South America.

The importance of the Cape Route can be summarized in the following statistics: The Route is used by 32 tankers per day; 75% of the Western World's total tanker fleet tonnage is engaged in transporting oil around the Cape; 80% of Western Europe's oil and a lesser proportion of British oil comes via the Cape; 80% of strategic raw materials essential to the West's furnaces are transported along Indian Ocean routes as is 80% of Japan's oil.

Co-operation with South Africa in the naval sphere has been rejected by the United States and Britain at the very time that Communist imperialism seeks to lay the ground work for ultimate control of Southern Africa, the Cape Route and the Indian Ocean. The West German report quoted above is but one of many such evaluations. A particularly important assessment comes from Dr. Igor S. Glagolev, a Soviet citizen living in the United States since 1976, who was an adviser on foreign affairs and SALT to the Central Committee of the Communist Party of the Soviet Union as well as a consultant to the Politburo of the Russian Communist Party:

"Seizure of control over the southern part of the African continent is the most important and immediate aim of the present Soviet leadership. The Soviet expansion in Africa developed in several stages. First, using the conflict between the Arab countries and Israel, the Soviet government established its influence over several Arab states. Then, using the tribal conflict in Nigeria, the U.S.S.R. began to influence Nigerian dictators for its own purposes. In the middle of the present decade, by taking advantage of the anti-Portugal Movement, the Soviet leadership has established its control over the former Portuguese colonies in Africa. The goal of the present, final stage is the elimination of the democratic development in the southern part of the African continent by means of subversion and military invasion by pro-Soviet forces . . .

The decision to begin an offensive for the conquest of Southern Africa was taken by the Politburo of the Communist Party of the Soviet Union near the end of the 1960s.

The then National Chairman of the Communist Party of South Africa, John Marks, as well as some pro-Soviet terrorists from Rhodesia, were summoned to Moscow. I participated in negotiations with them. The negotiations with the terrorists (who are called the 'Patriotic Front' of Zimbabwe) began at the Soviet Peace Committee and continued at the Central Committee of the CPSU in 1968. The terrorists asked and received Soviet arms and money. Later Marks attended a special conference organized by the Central Committee of the party and received Soviet instructions. His headquarters were in London and he was already controlled by the Soviet Politburo.

The present National Chairman of the Communist Party of South Africa, Yusef Dadoo, has also been controlled by the Soviet leadership for a long time. He attended international conferences of communist parties in Moscow in 1960 and 1969. He is one of the authors of the present programme of the Communist Party of South Africa which openly stipulates destruction of the structure of the South African society. In September 1979, Dadoo was awarded the Soviet order of 'Friendship of Peoples'.

The Soviet leadership controls through him not only the South African Communist Party but the African National Congress and the South African Indian Congress as well. Dadoo is president of the South African Indian Congress and vice-chairman of the Revolutionary Council of the African National Congress.

In general, the 'Institute of Africa' is the brains trust of the Soviet offensive in Africa. It is important to note this Institute began to consider invasion into Southern Africa as a major goal of Soviet foreign policy only in the 1970's. In the 1960's it paid much less attention to this region. In 1976, however, a deputy director of the Institute, Yablochkov, announced (at a secret meeting of the Permanent Interagency Council on the Foreign Policy of the U.S.S.R. and International Relations) that elimination of the Western influence in Southern Africa is the major task of Soviet foreign policy. I was a member of the Council and attended this meeting . . .

Pro-communist dictators in Angola, Mozambique, Ethiopia and in some other African countries usually rob a considerable part of their population. The land is taken from the peasants and given to the so-called collective farms, which practically belong to the government. The peasants are compelled to work at these collective farms for a very low income. Those who oppose the dictators are sent to concentration camps or killed.

The Soviet leaders instigated genocidal wars and terror of local dictators against the population of Biafra, Angola, Mozambique, Uganda, Equatorial Guinea, Ethiopia and other African countries. The year 1977 was very important for the preparation of the final Soviet attack against Southern Africa. The Soviet leaders took into consideration that the present U.S. administration would not support anti-communist and pro-Western governments in Southern Africa. On the contrary, the U.S. government actually lined up behind some of the demands of the U.S.S.R., the 'Patriotic Front of Zimbabwe', SWAPO and the African National Congress.

Nikolai Podgorny, who was then chairman of the Presidium of the Supreme Soviet, went along with the policy of the aggressive group of the Politburo and started its implementation. He went on official visits to Tanzania, Zambia and Mozambique. There, on behalf of the Soviet government, Podgorny concluded mutual agreements with the governments of respective countries concerning liquidation by military means of the present socio-political-economic system in Zimbabwe-Rhodesia, Namibia and the Republic of South Africa.

The 'Patriotic Front of Zimbabwe', SWAPO and the African National Congress were designated in the joint statements by the governments of the three aforementioned front-line states, on the one hand, and the Soviet Union, on the other, as the sole future rulers of Zimbabwe, Namibia and South Africa. Creation of new independent states in the region of South Africa was severely criticized. Similar agreements were concluded in Moscow in 1977 between the U.S.S.R. and Fidel Castro and between Nigerian minister of foreign affairs Garba and the Soviet government.

During the recent years the Soviet press openly described organization of military forces in Mozambique, Zambia and Angola for invasion into Zimbabwe-Rhodesia and Namibia. It maintains this invasion has already begun and the invaders occupy major parts of these countries.

Even the Prime Minister of the U.S.S.R., Alexei Kosygin, who formerly belonged to the seeming less aggressive group in the Politburo, demanded liquidation of the present social system not only in Zimbabwe-Rhodesia and Namibia but also in the Republic of South Africa, during his visit to Ethiopia in September 1979. Not only terrorist groups headed by Nkomo and Mugabe, but also regular military forces of the frontline states participate in aggressive actions in Southern Africa. Soviet arms are constantly supplied for these actions.

There is a Soviet inspired plan, published in the Western press, to use Nigerian regular troops for occupation of Southern Africa under the pretext of pacifying this region. It must be noted that Syrian troops occupied Lebanon, destroyed a considerable part of the country, and installed a puppet régime there under the same pretext.

Inclusion of pro-Soviet terrorists into the governments of countries of Southern Africa, and occupation of these countries by pro-Soviet forces, would lead to bloody civil wars, political and possibly physical liquidation of the present elected governments and parliaments of these countries, mass robberies, creation of concentration camps and suppression of the present system of human rights. All the supporters of democracy – i.e. the majority of the population – would be persecuted. Expression of independent opinions, which is allowed at present, would be forbidden.

The example of Angola and other Soviet-dominated African states shows that the white population of Southern Africa would probably flee before the communist take-over. The black population would not be able to do it and it would suffer the main human losses. Already now the pro-Soviet terrorists kill and mutilate mainly black civilians of Southern Africa, including women and children, priests and nuns. After the takeover the black population would be doomed to forced labour in the Soviet-controlled mines and in the state-owned collective farms.

The Soviet leadership would use the enormous natural resources of Southern Africa for a major increase of Soviet reserves of hard currency and for a more effective expansion of Soviet control in Africa, Asia and Latin America."

In 1979, General Magnus Malan, the then Chief of the South African Defence Force, wrote: "It had become a truism, however recently neglected, that if South Africa and its resources, both human and mineral, should fall to the Communists the very existence of the West itself would be jeopardized."

The rampaging of the Red Bear in the Indian Ocean hinterland State of Afghanistan has sounded the alarm bells in the capitals of the West more loudly and more insistently than ever before.

Now, after months of tough bargaining, Oman agreed in June 1980, to allow the United States the use of military "facilities" – initially two airfields and a naval base – in return for future military and economic aid. Similar arrangements have, in late August, been finalized with Somalia and one with Kenya is expected.

These facilities will help to alleviate the strain on the U.S. Pacific Seventh Fleet whose arduous responsibilities had increased to patrolling 50 million square miles of open ocean. Admiral Thomas Hayward, the Chief of Naval Operations, warned the House Armed Services Committee earlier in the year that "Your Navy is stretched thinner today than at any time since the late 1940s. The simple fact is that today we are trying to meet a three-ocean commitment with a one-and-a-half ocean navy."

Meanwhile, the Soviet Pacific fleet was growing both in quantity and quality. As the Russian fleet expanded, so too did its range. In little more than a year, the Soviet Navy had acquired secure logistical bases to challenge the Seventh Fleet's forward facilities at Guam, Subic Bay and Diego Garcia. In addition to the traditional Soviet home ports in Vladivostok and Petropavlovsk, Soviet vessels were routinely operating from the Dahlak Archipelago, an Ethiopian island group in the Red Sea. Two years ago, the South China Sea was virtually an American lake. By mid-1980 there were between 20 and 25 Soviet surface combat ships and two submarines permanently on station within the narrow confines of the sea, operating out of the former U.S. naval bases in Vietnam at Cam Ranh Bay and Da Nang, as well as from Ho Chi Minh city and Haiphong.

AS OTHERS SEE THE INDIAN OCEAN

"The extension of Soviet political influence that has taken place in the last decade represents the cutting edge of Sovereign policy backed by rapidly increasing military power of the Soviet Union itself, and the massive military aid extended to revolutionary, anti-Western forces in what has aptly been termed the 'arc of crisis'. This crisis area extends from South-East Asia to the Persian Gulf to the Horn of Africa to Southern Africa."

Senator Gordon J. Humphrey of the United States

"I think the Soviets are clearly striving for a force in the Pacific and Indian areas that will put themselves in a posture that should they, for whatever reason, choose to challenge the United States, they intend to be able to challenge and win."

Admiral Maurice Weisner, Commander U.S. Pacific Forces.

"We are beginning to see emerging from Soviet shipyards a deep water navy, designed for sea control rather than sea denial. It has sophisticated logistical support and increasing access to overseas bases. It poses a substantial and credible open-ocean surface threat to the trade routes not only in the North Atlantic but also in the other oceans of the world. Just imagine what one or two of these battle groups could do or threaten to do to our oil supplies if they were at large off the Cape of Good Hope."

Vice-Admiral Sir David Loram, British Deputy Supreme Allied Commander, Atlantic.

CHAPTER
15

India

India is bounded by a thrusting Russia and Soviet occupied Afghanistan, Sino-Soviet tension and a shaky and threatened Pakistan.

India's seventh General Election in January decisively brought to an end what had been called the country's period of chaos. With her two-thirds majority in the Lok Sabah, Mrs. Indira Gandhi will now be able to steamroller through any Bill she likes. Her re-entry upon the world stage at this delicate moment, however, is received with much less certainty, especially in Washington, London and Peking.

Mrs. Gandhi's previous inclination towards Moscow and her friendly relationship with Russian leaders following the border conflict with the Chinese threatens to tilt the Asian balance of power at a moment when India's role could be crucial.

For all its faults, the defeated Janata Party was just beginning to depart from the standard pro-Soviet stance which for two decades India had insisted was a policy of non-alignment. Friendship with neighbours, including China and Pakistan, were unthinkable under former governments. A move was afoot before the election to call for talks with Pakistan over the question of the Russians on their doorstep.

Mrs. Gandhi's reply to questions on the subject reflected her old preferences. She did not approve of the invasion of Afghanistan, she said, "since one presence invites another". The implication was clear. In favour of the election result is that India will get firm government at a time when the whole region is in a state of turbulence. Against it is Mrs. Gandhi's well-attested leanings towards Moscow which may have bad results so far as relations with Pakistan are concerned. She is likely to be far less accommodating towards Pakistan's military rulers than her predecessors.

After spending so many years in India, and having visited the country on four fairly recent occasions, the pro-Soviet tenor of Mrs. Gandhi's first foreign policy directive came as no surprise to the author of this book.

The directive said that India had no reason to doubt an assurance given by a friendly country like the Soviet Union that it would withdraw its troops from Afghanistan when the Afghan Government wants. The statement went on to criticize the United States, emphasizing that the Soviet action could not be viewed in isolation.

Of particular interest was India's expressed belief that it was Afghanistan's then President, Hafizullah Amin, who invited the Russians into the country on 26th December, 1979. When questioned on this Mrs. Gandhi said she had received information to this effect from a friend.

A few days later after saying that India did not support foreign intervention wherever it occurred, Mrs. Gandi added: "But in the case of Afghanistan the revolutionary council of that country invited the Russians to go in." This was also the hard line adopted by the Indian representatives at the United Nations, who gave an outspoken and unqualified endorsement of the Soviet case.

In various speeches Mrs. Gandhi indicated that the danger to India came from the offer by the United States to rearm Pakistan. Arms for Pakistan, said India's Foreign Minister, would be used against India and not for defence of Pakistan's Western border. Furthermore, there was the danger of an alliance between Pakistan, America and China which would leave India feeling themselves threatened,

India was totally opposed to the strong line adopted by the West in protest against the Soviet action, their argument being that warlike noises from the West would force the Russians into new adventures. Do nothing and the Russians will go away, was the Indian posture. Do something to show the Russians they can go no further, was the West's response.

India's Foreign Secretary, Mr. R. D. Sathe, began two days of talks with his Pakistan counterpart, Mr. Shah Nawaz, in Islamabad. He did so after America had pledged to back Pakistan against Soviet aggression and to build-up its military strength.

What worried the Indians was not President Carter's reaffirmation of the 1959 agreement between American and Pakistan, which covers Soviet or Soviet-controlled aggression, but the prospect of modernized armed forces on their north-west frontier.

They accepted that assurances concerning the use of these weapons were sincerely meant now, but in the past, assurances had proved to have no value.

Historically, their memories caused deep concern about any arms. They remembered 1954, when they were given similar assurances by the Americans. They said, whoever heard of a gun that can fire only in one direction?

Relations between India and Pakistan had been fairly even, if not warm, since they were restored in 1976 and it was decided to exchange Foreign Minister level visits once or twice a year. Mr. Sathe's visit to Islamabad returned Mr. Nawaz's trip to New Delhi of May 1979.

But the events in Afghanistan, and especially the American "knee jerk" reaction to them, as it was seen by India, had again altered the climate, while Pakistan's repeated denials that it was engaged in nuclear research for military purposes were disbelieved by the Indians.

Pakistan was so fired with new Islamic zeal that there seemed little chance yet of pursuing a subcontinental approach to possible outside aggression, as India would like. General Zia ul-Haq, Pakistan's military ruler, with the world spotlight on him, appeared to be playing his country's vulnerability, and the Afghan refugee problem for all he was worth.

India maintained that the Russian intervention in Afghanistan had been a god-send to General Zia, whose position before the December *coup* in Kabul, was, at the least, uncertain. For a military leader nothing could be better than a chance to acquire new weapons and aircraft for his armed forces and the promise of outside help if the Red Army started to head for the warm Arabian sea.

In February 1980, Mr. Gromyko, Soviet Foreign Minister, failed to win full Indian backing for his country's intervention in Afghanistan, they agreed to disagree on the question of possible Russian troop withdrawals from Afghanistan. Mr. Gromyko had to leave New Delhi after what amounted to drawing a diplomatic blank. India was at pains to say: "No door is closed, and that is a positive development." But there appeared to be no disguising the fact that despite Mrs. Gandhi's early statement on Afghanistan, there were now basic differences of approach to the problem.

At the talks, the Indians reiterated their broad view that there should be no interference in the internal affairs of other countries, and that frontiers should remain inviolable. The overwhelming point of dispute was India's opposition to the presence of foreign troops in another country. A joint communique, issued as Mr. Gromyko left, significantly made no mention of the troop withdrawal issue – another pointer to the fact that there was grave disagreement.

After the talks, however, India appeared anxious to discount any suggestion of a split between the two countries. "There may be differences of opinion and interim perceptions but the ultimate objectives are the same."

At the same time, India sounded a note of warning that international developments were further complicating the crisis over the Russian invasion. They referred to a "massive" build-up of American strength in the Indian Ocean area, especially on the island of Diego Garcia, as well as the agreement of Kenya, Somalia and Oman to allow Washington operational facilities.

They also referred to reports that some countries were training Moslem guerrillas opposed to the Afghan régime and said all these factors, in the Indian view, contributed to a worsening of the situation.

Dr. Kissinger called on President Carter to adopt "a Churchillian posture" to impress on America and the West the gravity of the situation in Afghanistan, Iran and other countries in the "arc of crisis". He felt it extremely unlikely that the Soviet Union would attack Pakistan over the opposition of India. "The real threat will therefore develop if the Soviet Union and India co-operate.

"The greatest danger is that India may seek, with Soviet co-operation, to dismember its neighbour by splitting off Baluchistan and the North West Frontier Province, and occupying Kashmir. Both India and the Soviet Union would then be surrounded by weak salient states. A serious policy must deal with that contingency.

"Since I do not see how we can build-up Pakistan rapidly enough to protect itself against these dangers, I have thought it desirable that for an interim period, American air forces be stationed there", Kissinger stated.

On 3rd March 1980, Mr. Ramehandra Daltatrya Sathe, India's Foreign Secretary, said India was convinced that the Soviet Union had no interest in threatening Pakistan's security. But, he added: "We can understand Pakistan's concern."

While it was natural that Pakistan should take steps to improve its defences, India was worried that piling up of arms would increase the danger of a superpower confrontation in the area.

Mr. Sathe, who led the Indian mission to Pakistan in February, 1980, said that if Pakistan felt threatened on its north-west frontier it had the option of moving troops from the India frontier. And—"I told General Zia when I was there that he had nothing to fear from India."

Asked what India had to fear from Pakistan's rearmament, the Foreign Secretary was at pains to point out that any undue accretion of strength to Pakistan would alter the present balance of forces. "Pakistan had about 19 divisions to India's 29 and 580,000 armed forces compared with India's total 850,000."

India's coastline was vulnerable and had to be protected, while it also faced 100,000 Chinese troops in Tibet. "Our ratio is not so heavily tilted that we endanger Pakistan's security," he remarked.

It was suggested to Mr. Sathe that Pakistan might feel reassured and thus possibly scale down rearmament if India were to declare that the protection of the integrity of its neighbour was a national interest.

Mr. Sathe agreed that India was concerned that Pakistan's integrity be preserved but had made no public declaration to this effect because such a general statement might be construed as a change in India's position on the Kashmir issue.

The Foreign Secretary said there had been no discussion with Pakistan on an arms limitation agreement, nor had it been proposed during his visit. He saw arms limitation as only a partial remedy to the problems between the two countries. The actual solution was in India's view, "a no-war pact which we have repeatedly offered Pakistan." It had not been accepted because Pakistan felt, or had been conditioned to feel, that such a pact was against its national interest.

India's policy after the "Russian incursion" was an evolving one,

Delhi had been taken by surprise, as had everyone else, by the assassination of Amin and the Russian response.

"When the Soviet ambassador informed me of their action, I expressed our anxiety at the possible repercussions. We experienced further anxiety at the reaction of the United States, which could have brought the cold war to our doorstep", Mr. Sathe stated.

Mrs. Indira Gandhi, the Indian Prime Minister, had, the previous day commented that it might be said that the Russians had been forced to intervene. Mr. Sathe was asked whether the Indian Government believed the Russian action was justified. He was not prepared to offer an opinion on the question of justification but commented: "They are there and that is the situation we have to deal with".

India has made it abundantly clear that it wished the Russian troops to be withdrawn but had not condemned the Soviet action "because we believe that condemnation is less likely to bring about a positive result than persuasion". Mr. Sathe added that India was encouraged that President Giscard d'Estaing and Herr Schmidt, the West German Chancellor, seemed to have adopted a similar approach.

Further support for Mrs. Gandhi's policy was expressed by Mr. S. N. Mishra, the Former External Affairs Minister. He said there was no significant opposition within India to the Government's reaction to the Russian intervention in Afghanistan.

Mrs. Gandhi – as Prime Minister of the largest non-aligned country in the world – made it clear that she believed the United States was at least as much to blame for the tensions surrounding Afghanistan as was the Soviet Union. She also strongly criticized the "spectacular" growth of the American presence in the Indian Ocean and added "we do not want any foreign influence in this region".

Western governments, she said had reacted excessively to the crisis "doubtless due to the influence of big business such as arms, shipbuilding and steel." The United States had in fact taken advantage of the situation to take "disproportionate measures". "It was important to realize that one of the reasons for the crisis was the *Rapprochement* between China and the United States against the Soviet Union which feels itself encircled."

She said that the Iranian example was enough to show the Americans that helping Pakistan might have consequences opposite to those it was seeking. "We do not want to enter into an anti-communist community with Pakistan, but we want to improve relations with it. It is very dangerous and it is not, in fact, in the interests of India, to have weak neighbours threatened with disintegration."

Mrs. Gandhi discounted the idea of an international force to control Afghanistan, basing this on the "fairly bad memory" India had of the United Nations force controlling Kashmir after independence in 1947. But whatever Mrs. Gandhi or her Ministers may say to the contrary, the fact remains that India has turned once more to Russia for the modernization of her huge military preponderance over Pakistan.

The relationship between India and Pakistan is certainly one of asymmetry in which Indian military power greatly exceeds that of Pakistan. Therefore, Pakistan has to be very careful to maintain her national security at a time when the Soviet threat from Afghanistan further aggravates the situation.

If Pakistan should drop her guard then the temptation for an adjacent country – India or the Soviet Union from Afghanistan, or both – to seize an advantage would be all the greater. Wars do not break out when neighbouring countries are each fairly strong. The lesson of the invasion of East Pakistan in 1971 by overwhelming Indian forces will not be forgotten in a hurry.

It is obvious that today Pakistan by itself cannot be said to represent a serious strategic threat to India. But Pakistan supported by a major outside power, such as China, might represent such a threat – particularly at the time of the year when the fourteen Himalayan passes are open. Indeed, China by itself is still a challenge to India, which bitterly remembers 1962, which was for them what Pearl Harbour was for the United States.

India perceives itself emerging as a great power. Therefore, a State that large and of that magnitude considers it essential to adopt a posture of basic preparedness against any possible and unknown contingency.

The large size of the army, 29 divisions and 45 squadrons of Air Force (660 combat aircraft) is big enough, India believes, to handle a joint Pakistan-China conflict. It is an army and air force designed to fight a two-front war with many Indian mountain divisions deployed up in the Himalayas facing China on a 1,500-mile common frontier.

The Soviet Union would like to see India invade Pakistan, in the hope that it could obtain overland transit arrangements and exclusive facilities at Karachi. But while India has not forgotten the Chinese invasion of 1962, why does she possess as many as 30,000 tanks! They cannot be used in the Himalayas, but rather in a fast moving action such as in Sind, which leads direct to Karachi and the adjacent Port complex. The terrain is eminently suitable for the use not only of tanks but also of armoured personnel carriers and self-propelled guns – all of which India possesses in abundance.

The Ratio of forces in favour of India is approximately:

Navy ....12 to 1
Army ....4 to 1
Air Force..................................6 to 1

Of course, the tragedy is that India and Pakistan seem unable to reconcile their differences sufficiently to enter into a mutual defensive pact which could be expanded to include all those other countries in South Asia now vulnerable to Soviet expansion.

As I pointed out in an earlier Chapter, events in Afghanistan should have brought home to India that it is now greatly in their interests to have a friendly Pakistan. With vision and imagination and diplomatic skill Britain should give the lead in bringing this about. The return of Pakistan to the Commonwealth would facilitate its achievement. From this would flow logistical, military and economic aid from the friends of both India and Pakistan without creating suspicion and fear on the part of India.

Yugoslavia

With the death of President Tito, Yugoslavia has now become another hot-spot on the map. Although well within the reach of Russian armed power, Tito, who was a Moscow-trained Communist, broke with Stalin in 1948, thumbed his nose at Moscow and pursued a policy of non-alignment and independence from Russia.

It was only Tito, with his immense command of Yugoslav loyalties and his known determination to fight back if attacked, who had deterred Russia for more than 30 years. Yugoslavia is a precarious and volatile nation and it was Tito who not only put the present federation together but held it together and made it work, after his own fashion.

As a communist state, Yugoslavia is — in Soviet language — "a conquest of socialism", even if from Moscow's point of view, an unorthodox and awkward one. According to the Brezhnev doctrine the Soviet Union therefore has the right and the duty to save it from itself, by military action if necessary, should it show signs of back sliding into the clutches of capitalism.

Because Yugoslavia is explicitly covered by the Brezhnev doctrine, any form of disintegration, and particularly any abandonment of Communism, would make it very difficult for the Russians to keep their hands off the country.

The Brezhnev doctrine was evolved at the time of the Russian invasion of Czechoslovakia in 1968, and lays down that:

"When internal and external forces hostile to Socialism attempt to turn the developments of any Socialist country in the direction of the restoration of the capitalist system, when a threat arises to the cause of Socialism in that country, a threat to the security of the Socialist Commonwealth as a whole — it already becomes not only a problem for the people of that country but also a general problem, the concern of all Socialist countries."

The Russian invasion of Afghanistan is an unpleasant precedent. It has already provoked firm Yugoslav reactions. A senior official said that the Soviet Union's credibility was seriously damaged. It had confirmed the Yugoslavs in the belief that Russia had never really given up hope of

Yugoslavia's population problem.
Appreciation to *NOW!* Magazine, 25th–31st January, 1980.

tying Yugoslavia to the Soviet Bloc. This had been proved in the past and the message had been driven home that this was still the case.

The anniversary of the death of Mr. Edvard Kardeli, architect of the Yugoslav political system, who died last year and whose memoirs were recently published, provided the opportunity for emphasizing this awareness. A senior Yugoslav official speaking at the ceremony, condemned the continuing practice of "forcing socialism upon other peoples" through "fraternal aid" or by military intervention such as "we are now witnessing in Afghanistan".

In his memoirs Mr. Kardeli, whom the Russians never trusted, recalled that in spite of formal agreements and the Russians' pledges to respect Yugoslavia's independence, he was convinced that they never gave up hope of drawing the country into the Soviet Bloc. He described the pressure to which the Russians had submitted him on several occasions from 1948 onwards, under Stalin, and then under Khruschev.

Another senior Yugoslav official, Dr. Vladimir Bakaric, recalling a visit to Moscow in 1948, on the eve of the break in relations between the two countries, quoted Marshal Tito as saying: "The Russians will bully you if you let them".

Russia has never given up hopes of regaining control over Yugoslavia. There is the danger that the Hungarian minority living in Yugoslavia but near the border with Hungary will request "protection" from Belgrade. In the south the Bulgarians will have no difficulty in stirring up trouble along the Macedonians, who in turn will demand protection from Sofia.

Tito's successors are going to find it difficult, if not impossible, to hold together the rich Slovenes and Croats in the north with the relatively poor Bosnians and Macedonians of the south. The Soviet Union's chance to interfere, indeed to be invited by proxy to invade, will thus not be delayed indefinitely.

Yugoslavia's battered economy was sliding into chaos. The country was facing a grave economic situation as a result of the overheated economy and the world energy crisis. Inflation was up to 30 per cent, unemployment to 15 per cent of the total labour force, the balance of payments deficit had risen to close on $6.5 million (about £3 million) and the country's debts with foreign banks totalled $13 million.

The Yugoslavs asserted that the EEC's failure to give better opportunities to Yugoslavia exports had inflicted serious damage on the country. As a result over 50 per cent of Yugoslav trade was with the Comecon (Eastern Bloc) countries.

This was something the Yugoslavians had for years been anxious to avoid but they said they had no choice because the EEC negotiations kept dragging on. The Russians could use economic pressure to hurt Yugoslavia.

Yugoslavia has never forgotten the weak and short-lived Western response to Soviet aggression in 1956 and in Czechoslovakia in 1968. There is, furthermore, the unfortunate matter of President Carter's remarks about Yugoslavia during the 1976 elections.

He was asked about his ideas on the subject during a televised debate with President Ford and his reply was clearly carefully considered. The full quotation is as follows:

Question: "The next big crisis spot in the world may be Yugoslavia. President Tito is old and sick, and there are divisions in his country. It is pretty certain the Russians are going to do everything they possibly can after Tito dies to force Yugoslavia back into the Soviet camp. But on Saturday, you said, and this is a quote: 'I would not go to war in Yugoslavia even if the Soviet Union sent in troops'.

"Doesn't that statement practically invite the Russians to intervene in Yugoslavia?"

Mr. Carter replied: "Over the last two weeks, I've had a chance to talk to two men who have visited the Soviet Union, Yugoslavia and China. One is Governor Averell Harriman and the other one is James Schlesinger.

"Mr. Harriman talked to the leaders in Yugoslavia, and I think it is accurate to say that there is no prospect, in their opinion, of the Soviet Union invading Yugoslavia should Mr. Tito pass away. The present leadership there is fairly uniform in their purpose, and I think it's a close-knit group, and I think it would be unwise for us to say that we will go to

173

war in Yugoslavia if the Soviets should invade, which I think would be an extremely unlikely thing.

"I have maintained from the very beginning of my campaign, and this was a standard answer that I made in response to the Yugoslavian question, that I would never go to war, become militarily involved, in the internal affairs of another country unless our own security was directly threatened. And I don't believe that our security would be directly threatened if the Soviet Union went into Yugoslavia I don't believe it will happen. I certainly hope it won't.

"I would take the strongest possible measures, short of actual military action there by our own troops, but I doubt that that would be an eventuality."

This statement has been of considerable embarrassment to senior officials ever since. It has never been disavowed, the way President Carter's promise "never" to impose an embargo on the export of grain has been disavowed.

We know from Major-General Cejna, the top-level defector from the Czech Army, that the Soviet General Staff has long since drawn up a plan for a full-scale invasion of Yugoslavia. The operation, code-named "Polarka" envizages a two-pronged armoured thrust via eastern Austria as well as southern Hungary.

Shortly before Tito's death there had been strains because of Tito's relations with China and because of what Yugoslavia had seen as a persistent attempt by Russia, using Cuba, to subvert the non-aligned movement. The Soviet invasion of Afghanistan increased the strains.

The Yugoslavs also suspected that from time to time the Russians stirred up the Bulgarians, Moscow's closest allies in Eastern Europe, to raise the question of sovereignity over Macedonia.

In the latter half of January 1980, the anti-Russian stance of the Albanian Communist leader, Enver Hoxha, had provided a measure of encouragement to the West. Indeed, his emphatic promise that Albania would fight alongside the Yugoslavs "as in the past" made Moscow's objectives in reaching a warmwater port in the Mediterranean far more difficult.

His statement also ended the uncertainty about Albania's political stance since he broke his close ties with China following the death of Chairman Mao.

His country had survived economically since its breach largely because it produces more than a million tons of oil annually. Its $2\frac{1}{2}$ million population are austere in their habits and a limited amount of foreign currency entered the country through strictly controlled tourism.

To have Russian sailors occupying Yugoslav naval bases on the Adriatic Sea at Split, Sibenik or the Gulf of Cattara would make it extremely difficult for the Atlantic Alliance to maintain its objectives in defending Greece and Turkey. For in addition to the Mediterranean ports, Yugoslavia has splendid air bases near Belgrade, Zagreb, Ljubljana, Mis and Skopje. Also Yugoslavia as a Soviet Satellite would render Italy more vulnerable to both internal and external Communist pressure.

Further, a Russian takeover of Yugoslavia would spell the end of independence for Albania, which controls the entrance to the Adriatic Sea with Italy and possesses the best natural harbour, Durozzo, in the Mediterranean.

Before deciding whether a Soviet invasion of Yugoslavia – either now or in the future – is on the cards, there are several factors to be considered.

How reliable is Hungary, without whose occupation the Red Army's invasion high road into the flat plains of the Voyvodina would be that much more difficult? There are now two Russian tank and two motorized rifle divisions in Hungary, two tank divisions in Poland and five divisions, including two tank divisions, in Czechoslovakia.

The tanks in Hungary are deployed in readiness for a dash down the Sava or Danube valleys to take over Zagreb and Belgrade. How much fight – as opposed to fire and brimstone – would the Rumanians put up under the Communist dissident, President Ceausescu?

Hoxha's move will certainly encourage President Ceausescu of Rumania to continue his resistance to Russian demands. He has been under heavy pressure from Moscow during the past few weeks as a member of the Warsaw Pact, to allow Russian troops to be stationed on his soil and to abrogate his mutual assistance treaty with Yugoslavia.

Indeed, thanks to the stance of Albania and Rumania's refusal to allow Russian troops to cross the disputed area of the Danube delta into Bulgaria, Moscow will be forced to proceed far more slowly in any action against Yugoslavia.

Rumania went on record as the only member of the Soviet Bloc to criticize publicly Russian intervention in Afghanistan. President Ceausescu followed up by putting the army on alert claiming that if need be, Rumania would rise "as one man to safeguard her independence and revolutionary gains."

Rumania is in a particularly vulnerable position, being formally a member of the Warsaw Pact, but not allowing passage to Soviet troops or manoeuvres on its soil. Since the Soviet invasion of Afghanistan, Mr. Ceausescu had taken military measures which Moscow obviously regarded as an affront. He had strengthened Rumania's territorial army and intensified military training of youth.

The Russians would have to move across nearly 400 miles of Rumania and Hungary and although the Hungarians would probably do as told, the Rumanians might not. Moreover the Soviet Army would have "a hell of a fight" on its hands. Yugoslavia has the third strongest army in Europe. It is well-equipped and could retire to the mountains from where its forces defied the Nazis in the Second World War.

All three Services of the Yugoslav armed forces are well trained and well equipped – though their weapons are neither modern nor standardized – and are intended exclusively for total national defence. The regular army is a first-class fighting force of more than a quarter of a million men, 130,000 of whom are conscripts. The 500,000 reservists are ready to join their units at anything from eight to 24 hours' notice. In addition, there is a territorial army of a further three million men, whose principal role is to wage a prolonged guerrilla war in the mountains where their fathers and grandfathers fought so gallantly and successfully under Tito against the Germans in World War Two. Furthermore, every citizen, irrespective of sex or age, is ready to resist attacks in one form or another. Therefore, if the Soviet Army were to invade in great strength, and with widespread paratroop drops, and succeed in seizing the main cities and towns they would be confronted by the whole population of the country, renowned for its expertise in waging guerrilla warfare. There would be no front in the accepted sense. The Soviet forces would find their land lines of communication completely cut.

There is a 16,000 strong trip wire border force of three armoured divisions, deployed at Sisak to the south-west of Zagreb, the capital of Croatia; at Kragnjevac in Serbia to the south of Belgrade; and at Skopje in Macedonia.

The task of the first two of these divisions would be to oppose the Russians invading the country through the good low-lying tank country in the Sava and Danube valleys from Hungary. The task of the third division at Skopje is to guard the Vardar Valley.

Of course successful resistance will depend on whether the three million Albanians in the south are able to maintain their independent stand. The Yugoslav navy is merely a coastal defence force, while the Air Force has 332 combat aircraft most of which are of old vintage.

There are wide differences of opinion on the combat effectiveness of the Yugoslav forces to deal with the massive and ruthless might of the Soviet war machine. But the lessons of Afghanistan will not have been lost on either Russia or Yugoslavia. The main problems are that the Yugoslav armed forces have not heard a shot fired in anger since 1946 and that much of their outdated weapons and equipment are a mixture of American and Russian-produced tanks, guns and small arms which, of course, require different types of ammunition and small arms. Then there are the internal dissensions with the minority of Slovenes, Dalmations, Macedonians, Albanians and Croats showing their exasperation from time to time against the dominant Serbs.

Yugoslavia is well alert to the threat of subversion and maintains an extremely efficient security system which keeps an eagle eye on subversive and terrorist elements in the country.

Having weighed up the pros and cons, the big question mark is, therefore, could Tito's death set off World War Three? The answer is probably not and certainly, not yet. World reaction to Russia's seizure of Afghanistan was almost universal and sufficiently pronounced and firm to deter Moscow from an invasion of Yugoslavia for the time being. But a great deal of activity will be required by the West.

The Kremlin's best policy now would be to let Yugoslavia weaken itself first. Moscow sees as its opportunity the succession system devised of a rotating leadership shared by men from Yugoslavia's six constituent republics. If the leader is a civilian or a general whom the Kremlin can get at — or has got at already — the Red Army's work will have been done for it.

Even more enfeebling for post-Tito Yugoslavia is its parlous (and worsening) economic situation. This could easily revive the country's ancient racial rivalries by widening further the gap between the rich north and the struggling south. Prosperous Slovenia already feels, culturally and psychologically, closer to Vienna (to which, for centuries, it belonged) than to Belgrade. Westernized Catholic, tolerant and entrepreneurial, this is a different world from a sister republic like Macedonia. These are the cracks in the Yugoslav stonework Moscow will seek patiently to widen before calling in any military steamroller.

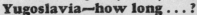

Yugoslavia—how long . . . ?

Appreciation to Garland and
The Daily Telegraph, 6th May, 1980.

On the whole those observers who know Yugoslavia best are the least anxious and the most confident that unity will prevail, for the simple reason that almost all Yugoslavs know that in unity lies their only hope for survival.

The elaborate rotating system of leadership devised by Tito may not last, they concede, but the essence of a federation based on equality and a communism tempered by non-alignment without, and relative

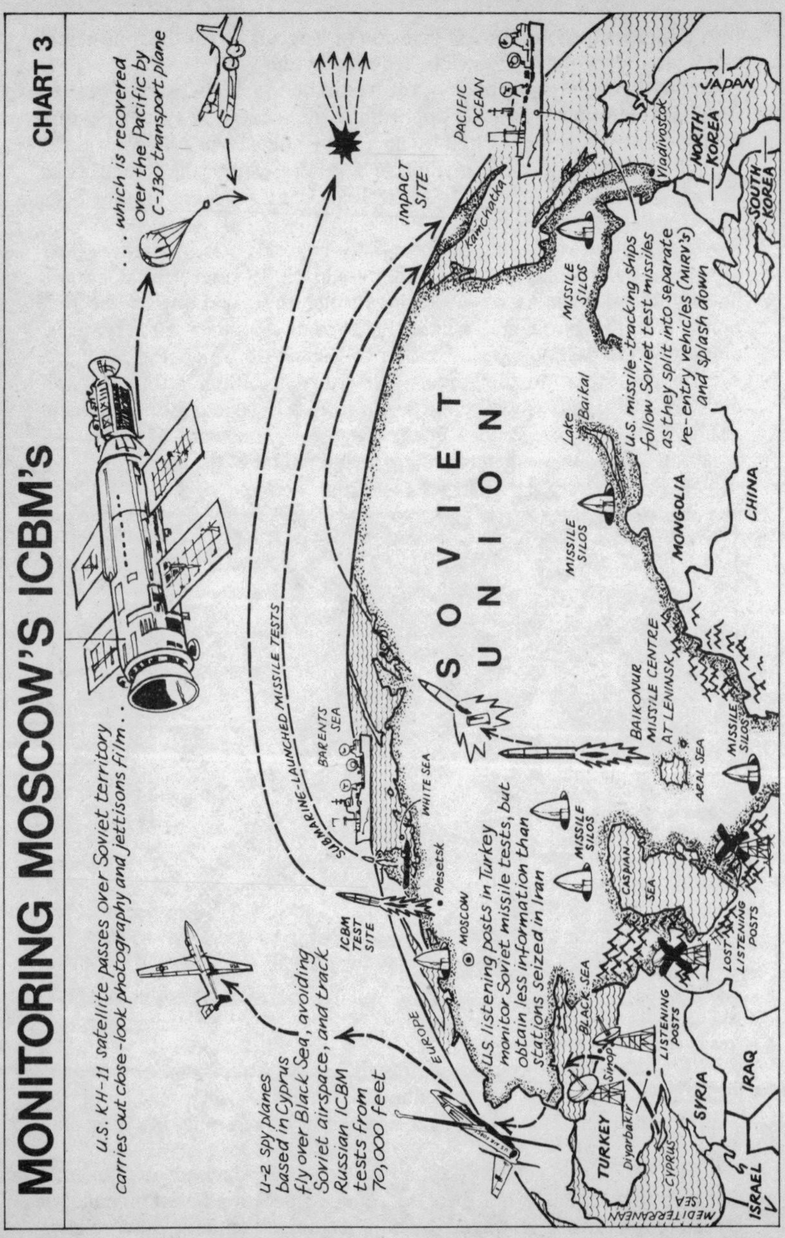
MONITORING MOSCOW'S ICBM's
CHART 3
U.S. KH-11 satellite passes over Soviet territory carries out close-look photography and jettisons film . . .
. . . which is recovered over the Pacific by C-130 transport plane
U-2 spy planes based in Cyprus fly over Black Sea, avoiding Soviet airspace, and track Russian ICBM tests from 70,000 feet
ICBM TEST SITE
SUBMARINE-LAUNCHED MISSILE TESTS
BARENTS SEA
WHITE SEA
IMPACT SITE
PACIFIC OCEAN
Kamchatka
EUROPE
MOSCOW
Plesetsk
SOVIET UNION
U.S. listening posts in Turkey monitor Soviet missile tests, but obtain less information than stations seized in Iran
MISSILE SILOS
MISSILE SILOS
MISSILE SILOS
MISSILE SILOS
BAIKONUR MISSILE CENTRE AT LENINSK
ARAL SEA
Lake Baikal
U.S. missile-tracking ships follow Soviet test missiles as they split into separate re-entry vehicles (MIRV's) and splash down
Vladivostok
NORTH KOREA
SOUTH KOREA
JAPAN
MONGOLIA
CHINA
BLACK SEA
CASPIAN SEA
LISTENING POSTS
LOST LISTENING POSTS
Sinop
Diyarbakir
TURKEY
CYPRUS
MEDITERRANEAN SEA
SYRIA
IRAQ
ISRAEL

Appreciation to Newsweek

freedom within now reposes on a consensus too strong to crack, This school of thought is adamant that nothing would solder any cracks more rapidly than a clumsy or premature Soviet attempt to exploit them.

We have to hope that that is right, and be careful to do nothing to make it wrong. It should be absolutely clear that the West respects and values Yugoslavia's non-alignment, and harbours not the slightest fantasy of reclaiming her for capitalism or enticing her into an alliance.

On that basis it can and should be equally clear that any interference with Yugoslavia's non-alignment or her political system from the Soviet side, and any military incursion into her territory on the pretext of whatever real or alleged "invitation" would affect the whole security and balance of Europe in a way that the West could not possibly accept.

Therefore, the West must maintain the utmost vigilance. NATO must prepare contingency plans for action if Yugoslavia's independence is threatened by Russia. Moscow must be put on notice now that an Afghanistan or Czechoslovakia type of intervention against Yugoslavia would be regarded as reason for placing the Western alliance on a war footing, and would also involve stringent economic retribution. It is absolutely essential to warn Russia of our intentions *in advance*, and not to keep them guessing. It is most important that we should implement this vital facet of deterrence now.

To conclude: What is China's appreciation of the likelihood of Yugoslavia or Rumania being the one of the wobbling 'dominoes' to fall?

The occupation of Afghanistan was particularly ominous for China, since it coincided with the ill health of President Tito, one of Peking's staunchest friends in East Europe. The Chinese appreciation is that if Moscow should attempt to subvert or control Yugoslavia now, after President Tito's death, Rumania would be the next target.

Combined with the possible subjugation of Albania – the former ally of China, but now an outspoken critic of Chinese policy – such a strategy on the part of the Soviet Union would mean complete Russian control of the Balkans as far as the Greek frontier.

The Chinese view is that if the Western response to the Russian invasion of Afghanistan proves to be as weak and short-lived as it was to Soviet aggression in Hungary in 1956 and in Czechoslovakia in 1968, then the Soviet Union is not going to be deterred from meddling in Yugoslavia. But they cannot afford a second Afghanistan – *yet*.

China

The West has not found it easy to establish relations with Communist China. During the eight years since President Nixon's pilgrimage to Peking and the sprouting of Chinese diplomatic missions all over the world, an unconscious fear lurked just beneath the surface that we might be falling into the trap of over-eagerness to grasp the hand of friendship. In a little over twenty years from the birth of Communist China on 1st October, 1949, that hand proved to be blood-stained and treacherous – which in the past has been exceeded only by the Soviet clinical terror.

In the event, the most conspicuous effect of Mr. Nixon's overtures to China was on the mind of the Russians. The possibility of a hostile combination against them caused the Kremlin to hasten its *rapprochement* with Washington. That decision was reinforced by the Russians' internal need to set "limits" to their defence expenditure and to *enlist the help of Western industrial technology*.

If indeed the West has fallen into a trap, it is surely to be evidenced in the technological transfusions, that the West has given *the Soviets* since 1972; not to mention what took place in the years before, reaching back to the early days of the revolution in Russia.

China has now abandoned the doctrinaire communist methods which produced the disastrous harvests of 1959-61. Today, an extra 100 million have been absorbed into agriculture and the world's most populous nation stands on the verge of major development.

The full effects of this change upon the communist system in China, cannot be entirely predicted. What *is* certain, however, is that the world – and Soviet Russia in particular – cannot afford to ignore China's long march to full employment.

Meeting with the Counsellor

It was on 12th February, 1976, that I first met Mr. Ting Wen-pin, Counsellor at the Embassy of the People's Republic of China. I had only recently been persuaded to enter the Newsletter field, with the aim of trying to warn the West of the rapidly growing menace of Russia's military might and her long and short term intentions. My Newsletter was called *International Summary*. The first two issues were published in January 1976, and I continued to publish two each month until the end of that year.

Mr. Ting Wen-pin was a double subscriber. My theme was, and still is, that the 1930s were now being repeated in the 1970s, but this time with Russia supplanting Germany as the main threat. The jackboot is still there, so is the goose-step – as I have said before in this book – 'Forwarned is forearmed'. The cover illustration of my Newsletter was designed to depict this, serving as a warning to imbalance over détente.

My meeting on 12th February, 1976, with Mr. Ting Wen-pin and his highly intelligent wife – who acted as his interpreter – was at his official residence in London at 11, Heath Row Avenue. Since that date there has been constant contact between us and I have continued to receive from the Chief London Correspondent of the New China News Agency their weekly News Bulletin and other literature.

On the 24th March, 1976, I dined with Mr. and Mrs. Ting Wen-pin when we discussed the threat from the Soviet Union and the importance of meeting it with a much stronger and more resolute NATO.

On the 8th June, 1977, my wife and I had lunch with the Counsellor and his wife at their residence, and on the 24th August they lunched with us at our home. On both these occasions we continued to discuss the Soviet Union's nuclear and conventional warfare capabilities and the apathy and weaknesses of NATO to meet the threat – *let alone deter it!*

On the 17th April, 1978, we again had lunch with the Counsellor and his wife. The points I made to the Counsellor were:

* America appeared to be blind to the fact that Africa was a theatre of power from which Russia intended to move the world in her direction.
* The stupidity of the United Nations in imposing an arms embargo on South Africa when it should be patently obvious that the arms and weapons that she required were submarines, surface warships and maritime aircraft to meet the Russian challenge at sea – the Cape Route. Such weaponry, I emphasized, could not possibly be used internally or for aggression by South Africa.
* Why did we not believe Admiral Gorshkov, creator of the vastly expanding Russian navy, and its chief for 23 years, when he said: "The Russian fleet can flag down and cripple the flow of *oil* and other strategic materials to the U.S.A. and Western Europe"?
* President Carter appeared to be virtually wallowing in the worst quagmires of national and international politics, and the danger was that he would drown before his term of office was up. He certainly looked like being a one term President.

* The U.S. eagle had lost its feathers in Vietnam, its beak in Helsinki, and its claws in Angola and the Horn of Africa. Next it would lose its sight, hearing and voice.

In September 1978, the Counsellor, in thanking me for sending him a copy of my book – *The Bear at the Back Door* – remarked: "The title is most appropriate."

Owing to a clash of dates it was not possible to accept further invitations from the Counsellor. In February 1979, he sent me a copy of the statement authorized for release by the Chinese Government consequent upon the invasion of Vietnam by China.

In my reply I made the following five points:

* In teaching the Vietnamese a lesson of chastisement for their intolerable provocations into the Chinese border area – as well as for invading Cambodia – China has taught the world that she is a growing superpower with a tenacious will of her own and has no intention of emulating the West's style of "turn-the-other-cheek" diplomacy.
* Harsh and resolute measures were essential. It was refreshing to see for a change the absence of frivolous talk and the implementation of real punitive action.
* The timing was certainly well chosen, namely when the Vietnamese army must have been stretched very tight with such a strong force tied down in Cambodia.
* Unless the Vietnamese realize that they will be taught some sharp lessons, the role they will play for their Kremlin masters will make the activities of the Cuban hatchetmen look like child's play. For all practical purposes, Vietnam was now a member of the Warsaw Pact.
* Even the most hawkish of the Kremlin gang must realize that to unleash an offensive on China's 900 million people would make Napoleon's march on Moscow look like an afternoon picnic.

The Counsellor replied to this on 9th March, 1979, and thanked me for "supporting the Chinese Government's action of counter-attack in self-defence against Vietnam." He continued:

"As you will have read from the papers and our statement of 5th March, our troops have started to withdraw to our own territory after attaining the goals set for our action.

"You quite correctly stated in your letter that you felt sure the Soviet Union would not interfere on behalf of their Vietnamese 'allies'. Our Government did not expect them to either. However, we had felt that we should always be prepared for the worst, and that is why China did take the necessary precautions, just in case."

The view from Peking

China chose the New Year of 1976, the very period when the West had just been celebrating peace and goodwill, to issue a stern warning as to why and how the West should be facing the holocaust of World War III. This country of nearly 900 millions will exceed the combined populations of the U.S.A. and the U.S.S.R. by the turn of the century and, with its finger on the nuclear trigger, is destined to play a decisive role in the Great Power struggle.

It was in 1976 that the Chinese leadership warned that there would be a vicious upsurge in Russia's military spending, which already accounted for about 20 per cent of the national income and 35 per cent of State budgetary expenditure. They pointed out that this was far higher than the expenditure in Hitlerite Germany before World War II. The Chinese deplored Western softness in the face of the evident Russian aim of world domination ("hegemony") and stated outright that the real dangers of détente had not been realized by the U.S.A. They regarded President Ford and Dr. Henry Kissinger as being far too soft and said that was why the Russians were "raising the ante" with more and more crippling demands at every opportunity and every round of the SALT II negotiations.

In November 1979, when former Premier Hua Guofeng visited England, he made no bones about it. He said the threat to world peace came from Russia. "Peace", he announced, "cannot be avoided by yielding". This, in a nutshell, had been Communist China's attitude to the NATO countries for some time. China feels threatened by Russia from the north and therefore strongly supports opposition to Russian expansionism from the West, which means NATO.

But what contribution had China herself been making? Her refrain had been: Stand up to Russia, send us your technology, lend us money. What was she offering in return? Really nothing, except the implication that a strengthened China would help to take the heat off Russia's looming arms superiority. But there were practical measures that China could take which would be welcomed.

One was to stop refugees from swamping Hong Kong which had again become a very serious problem. On a much broader plane, in the long run the West needed some reassurance that China was not again going to be subject to violent twists and turns of internal policies such as were characterized by the Cultural Revolution.

When Russia swept into Afghanistan, China called it naked aggression and an open challenge to Asia and the international community as a whole. Moscow had shown the world, said China, its wild ambition and appetite for expansion aimed at controlling the Iranian Gulf and major sea routes. They described the claim that the Afghan authorities had asked Russia to intervene as a clumsy concoction. The official reaction was: "How could President Amin invite Soviet troops to overthrow and execute *himself*?" In claiming that it was helping Afghanistan "repel an external threat", the Chinese reaction was that Russia was like a thief crying "stop thief". The only external threat to Afghanistan came from Russia, the culpable party.

Russia has now unmasked itself, said China. "No longer can it pass itself off as an angel championing world peace, nor can it absolve itself from the crime of direct military intervention to overthrow a foreign government – for the first time in a Third World country."

In the Chapter, "Pakistan Pre-27th December, 1979," I explain why Peking's appreciation of the situation was that the invasion of Afghanistan concerned much more than just the control of Afghanistan itself. China remains the joker in the pack. Afghanistan's tiny Chinese frontier, only 60 miles long and around 18,000 feet high, hardly presents a real geo-political threat to Peking. But this would change if any Soviet attempt was made to push into Pakistan. Indeed, establishing a direct Chinese military presence south of the Khyber Pass may in the end prove the only effective deterrence of further Soviet advance. Meanwhile the Afghan tribesmen must be supplied with arms and ammunition, transported from China by the Karakoram highway and then through insurgent channels to Afghanistan. When the weather is suitable the direct route will be across the mountainous Afghan-Chinese border.

The principal response by the United States must take the form of strategic co-operation, namely closer security ties with, and aid to China. There must be some change in Washington's China arms embargo.

The Afghanistan crisis brought the American arms issue sharply into focus. There are many kinds of American defensive systems and monitoring equipment which could help China guard its 4,500-mile border with Russia. Progress was made during March when Mr. Cyrus Vance and other senior State Department officials began talks in Washington with Mr. Zhang Wenjin, the Deputy Foreign Minister of China, on ways of responding to the Soviet occupation of Afghanistan.

The 10-day visit by Mr. Zhang, was a logical follow-up to the January 1980 talks in Peking between Mr. Harold Brown, the Defence Secretary and Chinese leaders. Mr. Zhang is the most senior official from Peking to visit the United States since Mr. Deng Xiaoping, the former Deputy Prime Minister, went there just over a year ago.

The latest round of talks focussed on parallel steps that Washington and Peking could take to strengthen Pakistan and counter Soviet expansionism in South-West Asia. The Soviet Union reacted angrily to the visit claiming that the United States and China were doing all they could to hamper peace in Afghanistan.

As the talks opened in Washington, the State Department gave its final approval for American manufacturers to sell various kinds of military support equipment to China, including cargo aircraft, early warning radar systems, trucks and training equipment.

The Administration's original agreement to sell Peking certain "carefully selected items of support equipment also suitable for military use" was announced in January after Mr. Brown's visit to Peking.

The Russian invasion of Afghanistan also brought a windfall for Peking in Indo-China. Peking had already drawn a comparison between Russia's invasion of Afghanistan and Vietnam's Soviet-backed occupation of Cambodia (Kampuchea) a year ago. When the world condemned Moscow for its role in Afghanistan, Peking's hand was then strenthened in seeking world-wide condemnation of Hanoi's aggression in Indo-China and understanding for the Chinese "counter attack" on Vietnam's northern border provinces during February 1979.

It was unfortunate that the Chinese Foreign Minister, Mr. Huang Hua, on his three-nation tour in mid-March, was unable to convince the countries belonging to the Association of South-East Asian Nations (ASEAN) that Soviet involvement in Afghanistan and Cambodia were two pincers of a Soviet claw to strike at Western Europe. This was why China thought the British proposal for a "neutral" Afghanistan was unworkable. What was needed was to force the Soviet Union to withdraw its troops from Afghanistan, and Vietnam to take its forces out of Cambodia.

The response that the Chinese Foreign Minister received was that though ASEAN's and China's aim was to have the foreign troops withdrawn from both the two countries the ASEAN countries could not accept China's strategic appreciation of Russia's role.

This ASEAN attitude is not unreasonable in the light of Mr. Huang Hua's refusal to discuss Peking's support for banned communist movements in countries belonging to ASEAN! It is not so long ago that China was a potential enemy. It occupied Tibet and the West fought against the Chinese in Korea. Meanwhile Malaysia is still fighting Chinese Communist terrorists long after the Malayan Emergency officially ended.

In a nutshell, China's position in relation to the Soviet Union's subjugation and occupation of Afghanistan can be summarized as follows:-

* Because Afghanistan is China's neighbour and they share a 60-mile mountainous border, China regards the Soviet armed invasion of Afghanistan as a threat to her security.
* Peking fears of being encircled by allies of the Soviet Union with hostile military bases became acute when Vietnam assumed the role of a Russian super-satellite, using military force in Cambodia and Laos, enabling Moscow to control Indo-China by proxy.
* The Soviet brutal repression of Afghanistan confirms China's earlier assessment of the untrustworthiness of the Soviet Union and the global scope of her aggressive designs. China had been warning all along, but to no avail, that the Russian communist

185

despots are set on expansion, with increasing reliance on sheer
military might and total ruthlessness.

* In China's view the outrageous occupation of Afghanistan is
  merely the forerunner of a major southward offensive in Asia
  and the Balkans.

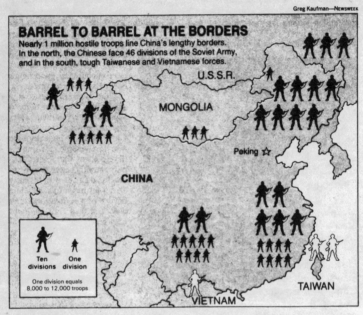

Greg Kaufman—NEWSWEEK

BARREL TO BARREL AT THE BORDERS
Nearly 1 million hostile troops line China's lengthy borders.
In the north, the Chinese face 46 divisions of the Soviet Army,
and in the south, tough Taiwanese and Vietnamese forces.

Appreciation to *Newsweek*, 9th June, 1980.

* By occupying Afghanistan those in the Kremlin can take
  advantage of the situation in Iran at any time to direct the
  momentum of their push towards the Gulf area while posing an
  immediate menace to Pakistan.
* China's appreciation of the situation is that if the Soviet Union
  were to succeed in subduing Afghanistan, followed by Pakistan
  and Iran, they would be in a position to sever parts of Central
  Asia from their political ties with Peking and then set up an
  independent Republic of Eastern Turkestan.
* China believes that Moscow will try to present the West with a
  fait accompli by means of exerting military pressure on Pakistan,
  Iran and Yugoslavia, leading to access for the Soviet navy to
  ports on the Arabian Sea and the Adriatic.
* Obviously China is worried about the danger of a war with
  Russia at a time when her own armed forces are so inadequately

equipped. Therefore she realizes that only the United States can muster forces strong enough to counter at short notice the Soviet Union's southward drive. Peking has many friends in the Third World and she will drum up their political support for any moves by the United States to stem the tide of Soviet expansion and further gains.

* Meanwhile, much to the advantage of NATO, China is "holding down" 46 Russian divisions on their border.

China's successful test firing of an intercontinental-range rocket, an ICBM, on 18th May, 1980, was a timely reminder to the world that military power on a global scale is a feasible objective for Peking. While shortage of equipment will hold in check her military arm for some time to come, the new missile test means that China might accelerate the growth of its nuclear striking force to ensure its own security – this, when, as they expect, Russia makes her move against Western interests.

With this Soviet objective in view – let us make no mistake – China intends to have a developing strategy in nuclear weapons in order to break the two superpowers monopoly and stranglehold in this field.

Zimbabwe-Rhodesia

In September 1976, a former Member of Parliament asked me if I would be willing to pay a visit to Rhodesia to assess the military situation, to familiarise myself with the country, its problems and its peoples and to meet a number of old friends who had settled in Rhodesia and who had expressed a desire to extend their hospitality to me.

I considered it prudent to seek Counsel's advice, because although it was then four years since I had retired from the British Army, I had to be careful that I would not be transgressing any rules or regulations.

In his six page Advice, Counsel pointed out a number of factors of which the following four were the main reasons that influenced me in deciding to refuse the invitation:

1.   *"By the Treason Felony Act 1848* (as amended) it is an offence to, *inter alia,* deprive, or imagine the deprivation of the Sovereign of her style title honour or Royal name as Queen of the United Kingdom, her Colonies, or other countries – I have heard it argued that the purported transformation of Rhodesia into a Republic was such a Treason as it attempted to deprive Her Majesty of her title of Queen in Rhodesia – my client would be well advised to do nothing to aid or abet (albeit post facto) this possible Treason as, by doing so, he could be an accessory after the fact (or within the terms of the Criminal Law Act 1967 a principal to an alleged crime). I have noted, of course, that the General proposes his visit to be a 'private one' – he must therefore proceed with the greatest possible caution if he does meet Rhodesian officials and be most careful not to say anything in public that could be misconstrued as giving 'aid or comfort' (to use a non legal phrase) to the Republican Government of Rhodesia. Treason, even if it is committed abroad, is punishable in the Country, if committed by a person owing allegiance to the Crown."

2.   "Sir Walter's passport will almost certainly be stamped with a Rhodesian entry permit – a stamp for which the Immigration authorities will certainly be on the look out."

"The British Passport contains the following caution:-

'This passport remains the property of Her Majesty's Government in the United Kingdom and may be withdrawn at any time'.

"This caution reflects the accepted maxim of Constitutional Law that passports are issued under the Royal Prerogative by the Passport Office (a sub-department of the Foreign and Commonwealth Office) and may be refused, revoked and impounded in the absolute discretion of the Crown. There is no formal machinery for appeal or, as far as I can discern, any means whatsoever, whereby a person aggrieved can obtain any review of a decision adverse to his interests.

"Sir Walter's passport unfortunately could be revoked or impounded before or after the projected trip."

3.   "Sir Walter in his letter of 12th September, 1976, states: 'I cannot take the risk of putting my Army Pension in jeopardy'. I fully appreciate Sir Walter's position, but can give him no comfort. It is settled Constitutional Law that an ex-member of the forces cannot sue for his pension – the authority for paying pensions is granted by virtue of Royal prerogative but such authority relates only to the grant of the pension, and in no case gives any member of the Army a right to any pension.

"Thus if the Crown decided to cease paying his pension Sir Walter has no legal remedy. He cannot sue for his pension, and, in my opinion, cannot complain to the Ombudsman".

"Obviously, any move by the Government to interfere with Sir Walter's pension would attract widespread publicity and I doubt if the Government would court such publicity, but there is nothing-in-law to stop them."

4.   "The difficulty I have in advising Sir Walter is the fact that in two instances his position is governed by unfettered Government discretion. If he follows my advice carefully he should commit no criminal offence, but I cannot advise as to how the Government will act where the discretionary powers are concerned."

In my book *The Bear at the Back Door,* I gave an account of my visits to Rhodesia in October 1977 and April-May 1978. I was careful to emphasize that "I was in Rhodesia as a visitor and was grateful for the opportunity to listen and learn. It was not my business to offer advice nor state my views. Indeed, I was not in a position to do so because their security forces have developed tactics and techniques far superior to anything I have encountered, I was an ordinary civilian and the Internal Agreement had, in my view, legalized the previous so-called 'Illegality' ".

Opposite page 79 of the South African edition of *The Bear at the Back Door* is a photograph taken at a cocktail party at the Wanderer's Club, Johannesburg, in October 1977. It was at this party that Air Vice Marshal Harold Hawkins, the Accredited Diplomatic Representative of Rhodesia in South Africa, drew me aside and suddenly asked me if I would be willing to fly to Rhodesia as the guest of Lieutenant-General Peter Walls, the Commander Combined Operations, who would brief me, accompany me on a tour of one of the operational areas, after which I would meet Mr. Ian Smith, the then Prime Minister. Harold Hawkins said that if I did not wish to accept the invitation then Peter Walls was prepared to fly to Pretoria to meet me. (Peter Walls and I had been operating in adjacent areas during the Malayan Emergency).

In explaining my predicament to Harold Hawkins I said I was perfectly willing to visit Rhodesia but on the strict understanding that my visit would be purely as a civilian under an assumed name, that it would receive no publicity whatsoever and that my passport would not be stamped with a Rhodesian entry permit.

A few days later my wife and I were guests at a large dinner party given by Harold Hawkins and his wife. At this dinner party was Ken Flower, the Head of Rhodesia's Central Intelligence Organization. After dinner Ken Flower explained to me that: my departure from Pretoria would be handled by South Africa's Special Branch and by the Airport Security staff; on arrival at the airport at Victoria Falls I would be met by his representative and an Army Officer in plain clothes; there would be no passport formalities; and finally, I would travel under the assumed name of Mr. Wilkins. There would be similar arrangements for my return journey.

Everything went according to plan. On arrival at Victoria Falls airport I soon saw the tall figure of Mungo Graham (Ken Flower's 'man') and a somewhat smaller figure who turned out to be Peter Walls representative, Colonel Peter Hosking. Mungo Graham was an ex-British Army Major. Sadly he died in Cape Town after a serious illness in August 1979.

He and Peter Hosking motored me at some speed from the Airport to our hotel at Victoria Falls, in time to join the tourists' trip by launch down the Zambesi river. The next day we flew from a grass airstrip to Wankei and spent a very pleasant day and night at the Wankei Game Reserve. Any Nosey Parkers of the media's fraternity would have been thrown off the scent by now. From Wankei we took off at dawn for Salisbury where my visit started in earnest. Peter Walls told me everything – no holds barred, no secrets hidden. The only awkward moments came during my visits to the 'soldiery' when it was quickly decided to reveal my real identity, otherwise it would not have been possible to brief me fully and make me privy to sensitive and classified information.

I recounted my visit and findings in my book *The Bear at the Back Door*. I decided that the best way of revealing the fact that obviously I had been to Rhodesia would be to write a letter to *The Daily Telegraph* of London giving my personal assessment of the situation and marking the letter as from Pretoria. I gave the letter to Harold Hawkins, whose secretary dictated it on the telephone to someone else's secretary in

190

London, and the next day the letter was hand delivered to the offices of *The Daily Telegraph*. The letter was promptly published on 24th October, 1977 and read as follows:

LETTERS TO THE EDITOR

RED SHADOW OVER RHODESIA

From Gen. Sir Walter Walker.

Sir, – Rhodesia is now standing alone, branded as an illegal régime by the Russians, the West and the United Nations, about one-third of whose members have come to power through bloody revolution. Rhodesia has become a bone in today's international power politics.

These Powers have decreed tiny Rhodesia as a threat to world peace and so her stable government which has done more to elevate the black man than any in African history is to be turned over to phoney liberators who we are asked to believe will restore human rights and dignity as in the Marxist-dominated Angola, Mozambique, Uganda, Cambodia, etc.

The real issue in Rhodesia is this: will the black government be truly elected from Rhodesia's 6,500,000 Blacks and Whites, most of whom are pro-Western moderates, or will a settlement be forced on Rhodesia by the British, the United States, the Russians and the Marxist front-line countries and the United Nations which will ultimately put Communist terrorist leaders into power?

If the latter were to take place then a bloody civil war would erupt in Rhodesia. Millions of innocent Blacks would die and if the Whites were ultimately forced to leave, Rhodesia would fall into the hands of the Russians just as has happened in Angola and Mozambique.

The Rhodesian pot is boiling. The characters in the cast are jockeying for positions and the outcome is in doubt. Meanwhile the British and Americans have proposed a new set of initiatives far more radical than Dr. Kissinger's initiatives and are busy rallying support for these proposals among the Black African States, the Patriotic Front and the United Nations. The new Anglo-American proposals would involve a United Nations police action in Rhodesia and set a dangerous precedent for United Nations troops to overthrow other pro-Western, anti-Communist governments.

The Rhodesian security forces, made up of no less than 82 per cent *black* Rhodesians *all* of whom are *volunteers,* is the finest counter-insurgency force in the world today. In addition the Selous Scouts are striking fear into the hearts of the terrorists. The best trackers and jungle fighters in the world, they can live in the bush for months at a time and are taking a heavy toll of terrorist infiltrators.

Aside from an invasion, i.e. the United Nations police force, or a

191

large-scale attack by East Europeans which would escalate a conflict, the Rhodesian army cannot be defeated in the field. This is precisely why the Russians, why the United Nations, the Patriotic Front and the new proposals put forward by Mr. David Owen and Mr. Andrew Young are all demanding the dismantling of the Rhodesian Army, for this is the only way the Communists can possibly take the country.

WALTER WALKER
Pretoria

On my return to England I was invited to address a meeting, which I did in one of the conference rooms of the House of Commons. The outcome of this was that I was prevailed upon to write a book. The warning that I wished to sound was that the Soviet Union, whether by blackmail, revolutionary war by proxy, or by brute force, intends to absorb the whole of Southern Africa, and thus deprive the West of vital minerals and control of Europe's lifeline round the Cape. It was obvious to me that, quite apart from the vital raw minerals, without which the armies of NATO would grind to a halt – likewise industry – Southern Africa as a whole contained key springboards and bases of fundamental strategic importance. Rhodesia was one such springboard for the eventual direct or indirect assault on South Africa itself. The fact that Zimbabwe is land-locked is neither here nor there – it is still *the* vital springboard for Soviet designs. Then there are the key naval and air bases that are of such strategic importance that their possession by the Soviet Union would not only enable them to control the sea lanes and trade routes in the South Atlantic and Indian Oceans, but also give them overwhelming superiority in global strategy. The Soviets would cut the world in two.

Having agreed to write the book, it was arranged that I should pay another visit to Zimbabwe, South West Africa (Namibia) and South Africa to enable me to check on certain facts and fill in one or two gaps in my knowledge. It was also agreed that I would be permitted to go everywhere and anywhere to meet anyone of my choice and that no secrets would be withheld from me.

For the reasons that I have already explained, my visit to Zimbabwe was again to be under the assumed name of Mr. Wilkins. Personally, I would have relished standing trial for treason. If a Trade Union leader like Jack Jones could go to Cuba, then Walter Walker could go to Zimbabwe. Similar parallels could be drawn, such as the KGB murderer, Shelepin, being invited to London as the guest of the British Trade Unions. Or the trade union leader, Clive Jenkins claiming that as a political institution, the KGB was no different from the House of Lords. Or Mr. Alec Kitson, of Britain's Labour Party's national executive committee, suggesting how pleasant it was to be in the Soviet Union where there is no unemployment and a continual growth of living standards. It would be a red-letter day if such people would go to Russia and stay there.

I do not intend to describe my second visit to Southern Africa, and Zimbabwe in particular, as my book *The Bear at the Back Door* gives a full account. When visiting the operational areas in Zimbabwe, the classified maps were uncovered for me so that I could see the deployment of their SAS and the Selous Scouts. On more than one occasion I was asked to autograph in Secret Operations Rooms, a document pinned on the inside of the door. The document turned out to be a copy of a letter written by me to *The Times*, London, published on 19th June, 1977. The letter read as follows:-

RHODESIAN RAID INTO MOZAMBIQUE

From General Sir Walter Walker.

Sir, It ill becomes any of us in this country to adopt a holier-than-thou attitude to the recent Rhodesian raid into Mozambique. It is no longer a secret that during the three year Indonesian confrontation against Malaysian Borneo I, as Director of Operations, was authorized by the then Labour Government to conduct cross-border operations several miles deep into Indonesian Borneo. Indeed, a *cordon sanitaire* was eventually established and virtually all contacts with our enemy took place on his side of the border.

Offensive action is the only solution to guerrilla or terrorist operations. A policy of containment is the passport to defeat.

Yours faithfully
WALTER WALKER

Charlton House,
Charlton All Saints,
Salisbury,
Wiltshire,

June 8. (1977)

If I had been Peter Walls, I would have carried out many more such external operations, using to the full the lethal weaponry with which I know his Air Force was equipped.

Before Britain's General Election, early in 1979, I wrote to a number of Members of Parliament urging that Mrs. Thatcher should announce during the run-up to the Election that as a result of the overwhelming referendum vote in Zimbabwe-Rhodesia the Conservative Government, on coming to office, would immediately lift sanctions and recognize the internal agreement. I also wrote to Mrs.Thatcher. The majority of the replies that I received could be summed up in one sentence: "Believe me the attitude of the Conservative Party leadership on Rhodesia causes me as much distress as it does you." It seemed to me that the Conservatives were "up the creek" without a paddle.

Mrs. Thatcher sent Lord Boyd to report on the April 1979 election that resulted in Bishop Muzorewa's victory. His verdict was that the election was free and fair. On becoming Britain's new Prime Minister, Mrs. Thatcher's first instinct was to recognize the Muzorewa Government; but the Prime Minister and the Foreign Secretary proved to be political cowards. Informed opinion, of course, knew it was Lord Carrington who talked Mrs. Thatcher out of it on the grounds that the Americans wouldn't like it, nor would the Third World, and certainly not the Commonwealth. *What of the Commonwealth! Brotherhood in defence is the acid test of its value.*

I wrote to Mrs. Thatcher and expressed my views which, incidentally coincided with those of Mr. R.F. Botha, South Africa's Minister of Foreign Affairs: "A Rugby Football game in which the winners must be made to lose."

Appreciation to *Sunday Times Business News,* London.

Lord Carrington's hand in the game did not surprise me. After all, this is the man who, when Minister of Defence, was panicked in December 1973 into slashing £178 million off an already perilously low defence expenditure, in spite of the lessons of the Arab-Israeli war, and the pledge by the European members of NATO to make a greater contribution to their own defence, I pointed this out in a letter published in *The Daily Telegraph* on 27th December, 1973.

At Lancaster House, the London Conference, the Marxist terrorist leaders – Mugabe and Nkomo – gained most of their objectives and the elected government of Bishop Muzorewa were forced to make the most of the concessions. Mugabe and Nkomo knew that by adopting the tactics of those used at the Vietnam peace talks, filibustering and prevarication, minor concessions followed by exorbitant demands, an exhausted and besotted British Government would settle for a compromise in order to get a settlement at any price.

Many people regard the talks on Rhodesia as the Foreign Secretary's finest hour. But Andrew Alexander in an article in the 23rd-29th November, 1979 issue of *NOW!* magazine offered a more critical assessment of this politician and his methods. We are told that in Mr. Heath's clash with the miners Carrington was the most eager to use the occasion for an election, convinced that he knew the mood of the electorate. Heath lost the election.

Andrew Alexander tells us that Carrington was then acquiring a reputation with some of his political colleagues for "not being as direct as he seemed." The article goes on:

"This reputation must certainly have been enhanced by his handling of the Rhodesia crisis. For the closer Carrington's behaviour is scrutinized, the less straightforward – indeed cunning — it appears to have been.

The Lords debate on sanctions in November last year found Carrington eloquent in his defence of the internal settlement. The difficulties were not Ian Smith's fault; the prospect of an election was impressive; and the Government's constant reiteration of the Anglo-American proposal was unhelpful, tiresome and a threat to progress.

It was one of the most pro-Salisbury speeches from the Tory Front Bench that peers had heard. True, Carrington concluded that sanctions must be continued for a while, not least because a clash between the Upper and Lower Houses would be an ugly affair. But listeners could not doubt where Carrington's sympathies lay.

Or could they? It was at about this time that Carrington was privately cornered and quizzed by some Tories on Southern Africa. The private and public views of the future Foreign Secretary proved remarkably different. It was not clear where he differed from the Ango-American plan. There was a curious (and unexplained) insistence that Britain must make sure that Rhodesia was not "our Vietnam". As to general policy, what mattered was keeping in with Black Africa generally, especially the Nigerians. The "realpolitik" element struck his hearers as positively crude.

And whom was he backing as the future leader of Rhodesia? Carrington was reluctant to nominate his favourite. But eventually he admitted it was Nkomo. That at any rate was not so surprising. The Foreign Office, after all, was backing Nkomo; and Carrington had always been a man for listening to the civil servants.

The sheer, almost grotesque inconsistency between the man's private and public views was in fact explicable. The fear that the Lords would vote against sanctions renewal was real. Had Carrington sought to dissuade them and yet acknowledge his pro-Nkomo sympathies, there would have been a massive revolt.

There was however the problem of Mrs. Margaret Thatcher. Her sympathies were for swift recognition of the new régime after the elections. A taste of her – and his – views had been provided many months before by a remarkable incident at a meeting of Shadow Cabinet Ministers. Carrington aired the view that it was only a matter of time before Black Africa proposed to the United Nations that mandatory sanctions should be imposed on South Africa. Britain, he suggested, should be prepared to go along with that. Mrs. Thatcher blew up. Carrington hastily, and typically dropped the subject altogether. She, it must be presumed, had forgotten that fleeting incident when she came to appoint him Foreign Secretary last May (1979).

Given his views on Southern Africa generally, and on Rhodesia, it should have been difficult if not impossible for Carrington to subscribe to the Tory election manifesto with its promise to recognize the Muzorewa Government provided that the election had been fair.

Bringing his leader round to his view was not a task which daunted Carrington. He had an understandable confidence in his own powers of persuasion. Indeed Carrington's more critical colleagues argue that he has only one substantial quality; persuasiveness. And that he had in abundance.

Once the leader was whisked away from London and her normal supporters, bringing her round to the Foreign Office point of view did not prove difficult. The Iron Lady proved to be very malleable."

Comrade Mugabe's Great Debt

In the Rhodesian election in March, Comrade Robert Mugabe – an avowed Marxist – won 57 of the 80 black seats in the 100 member House of Assembly.

The result came as no surprise to Mr. Ian Smith. He was the one man who had predicted correctly the outcome of the process that Lord Carrington had set in motion at the Lusaka Commonwealth conference in August 1979. Ian Smith said in London at the time of the Lancaster House talks which began on 10th September and ended on 21st December: "Between them the guerrillas will walk it." How right he was.

Mr. Smith and Comrade Mugabe had one thing in common. Neither had any respect for the political abilities of Bishop Muzorewa. Both knew that in a real election the odds were that the vote of the Shona people – about 80 per cent of the total – would mass around Zanu and Comrade Mugabe. Mugabe was determined to emerge on top, if not by fair means then by foul.

The prospect of a Marxist administration in Salisbury was not what the Conservatives had in mind when the party made a General Election pledge "*to achieve a lasting settlement to the Rhodesian problem based on the democratic wishes of the people of that country.*" Yet a Conservative Government brought to its knees and finally overthrew an existing non-Marxist Government, tolerable by African standards. It undermined the Bishop and stripped him of power, authority and legitimacy.

In the House of Commons, Sir Ian Gilmour, then Lord Privy Seal, dismissed a charge by Mr. Julian Amery that the emergence of a government led by Mugabe was a major defeat, and said in the manner of a self-satisfied headmaster: "There is no evidence at all that Mr. Mugabe is under Soviet influence – quite the contrary."

Yet the sanctuary for Comrade Mugabe and his terrorists had been the Russian tool, Mozambique, whose President, Machel, is a committed Marxist and under the strong influence of his Russian paymasters. Robert Mugabe is a close friend, associate and admirer of Samora Machel and heeded his advice.

The former Portuguese province of Mozambique, right next door to Rhodesia, was pushed quickly down the slippery slope leading behind the Iron Curtain and is already bankrupt and hungry, dependent entirely on the West and South Africa for aid. But the strongest backing has come from the Soviet Union. Obviously the Lord Privy Seal was either ill-informed or was playing to the Socialist gallery in Parliament.

If Mr. Mugabe is not under Soviet influence at this moment there is plenty of evidence that he has been under Soviet (and Communist Chinese) influence in the past. How, otherwise did he get the arms and military training for his terrorists without which they could not possibly have penetrated into Rhodesia, or, if he had, could quite easily have been dealt with by the forces of the Rhodesian Government? Did Sir Ian think these terrorists made heavy machine guns and mortars for themselves?

If Zimbabwe's Premier does not repay his debt to the Soviets, he will be a most ungrateful man. *The Soviet Union does not like ungrateful people, and if Mr. Mugabe does not show his gratitude in the future he is likely to be replaced by somebody else who will.*

Mr. Julian Amery also said – again quite correctly – that to bring Soviet influence within 200 miles of the mineral resources of South Africa was comparable to the danger posed by the Soviet take-over of Afghanistan. Sir Ian Gilmour, quite incorrectly, denied there was any parallel with Afghanistan. The Lord Privy Seal then proceeded to make an even bigger ass of himself by pronouncing, in reply to another Member of Parliament, that the defence of the trade routes round the Cape had nothing to do with Zimbabwe, because it is a land-locked country. This is the sort of reply that one might expect to receive from a private soldier taking his third class certificate of education.

Russia's intention is to ensure that after Zimbabwe has absorbed 'democracy', a totalitarian Marxist dictatorship is to emerge as International Communism gains control and begins to use Zimbabwe as a forward base from which to attack the next target – South Africa, the Free World's last great base in Africa.

Mr. Igor Glagolev, one-time adviser to the Russian Government and Communist party, said in Washington on 4th March that "the victory of Mr. Robert Mugabe in the Zimbabwe elections represents a major advance in the Soviet Union's ambitions in Southern Africa." Mr. Glagolev, who defected in 1976, said that from his own personal knowledge, Mr. Mugabe *was armed and financed by the Soviet Union and subject to its wishes.*

If, as I doubt, Zimbabwe becomes a happy and united country, grown fat and prosperous on its cheerful toil, who will scruple at Sir Ian Gilmour's sunny, carefree manner and headmasterly wit on this historic occasion in the House of Commons? But if it turns out that he was a smiling Charybdis at the gate of Hell, who will forgive him and who will not forget him?

Robert Mugabe is an intelligent man, very bitter, very radical. He has seven degrees, three of them acquired in detention. The image of the Che Guevara of Rhodesia's "Revolutionary War" was carefully nurtured. But he has never undergone serious military training or fired a shot in anger in his life. He never infiltrated Rhodesia with his terrorist forces, as was sometimes claimed. Militant he certainly is, but a military

197

man never. His arsenal is in his mind. He is a revolutionary theorist, not a soldier.

Premier Mugabe is clever and well-informed. He knows perfectly well that the Soviet Union has done relatively little for Africa except provide weapons, military advisers and Cuban soldiers. It has shown very little interest in helping the poor and the starving. But it does provide a model of a political system that takes power into the hands of one party.

The Russians and their allies will move in with large embassies. They will offer advice, scholarships, technical assistance as well as arms. They will find allies among young intellectuals and they will be looking for ways of promoting discord between blacks and whites. They intend to reap the fruits of their support for "wars of liberation."

They are acutely aware of the West's dependence on African raw materials and the sea lanes around the Cape, and they intend to dominate them. The Soviets intend to prepare for the day when the assault on South Africa begins in earnest in a revolutionary war by proxy.

"Do you suppose, Abdul, that Lord Carrington is going to have as much success helping us as he had helping Bishop Muzorewa?"

Appreciation to *Sunday Express*, 9th March, 1980.

At the right time, Premier Mugabe will fulfil his promise that once in power he will nationalize essential industries, abolish private land ownership and transform the social structure of his Zimbabwe. It suits his purpose to sound conciliatory today. But like a boa-constrictor he will slaver his prey before he crushes and devours it.

As the likelihood of a Mugabe victory became more apparent, one incredulous white business executive ordered a large whisky and muttered, "A Communist government in Rhodesia? Supervised by a British Tory Government? Full *Marx* to Lord Soames."

An executive of a large multi-national corporation with extensive Rhodesian interests said he was absolutely despondent at the election result. "Mugabe will quickly become another Nyerere. The victory at the polls is really a victory for Russia," he said, adding that Rhodesia would become "a springboard for Communist incursions into South Africa." Mr. Mugabe would "tear up the constitution in six months, and the whites would be excluded from Government," he forecast.

Both white and black farmers, however, were more optimistic, Mr. Dennis Norman, president of the 5,300-strong Commercial Farmers' Union said: "We had discussions with Mr. Mugabe before the election, and his socialist policies are not as red-blooded as originally thought."

Mr. Ian Smith is obviously worried about the political philosophy of the ruling Zimbabwe National Union. "The question of reconciling our differences and living with past enemies has never been a problem for white Rhodesians, but accepting a different political philosophy – and one always alien to the Western World – was the problem," he said.

Mr. Smith said "Providing Mr. Mugabe and his party live up to those commitments, then there is clearly hope." But he added: "We will only be in a position to make a meaningful assessment after we have had the opportunity of examining the track record of Mr. Mugabe and his party. We must wait and see."

Making an interesting observation, Mr. Smith said, "At Lancaster House I was impressed by the ability and performance of both Patriotic Front leaders and their delegations, which constantly outwitted and out-manoeuvred the British."

Calling on the white community to forget the past, he said: "You never solve a problem by running away from it. Therefore I urge you to resist hasty action. I believe we have overcome greater problems in the past. Therefore let us join in with the plea to resist recrimination for deeds gone by, and work together with our fellow countrymen and make a success of this new venture."

The former Prime Minister thought the inclusion of white representation in Mr. Mugabe's Cabinet would give confidence to the white community. "I believe we have a big part to play – politically we have the most experience." Mr. Smith denied categorically that Mr. Mugabe had made a white presence in the Zanu government conditional on his resignation.

Noting the chaos and bankruptcy which had resulted in other African countries where whites had left prematurely, Mr. Smith said: "Everyone accepts that it is vital to retain the white man in this country

... It is absolutely vital for the future success of this country."

Mr. Smith, an avowed opponent of Communism, said: "The Communist battle is for the whole of Southern Africa. They hope to use Rhodesia as one of their launching pads. I've got a feeling they believe the ground is more fertile than it was before."

The man who could talk from experience was bitter about the British, "We have been betrayed all along the line by them ... We were betrayed at Lancaster House. What is obvious is that the British are going to wash their hands of Rhodesia, come what may."

In my view, it may have been expedient that the Government should throw Rhodesia to the wolves, but how could any Conservative believe that this was, in Lord Carrington's words, the "morally right" thing to do?

Since when did Conservatives regard "one-man, one-vote" as the touchstone of morality? How could Conservatives think it right to bully, threaten and cajole a brave and civilized white community (which was acting, by them, in conjunction with pro-Western blacks) into letting the Marxists in? The Lancaster House agreements may have been adroit as a way of removing Britain from off the hook, but they were nothing for a Conservative Government to boast about.

There is also a nasty smell about the whole business. The London *Daily Telegraph* published a letter on 7th March, 1980, which said: "I wonder if it is realized, that at the Lancaster House Conference the Government of Zimbabwe-Rhodesia was prevailed upon to accept an outline Constitution, and that the outline was what the Members of Parliament were provided with less than a day before they voted for the new 'Independence' Constitution.

"Not only was it a Soviet-type Constitution as opposed to a democratic Constitution, but they did not know precisely what they were voting for.

"I have now managed to obtain a copy of the final version, and find that the detailed 'clarification' has introduced a number of points that one would think the majority of British M.P.s would consider to be unacceptable.

"In the first third of the Constitution alone I found 20 provisions of the general type:

The Government may order people to be killed "in order to prevent commission by that person of a crime."

Any company, property or land may be compulsorily acquired, for its utilization for purposes defined by the Government as "beneficial to the public generally."

Freedom of conscience and freedom of religious institutions shall no longer be allowed if the Government deem this to be in the interests of "defence, public safety, public order, public morality or public health.

"Anyone may be deprived of his personal liberty by order of the Senate or House of Assembly."

People shall be required to perform forced labour in any circumstances that the Government may define as an emergency.

"One might also wonder how it comes about that Britain seeks to impose upon Zimbabwe-Rhodesia a régime that involves infringement of the terms of the Genocide Act on the part of the politicians and officials involved."

It was jubilation in every black African capital as the results of the elections were received. Only from Rhodesia's southern neighbour, South Africa, came a sombre note of caution.

President Nyerere, unofficial leader of the five "front line states" which backed the Patriotic Front during the guerrilla war, and a consistent and vocal critic of Britain, had predicted that the Rhodesia elections would not be fair. If the Patriotic Front won in spite of what he had described as "British perfidiousness", the teetotal President said he would drink champagne. In the Tanzanian capital Foreign Ministry officials said the champagne had been on ice for some time, and they would be celebrating.

President Nyerere admitted he had been wrong. "It's not the first time I've been proved wrong," he said, "and it's not the first time I am very happy to be wrong." With President Machel of Mozambique, was a steady supporter of Mr. Mugabe, giving him refuge, material help, and political backing.

But President Kaunda of Zambia had hoped to see Mr. Joshua Nkomo, the Zapu leader, winning the election. Dr. Kaunda sent a message congratulating Mr. Mugabe, and assuring him that Zambia would accept any government he formed. Moreover he said he hoped Mr. Nkomo would still play a part in an independent Zimbabwe, and pointedly passed on a recommendation of a meeting of Foreign Ministers that unity between the two wings of the Patriotic Front should be sought.

Dr. Kaunda praised China and Russia for their support of the Patriotic Front guerrillas during their armed struggle, and said he hoped and prayed there would be no outside interference in Rhodesia. He made it plain he feared some action by South Africa.

Botswana, Uganda, Kenya and a dozen other African countries all sent messages of congratulations to Mr. Mugabe, though the leaders of the three States would be privately deeply concerned at the prospect of a Marxist country in the centre of their continent.

Mr. Pieter Botha, the Prime Minister of South Africa, dourly accepted that the election result was the decision of the people of Rhodesia. "They will have to work it out for themselves and live with it," he said.

He gave this warning to Mugabe not to overstep the mark: "Any neighbour which allows its territory to be used for attacks on or the undermining of South Africa and its security will have to face the full force of the Republic's strength."

201

An intriguing question will be the effect that the results of the elections will have on the outcome of negotiations between the South African Government and the United Nations about the future of South West Africa (Namibia) and the establishment of a demilitarized zone with Angola.

It was probably less Mugabe's personal appeal than his image as commander-in-chief of his guerrilla forces that encouraged such extensive support.

The blacks of Rhodesia, like the whites were desperate for peace after a bitter war which claimed more than 20,000 lives and affected practically every family in the country. They sought it from Bishop Muzorewa in the April 1979 elections, but he failed to deliver, and was perceived to be no more than a front man for the existing white structure.

Mr. Mugabe and his men effectively put it across that only they could bring peace. They were the men with the arms and, beyond a defeat by force, were the only people who could silence the guns. Intimidation on a large scale there undoubtedly was, and Comrade Mugabe's forces, thousands of whom remained deliberately outside the cease-fire camps, were among the main offenders. But even allowing for 10 seats' worth of intimidation, Zanu (PF) would still have had a convincing victory.

Mr. Mugabe's appeal probably had roots also in an underlying racial resentment among blacks, not a hatred directed against individual whites, but a reaction to the fact that the white establishment continued to control all aspects of life in the country nearly two decades after most of Africa was decolonized.

A white Rhodesian who had played an important part of life in Salisbury said there had been massive violations of the Lancaster House agreement by the Patriotic Front as it filtered thousands more trained men over the border. This had programmed vast areas at the barrels of its guns and threatened a continuance of the war if voters favoured any of the other parties. For some strange reason, he said, this did not seem to qualify as undue intimidation. It suited the book for the election to be labelled "reasonably free and fair."

This public figure said white Rhodesians had every reason to be bitter with what had happened during the past two years. Reluctantly at first, then more readily as time passed, they had gone along with a traumatic transfer of political power to the black people. They had kept the economy going despite continued sanctions, maintained an efficient administration and above all, fought the war alongside increasing numbers of their black comrades, despite world pressures that must surely never have been paralleled in modern times, not even in the Israeli State.

This man said that the news of Mugabe's landslide victory stunned the nation. He gave it as his view that pressure from intense political intimidation, anxious to see an end to the terror of war and deeply con-

202

scious that whites would have preferred to see the Bishop win again, the black man took the line of least resistance. Far better to say the Bishop was going to win than to have to explain why he might not.

This old Rhodesian hand said all the old arguments had been revived. Mrs. Thatcher should have recognized the Government of National Unity shortly after the May 1979 election. By not doing so the Patriotic Front's case was strengthened and the new Government almost totally emasculated.

Given enough time to prepare their men in the field (which Carrington did so successfully with his incredible efforts to keep the P.F. from defecting) they had an ace up their sleeve: "If you want the war to end vote for us. If the P.F. does not win the election we shall start the war again." Then finally: "Don't think we will not know how you voted. We will, and then, if you have done the wrong thing, we will kill you." It was as simple as that and there were many white Rhodesians who predicted this as far back as October 1979.

The Left-White Merger

So what of the future? Will the British "red on the map" that Rhodes dreamt of as stretching from the Cape to Cairo become a broad Communist red band girdling south-central Africa from the Atlantic to the Indian Ocean? Will comrades and commissars and collective farms and industries swamp the drive and initiative that has characterized this stubborn little country for nearly a century?

Our Rhodesian said he wished for a sure answer. Contacts between old enemies had been made with incredible swiftness. Generals and brigadiers had rubbed shoulders with men only recently classified as Communist terrorists. Guerrillas in large numbers were in training with army units. Mr. Mugabe had said all the right things and was clearly aiming for a rapid reconciliation. Above all, the war was over. Clearly this would not have been the case if the Bishop had won the election.

In this spokesman's opinion the black man in the tribal lands would quietly return to his old ways. He would try to forget the war, the mutilations, the killings, the beatings, the terror in the night. He would pray that he never had to suffer another election like the last one.

The black man in the towns, on the farms and in the mines had become an integral part of a sophisticated economy. He had been rather more shielded from the worst effects of the war than his brothers in the tribal lands but had suffered nevertheless. In most cases he maintained close links with his tribal home. He probably had a house, land to cultivate and the ultimate in wealth and status – cattle. All these material assets had suffered.

His aspirations would be difficult for any Government to meet; certainly in the short term. Higher wages, full employment, quick promotion combined with promises of free education and medicine, slip easily past a politician's lips. To implement them would be another thing altogether. Higher wages meant less jobs. Too rapid promotion led to inefficiency and inefficiency quickly led to lowered production and less money. Less money meant that free educational and medical services must suffer.

Our Rhodesian spokesman said the whites who had soldiered through the traumas of the post-UDI years were still suffering from post-election shock. They had been deeply hurt by what they considered nothing short of treachery by a British Government that had promised so much while still in opposition and then promptly gone back on its previous undertakings. They feared the economy would be destroyed by the totally unrealistic socialist principles that they believe had threatened the ruin of neighbouring countries like Mozambique and Tanzania.

The first appearances of the Prime Minister-elect on T.V. and radio and the restrained, disciplined exuberance of Zanu supporters had done much to re-establish confidence. But there was caution. "A leopard cannot change his spots," many argued, but even in Rhodesia there were secret hopes that this leopard would prove the exception with everything turning out right in the end.

The overtly conciliatory tone of Comrade Mugabe's victory night speech and his impressively articulate manner, succeeded in reassuring many whites that the advent of Marxist rule was not an immediate disaster. Mugabe was hated and feared by the whites as the commander of the ruthless Zanla guerrilla forces during seven years of bitter war,

"Try our new local cocktail?"
Appreciation to *The Argus*, S.A.

when he spent time in detention and living in exile. He was probably better known in Europe, particularly as a result of the Lancaster House negotiations.

His television appearance, grey-suited and wearing his favourite red tie, his softly spoken and deliberate speech, and above all his words of reconciliation, did much to allay the fears for the minority white community. Mugabe told his audience that peace and security could be achieved only if individuals *felt* a definite sense of security and had an assurance of national security from the government.

"In this regard, I wish to assure you that there can never be any return to the state of armed conflict which existed before our commitment to peace," he said. "It is now time to beat our swords into ploughshares so that we can attend to the problems of developing our economy and society."

The promise of an end to the war brought by Mugabe's comprehensive victory meant as much to the 220,000-strong white community as to the country's 6,800,00 Africans, whose fervent desire for peace, probably more than anything else explained the massive vote for Mugabe.

For the whites it spelt an end to the call-up which affected nearly every adult male, and many women, for up to eight months of the year. Compulsory military and police duties were a considerable handicap to any employer.

Significantly, Mugabe said he had asked Lieutenant-General Peter Walls, the Rhodesian Commander of Combined Operations and for long the mortal enemy of the guerrillas, to stay on to supervise the formation of a national Zimbabwean Army to include the Zanla forces, Mr. Joshua Nkomo's Zipra guerrillas, and the Rhodesian security forces. He said the need for peace demanded that all the forces in the field be integrated immediately. "Accordingly I have authorised General Walls, working in conjunction with the Zanla and Zipra commanders, to preside at the integration process."

The size and structure of an army which will have to be drawn from three forces will present considerable problems. Zanla is tribally Shona and Zipra Ndebele. As the elections showed, the country is politically divided on tribal lines.

An even more difficult problem is presented by the Rhodesian forces, which have spent seven years at war against guerrillas. They include several thousand white regulars and an air force in which the pilots and senior personnel are all white.

Limited attempts at integration have been made in the past by the Rhodesians, with white NCOs serving in black units. But the more radical integration of the sort that is now being conducted still has to stand the test of time and tribal conflict.

One very senior General said to me when I was in Rhodesia: "You

205

see that black Sergeant over there. His whole family have been wiped out and his village burned to the ground. His wife, sisters, and daughters were raped, tortured and terribly mutilated before dying in agony. The men of his village were subjected to unimaginable atrocities and then burned alive. Do you mean to tell me that he will serve alongside former murderous terrorists. He will choose his time and place to seek revenge."

Britain has been asked to help in training the future national army. It will be said that this will only help to make the army more efficient for eventually attacking South Africa. That's as may be, but it is preferable to having Russia do the training.

I believe the true situation could not have been better expressed than by that well-known and well-informed Member of Parliament, Patrick Wall, who, in a letter to *The Daily Telegraph* gave this summary:

The pressure on Mr. Mugabe to Africanise all levels of the defence forces, civil service, judiciary, etc., will be overwhelming. Should, as seems likely, the standards of justice, local government and commercial practice decline, then the gradual white exodus will continue.

Once again, the U.S.S.R. will have harnessed genuine African nationalism to its long-term requirements namely, the elimination of Western influence in Southern Africa and a final confrontation with South Africa.

Can anyone doubt that if Zimbabwe should turn Marxist, South Africa would not agree to U.N. supervised elections in Namibia and thus run the risk of U.N. economic sanctions. In consequence, Prime Minister Botha's startling reforms in South Africa itself would then have to be curtailed.

The key issue today is the Battle for Resources and the Soviets are already well placed to control the two vital areas; the Middle East for its oil and Southern Africa for its minerals. In the days of my youth, Captain Liddell Hart propounded the strategy of indirect approach, which is said to have considerably interested Herr Hitler.

Today the Soviet Union are using the same strategy by a clever use of Cubans, East Germans, etc. in Africa and in Central America they have, or are about to, secure key areas on the world's trade routes. The next step will not be achieved by invasion, as in Afghanistan, but by increasing local tensions and by the use of national forces, such as the Tudeh Party in Iran and ANC/PAC in South Africa.

Unless the West calls a halt to this strategy of indirect approach, it will be too late and we will face World War III deprived of key raw materials."

If Mrs. Thatcher was embarrassed when she found that she had helped a Marxist into power in Salisbury, spare a thought for the red faces near Red Square. Educated on Charles Dicken's Eatanswill and the dogma of the wickedness of British diplomats, Moscow Radio and the *Tass* news agency were both convinced that Lord Soames had the elections fixed. Bishop Muzorewa was as good as in!

The results would be submitted to "members of Britain's Conservative government" for approval, the *Tass* political observer reported. "The British colonial authorities in Salisbury are not concealing the fact that they do not intend to take account of the results of the voting if these results are not in keeping with the long-term aims of neo-colonialism in Africa."

Moscow's World Service's man-on-the-spot found that the intimidation of voters had assumed "most arrogant forms." He declared:

"It is said that the voters are even made to dip their hands into a specially prepared solution. Before casting the ballot, they place their hands in a box exposed to ultra-violet rays. This procedure is used to intimidate the voters and establish who cast the vote for the .Patriotic Front."

Earlier in this Chapter, I refuted the claim that Rhodesia was Lord Carrington's finest hour. On the same day that the House of Commons was being subjected to Sir Ian Gilmour's headmasterly wit and abysmal ignorance of military strategy, the Foreign Secretary was also displaying a distinct lack of knowledge in the House of Lords. According to the Parliamentary Correspondent of *The Daily Telegraph,* Lord Carrington told Lord Shinwell he was wrong in saying Mr. Mugabe had Russian connections. He had got his weapons, said the Foreign Secretary, from the Chinese and it was Mr. Nkomo who got guns from the Russians.

From *where,* then, did Comrade Mugabe's terrorists obtain their Russian weapons?

It was after the death of Mao Tse-tung in 1976 that Chinese aid dried up and Mugabe struck a deal with Moscow that gave him access to Soviet arms. Russia's puppet, Comrade Machel of Mozambique, had not only provided a sanctuary for Mugabe's terrorist army, but 600 of Machel's own Frelimo intelligence personnel had been operating inside Mugabe's Zanla. Evidently, Britain's Foreign Secretary was unaware of this.

In the 7th-13th March 1980, issue of *NOW!* magazine, Anthony Shrimsley's verdict of Lord Carrington's diplomacy is that it was a disastrous failure. Lord Carrington is responsible for installing the first Marxist government in Africa to be elected by ballot. For those who did not have access to *NOW!* magazine before its untimely end, I give below the text of Anthony Shrimsley's report and with those views I agree entirely:

"If Lord Carrington is proud of himself, he should not be. The triumph of Robert Mugabe in the Rhodesian elections is perhaps the biggest landmark in the Foreign Office's consistent strategy of pandering to extremism since Neville Chamberlain's ignominious return from Munich.

And, as the reality sinks in, more damage will, I suspect, be done to the Government at the grass roots of the Tory Party than has been inflicted by the dithering over industrial relations or worries about the economy.

The result of Lord Carrington's diplomacy is a disaster – and it will remain a disaster even if political realities encourage Mr. Mugabe to tread a cautious path for a year or two.

Nor is this verdict hindsight. The dangers of the British policy of selling out Bishop Muzorewa were always apparent to those who chose to look. For the record, I wrote on 14th December, as the Lancaster House constitutional conference closed to almost universal applause, that a Patriotic Front dictatorship was the most likely result of the elections.

But, it will be argued, the huge turn-out in the election demonstrates that democracy has spoken in Zimbabwe.

Pardon me! But I do not agree. What has spoken in Zimbabwe is a combination of tribalism – which was always pointing in the direction which has led to the actual result – and the realization by those who might have supported Bishop Muzorewa that he was doomed to defeat.

He was doomed because his prestige and his position were destroyed by the British Government, quietly urged on by an American State Department whose capacity for misunderstanding

207

Africa is these days almost as great as its capacity for misunderstanding Moscow, Paris, Teheran or any other corner of the globe.

Since Mr. Andrew Young and Dr. David Owen started their misconceived "Anglo-American" strategy for Rhodesia, the alleged objective was to bring about a transition from Mr. Ian Smith's illegal régime to a majority African state which would not be a magnet for Russian influence.

The purpose was said to be to prevent a takeover by the guerrilla forces, especially by those of Mr. Mugabe who was regarded as too revolutionary and too Marxist by half.

Dr. Owen and Mr. Young failed. Mr. Ian Smith almost succeeded. His internal settlement led to an election victory for Bishop Muzorewa and a form of government which gave majority African rule and a greater degree of self-rule for the Africans than they are likely to find under Mr. Mugabe.

When Mrs. Thatcher was elected in Britain her first instinct was to recognize the Muzorewa Government. She was talked out of this by Lord Carrington and by other supposedly wiser people who explained that the Americans wouldn't like it and there would be trouble with the guerrillas and with the Commonwealth.

Leave it to the experts, they said, and we will engineer things in such a way that Mugabe walks out of the constitutional conference, or is at least outflanked by jolly Joshua Nkomo. That way (they said) we will have a nice neat coalition of Nkomo, Muzorewa and Smith. Mugabe, even if he won the most seats, would become the Opposition leader, or find himself fighting a guerrilla war against the combined military forces of the Rhodesian Army and the Nkomo freedom fighters.

Meanwhile Muzorewa would have to give up the Premiership and do as the whites told him. Muzorewa was thus labelled as a white puppet – and his support slid to Mugabe. Lord Carrington has, therefore, succeeded in organizing the fall of a sympathetic régime and its replacement with the first Marxist government in Africa to be elected by ballot.

And instead of splitting the guerrillas, or even integrating them into the army, Lord Carrington's strategy has integrated the army into the guerrilla forces. Mr. Mugabe now has under his hand the instrument with which he will, in due course, turn the new Zimbabwe into a one-party state under military control.

Indeed, with Mr. Nkomo's support, Mr. Mugabe would even have the two-thirds Parliamentary majority he needs for the constitutional changes which are now inevitable.

There will now, no doubt, be a scramble by Britain and America to pour aid into the Mugabe régime in order to outbid the Russians. That is, I fear, the only sensible course left in the face of the shambles which is the consequence of Britain's pathetic failure. But for all the pious words, which are being – and will be – uttered at Westminster, a failure is precisely what this has been."

So much for this assessment of Lord Carrington's diplomatic feat. There are moments in the life of nations when those who lead them are unmasked by circumstances. Those who seemed great in small days, in great days prove infinitely small.

It was Field Marshal Lord Montgomery who said war he knew to be a tough and dirty business, but since the war, he had come to learn that it was pat ball compared to politics.

I mention this because on reading *The Crossman Diaries*, I came across this passage:

"*Crossman to Wilson* (Prime Minister of the Labour Government): I explained how Carrington had given me every detail of what went on at the Shadow Cabinet Meetings."

On an earlier page Crossman describes how he had secret meetings with Carrington at the latter's request:

"Even though Carrington had talked to me with such freedom about what had happened and who had taken the decisions on his side I shouldn't have talked to him so freely about our goings-on. I think there'll be a good row about this and I shall have to tell my colleagues what I think happened."

I am not in a position to vouch for the authenticity of the Crossman Diaries, but I am at liberty to quote from them.

Within two weeks of the election the relationship between the two political parties, Mugabe's Zanu and Nkomo's Zapu, had already become strained. The real test comes now after Independence. By 18th March Mr. Joshua Nkomo's Patriotic Front Zapu party, was far from satisfied at the role it had been given in the government of Mr. Robert Mugabe. Mr. Nkomo, veteran of Rhodesian nationalist politicals, having turned down the offer of the Presidency because of its non-executive nature, accepted the "important" Ministry of Home Affairs.

But the internal affairs portion of the portfolio had been re-allocated to the Minister of Local Government and Housing, Mr. Eddison Zvobgo, previously Mr. Mugabe's chief spokesman.

The ministry Mr. Nkomo had been left with, though including responsibility for the British South Africa Police, was not what it promised to be. The Police Special Branch, a key part of state security, is to come under the Prime Minister's office.

Apart from Mr. Nkomo, only three other prominent members of Zapu had been given cabinet posts: Mr. Clement Muchachi, Public Works; Mr. George Silundika, Posts and Telecommunications; and Mr. Joseph Msika, Natural Resources and Water Development. One senior Zapu source said: "All we have been left with are stones to govern – not people."

Many Zapu supporters had complained that though Mr. Mugabe professed to bring his Patriotic Front allies into government, the reality was that his concessions to the White community showed him to be "little better than Muzorewa."

Mr. Nkomo's well-trained Zipra guerrillas were very disappointed at the way things had gone.

This was likely to prove a real problem as about 6,000 highly-trained Zipra guerrillas were then still active in Zambia. Their future had still to be determined and the Zipra commander, Dumiso Dabengwa, had arrived in Lusaka with a senior logistics officer to report on the situation in Salisbury.

It was believed that Mr. Nkomo was prepared to allow the return of the Zambian-based Zipra forces if they were to be integrated into the Zimbabwean Army. Mr. Mugabe would sooner have them in civilian life. Zapu sources said that they had been encouraged by Mr. Mugabe's eve of election promise to bring them into government come-what-may.

Since the election, the relationship between the two parties had not always been easy, with some members of Mr. Mugabe's central committee pressing for the total exclusion from government of Zapu, which won 20 seats to Zanu-PF's 57. Senior members of Zapu pointed out that they fought the war in alliance with Mr. Mugabe's Zanu, that they were

209

behind the Lancaster House settlement and had won a quarter of the black seats in the new parliament. They believed the real test would come after Independence.

They did not exclude the option of pulling out of government if "we are not given a proper deal," but added that they felt it was better to be in Government than in opposition. But Zapu discontent, particularly in the party stronghold of Matabeleland, could lead to a cabinet split and at worst, civil war, unless Mr. Mugabe could satisfy Mr. Nkomo and his followers that they had been given their fair share of government.

A wave of industrial unrest and strikes, something almost unknown in Rhodesia with its high black unemployment, had already swept through Salisbury. Workers at six factories had gone on strike over wages, working conditions and alleged abuse by white officials and managers. Most of the disputes were settled, but a major walk-out by about 500 workers continued at the Seki township plant, of Cone Textiles, just outside Salisbury.

The new Minister of Labour and Social Welfare, Mr. Kumbirai Kangai, said that the basic cause of the industrial unrest was "a malicious rumour" that all pension funds were to be nationalized by the new government and that workers would lose their contributions.

"I wish to strongly refute this rumour," he said. "I now give a categorical assurance that all money paid into pension funds by workers are fully safeguarded." As for wages and other disputes, he added: "There is a laid-down procedure, for the airing of workers grievances, which must be observed."

For the record

The situation can best be summarized as follows:-

* Britain's last attempt at a colonial policy of divide and rule has failed.
* Tribalism proved decisive. The Matabele on the whole voted solidly for Joshua Nkomo and the majority Shona tribe for Mugabe.
* Bishop Muzorewa lost his Shona support because first, he was perceived to be a tool of the whites and second, he was seen as the man who gave in to the British at the Lancaster House talks, while Mugabe and Nkomo held out for more and more concessions.
* The traditional tensions between the Shona and Matabele will cause Premier Mugabe some very severe headaches.
* To compare Mugabe with Kenya's late President, Kenyatta, is tempting, but holds no water. Kenyatta became disillusioned with Marxism and was a strong believer in free enterprise.
* Mugabe's Marxism has been postponed, *not put aside*. The change is tactical rather than strategic. There are three reasons

for this: Firstly, his internal party-wing threatened in November 1979 to oust him from the leadership if he did not shed some of his Marxist doctrines. Secondly, he has to secure his economy and, above all, agriculture, before taking any drastic action. Thirdly, he needs the whites badly – for the time being at least – particularly in the police and military forces for the maintenance of law and order.

* The two Marxists, Comrades Machel of Mozambique and Mugabe of Zimbabwe, now control a swathe of Africa from the Limpopo to the sea.
* South Africa has acquired yet another Marxist neighbour.
* The peace of Southern Africa is at stake. Events will prove that Britain handed this vital corner of the world into Marxist hands.
* Britain sold the white man down the river. One can but hope that the West will now at last recognize that South Africa is a bulwark against communism and shield it from direct or indirect attack by the Soviet Union.
* While General Peter Walls and his white officers were in control of the armed forces, Comrade Mugabe meant it when he says that no terrorist infiltration will be allowed to originate from Zimbabwe territory.
* But now General Peter Walls has served Mugabe's purpose, Zimbabwe will in the future be used as a base for terrorist attacks against South Africa. Let it never be forgotten that Mugabe's terrorists were responsible for some of the worst atrocities in a bitterly fought war.
* A Marxist net is being pulled around South Africa. Already numbers of terrorists are being captured in South Africa when entering it from neighbouring countries. Big caches of weapons are being uncovered.
* Sam Nujoma's SWAPO terrorists will step up their atrocities against Namibian blacks in raids over the border from Angola. Meanwhile Nujoma now entertains high hopes for success in Namibia of a similar kind to that of Mugabe in Zimbabwe.
* Jonas Savimbi and his anti-Marxist UNITA forces have wide and deep support from Angola's country population and are meeting with success in southern Angola. As I have explained in the Chapter on Unconventional War, this success must be exploited by the West.
* South Africa will now be less willing than ever to allow a Marxist SWAPO party to come to power in Zimbabwe's next-door neighbour – Namibia.
* Sooner or later Mugabe will be forced to yield to black-nationalist pressure. The 64 thousand dollar question is: Will he be able to buy enough time to put his own house in order before events sweep beyond his control?

211

* Zimbabwe is certainly another 'domino' to fall and will prove to be one more nail in the coffin of the West.

The only bright side of the picture is the brilliant performance of the Commonwealth monitoring group. The West, and the people in Britain in particular, owe a great debt of gratitude to the soldiers and policemen who kept the peace in Rhodesia during the run-up to the elections. Quietly, with no weapons to speak of and no show of strength, they won the trust of the Africans and defused what might have become a highly explosive situation.

The British may no longer have an empire to speak of, but the brief, three-month revival of colonial rule in Southern Rhodesia proved they can still be first-class imperialists in case of need, and even better decolonizers.

Lord Soames and his small team of officials arrived before the ink was dry on a shaky ceasefire agreement breaking off a vicious terrorist war which had cost more than 20,000 lives. The armistice left three undefeated armies — The Rhodesian security forces and the Zanla and Zipra armies — in the field.

To keep them apart, the Governor was given the thin jungle-green line of 1,400 mainly British soldiers in the Commonwealth monitoring group, who parcelled themselves out among the 16 terrorist assembly camps and scores of Rhodesian military bases.

This handful of soldiers could easily have become hostages in camps bristling with weapons up to and including field artillery and awash with ammunition in the hands of nervous terrorists who knew they were most exposed when concentrated.

Instead, the soldiers with the red, white and blue shoulder flashes and the white crosses on their Land-Rovers won the confidence of the terrorists, played cards and football with them, drank beer and swopped yarns with them, exchanged items of uniform and lived among them devoid of a single noteworthy incident.

It would be difficult to gainsay what Lord Soames wrote in his letter of thanks to them: "The task which you have been performing is unique in the annals of military and political history ... Nobody has ever before even attempted what you have now achieved with such notable success."

The monitoring operation, organized by the British and ably supported by Australians, New Zealanders, Fijians and Kenyans, was a brilliant success, and can do nothing but good.

But the public relations masterstroke of the whole affair was the brief intervention of 570 British policemen, one to each rural polling station, to reinforce the message that the ballot was secret.

To see a young Metropolitan Police sergeant "walking the beat" along the length of a queue of amazed African voters for the benefit of photographers, hands behind back, feet at ten-to-two, helmet on head and strolling at the regulation two and a half miles an hour in the sweltering heat of the Lowveld bush, will be an imperishable memory.

The Left-White Merger – Postscript (1980)

At the beginning of July, internal tensions between the rival factions in the black majority government began to surface in public, having grown considerably since independence. One Cabinet Minister called for the political diminution – or "crushing" as he put it – of Joshua Nkomo, whose position was clearly being undermined, adding greatly to the potential for full scale tribal civil war.

The flow of whites out of the country was increasing dramatically as the future looked more uncertain. Small things, like the use of the word *comrade* by the broadcasting media was not helping matters, but from the very beginning of black rule, doubts were cast over the future of the whites in government. Within weeks of taking office the Minister of Manpower Planning and Development, Edgar Tekere, who with Finance Minister Enos Nkala was leading the more radical element within the Cabinet, made a major contribution to the white exodus figures when he announced that the Lancaster House agreement was nothing more than a "scrap of paper". Specifically Tekere said white representation in parliament would go. Then it seemed *he* would – *on a murder charge!*

Moves to oust the 20 whites led by Mr. Ian Smith in the first Zimbabwe Parliament had been made on 13th May – the eve of its official opening. The Minister of Justice and Constitutional Affairs, Simbi Mubako, said it was "repugnant" for whites to hold a fifth of the seats. Under the Constitution negotiated in London last year, there is the provision for 20 white seats over the next seven years unless the House votes unanimously to overturn the clause. Marxist pressures, however, are not held in check by democratic constitutions!

We need to reflect that in almost all of the African States which have been granted independence by Britain, dictatorship and rule by fear has come about. Short of intervention by the hand of Providence, Rhodesia will prove to be no exception. In ridding itself of Rhodesia to an avowed Marxist, Britain has created yet another vacuum into which the Soviets *will,* by stealth, seek to infiltrate.

I must reiterate a warning which I have given on previous occasions: Rhodesia is but a bridgehead in Russia's master plan to absorb the whole of Southern Africa, including its great mineral wealth, so to complete the encirclement of, and the preparation for the assault on, South Africa, thus to dominate the Cape Route and bring NATO to its knees without firing a shot in this *international* war.

Two of the key factors are how long Mugabe can hold the hot heads and hard-liners and whether the white-dominated infrastructure will hold on long enough for the Africans to acquire the necessary skills and experience.

Mugabe's careful manoeuvring is consistent not only with the standard Communist pattern but also with his past statements. His apparent moderation is the classical textbook Communist approach, using the honeymoon period to infiltrate the basic instruments of power and then to seize total control.

Meanwhile Nkomo is playing a cat and mouse game. If Mugabe fails to "deliver the goods" to the blacks quickly enough there will be a blood bath. And Nkomo has the better trained and equipped soldiers. This tactic is, of course, a hangover from the tribal days when might and physical power were respected – only the strong survived to dominate the weak. The Matabele (Nkomo) always dominated the Shona (Mugabe) – these are the two major tribes in Rhodesia.

Therefore, what we now have is the makings of an Eastern Bloc backed tribal war for the ultimate survival of either Nkomo or Mugabe, who owe allegiance either to Russia or China and other Eastern Bloc nations for their political and military support. This ensures a civil war between Nkomo's Matabeles and Mugabe's Shonas for ultimate power in the country.

The ultimate victory will go to the Eastern Bloc. They are in a "can't lose" position. Without the support of the West this is the fate of the country, no matter how long it may take. And the world is faced with another totalitarian, one party, Eastern Bloc country, this time right on South Africa's northern border.

The sequence of events now being planned is:

* Solicit Western aid.
* Consolidate gains.
* Prepare for the coming renewed offensive against South Africa.

South Africa fully accepts that it will have to fight its own battle for survival. The first blow was struck at the beginning of June, when trained saboteurs successfully carried out the biggest act of urban terrorism so far in South Africa, with the sabotage of vital installations – two Sasol oil-from-coal plants.

As I warned in my book *The Bear at the Back Door* (pages 15 and 70), the king-pin behind the scenes in Southern Africa is the Russian Ambassador in Lusaka, Zambia. It is he who is playing a major role in the African National Congress (ANC) planning and strategy and who is conducting a comprehensive surveillance and monitoring of energy and other vital installations in the Republic of South Africa. As a senior KGB officer, the Ambassador is the great planner of the Communist onslaught and one of his publications has been described as "a primer for subversion".

Protection against the sabotage of vital installations by sophisticated explosive devices is one thing. Protection from attacks by rockets is another. I have no doubt that South Africa will get the measure of both. Not only do they possess a most impressive military machine but their home-produced weaponry is devastatingly efficient. A missile system second to none, an artillery rocket matching anything in the armoury of the great powers and a naval missile, launchable from small vessels with deadly accuracy over 30 kilometres and capable of putting a 2000-ton destroyer out of action with a single shot.

South Africa will not be easily invaded by either East or West. Indeed, potentially it is as valuable as an ally, as it is deadly as an enemy.

CHAPTER
19

Norway & Denmark

Just as Turkey is the soft underbelly of NATO's Southern Flank, so are Norway and Denmark the fragile umbrella of NATO's Northern Flank. But whereas Turkey has the largest army of NATO's European nations, Norway and Denmark have the smallest.

Having been NATO's Commander-in-Chief of this vulnerable Northern Flank from 1969-72, I am, perhaps, in as good a position as anyone to comment on the sharpening of Russia's recent (February 1980) warnings to Norway over NATO exercises on their soil and the creation of an "arc of crisis".

I will not succumb to the temptation of saying "I told you so" and then giving chapter and verse, because all my warnings and attempts at remedial action are expertly described by Tom Pocock in his last chapter entitled *The NATO Jungle* of his biography of me entitled *Fighting General**. Thirty-two pages in this fascinating chapter describe not only the land, maritime and air threats from Russia, but also the attempts made to dismiss me, or declare me *persona non grata,* for having sounded the tocsin so consistently and stood up to the Russian bully, as well as to a rag-bag of NATO politicians and Services chiefs, most of whom appeared to be infected with dry-rot.

In their bluntest warning yet to Norway, the Russians, on 19th February accused the Oslo Government of deliberately trying to worsen Soviet-Norwegian relations and of helping the Americans create an arc of crisis on the Soviet frontier in the north to complement that in the south.

An article in *Pravda* signed, with a pseudonym used to express the views of the Soviet leadership, said Norway was joining in Washington's anti-Soviet course "without giving thought to the possible implications of this step".

Following the increasingly sharply-worded daily attacks on Norway in the Soviet Press over the NATO exercises there in March, the party newspaper accused the Norwegian Government of deliberately allowing itself to be drawn into "unfriendly acts" against the Soviet Union.

* Out of print.

The paper said this was no coincidence since Norway supported the NATO decision to deploy new nuclear missiles in Western Europe, which it said were intended to achieve military superiority over the Soviet Union. Norway also supported the campaign to disrupt the Moscow Olympics and had cancelled planned meetings and contacts with the Soviet Union.

"The ruling circles of Norway are actually serving as accessories to the adventurist line pursued by the Carter Administration aimed at destroying international détente and unleashing a cold war."

The Russians were particularly worried about the current discussions between Norway and the United States on the stationing in Norway of enough American weapons and vehicles to equip a brigade of 8,000 American soldiers.

Pravda repeated charges the Russians had made recently that military bases were being set up on Norwegian soil which would remain after the NATO exercise "Anorak Express" was over.

"Norway's transformation into an arsenal of foreign offensive weapons openly aimed at the Soviet Union cannot be described otherwise than as a departure of the Government from the principles of its own declared policy of not stationing foreign troops and nuclear weapons on Norwegian soil in time of peace – despite the assurances about a consistent observance of these principles repeatedly given by Norway."

Norway rejected Soviet charges that it was departing from its policy of not accepting foreign troops and nuclear weapons on its territory in peacetime. Mr. Thorvald Stoltenberg, the Norwegian Defence Minister, said the question of storing military equipment had been a subject of consultation for two years and was nothing new. The storing of tactical nuclear weapons had not been raised in the consultations.

He added that NATO exercises of the "Anorak Express" type had taken place regularly over a number of years and that the Soviet Union, as usual, had been notified in the normal way.

The NATO exercise referred to by the Russians took place in Northern Norway, at a considerable distance from the 120-mile frontier with the Soviet Union. Beyond it there are two Soviet divisions, about 40 airfields and the big Soviet naval base in the ice-free port of Murmansk.

British units, including 3 Royal Marine Commando Brigade took part with the Norwegian Army, American marines and other allied forces, totalling about 24,000 troops, in the "Anorak Express" exercise under the Arctic winter warfare conditions.

The main aim of the exercise was to deploy the Allied Mobile Force (Land) (AMF(L)) into one of its possible emergency task areas. The sharp attacks in the Soviet Press, expressed concern at exercises so near the Soviet border and at the stockpiling of heavy weapons for use in wartime.

General Sir Anthony Farrar-Hockley, Commander-in-Chief Allied Forces Northern Europe said that, on the contrary, by holding this exercise several hundred miles clear of the border, Norway was showing sensible restraint.

Moreover, Russian propaganda about nuclear stockpiles in Norway was a blatant lie. He emphasized the importance of this type of exercise in Norway where the difference in environment was not only the snow but where the temperature can drop to below minus 20°C in a matter of minutes. Soldiers had to learn to survive before even being able to think about combat.

The Allied Mobile Force is a brigade-size force. It would confront a move by the Soviet Union by ensuring the immediate involvement of as many allied countries as possible. It is expected to be deployed in Greece and Italy but the most likely areas of activity are considered by NATO planners to be the extreme flanks — Turkey and Norway. Regular exercises are held in these countries, although the composition of the force varies. It is equipped and organized to fight alongside the forces of the host nation.

It is here in Norway that the defence of Britain begins. Soviet air-craft and ships have to come out through the gap between Norway and the North Cape, or out of the Baltic Sea. The battle for Britain and the Atlantic would be much more difficult to conduct and win if the Norwegian bases were lost or neutralized.

The British element of the "Anorak Express" force consists of one infantry battalion as well as artillery, reconnaissance, signals, intelligence and logistic units. Similar sized detachments are provided by Canada and Italy. West Germany, Belgium and Luxembourg also have units available for the force.

Troops are normally stationed in their home country and are trained to move rapidly to a force concentration area before being committed to action. The commander of the force is rotated among the NATO countries involved, and at the time of "Anorak Express" was a Major-General of the United States Army. The commander has a small international headquarters usually based in West Germany.

Rapid reinforcements of the area is a major consideration. It would be done mostly by prepositioning stocks of heavy equipment and stores to enable outside reinforcements to be moved quickly by air and sea. Discussions for assembling stocks had been going on for some considerable time with Norway and were expected to end soon.

I will now proceed to explain why Russia is so sensitive to such military exercises in Norway. In the process it will become apparent why Norway, and Denmark also, qualify for inclusion in the row of "dominoes" that can fall into Russia's lap.

Norway is being outflanked at sea by the Russian Arctic Fleet. Norway and Iceland — the latter being the cork in the bottle — hold the key to the sea-lanes leading from the Soviet strategic base of the first order at Murmansk, right out into the Atlantic. If Malta mattered in the defence of Southern Europe, Norway matters more. This is why Britain had to "keep cool over cod".

The importance of Iceland was readily appreciated by the British War Cabinet in 1940, when they ordered its occupation. Winston Churchill wrote in his memoirs: "Whoever possesses Iceland holds the pistol firmly pointed at England, America and Canada! It was not by chance that the Royal Navy first encountered the German battleship *Bismark* in these waters.

What the Communists in Iceland are after is not just a breach between Iceland and Britain, but the neutralization of the vital NATO base at Keflavik, manned by U.S. forces, whose task it is to monitor Soviet naval and air movements in the North Atlantic.

Iceland's withdrawal from NATO would be a major blow to the West, because it would leave a vacuum for increasing Soviet influence on an island from which such a large sector of the North Atlantic can be dominated.

It is a fact that nowhere in the Alliance is the imbalance of standing forces – land, amphibious, sea, air and nuclear – greater than it is on NATO's Northern Flank. The Soviet Union far exceeds NATO's capability on the Northern Flank. The situation is aggravated by the refusal of Norway and Denmark to allow the stationing of foreign troops and nuclear weapons on their soil in peacetime. *How on earth do they expect to be reinforced in time* in the face of the threat, particularly at sea?

In a letter published in *The Times,* London, on 19th March, 1976, I emphasized Russia's ability to launch a surprise attack on NATO's Central Front in Western Europe. The description I gave of the speed, devastating power and velocity of a Soviet surprise onslaught would apply to an even greater degree against NATO's highly vulnerable and neglected Northern Flank, particularly North Norway.

One of the reasons for this is that NATO's forces on the Central Front are so deployed that the Soviets could not launch a limited aggression against one NATO ally alone without becoming involved with another. This would involve major aggression and lead to general war.

In my view the initial danger lies at the extremity of NATO, namely North Norway in the Arctic. Here the Soviets have the most to gain at the smallest risk. If they were ever to decide to fight a general war in Central Europe, they would be in a far better position to do so if, as a first step, they had tested the resolution of NATO by launching a surprise attack in overwhelming strength against North Norway, where the imbalance of forces is so pronounced.

A swift, decisive limited aggression could be completed successfully before the NATO allies could enter into, let alone conclude, their consultations, and NATO would be presented with a *fait accompli.* How would and could NATO react?

The factors that the Soviets would already have taken into consideration when surveying the NATO scene and deciding how the Alliance might react to such an attack, would be:

One, The West's opposition to defence spending because of their people's preoccupation with the day-to-day problems of jobs, housing and food, has now undermined their will and determination and their defence capability.

Two, NATO would fear the escalation to general war and the further escalation to a nuclear conflict.

Three, Norway's outdated Bases Policy, whereby the stationing of NATO troops and nuclear weapons is prohibited on their territory in peacetime, is a self-inflicted wound. (The same applies to Denmark).

Four, the lack of stockpiles in Norway for external reinforcements is another self-inflicted wound.

Five, External reinforcements would be unable to reach Norway in time. Indeed, Russia has already won a bloodless victory in the North due to Britain's series of defence cuts which will result in greatly reduced reinforcements being available for the Northern Flank. It is pathetic that some British reinforcements will now have to go to war by requisitioned car ferries which will be obliged to scuttle into some remote Norwegian fjords, hopefully ahead of the Russians.

Six, the inability of NATO councils, and their lack of moral courage, will prevent them from reaching political decisions in time.

Seven, Russia's Northern Fleet, their smallest at the end of World War II, is now their biggest – the super fleet of a super navy of a superpower – and is capable of deploying well over 100 submarines in the Atlantic with ease. In World War II the picture was grim enough for the Allies when there were only 50 enemy submarines.

Eight, in the face of this maritime strength, Norway would not and could not be reinforced. She is already outflanked at sea. It is the intention of the Soviets to push their naval defence line outwards to Iceland and the Faeroes. If this is a likely development, then it indicates that the Russians would, to an increasing degree, come to regard the Norwegian Sea as a Soviet lake behind which, of course, Norway will lie.

Nine, by occupying the vast but sparsely populated area of Norway's Northern province, Finnmark, Russia would secure airfields, ice-free naval dispersal areas in the fjords and easier access to the West's jugular vein in the Atlantic, while NATO would lose important surveillance units and radars.

Ten, Russia's Delta class submarines which carry nuclear missiles with a range in excess of four thousand miles, already give them the capability of covering the entire NATO land mass from submerged positions inside their own protected waters. With North Norway in their hands the protection afforded would be greatly enhanced and the threat to the West greatly increased.

It behoves the West to bear in mind that by the time the American equivalent submarine, the Trident, goes to sea, the Russians will already have 25 Delta submarines at sea, each with megaton warheads.

In the face of the ever-growing Soviet threat, the development of Norwegian defence policy, and Denmark's for that matter, is taking place at far too lazy a tempo. *God helps those who help themselves,* so Norway should now change its bases and nuclear policy which was adopted more than 23 years ago. They should also give their already well organized Home Guard a more mobile and offensive role. This alone would help to act as a deterrent to any Russian adventure.

Opposite Denmark the military activities of the Soviet Union and Warsaw Pact countries have escalated substantially. Formation flights by up to 40-50 Soviet warplanes are carried out to within a handful of miles of Danish territory. The strategic aim of the Warsaw Pact countries includes plans to over-run Denmark in order to secure a safe passage for the Baltic Fleet to sail out into the Atlantic and marry up with the Soviet Northern Fleet. Denmark, or a greater part of it, and Norway are already behind the battle-front in the eyes of Soviet Generals.

The Baltic is an inland sea, dominated by the warships of the Warsaw Pact. The cork in the Baltic bottle is Denmark. The shallow and narrow straits which provide the only exit from the Baltic are within sight of Danish territory.

Within the Baltic, Western naval forces are outnumbered by something approaching six-to-one. In recent years, the Soviets have taken to conducting large amphibious exercises, in which their troop transports and warships head directly for the Danish coast, only to turn south at the final moment and land on East German beaches, which bear a striking similarity to the Danish beaches. Soviet attack aircraft have made simulated runs.

If a combined Soviet airborne and naval assault were undertaken it would be met by a standing Danish army about half the size of the New York police force. Neither Denmark nor Norway, the other Scandinavian NATO ally, allows the stationing of allied troops or nuclear weapons. The relatively feeble local forces are expected to hold off the assaulting Soviet until the arrival of allied reinforcements.

All of which raises what must seem to the Soviet general staff a credible scenario for a brief, blitzkrieg war in Europe. Given the U.S.-NATO doctrine of "flexible response", assume a surprise attack with conventional weapons across the North German plain towards the Rhine, which some military experts believe could be reached in 72 hours.

Simultaneously, airborne-sea-land assaults are launched to occupy the northern tip of Norway and Denmark, which dominate Soviet sea passages to the Atlantic. After 72 hours the Soviets achieve their minimal objectives. The Soviets offer the Germans, the Danes, and the Norwegians a cease-fire and peace agreement – in exchange for with-

221

drawal from NATO, disarmament, neutrality, and unlocking of the naval gates to the Atlantic.

Would the densely populated countries of West Europe prefer to be over-run by Russian troops, and their homelands made conventional or nuclear battlefields rather than opt for concessions, peace and neutrality? Would an American president reject negotiations and engage in atomic war in Europe, which would rapidly escalate to strategic war with the Soviet Union, which has probably established nuclear superiority?

Soviet conventional superiority continues to grow, her strategic forces to expand. *There is no precedent in history for such a build-up of naval and military power where that power was not eventually used.*

Russia's Arctic Superfort at Murmansk*

High on the top of the world, the Soviet Union has assembled a mighty arsenal of warships, nuclear submarines and long-range bombers capable of striking the U.S. At Murmansk is the largest military base in the world, and it lies directly on the shortest route between the most densely populated centres of the United States and the Soviet Union.

In Murmansk and at Severomorsk, on the same fjord, or nearby in other parts of the Kola Peninsula, Russia has built up a massive combination of military forces capable of fighting at sea, in the air or on land.

Based in this area is Russia's Northern Fleet, the largest of its four fleets and said to be the Soviet Navy's most powerful strike force.

The fleet contains 69 surface-combat ships and 47 support ships. Listed among its combat vessels are one aircraft carrier (presently in the Mediterranean, March 1980), 9 guided-missile cruisers, 2 light cruisers, 7 guided-missile destroyers, 6 other destroyers, 39 frigates and 5 other frigates with guided missiles. With several hundred smaller ships, the fleet has a manpower totalling in the region of 116,000.

Assigned to the Northern Fleet are 102 nuclear powered submarines, about two-thirds of Russia's nuclear-submarine force. One half of the entire underseas fleet is in this area, including 48 ballistic missile submarines – 26 with cruise missiles – and 26 torpedo-attack submarines. No land-based strategic missiles are known to be on the Kola Peninsula; but some missiles of the Delta-class submarines can reach the United States from the Barents Sea.

Also assigned to the Northern Fleet are 15 to 20 Backfire bomber aircraft with a combat range of more than 3,000 nautical miles that puts them within easy reach of NATO's military centres in Western Europe. With inflight refuelling capabilities, the Backfires also could reach the United States.

* Reprinted from *U.S. News & World Report,* 3rd March, 1980. Copyright (1980). U.S. News & World Report, Inc.

Ground troops include motorized rifle divisions at Murmansk and Kandalaksha and a naval infantry brigade, comparable to the U.K. and U.S. Marines. With artillery, rocket and anti-missile forces there may be up to 40,000 fighting soldiers in a combat role. Their offensive capability is enhanced by the addition of modern amphibious vessels.

What makes Murmansk so important is its geographical location and the warm Gulf Stream that keeps a narrow strip of Arctic waters ice-free all the year round. From bases in the region, Soviet submarines can move quickly into the Barents Sea, where they could launch their 4,800 mile range missiles at U.S. targets.

The same area is the departure point for missile submarines with shorter ranges and hunter-killer boats that have the mission of destroying NATO submarine forces. From the Barents Sea, these underwater vessels could head for the Greenland-Iceland-United Kingdom gap *en route* to the Atlantic Ocean. Murmansk is only 60 miles from the northern tip of Norway, a NATO member.

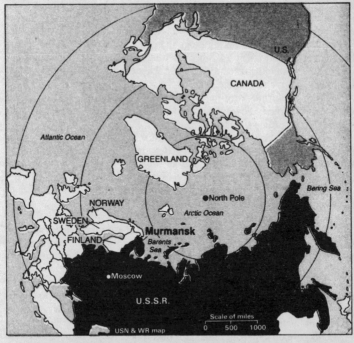

Murmansk became famous in World War II as the port of delivery for military supplies from the U.S. and Britain to Russia. Between 1941 and 1945, an estimated 7,500 tanks, 100,000 trucks and armoured vehicles, aircraft and other supplies passed through there.

Invading German troops came within 40 miles of Murmansk, and the city endured a relentless bombing that destroyed 70 per cent of its built-up area.

Murmansk is not only a military base. It also is an operational base for assaults on the frozen Arctic Ocean by Russia's three nuclear-powered icebreakers; the 20 year old, 16,000-ton *Lenin* and two more modern ships, the 23,000-ton *Arktika* and the *Sibir*.

The *Arktika* gained fame in 1977 as the first surface ship ever to reach the North Pole. Later the *Sibir* led a merchant ship from Murmansk across the high latitudes to the Soviet shores of the Pacific Ocean.

Opening this new route could cut the normal summer time journey by 1,300 sea miles. Murmansk is also the hub of a Soviet effort to gain greater flexibility for its expanding blue-water Navy. Already the Barents and White seas are linked to the Baltic by a 200-mile canal.

Thus warships of the Northern Fleet are able to move from Murmansk to their major repair bases at Leningrad quickly – and beyond the sight of NATO reconnaissance. A future goal, now closer at hand as a result of the *Sibir's* exploration, is a sea-lane of about 4,300 miles linking Murmansk and the Bering Sea and open the year round. This would help speed development of Siberia's wealth because heavy equipment and supplies could be transported there whenever needed instead of during only a few months of the year.

More important from the military view, a sea route across the top of the world would allow warships to move quickly from west to east or vice versa, according to strategic needs.

As part of their planning for this future, the Soviets acquired a huge floating dock built at Goteborn, Sweden. It can handle an 80,000-ton warship or four nuclear submarines at one time. A similar floating dock is in position at the Pacific Coast end of the Arctic route. When both are operational, warships can be moved as needed, with repair facilities at both ends of the sea-lane.

Murmansk is also the major base for Soviet development of the 24,000-square-mile Spitsbergen archipelago. These islands are owned by Norway, but 39 other nations possess equal rights to develop resources in the area under a 1920 treaty. The treaty bans military activity in the archipelago.

Coal is the only Spitsbergen resource that currently is being developed. Norway and the U.S.S.R. each mine about 450,000 tons a year. Oil has been sought, but exploratory holes have been dry. Seismic surveys indicate there are offshore oil deposits.

Offshore oil exploration has not begun because of disputes between Norway and Russia. Oslo claims that the 400-mile-wide span between the archipelago and Norway is continental shelf and not subject to the 1920 treaty.

There is a wealth of oil and natural gas off the coast of Norway, as well as in the Barents Sea, between Norway and Spitsbergen. It looks like another Middle East. It is a continuation of the flush North Sea deposits, which become flusher and bigger further North and which extend even into the Kara Sea, further east, off the Arctic coast of Russia.

The Soviets want to share with Norway the Norwegian part — about 90% — of this oil province, and have said so to the Norwegian Government. The Soviets, however, do not offer any *quid pro quo*, like sharing the natural gas wealth in the Kara Sea, which they control.

At stake, therefore, are these offshore oil reserves that some authorities claim could rival those of the Middle East. Just as important are the waters traversed by the huge Soviet fleet on its way to the Atlantic from Murmansk. Moscow would like a crack at these potentially huge oil deposits. But Moscow does not want Western oil rigs interfering with or watching Soviet nuclear submarines as they slide out of Murmansk and into their position for firing nuclear missiles on the shortest path across the Atlantic.

If the continental shelf is governed by the treaty (the post-World War I treaty that gave Norway sovereignity over Spitsbergen, which the Soviet Government signed in 1925), U.S. and U.K. oil companies could drill into a possible bonanza of great dimensions.

Invasion from "The Sea of Peace"

The Soviets utilize the waters between Spitsbergen and the North Cape of Norway, including the Norwegian waters in the area, for the movement of their nuclear submarines and their nuclear bombers to the Atlantic within hitting distance of the United States, Canada and Great Britain. Hence the Soviet concern of a possible new Western presence off Soviet shores.

The Baltic — *the sea of peace* as the Russians have christened it — has seen a consistent growth in Warsaw Pact activity in recent years. East German and Polish amphibious craft and ships conduct exercises increasingly near to Danish waters and aircraft from these countries patrol ever closer to Danish airspace.

As if to underline this increased activity, East German craft in the Spring of 1979 embarked upon a new ploy, attempting in broad daylight — and in full view of Danish television cameras — to net a (albeit anti-quated) Danish torpedo during practice firings, cocking a snook at NATO's Baltic muscle.

The Russians are also involved in greater manoeuvre activity, and are known to have had six Golf submarines, each equipped with 3 Serp nuclear warheads (range 750 miles), in the "peaceful" Baltic since 1976.

The arrival of the nuclear age has not diminished Denmark's age-old strategic importance as the guardian of the Baltic Straits, even if Danes no longer exact dues from ships entering or leaving the Baltic as they did for 400 years until 1857.

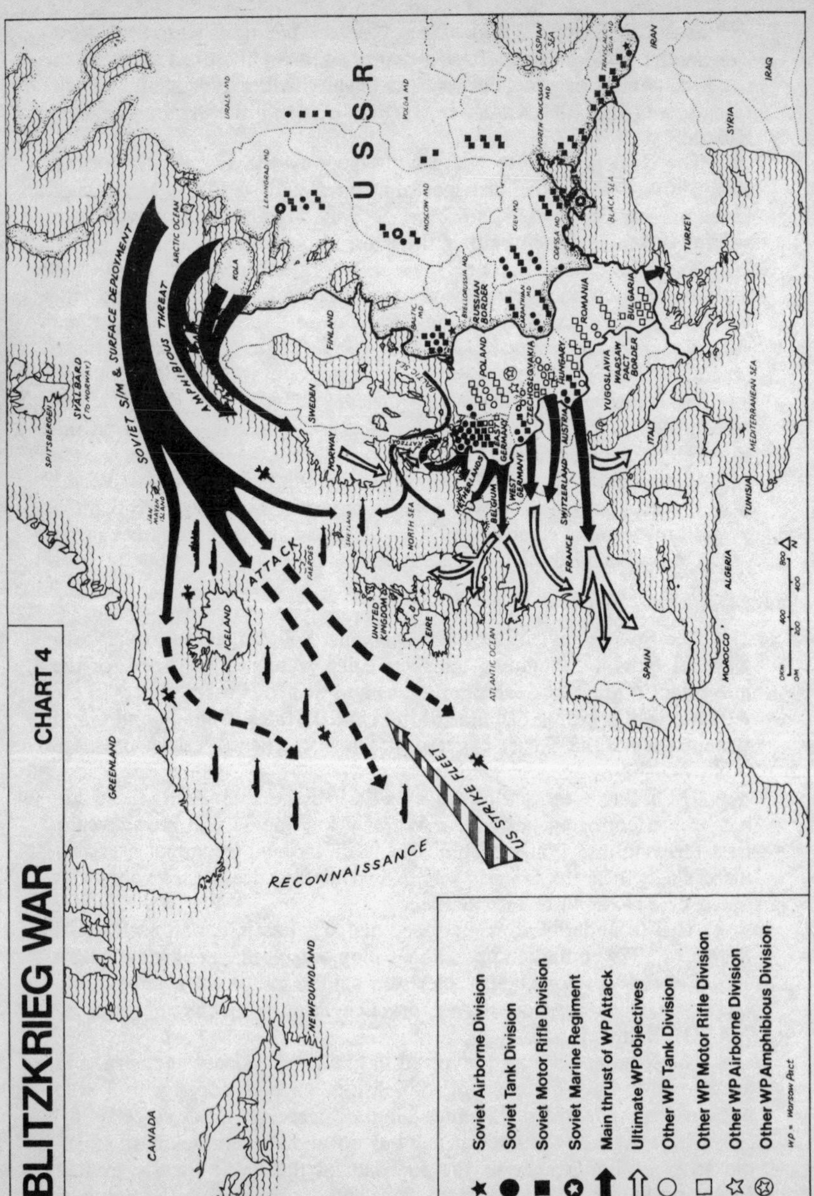

BLITZKRIEG WAR

CHART 4

Legend:

★ Soviet Airborne Division
● Soviet Tank Division
■ Soviet Motor Rifle Division
✪ Soviet Marine Regiment
➡ Main thrust of WP Attack
⇨ Ultimate WP objectives
○ Other WP Tank Division
□ Other WP Motor Rifle Division
☆ Other WP Airborne Division
⊗ Other WP Amphibious Division

WP = Warsaw Pact

Appreciation to War Monthly

After the Second World War a "Nordic balance" was created in Scandinavia, with neutral militarily powerful Sweden flanked on the one side by Finland allied to the Soviet Union, and on the other by two non-nuclear NATO member states, Denmark and Norway.

NATO sees Denmark's role in a conflict with the Warsaw Pact states as that of a delaying element, holding the aggressor while NATO retaliates. NATO command in Denmark anticipates that any significant Warsaw Pact conventional attack on central Western Europe would be prefaced by a rapid air, land and sea pincer attack via the Baltic and Schleswig-Holstein.

This would give the East control of Jutland, the Danish Islands and the Baltic Straits, and thus secure an exit for their ships to the North Atlantic. Denmark's role is thus to prevent the Baltic Straits being taken for as long as possible, as well as helping in the North Atlantic to hold the strategically important Greenland-Iceland-Scotland line.

In this light NATO sees the further strengthening of Norwegian, and particularly Danish, defences and military capacity – without a nuclear presence – as of great importance. Denmark's dire economic situation has prompted the Government to make cuts in military expenditure within the past few months much to the dismay of Denmark's allies – and the overt satisfaction of the Soviet Union. Not only was military expenditure cut by 100m Krones (£8.3m) in the Government's austerity package last December, but Denmark also angered NATO by asking for a six-month postponement of the decision to site Cruise and Pershing missiles in Western Europe to counterbalance the Soviet missile build-up in Eastern Europe.

The Postponement suggestion, which was to allow for new talks on disarmament with the Soviet Union, broke the apparent consensus within NATO on modernization, giving Denmark another black mark. The third action to tarnish Denmark's image within the alliance was the Government's proposal for a zero-growth rating in its new defence budget for 1981-85.

Although the Defence Minister had insisted that the zero-growth formula was only "a basis for negotiations" on a new defence Bill, the very thought perturbed General Bernard Rogers, Supreme NATO Commander, Europe, who during a visit to Copenhagen, called upon Denmark to increase military expenditure by 3 per cent.

The defence debate in Denmark, it should be emphasized, in no way reflected a Danish desire to withdraw from NATO and take on its past garb of neutrality.

Notwithstanding, it was the Danish politician, Mogens Glistrup, who had the temerity to suggest that the army should be "done away with" and the defence budget allocated to placing loud-speakers along the border to proclaim *"We surrender"*, as the Soviet armies approached.

The latest opinion polls showed that 57 per cent of Danes were *for*

227

NATO membership. There was more concern over Danish willingness to contribute effectively to the alliance. Denmark contributes a meagre 2.4 per cent of GNP to defence, its soldiers are among the highest paid (and some say worst disciplined) in the world. Rumours of frequent desertions by brave Jenses (a "Jens" is a Danish "Tommy") on military exercises in Jutland did not amuse NATO circles.

Broadly, the Danish Government wants to reduce military manpower by purchasing ultra-modern technology for the Navy and the Air Force, on which Danish defence would be concentrated, at the cost of a depleted Army.

The Danish defence force is compact if lilliputian in size. The total wartime strength of the three services and the Home Guard amounts at present to about 200,000.

The so-called zero-growth proposal which the Defence Minister was using as his basis for the new defence package would effectively concentrate Danish defence in Jutland and mean a cutting of defence personnel by 5,200, the disbandment of a brigade on the eastern island of Zeeland (on which Copenhagen is situated), two Air Force Squadrons, and the Navy's five frigates, as well as the closing of several bases.

In the current uncertain international situation a freezing of the budget, implying cuts of one quarter of Denmark's fighting men, a third of its combat aircraft and ships, was not attractive to the rightist and centrist parties led by the Liberals and Conservatives, whose support the Prime Minister would need for the passing of a new defence Bill.

The price these parties would ask would in all likelihood not fall far short of a 3 per cent rise. The talk of extending NATO bases and depots in Denmark for eventual use by NATO forces numbering up to 20,000 revived old Danish fears of loss of sovereignty, foreign occupation and nuclear involvement, all skeletons in the cupboard pointing to an increase in Danish military expenditure.

I said earlier that by occupying the vast but sparsely populated area of Norway's Northern province of Finnmark, Russia would secure airfields, ice-free naval dispersal areas in the fjords and easier access to the West's jugular vein in the Atlantic, while NATO would lose not only the above but also important surveillance units and radars.

Obviously Russia has a contingency plan for a rapid invasion of Finnmark by surprise attack, using tanks, motorized infantry, parachutists, airlanded troops and amphibious forces backed up by air and naval support. They would be trained for this contingency plan under adverse winter conditions by day or night and could deploy without giving any prior warning. They would achieve suprise under the guise of manoeuvres or by keeping their invasion forces at sufficient combat strength over a long period to obviate the need for reinforcements. NATO would be presented with a *fait accompli*. Would the

President of the United States commit suicide on behalf of Finnmark by pressing the nuclear trigger?

The same would apply to the Danish island of Bornholm in the Western part of the Baltic Sea. The Soviets could take it out at any time of their own choosing.

What a test these two contingencies would be for the will, determination, resolution and effectiveness of NATO. They would be prime examples of NATO being nibbled to death under conditions of nuclear stalemate.

CHAPTER 20

Unconventional War

President Carter asked Congress to authorise the expenditure of $142.7 billion for America's defence forces for 1980. This enormous sum is necessary because the Soviet Union has been spending much more than this on her military might throughout the past decade. Even this expenditure will prove inadequate to assure the security of the U.S.A. because military weapons, however powerful, cannot successfully fight the war which communist Russia and her satellites are waging and winning.

One of the most serious gaps in the West's defences is the failure to mount a full-scale political and propaganda strategy. We have no political warfare strategy for supporting liberation movements and undermining from within the Soviet Union and her Warsaw Pact and non-Warsaw Pact satellites. It is no good defending ourselves in the military field alone.

To prevent military war, the West must win the war of subversion and propaganda which we are losing by default. To achieve this, a dramatic change in our attitude is needed. All our eggs must not be placed in the military basket. We must conduct a psychological and political offensive for which there is no shortage of targets and subjects. In dealing with each in turn, I take cognizance of a number of highly specialized reports published during the last nine months and I am indebted to one eminent investigative journalist in particular.

1.   Angola

As a key base for Soviet plans to destabilize moderate governments in Central and Southern Africa, Angola features as a pivotal point of strategy, offering one of the most promising opportunities for Western counter-action in the form of unconventional warfare. Angola provides camps and a training ground for guerrillas from Zaire, South West Africa (Namibia) and South Africa. This is also where Cuba's heaviest foreign investment has been committed. If indeed President Castro's expeditionary force of some 20,000 men were to sustain significant reversals and casualties, the blow to Cuban morale would undoubtedly lessen the appetite for foreign adventures elsewhere and help to generate opposition in Cuba to the régime's torturous policy of fighting the Russians' battles for them.

There is another factor that could be brought to bear upon the situation. During the 1975-76 civil war, the U.S., without a true grasp of geo-strategic realities, failed to out-manoeuvre the Soviets in their massive backing for the victorious MPLA, by providing support for the anti-Soviet guerrilla forces in Angola. These forces of Dr. Jonas Savimbi's UNITA movement which operate in the south and in a lower profile, to those of the FNLA in the north, did not abandon the fight. According to intelligence reports towards the end of 1979, the Cubans were forced into retreat by removing well over 300 civilian advisers in around 30 municipalities as their lives were in danger. Numbered among these personnel were secret police operatives acting for the Angolan security service.

The Soviets were evidently put to some length over the reversal in Angola in that a top-level military mission arrived in Luanda in December 1979. One month before that, East European reinforcements for Angola were high on the agenda in strategy talks between Fidel Castro and General Alexei Epishev, chief of the Soviet Army's main political department.

On the internal political front, in Angola, the unequivocally pro-Soviet President, José Eduardo dos Santos, has not been popular with the ruling MPLA, due to excessive fawning on the Russians. He was of course hand-picked by the KGB and trained in specific military and ideological techniques. Speculation has also been rife in Luanda that Dr. Agostinho Neto, the predecessor to dos Santos, was assassinated by the Russians while undergoing medical treatment in Moscow, to engineer the installation of the KGB's man.

Against this background, Dr. Savimbi's case for Western support which he has been making forcefully to Washington and London has been supremely important. Inexplicably however, U.S. National Security Adviser, Brezezinski, refused to see him and London made convenient political excuses for not having him around during the Lancaster House conference last year. What is the long term strategy of NATO governments in respect of unconventional war? Do they in fact *have* a strategy and if so, are they actively implementing the strategy? Dr. Savimbi is, on the personal impression of the investigative journalist, the most attractive, intelligent and democratically minded of the black African leaders. His advise to NATO governments has been outstanding and if acted upon, would begin to destroy the Soviet Bloc's prevailing sway in unconventional warfare.

Western military observers who visited areas of north-eastern Angola at the turn of the year (1979-80), which areas were controlled by Dr. Holden Roberto's National Front for the Liberation of Angola (FNLA) returned highly optimistic about the prospects for mounting an effective guerrilla campaign against Soviet and Cuban occupational forces.

Combined with the proven success of Senhor Jonas Savimbi's anti-Soviet UNITA movement in· southern Angola, these reports indicate that Western support for a new offensive against the Marxist MPLA régime in Luanda now offers a low-cost (and potentially highly profitable) way of responding to the Soviet invasion of Afghanistan.

Between them, the FNLA and UNITA are believed to control about two-thirds of Angola, up to four years after the supposed end of a civil war that was won for the MPLA by Cuban troops and Soviet hardware; the Cuban garrisons and the MPLA's forces are confined to the towns, and are making little effort to evict the guerrillas from their vast "liberated zones".

A successful guerrilla offensive in Angola might eventually compel the MPLA to negotiate a democratic settlement. But as the investigative journalist pointed out, it would also accomplish the following broader objectives:

1.   The imposing of psychological defeat upon the Russians and Cubans, which is of prime importance to the stemming of their insurgent operations and causing them to reconsider their expansionist policy – *a Cuban division is positioned in South Yemen next to Saudi Arabia* – and increase the wave of revolt in Cuba itself.

2.   The Soviet Bloc subversion in countries bordering with Angola needs to be reduced or taken-out at its source. Support for the FNLA and UNITA by the West would disrupt the training of guerrillas and the movement of arms and supplies from Angola.

3.   With regard to geo-strategic aspects and any potential ground or air offensive on South Africa, the increase of pro-Western resistance in Angola would create the opportunity to prevent the Soviets use of deepwater ports and air-base facilities in any future conflict.

There is beyond question, great potential for launching a guerrilla offensive in Angola. The terrain and the vast region offers all the protection required and the airdrop of weapons and supplies could be achieved with relative safety.

When it comes to the local political life, the FNLA, like UNITA, has a ready-made cause in Angolan nationalism which would readily expel the "new colonialists" from the Soviet and communist empire. Although the FNLA fighting men require retraining "from scratch" in order to launch intensive operations, the military observers who have been to the areas they control, reported that a powerful motivation was present among the FNLA's fighting men.

Estimates of the number of armed cadres at the disposal of the FNLA vary – not least from the claims of the FNLA chief, Dr. Roberto, himself – but generally the figure has been put at 60,000. The fact is, however, the FNLA needs assistance. It has been severely lacking in financial resources and modern weaponry and has some enormous logistical problems. It has no weapons larger than the 88mm mortar, and most of the sidearms in use are ageing. A small amount of money is raised by the sale of ivory and coffee which comes as contraband from Angola. Something more is demanded of the West, unless our governments actually *desire* to see the siege of Southern Africa develop to the point where it cannot be reversed?

The leaders of the force are based in Zaire (where there is a large Angolan refugee community) but the inconsistent actions and widespread corruption of the local authorities interrupts the flow of supplies and men over the Zairean border.

While Dr. Roberto, aged 63, lacks in personal charisma and driving power in comparison with UNITA's Sr. Savimbi, the potential of the FNLA, given proper training and the increased support of the West, is considerable and should not be disregarded. For instance, with training, FNLA units could launch a highly-effective urban guerrilla campaign, inflicting significant reverses on the friends of Russia by engaging company-sized units, breaking them up and destroying their morale.

With its cells in Luanda, the FNLA has the capacity to provide the base for the campaign and given Soviet-designed weapons (which China has supplied in the past), the FNLA could seek-out supplies of MPLA and Cuban forces ammunition.

Of course, to maintain an effective flow of Western support to the FNLA, an alternative base to Zaire would have to be sought, where training for the military and the airlift to the guerrilla forces in the bush could be conducted without interference and theft by the local administration. One possibility here, if the French decide to play a significant role, is that Senegal or Gabon might agree to provide the base for these operations.

No doubt such counteraction to the spread of communist influence and domination would be objected to on the basis that the United Nations and most of its members recognize that Angola has a legitimate government. But so did they recognize the government in Afghanistan. It is encouraging that NATO governments are now giving serious consideration to the support of Angolan resistance, as part of a "land reclamation" policy for Third World countries which have fallen victim to Soviet expansion over the last five years.

2.   *Iran*

If there is anything positive that can be seen to be emerging from the humiliation of America over the taking of the hostages, it is the early signs of recovery from the mental paralysis that Washington has displayed in foreign affairs since Vietnam. The appeal by President Carter for a united front by the West against the Iranian action is obviously of vital importance. But to what extent is this stand to become a *counteraction* to the foreign involvement which is seeking to ignite Islamic fervour throughout the Arab world against the West and its vital interests?

It is known in Washington that the extremely well-organized assault on the Grand Mosque in Mecca, involved over 70 Yemenis, who had undergone Cuban instruction in Aden (which now operates as Moscow's launch-pad for disruptive action in the Gulf region). An analysis of photographs of the "Moslem students" who were involved in the occupation of the American Embassy in Teheran and of the mass executions by the Revolutionary Guards of Kurdish prisoners, have yielded important information on foreign involvement in the pseudo-Islamic and Marxist revolution. It is believed that a PLO unit has also been involved in Kurdistan.

Economic complicity between the Iranians and the Palestinians is also confirmed by the reported transfer of around $10 million through the Central Bank in Teheran to the PLO in Beirut.

When the *overall* situation is viewed, a picture of very considerable confusion is to be observed. Rival interests seek to spread the Iranian style revolution to the Arab Gulf region – but fortunately for the West, in some ways, they are locked into various murderous feuds.

The radical nature of Iraq, constitutes the major disrupting element with its aim of becoming the leading power in the Gulf. It has an all-out part "holy" war going with Iran and it continues to feud with Syria and South Yemen. Moscow of course seeks to maintain its influence and domination over them all. At odds with Libya, there are also deep splits within the PLO itself, which relies to a large extent on Syria for its bases and the supply of arms. All of this constitutes a basis for subtle and imaginative strategy, if indeed the West can bring itself to restore some positivism to its previous defeatist and retreating foreign policy.

While the same spirit of fanaticism may drive the heritics within Islam and the Soviet imperialists to hate the West, the lesson of history is that the camp of those who disrupt true civilization is always divided – hence, the just receive their due. Islam and communism are uneasy bedfellows which is a situation that can be exploited. The opportunity that presents itself to the West should not fail to be seized.

Experienced opinion views the situation in Iran as offering hope of changing the régime to one, more in favour of moderation and the West. Such a change is less likely to be effected by air-strikes from U.S. aircraft carriers *Kitty Hawk* and *Midway* (which only enabled Khomeini to rally support against "foreign aggression") than by the strategy of unconventional warfare. But events are overtaking us from Iraq.

A long hard Winter without sufficient heat and an adequate supply of food would bring a greater inducement for internal revolt, and the sabotage of Teheran's hydro-electric scheme would help considerably in this respect. *The slogans of Khomeini cannot be eaten* – all that the West has to do is maintain a cut on food supplies. Another way of bringing on difficulties for the régime would be if America were to jam radio and telephone communications in the country, which would be entirely practical as they are channelled through satellite systems.

There are many members of the late Shah's Imperial Guard (just one-tenth only who returned to their barracks after the revolution) who are now active in the underground and resistance networks, one of which – the Free Iranian Liberation Army (ARA) – is stated by the special investigative journalist as having strong representation among exiled army officers in Cairo and several European capitals.

The Kurdish rebels offensive which has remained undefeated has received armed assistance and direction from a number of former Iranian army officers, including General Oveissi, the former martial law commander in Tehran. They will certainly need continuous support in order to achieve their objective. There are people in Iran, like Admiral Madani, who could be the leaders of a counter-revolutionary force, but they cannot expect to succeed without the active and full support of the West – meaning the supply of specialist guidance more than financial assistance, which will be forthcoming anyway from Arab sources.

There could be increasing opportunity to reverse the 'domino' process in this part of the world, but indeed, it remains to be seen if America and the West are determined enough to ensure that the process *is* reversed and remains this way in such a critical zone – Soviet borders considered.

3.   *Soviet Muslims*

When I was in Pakistan in June and July last year, I pointed out to the Minister for Information and Broadcasting, Major-General Shahid Hamid, that in the July issue of the mass circulation American magazine *Reader's Digest*, Mr. William Griffith had stated that "as many as 40 million people – 15 per cent of Russia's total population – are Muslims. These people, most of them located in Soviet Central Asia, have a much higher birth-rate than the European Russians, and by the end of this century, may account for as much as 40 per cent of the teenage and young-adult population of the USSR.

"If Islamic militancy spreads, Moscow's hold over huge numbers of its citizens could be dangerously threatened."

I asked Shahid Hamid if he agreed with this and if so, could one take comfort in the fact that should there be a real Islamic revival could it misfire against the Soviet Union, because one in five of their soldiers are Muslims from the Southern States? I also asked him if the combined effect of a Polish Pope and an Islamic revival would act as a bulwark against the spread of Soviet communism?

His reply was that little comfort could be taken in all this because "the Muslim soldiers in the Soviet Army," he said, "are second and third generation citizens. Their religion and creed is not Islam, but *communism*. This is taught in the schools as well as in the Army and injected into them every day and night. There are commissars in every military unit whose task it is to continue with the brain washing of the soldiers, sailors and airmen."

Hamid emphasized: "The Mosques are empty and attended only by old people. The Mullahs have been thoroughly indoctrinated to spread the Communist gospel."

These comments emphatically contradict the views of the investigative journalist who wrote that the "Moslem reactions to the invasion of Afghanistan could create serious troubles for the Russians inside their Central Asian fiefdoms (and their armed forces) as well as in the wider world of Islam."

Hamid is a very devout Muslim and a walking encyclopaedia on all facets of his religion. It is very important to put in perspective the likelihood or otherwise of serious discontent and a flare-up of Moslem unrest. Only then can one judge the effects of a Western psychological warfare campaign leading to more positive action in the form of unconventional warfare.

Accordingly, the divergent views and findings are given below. While I have no hesitation in agreeing with the conclusions I must, however, emphasize two points. First, the more Russia's internal position and empire threaten to decay politically, the more ruthless will be her use of force in order to reverse the process. *The Brezhnev doctrine is the writing on the wall.*

Second, unlike the CIA, the KGB – the dreaded Soviet Secret Police – has a major and sinister role *inside* the Soviet Union itself. This much feared octopus-like clandestine terror apparatus is an organ of mass repression aimed against its own populations and it ruthlessly destroys all opposition inside the USSR. It engulfs the lives of nearly 250 million individuals in the Soviet Union and countless others in its satellite empire.

The best single definition of the KGB is the "Sword and Shield" of the Soviet Communist Party. The sword by which the party rulers enforce their will on the people and the shield that protects the rulers from any opposition.

The KGB is also dedicated to attacking ceaselessly and exterminating the non-Communist system in the West by disruption, subversion

236

and assassination. This hateful, malignant and virulent virus is the world's greatest spy machine, with more than 90,000 external agents — the Soviet's storm-troops.

I now relate the report of the investigative journalist, dated January 1980, who submitted, that the Soviet leadership is aware of the risk that the brutal repression of an Islamic people will add to the simmering discontents of the 40 million Moslems of the Soviet Union, most of whom are concentrated in the 'autonomous' republic of Soviet Central Asia.

Russia, he said, has sent many Asiatic Moslems among the troops it has put into Afghanistan and already there have been reports of defections among some Tadzhik soldiers to the Afghan rebels. As happened in the 1956 invasion of Hungary and also in 1968 of Czechoslovakia, Moscow keeps its troops in ignorance when they are dispatched to invade other people's freedom. In the case of the semi-literate Azbeks and Turkomans and Tadzhiks who are serving in Afghanistan with the Soviets, they have been told that they are acting to assist a 'progressive government' which had been attacked by 'imperialist' forces.

As the Moslem conscripts have become aware of their real assignment in Afghanistan, the Third Chief Directorate of the KGB — which is the department that ensures the security of the armed forces is maintained — will have been working strenuously to suppress any possible defections. Also, in order to prevent a flare-up of Moslem unrest in the southern republics, the Ministry of Internal Affairs, or MVD, have conducted a 'Vigilance campaign'.

In particular, warnings of a supposed Western psychological warfare campaign, were passed to the top security officials in Uzbekistan — General Levon N. Melmukov of the KGB and Major-General Kudrat Ergashev of the MVD — despite the fact that no such action had been actively considered.

The reason for these warnings, link with the KGB's strategy for the instigation of violence and anti-Khomeini demonstrations in Iran's Azerbaijan. The outcome being, that just this sort of development would provide the Russians with substantive reason to invoke the Soviet-Iranian 1921 treaty — which remains in force — that gives Russia the right of intervention in Iran if events in that country are considered by Moscow to threaten its own security. But *war* now flares!

Major-General Marius A. Yuzbasyov, the local KGB chief in Azerbaijan, is known to have been given both an offensive and a defensive assignment and for a considerable while has recruited agents to operate in Tabriz and other cities in Iran as *agents provocateurs,* to deliver the 'events' when required.

While official recognition is given to Islam both inside and outside the Soviet Union, in reality, Moscow is determined to uproot and exterminate all traces of religion in the long term. In Tashkent, the Mufti

237

never departs from the party line – the control of Islam is more complete than with any other religion in Russia. However, in South Yemen, a Soviet puppet régime, supported by the Russian military, is bolder and the religious extermination policy made operative.

But there is a significant and growing Sufi Islamic underground movement, or kind of 'parallel Islam', in the Soviet Union. Included in this world – which is denounced by the 'faithful' party-approved as "a fanatical anti-Soviet force" – are many young people from the Central Asian republics. There are literally thousands of unlicensed mullahs and hundreds of unrecognized mosques, while Arabic and Koranic lore is taught in undercover religious schools, or medressehs.

Quite obviously, the opportunity for *real* opposition in the Soviet totalitarian republics is severely restricted. Nevertheless, there *is* a potential among the Soviet Muslims to mount resistance on an ever increasing scale, as the Russian bear paws its way through the sacred Islamic region of the Middle East, with all the ensuing consequences. As the investigative journalist reminds us; the lonely campaign that has been waged by one of the Soviet Union's Moslem minorities, the Crimean Tatars, over more than a third of a century is an example of what can be achieved against great odds through courage and national pride. Well over half a million people deported by Stalin in 1944, lost their homeland and nationhood. The United Nations is deaf to their petitions.

If now the Afghan Moslems are to suffer to the degree that the Soviet Moslems have suffered, reaction to the invasion of Afghanistan could create severe trouble for Russia and their Central Asian fiefdoms.

4.   *Russia's Persecution of the Crimean Tatars*

One side of the Soviet Union that the people who went to the Moscow Olympics were not allowed to see was the murder of a nation and its history – the Crimea of the Tatars.

On the persecution of the Tatars, the investigative journalist reported at the end of January this year:

"People should understand that we are witnessing nothing new in Afghanistan. If the Russians behave as they behaved in the Crimea and throughout Central Asia in the past, then in 10 years the Afghans will be forced to write with the Russian alphabet and the tribes that refuse to bow down will be deported to Siberia."

These are the words of the leading Crimean Tartar spokeswoman who, having been sent into exile, now makes her base in New York and is seeking to enlist Western and Islamic support for the plight of her people.

Soviet policy in the Crimea – a strategic peninsula which contains one of Russia's main bases for training foreign terrorists at Simferopol –

follows in the Tsarist tradition. It is aimed at total Russification. This entails the systematic elimination of Islam.

In the city of Stary Krym, there were once 112 mosques; not one remains. There is not a single Moslem cemetery left in the whole Crimea. During raids by KGB and Ministry of Internal Affairs (MVD) officials, Korans and other religious literature are confiscated.

As the journalist concluded; the continuing resistance of the Crimean Tartars to Soviet communization, at a time when Moscow is engaged in a wide-ranging conflict with Islam, may well have a contagious effect on the other Moslem people of the Soviet Union.

5. Western Counter-Action

These specialized reports have performed a great service in revealing unconventional warfare — running the whole gamut from propaganda through subversion to guerrilla action — *as* significant as conventional, Euro-strategic or strategic inter-Continental nuclear warfare. But in this area, NATO today is arguably weaker than in any of the others.

Yet, as we know, the resources required are not great; the cost (compared with that, say, of an aircraft carrier) is very little; and a great deal of invaluable real estate may be held or lost as a result.

The Soviet leadership makes no secret of its intent to support revolutionary groups wherever they may advance Moscow's interests, and by whatever means fall to hand. By contrast, NATO governments are giving (at best) only half-hearted support to anti-Soviet resistance groups in Third World countries whose Marxist régimes were installed by unconventional warfare or direct Soviet and Cuban intervention.

The question is indeed correctly posed: Is it not time to correct the imbalance?

These factors have been under intense discussion among defence specialists in several NATO capitals, and there is increased support for the view that there is no reason — either moral or practical — why the recent expansion of the Soviet empire into countries like Afghanistan or Angola should be regarded as irreversible.

This Chapter has already described how Angola offers one of the most promising opportunities for Western counter-action.

6. CIA Weakness

Ever since America's defeat in Vietnam, Congress has strapped the Central Intelligence Agency (CIA) into a straightjacket. Covert and clandestine activity — operating by stealth — cannot be conducted until the CIA is put on a freer rein. The CIA must no longer be hamstrung by the crippling restraints that were imposed on its ability to undertake intelligence collection and covert action. Obviously the progressive Establishment and the media would oppose any move in this direction and label covert operations as "dirty tricks". Yet in situations like Iran, where diplomacy has failed and armed force proper was not, or could not be used, covert operations are the only form of leverage available to a great Power. The CIA has been unable to exploit developments in Cuba, Iran and Afghanistan. Indeed, today the CIA stands accused of being too cautious rather than too aggressive.

As another distinguished British journalist – Peregrine Worsthorne – wrote in *The Sunday Telegraph,* London, of 9th December, 1979: "As is becoming increasingly clear, Ayatollah Khomeini rules over a deeply divided people. His enemies, secular and religious, are quite as numerous as his friends. Instead of moving aircraft carriers around in the Mediterranean with the maximum publicity – an idle and counter-productive threat if ever there was one – Carter should have moved against Khomeini as Nixon, with far less provocation, moved against Allende – covertly, by stealth. But the means of such operations, which are absolutely essential for American influence in the Middle East, no longer exist."

7.   Life In The Soviet Union

We must open peoples' eyes to the realities and grimness of life in Russia and its communist satellites. The evidence is readily available but the West's information services are so ineffective that it is not being widely and constantly publicized.

The idea that there exists an egalitarian society in the Soviet Union is totally false. The Marxist upper class is more apart from the ordinary classes as ever an upper class was in any country in the 19th century. The whole structure is an imperial military outfit with a technological and administrative upper class. The power of government is monopolized by a small clique of politicians and military men and policemen in a remote bureaucratic presidium. So much for all this egalitarian cant.

Idealistic youth leaving school knows little of the grimness of life and history of barbarity in Soviet Russia, a record of bestiality unparalleled. Soviet Russia is a monstrous tyranny where mental and physical control of the whole population is practised.

There are today *one million* political prisoners in jails and in bulging forced labour camps in Russia, located in remote areas with a terrible climate. This slave labour is kept in a state of semi-starvation while forced to do heavy manual work. The death rate is appalling, more than 20 million have been shot, perished or exterminated over the years.

There is the scandalous abuse of psychiatry for political and penal purposes, such as the terrifying punishment of psychiatric drugs administered to sane people in mental hospitals or asylum prisons for the suppression of the human mind, because their political views differ from those of the authorities.

Russia is a closed society with rigorous security, censorship, a controlled press. They do not allow free elections. There is no opposition in Parliament, therefore no need to heed public opinion.

A strike is treated as a crime, an act of sabotage against the State and strikers, if they are too numerous or too resistant to be arrested, are simply shot down. In Hungary and Czechoslovakia the opposition was crushed by Russian tanks. Poland listens for them now.

Their so-called 'unions' have nothing to do with free collective bargaining, or with freedom of any kind. This is totally inadmissable and regarded as an act of defiance. Their principal task is not to represent the workers, but to control them, and to enforce labour discipline. Whenever the workers lose their chains, *other chains* more heavy are clamped upon them.

The tourist is easily misled because he is only allowed to see the specially subsidised hotels and the special shops reserved either for tourists or the élite among the party members. There are very few people indeed in the West who have actual experience of the grimness of life for 90 per cent of the Russian people.

The evidence is available if we know where to look for it. It should be dug out and shouted from the roof tops. There are reliable defectors and dissidents who have written frankly of the quality of life in the Soviet Union.

Russia, industrialized in 1917, is a ghastly economic failure. Though the richest agricultural country in the world and pre-revolution a grain exporter, her agriculture is now so abysmally inefficient that she cannot even feed herself, let alone assist the hungry elsewhere.

8. *Soviet Internal Weaknesses.*

One third of all Russia's machine products, one fifth of all its metallurgic products and one sixth of all its chemical products are absorbed by the military. Of its energy resources, one sixth is used by the Soviet Forces. This lopsided allotment of resources, while giving the Soviet Union a powerful military machine, has warped its civilian economy and slowed its modernization – above all in agriculture.

Farming is the weakest and least productive sector of the Soviet economy. Under the Communist system of state and collectivized farming, the average Soviet farm worker produces only 5.5 per cent as much as his American counterpart. Although Soviet planning calls for large-scale mechanized farming and huge amounts of money are poured into modernization attempts, many of the farming methods remain anti-quated and inefficient. Wooden ploughs and flails are still used on some farms.

As a result of the agricultural failure, the Soviet Union is forced to import large amounts of grain, and meat supplies are always short. The Soviet consumer sector, although fairly modern, is inefficient and produces less than is needed. Political straight-jackets prevent needed reforms. Technology that turns out first-rate space rockets and intercontinental missiles has been unable to develop an industry capable of supplying enough canned and frozen foods. It's always feast or famine for civilians in terms of fruits and vegetables.

Russia lags far behind the U.S. in the production of computers, which are important to the military as well as to the civilian economy. A CIA study reports: "In 1974, the U.S.S.R. had an estimated 12,500 computers installed and in use, compared with 207,000 units for the U.S. By 1977, this gap had widened substantially – an estimated 20,000 in the U.S.S.R. compared with 325,000 in the U.S. The Soviet gap in production is complemented by a gap in technology. In technical capabilities and performance, general-purpose computers now in production in the U.S.S.R. are approximately equivalent to those marketed in the U.S. in the late 1960s."

An even greater drawback in the future is the fact that Russia is facing an energy pinch. At present, it produces enough oil for its domestic needs, but the CIA predicts that a production squeeze will force the Kremlin to become an oil importer from 1985. Soviet officials challenge this forecast but admit, nevertheless, that Russia's oil output in 1979 rose only 3 per cent, after years in which the increase had been 8 per cent or more.

Like other raw materials, oil and natural gas are becoming increas-ingly expensive to find and develop. New fields in Siberia are far from the markets; pipelines are difficult and expensive to lay down in inhospit-able terrain. Labour costs continue to mount, and young workers are not eager to live under the extremely difficult conditions.

All across the board, economic difficulties are mounting for Russia. Labour is no longer plentiful. An actual shortage is developing. Families in the heavily industrialized republics – Russia, the Ukraine and Belorussia – are having fewer and fewer babies. The population's growth rate is very close to zero. In Moslem areas, large families are still the norm, but they are far from the industrialized areas where workers are needed.

A sign of the labour shortage: A popular food *centre* in Moscow closed its doors for repairs in July 1979. It was supposed to be shut for six weeks. But it was still closed in February 1980 because of a lack of workers, many of whom had been drafted to work on building sites for the Olympic Games.

The productivity of Soviet workers is low by comparison with almost all other industrial nations. And the rate of increase in labour productivity has been declining. In 1979, the output per worker in factories rose only 2.4 per cent, compared with a target of 4.7 per cent. In the construction industry, productivity increased only 1 per cent. Also, agricultural production per worker dropped by 4 per cent.

Some of the country's economic and industrial weaknesses are felt by its military sector. Training soldiers is a problem because most of the draftees have little experience with machinery. The Russians have trouble keeping their equipment operational. Their ships spend far more time in port than do their American counterparts. Tests done by Americans show that the engines and gears on Russian tanks are not very durable by U.S. standards.

Going into the 1980s, Soviet leaders face a grim economic outlook. Over all, the economy is expected to grow by no more than 3 per cent annually, compared with gains of 6 per cent or more in the 1950s. The rate of capital growth is expected to decline.

To summarize:

A close look behind Russia's facade of invincibility reveals many serious weaknesses: An economy that is still backward, even by the standards of Eastern Europe. A collectivized system of farming that ranks among the least efficient – and most disaster-prone – among developed nations. A labour shortage that promises to become acute in the 1980s. And the prospect of an oil shortage.

It is imperative that the West should exploit this situation through psychological warfare and economic restrictions, for despite these grave weaknesses, there can be no doubt about Russia's military might.

9. *We Are Losing The Information Battle*

How many of the young remember that before World War II Russia had annexed the Baltic States and parts of Finland, Rumania, Poland and Czechoslovakia. And after the war, Albania, Bulgaria, Rumania, East Germany, all of Poland, and Czechoslovakia, and Hungary became completely Russian-dominated, and are now unable to maintain their independence and the individual freedom of their people? But the human spirit cannot be suppressed for ever.

In Poland there is a whole sullen, pinched and resentful nation.

For some years now the food shortages have been getting worse, the queues longer, the complaints about bureaucracy and muddle in the Communist economic system louder and the indignation at the privileges for the party hierarchy deeper. The Poles are used to being told that belts would have to be tightened for a little while longer. They have been told flatly it will be so for a decade – unless they work harder, unless

243

there is a dramatic improvement in efficiency and management, and less corruption. The industrial crisis in August threatened to explode.

The Polish people know only too well that, whatever they do, these evils and injustices are with them for as long as the Communist system is imposed on them. There is to be no lightening of their yoke. The bitter irony of it all is that things would have been far worse, perhaps beyond breaking point, but for Western credits of £8,500 million – and another of £2,500 million is being sought this year. Much of this has run away into the sands of Communist mismanagement, and much into Communist pockets. Debt repayment will be a crushing burden.

But for the efforts of the Catholic Church in restraining the people and forcing concessions from the Government there would have been a terrible upheaval long since. In the people's minds the Church, not the Government is the real authority. This is even more so the case now that there is an ebullient and very Polish, Polish Pope. But how can Russia, whose people are similarly deprived, send out mighty, modern conquering armies into so many countries when it has so many festering backyards? As Solzhenitsyn says, it is in the nature of Communism, which is a danger and an evil so unique in history that the flabby self-indulgent West cannot, or is afraid to, comprehend it.

What is the situation in East Germany?

Machine-gunning of fugitives by East German guards at the dominated blood-stained Berlin Wall should have given the West a disturbing echo to the hand-clapping at the Helsinki propaganda jamboree. The contrast between the glossy, pious, fine-sounding phrases and the emotional mush at Helsinki, and the realities along the Iron Curtain, should be a warning to the peace-makers that this kind of thing still goes on after years of so-called "peaceful co-existence", that deceitful propaganda slogan. East and West may talk of détente, but along the Berlin Wall the sound is still the staccato of the machine gun; and the East German bullets are not made of rubber.

Although it is no longer fashionable to talk about Winston Churchill's 'Iron Curtain', it still exists: an endless girdle of walls, wire, watchtowers, fortifications and minefields, right across Germany through to the very heart of Europe. Nor is it fashionable to talk about outright Russian aggression, yet the tanks which relentlessly crushed plaintive efforts to obtain freedom in Budapest, Prague and Warsaw, are still there and in ever-increasing numbers.

The fashionable words now are détente and disarmament, and yet the Russians who bellow about them loudest continue to pump billions into their armament programme, while the State with which diplomatic relations have been established – East Germany – continues to make its 600-mile-long border with West Germany even more escape-proof – new automatic shrapnel-firing devices and new electronic fences and bunkers. The unsmiling border guards continue to chalk up on their score boards the hundreds of killed and wounded whom they have shot in the back.

By supplying the Soviet Union police state with food, machinery, plants, mills, technology, know-how and credit, the taxpayers of the West are enabling Russia to pour more and more money, faster and faster, into her vast armaments industry. They are assisting her not only to get a foothold in Western Europe, the Middle East, South Asia, and Africa, and to rule the waves and dominate the skies, but also to communize the world and establish herself as the unparalleled world power.

The crocodile tears shed by Brezhnev at Helsinki were not worth the blotting paper on which they fell.

If the man in the street, the Trade Union Worker, the shopkeeper, the business man, the teacher, and those who ventilate their ignorance over television and radio, were to learn more of the facts of life, then, if only for selfish reasons, they might be more willing to make the relatively small sacrifices necessary in order to secure the safety of our own infinitely happier society.

The soldiers in this communist war do not wear military uniforms. They are teachers and students in universities and schools, agitators organizing strikes in essential industries, theologians undermining faith and tradition, the media publicizing every fault they can discover while remaining silent about the infinitely greater crimes of the communist enemy, guerrillas, terrorists, and propagandists travelling the byways of the world armed with propaganda literature describing the Soviet Union as generous and humane while the West is avaricious, inhuman and malignant.

It was Lenin who said: "We shall find our most fertile field of infiltration of Marxism within the field of religion, because religious people are the most gullible and will accept almost anything if it is couched in religious terminology." Indeed they are — *when devoid of truth*.

It was Winston Churchill who said: "From what I have seen of our Russian friends during the war, I am convinced that there is nothing for which they have less respect than weakness, especially military weakness. We cannot afford to work on narrow margins offering temptations to a trial of strength."

It is power and the will to exercise it that impresses the Soviets. It is weakness that will encourage them to adventure. Resources must be found for defence. Some can be found within the overgrown national defence departments and the over-staffed and over-stuffed NATO headquarters. Like many arms of central and local government, they have come to be run for the benefit of staff, and shop stewards, while the fighting units are starved of resources.

But much more than this is needed. Consciousness of the threat must be more widely inculcated and its implications drawn. Of course, defeatists will cry "Jingoism", just as Churchill was denounced by the

Socialist and Conservative parties alike in the 1930s. But weakness encourages conflict, while only resolution will avert calamity.

Détente has failed because to the West it means the suspension of Soviet aggressiveness, whereas to the Soviets it means the suspension of Western reaction in the face of their aggressiveness.

I have described where Soviet weaknesses exist. The lesson to be learned is that whereas the U.S.S.R. exploits all the weaknesses of the democratic camp, Western leaders not only abstain from exploiting Soviet failures, but even are misguided enough to think they should *help* the Soviets to surmount them!

WHITHER POLAND?

LISTENING FOR THE TANKS

Appreciation to Oliphant in *The Washington Star* and Universal Press Syndicate.

CHAPTER
21

Other Flash Points

Cuba

The cost to the U.S.S.R. of using Cuba as a builder of the Soviet Empire is estimated at $8 million a day. But the long-term benefits to the Soviet Bloc are enormous: commercial, strategic, psychological – in a nutshell *geo-political*.

Castro has been used to aid and inspire revolts in Africa, Latin America and the Middle East ever since 1961.

In 1961, just two years after seizing power, he sent a handful of troops to Ghana to provide training in guerrilla warfare.

In 1963, he sent tanks, arms and advisers to Algeria, which was then involved in a border dispute with Morocco.

In 1965, he sent troops to the Congo.

In 1973, he ventured into the Middle East when he gave military support to South Yemen.

With this pattern established, the U.S., the U.K. and the West should not have been surprised by the major Cuban involvement in Angola in 1975 and Ethiopia a year later. In Angola 20,000 Cuban troops fought on the Communist side and 16,000 troops were sent to Ethiopia.

Cuba has more than 1,000 troops in a dozen other countries. In addition to this, Cuba has approximately 11,000 civilian advisers in such Third World nations as Mozambique, Jamaica, Libya, Iraq, South Yemen and Vietnam.

Latin America has been and is a prime target: Nicaragua, El Salvador, Guatemala and Honduras. Cuba is exporting revolutions to the whole of Central America and the Caribbean as well as Africa.

The revelation in September 1979 that Russia had a 'combat brigade' in Cuba should have been a clear signal to the world that the Soviets are in the process of destabilizing the Caribbean. Despite his earlier insistence to Moscow that the *'status quo'* was unacceptable, President Carter climbed down and lost face when the Soviets replied with a resounding *Nyet*. The Russians and their tanks and other offensive weapons remain in Cuba.

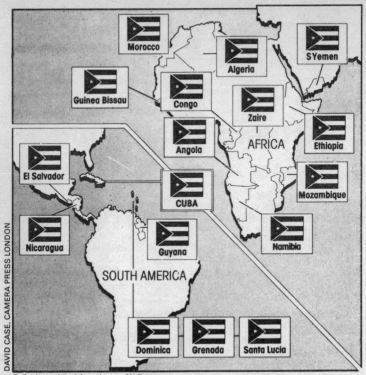

Cuba's world-wide sphere of influence

Appreciation to *NOW!* Magazine, 4th–10th January, 1980.

There were those who said that what was now needed from America was some dramatic demonstration of her capacity and willingness to exercise power as ruthlessly as does Russia. Imagine the impact, they said, on the world if President Carter did to Cuba what President Brezhnev has done to Afghanistan – invade the island and depose Castro.

But the Soviet leaders were sending some hard-line signals on Cuba to dissuade President Carter from taking any military action to force the removal of Russian combat troops from that strategic island.

The message was in the form of a massive airlift operation to the Horn of Africa and the tip of the Arabian peninsula. Elements of seven Soviet combat divisions were airlifted aboard giant Antonov-22 transports from southern Russia and Bulgaria to air bases in South Yemen and Ethiopia. The airlift involved more than 350 flights and the airlifting of major combat elements of two full divisions and the skeleton staffs of five other divisions. Included were airborne mechanized units, light armoured units, supporting arms and logistical units. Several of the units contained troops specially trained in handling nuclear weapons.

The significance of the operation, the largest ever attempted by the Soviet Union outside the Soviet Bloc nations since the end of World War II, was that it demonstrated the Kremlin's capability to extend its military power into the vital area that contains the world's major shipping lanes for Middle East oil.

In the terms of geo-politics, the Russians sent a loud message to President Carter that the Soviet Union has the military capability to disrupt the oil supply routes from the Middle East to the U.S., Japan, and Western Europe should the U.S. use military force in Cuba.

The efficiency of this Soviet operation shows that Russia is now capable of airlifting at least two fully equipped divisions to the tip of the Arabian peninsula or the Horn of Africa in less than 72 hours.

A Soviet defector, who came over to the West in 1979, has warned that the Kremlin's timetable for bringing nuclear bombs into Cuba for their MiG-23s is at hand, and that 1980 is the year for the introduction of their 5,000-mile-range Backfire bombers. Runways of two airfields in Cuba have been lengthened and strengthened to handle the Backfire bombers, and storage facilities for nuclear bombs have been built and are now ready for use. Whether nuclear bombs are already in Cuba and are stored in areas guarded by elements of the Soviet combat brigade is now being debated in U.S. intelligence circles.

The only way these nuclear bombs can be detected is by over-flights of SR-71s carrying special equipment to detect fissionable material. President Carter has not yet authorised such flights. The continuing Soviet military build-up in Cuba is an integral part of the Kremlin's grand strategy of positioning its forces to control the strategic waterways of the world and thus change the balance of power in their favour.

The Soviet lightning onslaught in taking over Afghanistan was a key part of that strategy, as it brings Soviet military might nearer to the strategic Strait of Hormuz, through which 60% of the oil to the West now passes. Under the Russians grand design, control of this strategic waterway, along with the Caribbean region, will put Soviet leaders in a position to cut off oil supplies to the United States, Western Europe and Japan. This is why the link between Afghanistan and Cuba is a most pressing problem.

What is the answer short of a naval and air blockade of Cuba? Surely this is the ideal opportunity to wage unconventional warfare in the form of:
* A Radio Free Cuba similar to Radio Free Europe.
* Publicizing the plight of political prisoners in Cuba.
* Assisting African guerrilla organizations fighting against Soviet-Cuban-East German forces.
* Bringing to the attention of the United Nations the Security

249

Council and world public opinion the extent of the involvement of Soviet-Cuban-East German forces and advisers.

* Seizing every opportunity to exacerbate differences between Castro and the Soviet Bloc.
* Establishing a university of revolution where potential insurgents could be trained for subversive action against Communist oppression. There would be no lack of applicants from Poles, Czechs, Slovaks, Hungarians, Bulgars, Rumanians, Ukrainians, Belorussians, Lithuanians, Latvians and Estonians.

Soviet forces — armour, infantry and airborne, with strong air, naval and amphibious support — are now so poised that they could intervene almost anywhere in the world and with such strength and speed that the United States could not possibly respond with anything like the same force and rapidity. Indeed, were they to attempt to do so they would suffer such a crushing defeat that they would be humiliated in the eyes of the world, and the Third World in particular. They would lose such face that their whole position as a super military power be undermined.

The Soviet Union is now in a position almost to relish and entice American intervention with the aim of inflicting on them a crushing defeat on the battlefield.

Israel — Palestine

While the reasons for conflict between the peoples now living in Palestine are very deep, reaching back into distant history, the Arab-Jew protagonists will now ignore the broad geo-strategic situation at their peril! If settlement of the Palestinian question is not reached soon, events may overtake them both.

It would seem, the inevitable price that the PLO must pay for Palestinian nationhood, is a clear commitment to recognition *of* and peaceful co-existence *with* Israel. Equally the Israelis have to accept that recognition of Palestinian nationhood is the price that they *must* pay for peace with the Arab world as a whole.

Unfortunately the problem is not as clearly defined as this. First of all, straight answers have to be given to the following straight questions:

* Can the solution be found in the establishment of a PLO-Palestinian State dominating both Israeli and Jordanian vital territory, when the PLO is led by men who declared their support for the ruthless take-over of Afghanistan by the Soviet Union?
* Is the lesson for Israel from the Soviet invasion of Afghanistan that the creation of a Palestinian state would lead to a direct Soviet presence in the Middle East?
* If so, is it in the interests of the West to encourage the emergence of a Soviet dominated PLO mini-state on the West Bank?
* Would a Soviet satellite nine miles from the Mediterranean coast further the West's interests in the Middle East?

* Can the defence of the West's vital strategic and oil interests be left in the sole charge of the Arabs?
* Is the only way to prevent the creation of a PLO State by keeping the West Bank under Israeli control?
* If so, can this control only be exercised effectively by setting up settlements at various strategic points?
* Could Arab and Israelis co-exist in the West Bank by creating separate blocs of Jewish and Arab settlements and by the Jews refraining from settling in Arab towns?
* Until a substantial Western presence can be established in the region who would prove to be the West's most steadfast ally? Israel, the one democracy in the area, or Arab dictatorship and semi-feudal sheikdoms?
* Does European recognition of the PLO depend upon the latter giving simultaneous recognition of Israel's right to exist?
* Do the PLO and the Palestinian people recognize Israel's right to exist within secure 1967 borders?
* Is the Palestinian leadership totally committed to the destruction of the Jewish State?
* Does Israel recognize the PLO?
* Does Israel recognize the right of the Palestinians to an independent state?
* Lord Carrington has stated that the PLO as such is not a terrorist organization. Does Mr. Arafat have a terrorist record? Does Mr. Arafat co-operate closely with the Soviet Union in military and political matters?
* Is there not a parallel here with Zimbabwe where the British legitimized terrorism in Rhodesia as a means of attaining a political goal? (This is not a new tactic as some of the New Commonwealth was built on similar foundations).
* Is there not also a parallel here with Northern Ireland? i.e. If the Israelis see the PLO as a terrorist body dedicated to the destruction of their state, would they not be viewing the idea of negotiating with it much as Mr. Ian Paisley would view negotiations with the IRA?
* There are those who say that Israel cannot expect to retain territories, acquired by force.

As a result of war, Texas, New Mexico, Arizona and a large part of California are now part of the United States: Latvia, Lithuania, Estonia, Finnish Karelia, parts of East Prussia, Hungary, Rumania, Czechoslovakia and a number of former Japanese islands in the Pacific are occupied by the Soviet Union. Poland occupies part of East Prussia, China occupies Tibet.

As a result of an attack on Israel by Jordan in 1967 Israel occupied part of the West Bank. One is curious to know what makes Israel the odd man out, or in today's terminology, "a special case."?

Has not Israel shown its good faith by giving back to Egypt all territories, including precious oil supplies, in return for peaceful co-existence?

* Has not recent history shown that any country in which the PLO has been involved, such as Jordan in 1970, later Lebanon and, last year, Iran, has become in a very short time a battle-ground where blood has been shed indiscriminately?

* Can the Palestinian problem only be solved through co-operation and co-existence with Israel?

* Should Jerusalem be undivided and can Israel claim total sovereignty *and* expect peace?

Dr. Everett M. Jacobs of the Department of Economics and Social History, University of Sheffield, writing to *The Times,* London, poured scorn on Lord Carrington's statement in the House of Lords. The letter dated 24th March, 1980, quotes from an exclusive interview given on 11th February to a Venezuelan newspaper by Yassir Arafat, chairman of the PLO and leader of the Al Fatah terrorist group. The letter says:

"It is unbelievable that Lord Carrington could have meant it when he said in the House of Lords on 17th March that he was unaware that the aim of the Palestine Liberation Organization was to destroy Israel completely, and that he did not think the PLO was a terrorist organization 'as such'.

Yassir Arafat, chairman of the PLO and leader of the Al Fatah terrorist group, put the record straight as recently as 11th February in an exclusive interview in the Venezuelan newspaper, *El Mundo.* He said: 'Peace for us means the destruction of Israel . . . We are preparing for an all-out war. This war will last for generations. Since the birth of Al Fatah in 1965, we have become the most dangerous enemies that Israel has. We shall not rest until the day when we return to our home, and until we destroy Israel'.

He continued by outlining specifically the PLO programme and methods: 'The destruction of Israel is the goal of our struggle, and the guidelines of that struggle have remained firm since the establishment of Al Fatah in 1965: 1. Revolutionary violence is the only means for the liberation of the land of our fathers: 2. the goal of this violence is the destruction of Zionism in all its political, economic, and military forms, and its expulsion from Palestine; 3. our revolutionary activity must remain independent of any party or state control; 4. this action will be of long duration. We know that the intention of some Arab leaders is to resolve the conflict by peaceful means. When this occurs, we shall oppose it.'

No one has challenged the accuracy of Arafat's statements which, as Lord Carrington must have known, only repeat what numerous PLO spokesmen have said many times before. I fear that Lord Carrington's diplomatic blindness is part of the EEC disease that has recently been affecting this country."

On 13th June, 1980, the EEC heads of government signalled an historic shift in the European attitude to the Middle East conflict by stating for the first time that the PLO must be associated with peace negotiations – but they stopped short of actual recognition of the PLO. There is now an implied invitation to Moscow that Europe wishes to see the Soviet Union involved in any Middle East settlement.

The wisdom of embarking upon this course from a position of military weakness and without full U.S. support, must be questioned. If Europe as such had a military presence in the area it might afford the luxury of an independent Mid-east policy. It has not.

In the growing confrontation between East and West the PLO are openly on the side of the Eastern Bloc. Their links with Moscow are close and of long standing. At their Damascus conference in early June, Fatah leaders formally declared the United States to be their 'main enemy'; they reaffirmed their intention to destroy the Israeli State and their aim for the overthrow of the Sadat régime in Egypt.

It would appear that those of our friends among the Arab countries are caught in a series of vicious circles. They want American protection and yet are afraid to grant them the bases or facilities necessary for that protection. They resent American support for Israel, yet as they champion the Palestinian cause, they have considerable fear of a left-wing Palestinian state.

Syria

The level of violence in Syria reached a point early in 1980 where it appeared no longer a question of whether President Assad's régime would fall – but when? Assad belongs to the minority Akamite sect which has maintained a firm grip on the state. The Sunni Moslem majority are fighting to put an end to the corrupt and inefficient Alamite domination, which represents only 12% of the population. In 1979 at the military academy at Aleppo sixty Alamite cadets were slaughtered.

Large-scale violence broke out on 8th March in northern Syria, with attacks in Hama and Aleppo on government buildings and police stations. The unrest lasted for nearly two weeks spreading east to the Euphrates and west to the Mediterranean and even to a Alamite mountain stronghold.

The strategy of the Sunni opposition is to increase the violence against the Alamite security brigades to the point where the latter loose control and are forced to call in the conscript army, mostly Sunni, to fight the population – their kith and kin. It was not long before the government had to withdraw an armoured division from the Israeli front in the hope that a display of tank strength would act as a deterrent, and intimidate the people. Meanwhile the Russians continue to supply weaponry. What is their intention? On 10th September, 1980, Syria and Libya became a single state and urged a confrontation with the Israelis.

Iraq

Iraq's Ba'athist government is once again engaged in its long-standing clandestine feud with its arch rival Syria. Both Syria and Iran are inciting the simmering unrest among Iraq's large Shi'ite Moslem community with the aim of sparking off revolt. Already the régime, under President Saddam Hussain, has survived at least two serious attempts at a *coup* during the past year. On 27th April, the mounting psychological warfare between Iraq and Iran reached a new climax when the Iranians announced the 'death' of President Hussain, who they said had been shot by Islamic fundamentalists. Undoubtedly the Shi'ites from Syria and Iran are plotting to create another Islamic state, adding to the volatile situation that exists in the region.

So much for the stability of the three neighbouring countries – with Iraq in the middle flanked by Iran on the East and Syria on the West. At the head of the Persian Gulf is Iraq's port of Umm Qasr which Russian warships have used for the past 10 years. Once developed as a naval base it would be capable of supporting a permanent Russian naval squadron in the Gulf.

Somalia

A strong Somalia could upset Russian strategy because it is the lynch pin between two proposed arcs of defence in the Indian Ocean, Red Sea and the Gulf. The United States intention is to establish a permanent naval and air presence along an arc from Diego Garcia in the southern Indian Ocean to Mombasa in Kenya and Somalia's Soviet built naval and air base at Berbera in the Gulf of Aden.

The intention is that this arc of defence should be linked to the expanded military presence which the United States is proposing to establish with some of its NATO partners in the Gulf area.

In late August 1980, the report came that America and Somalia had agreed on the use by the U.S. of the former Soviet base at Berbera.

Any encirclement of Saudi Arabia by the Soviets must use South Yemen as the flank; a flank which would not be secure with an American naval and air presence at Berbera. One can be certain that the planners in the Kremlin will not have overlooked this. To the Somalis the word SALT does not mean "Strategic Arms Limitation Talks" but rather *"Soviet Army Landing Tomorrow!"*

Japan

That ubiquitous and eminent journalist Clare Hollingworth – to whom I gave more than one lift in my helicopter in the early 1970s, when I was Director of Operations, Borneo – succeeded the expert Brigadier Thompson as Defence Correspondent of *The Daily Telegraph*. On 19th March, 1980, she wrote an excellent article on Japanese fears for their oil supply from the Gulf in the face of the mounting threat to Japan from Russia. The article is so precise that I have no hesitation in reproducing it in full:

"Fears are mounting in Tokyo that the American nuclear umbrella can no longer be relied upon as the Russians continue to demonstrate their ability to cut Japan's vital sea route to Middle East oil.

254

CHINA

Ch'ŏngjin

NORTH
KOREA

Hamhŭng

SEA OF JAPAN

Wŏnsan

Pyŏngyang

CEASE FIRE LINE
27th July, 1953

Panmunjŏm

Kansŏng

SEOUL
Inchŏn

SOUTH
KOREA

YELLOW
SEA

Ch'ŏngju

100 miles

Kunsan

Taegu

Pusan

Mokpo

Tsushima

JAPAN

The Gulf oilfields supply over 70 per cent of Japan's energy requirements. The remainder comes from China and Indonesia which supply crude oil, while Brunei ships liquid gas to Japan.

The Japanese, taking a view on the collapse of the American-backed régimes in South Vietnam and Cambodia, doubt the United States' willingness to come to the defence of Japan in the event of an attack by Russia.

Defence officials feel the mutual defence treaty with the United States will not be implemented unless American vital interests are also at stake.

Now there are even doubts over Tokyo's three non-nuclear principles of not possessing, not manufacturing and not permitting the entry of nuclear weapons into Japan.

THE NEXT DOMINO?

Flotilla scare

Recently the Russians sailed 10 warships through the vital Tsushima Straits between Korea and Japan — the largest Soviet flotilla to pass through Japanese seas since the 1939-45 war — doubtless to demonstrate their ever-increasing military threat to the Japanese Archipelago.

There are reports of 4,500 Russian marines in Vladivostok who have exercised in assault landings on the disputed Kurile islands to the north of Japan where the Russians have deployed 13,000 troops equipped with T.62 tanks and helicopter gunships.

The airfield and runways, together with other facilities at Burevestnik on the disputed island of Etorofu, have been expanded recently.

Troops poured in

But the most ominous Soviet move from Tokyo's viewpoint concerns the Russian troops now deployed along the Eastern Pacific coast of the Soviet Union, with headquarters at Vladivostok and Kharbarovsk, which have recently been reinforced to the level of 20 divisions.

They are deployed in such a manner that they can move against Japan as well as China, while two divisions on Sakhalin and one of the Kamchotka Peninsula are deployed only against Japan.

Meanwhile the Backfire bomber and the SS20 mobile missile have been deployed in the Sikhote range, adding to the deepening concern of the Japanese High Command.

Against the Bomb

Indeed, the recent massive build-up has begun to disturb the 116 million Japanese who are still reacting against the militarism of their parents.

Senior officials, however, believe that it is still too early so far as public opinion is concerned to make a definite proposition that the Japanese should begin to consider the production of their own nuclear weapons.

Later this month (March 1980), Mr. Saburo Okita, Foreign Minister, will visit Washington with, it is hoped, concrete proposals to increase Japan's defence capability in response to recent pressures from Mr. Harold Brown, President Carter's Defence Secretary.

Defence cuts halted

During a visit earlier this year, Mr. Brown appears to have prevented the Japanese Government cutting its defence expenditure from 0.9 per cent, of the gross national product to 0.8 per cent.

He reminded the Japanese that members of Nato were pledged to increase their defence spending by three per cent annually in real terms.

It is likely the Japanese will acquire several Orion P.3 anti-submarine aircraft, as well as F.15 fighters. But new sophisticated weapons cannot compensate for under manning.

More than one of the four divisions which form the vital Northern Army Command on the Island of Hokkaido to check any Russian attempt at invasion is 25 per cent under-manned, and short of weaponry. Other units in less sensitive areas are in an even more parlous state."

South Korea

In Chapter 4, *America — No Longer a 'Paper Tiger'?*, I have referred to the fact that Communist aggression in Korea was thwarted, but not defeated in 1953. U.S. leadership, I stated, spurned the advice of General Douglas MacArthur, who told both Houses of Congress that there could be "no substitute for victory".

How precarious is the armistice was shown two years ago by the discovery of two tunnels which the North Koreans had dug under the demilitarized zone into South Korea. The plan, it seems, was to enable two divisions of North Koreans, dressed in South Korean uniform, to stage a simulated revolt. They would then have called for North Korean help, and tried to seize the capital, Seoul, to present the Americans with a *fait accompli*.

Apart from the risk of such Trojan Horse manoeuvres, Seoul is only 40 kilometres from the armistice border with North Korea. North Korean MiG fighter bombers could be over Seoul in three minutes. From Pusan, in the south-eastern tip of South Korea, to the Japanese island of Tsushima is less than 50 miles.

South Korea is a pivotal country in East West relations. Its invasion by Communist North Korea in 1950 brought about the first "hot war" since the 1939-45 conflict. Across the frontier on 25th June, 1950, North Korea launched its sudden offensive against the South. The war cost 2,500,000 lives, 94,000 of them in the United Nations command, and the eventual result was a "draw" on a line where the war began. The war influenced the whole course of Western rearmament against Communist aggression, including the rearmament of West Germany and its inclusion in NATO.

South Korea is strategically and politically important and its defence is as vital to the security of the Free World as the defence of Western Europe. Why? Because Korea is not only the key to the defence of Japan but also to the security of the Pacific as a whole. Indeed, if South Korea were to fall to communist North Korea the whole balance of global power would be changed.

Across the demilitarized zone (DMZ) established by the armistice agreement of 1953, the Russian equipped powerful armed forces of communist North Korea stand poised as a constant threat. Yet, in the face of this threat and the maintenance of a precarious balance of power and all that is at stake, President Carter began his term of office by making the incomprehensible strategic decision to withdraw U.S. combat *ground* forces by 1982.

The risks of withdrawal were only too clear to the principal experts in the area. The U.S. General Steinlaub was sacked from the Korean Command for his public disagreement with the President's decision. Before the American Ambassador, Schreiner, retired in 1978 he was so deeply concerned that he expressed his fears to the Senate's Foreign Affairs Committee. It was only recently that the run down of American forces was halted and the total withdrawal of ground forces rescinded.

For 27 years the demilitarized zone has been one of the most sensitive of all frontiers. Unlike the Berlin Wall it has no gaps through which men on legitimate business may pass without risk of death. No man, except for a few observers, ever passes. The opposing forces stand eyeball to eyeball and shots are frequently exchanged.

Today, according to General O Kuh-yol, Chief of Staff of the North Korean Army, his forces' combat capabilities are far stronger,

257

and they are forward-deployed. On the eve of this year's internal violence in South Korea, General O Kuh-yol told his troops that settlement of the question of Korea's reunification could not be put off.

The South Koreans said that between 20th and 25th May the North Koreans gave every indication of preparing to attack. But the Americans, whose intelligence must be counted as more credible, believed the South Koreans were crying "wolf" to divert attention from their domestic crisis. Nevertheless, Washington believed the situation to be critical enough for America to station an aircraft carrier near Korea and to warn Pyongyang, the North Korean capital, that any attempt to invade the South would be met with full American force.

The view of the United Nations command is that the North Korean may be tempted to exploit South Korea's trouble by providing arms, ammunition and other assistance to stimulate a local insurgency in South-Western Korea.

For the first time in 16 years the country is experiencing a negative economic growth rate. Bitterness is running deep. The military argue that democracy is a luxury South Korea cannot afford in this situation. If the price is South Korea's international standing, then relatively little will be lost.

The alternative could be another Vietnam *and* another 'domino'.

Thailand

Of all the non-Communist states in South-East Asia, Thailand is in the very front line against Vietnamese expansion. Hanoi's army is poised along the joint Thai-Cambodian (Kampuchean) frontier, and there have been rising fears that the war in the neighbouring territory could quickly spill into Thailand if the Vietnamese felt this was in their interest.

But even as I write, 23rd June, 1980, these fears are being realized, for Vietnamese troops have launched their first invasion of Thailand in modern times and from the Thai-Cambodian border, over the Thais voluntary repatriation programme for Cambodian refugees, which the Vietnamese know would include troops and supporters for the Khmer Rouge cause.

Militarily, Thailand's 140,000-man army lacks the punch of experienced leadership and sophisticated weaponry, and there was bitter disappointment earlier this year over the low military sales credit from the United States. "What can you buy with that?", the former Prime Minister questioned – "It is for the United States to decide how important Thailand is to them and to consider our strategic importance. At this time, Thailand is the key."

About a quarter of Thailand's 40-million people now live below the poverty line. The discontent of the rural poor is fanned by communist rebels in the north and south of the country, and the key to political stability and internal security lies in improving their lot. The previous

Defence Minister and Army Commander-in-Chief, General Prem Tinsulanonda, who became Prime Minister in March of this year, will face a difficult task in trying to steer Thailand through one of the most troublesome times in its history. The principle hurdles are the threat to the Thai Kingdom's security from the conflict in Cambodia and, internally, from the communist insurgents, plus simultaneously the pressure to work miracles with the deteriorating economic situation, rising prices, increasing unemployment, and the strain placed on the country's limited resources by the scope of the refugee problem.

While China and the Association of South-East Asian Nations (ASEAN) agree about the invasion of Cambodia and the Russian hand in it, they disagree about the solution. The Chinese view is that the Vietnamese occupation force should be slowly bled to death by providing support for the anti-Vietnamese guerrillas.

Towards the end of March the new Thai government made it clear that it does not share China's belief that the conflict in Cambodia can be allowed to drag on. It is worried that, by supporting the Khmer Rouge guerrillas, some of whom operate from Thailand, China is contributing to Thailand's refugee problem without causing much real damage to Vietnam. At the same time, there is the danger of the conflict spilling over into Thailand. The Thai Prime Minister, wants an international conference to be called to find a political solution to the Cambodian problem. Prince Sihanouk was in Europe urging just the same thing.

When China's Foreign Minister, Mr. Huang Hua, was in Singapore on 19th March, he described Soviet strategy in Asia as being shaped like a dumb-bell: Afghanistan and Cambodia are the weights; *the Malacca Strait is the bar connecting them.* Sooner or later, he said, the Russians will decide to grasp the bar – a correct evaluation in my view.

On 9th September, 1980, the report came that the Thai Prime Minister, concerned about a "probable" *coup,* was to stay on as C-in-C of the Army.

Northern Ireland

In 1972 I went on record as saying that I thoroughly disagreed with the flabby way operations were conducted from the very outset of the troubles, as a consequence of which the campaign was bound to be long drawn out, with a heavy toll of lives and material damage.

I warned that Russia's avowed aim to subvert Ireland and convulse Britain. I said that by creating a Cuba out of Ireland, NATO would become outflanked in the truest sense of the word, and Britain would be directly in the firing line.

Eight years of terror later, one could only wish that these prognostications had not been proven correct. The truth, however, is manifest before us – as a people whose love of freedom and true civilization is unbounded, we have failed to issue the necessary directives to effect a resolute defence of the Realm. We are thus moving into the *second decade* of the present troubles, with the daunting prospect of an ever widening conflict in view.

In February and March this year, there were shooting incidents that brought the Irish conflict to the plains of Lower Saxony and Westphalia in the Federal Republic of Germany. There can no longer be any doubt that an extension of IRA terrorism into West Germany presents the British Army with a security problem potentially as serious as the one it has faced for so many years in Northern Ireland. These shooting incidents have added a new dimension to the campaign. Where will they spread to next?

During her visit to Northern Ireland last year, Mrs. Thatcher was reported as saying, "If we do not defeat terrorists then democracy is dead". Since then we have witnessed the occupation by Iranian terrorists of the Embassy in London and the successful action by the Special Air Service Regiment, who killed five out of six terrorists and rescued the hostages.

Britain's Home Secretary, Mr. Whitelaw, stated on 5th May that we are not prepared to tolerate terrorism in Britain. In the name of all reason then, *what* is not only being tolerated but is *flourishing* in Northern Ireland? Although separated by water, this land is part of the United Kingdom in which, not so very long ago, Mr. Whitelaw was Secretary of State, and for which as a result of direct rule from Westminster he *still* has considerable responsibility.

We are bound to ask, why it is that terrorism has been allowed to go on for over ten years in Northern Ireland – is it a case of what happens there does not matter so long as it does not spread to the mainland?

CHAPTER 22

Peace, War or Surrender?

The Soviet Union's First Strike 'All Arms' Capability.

I am convinced that Russia is intent on possessing an overwhelming surprise first strike 'all arms' capability. We have the evidence of the great Soviet Intelligence agent, Colonel Oleg Penkovsky, who transmitted to the United States, through his British contact, Greville Wynne, at least 5,000 Kremlin documents which set forth this strategy in complete detail. He summarized these official military documents in the following words:-

"A future war will begin with a sudden nuclear strike against the enemy. There will be no declaration of war. Quite to the contrary, an effort will be made to avoid a declaration of war. When conditions are favourable for delivering the first nuclear strike, the Soviet Union will deliver this strike under the pretence of defending itself and preventing the U.S. from attacking the U.S.S.R."

I discuss this again later when dealing with the translations of Soviet strategic studies.

Whether or not the Russians would, in fact, ever deliver the first nuclear strike is the 64,000 dollar question. But what is quite certain is that they are determined to possess the *capability* to launch a surprise first strike, so overwhelming in its power of destruction of American underground missiles, that the United States would not have enough left over to retaliate with a counter-punch that would inflict sufficient damage on the Soviet Union as to make the price paid unacceptable to them. Thus the Soviets would be able to use *nuclear blackmail* to impose their will on the world.

This is the kind of power now in the hands of the Kremlin imperialists (let us not say Kremlin 'hawks' for that presupposes there are 'doves' also, which as a theorem, is precluded by Soviet doctrine for global hegemony). The West must come quickly to the realization that a

U.S. MILITARY INFERIORITY CHART 5

STRATEGIC AND INTERMEDIATE OFFENSIVE WEAPONS COMPARISON

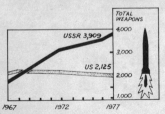

USSR 3,909
US 2,125

TOTAL WEAPONS
4,000
3,000
2,000
1,000

1967　1972　1977

JAN 1978 BALANCE	US	USSR
Intercontinental BMs (ICBMs)	1,054	1,450
Sub-launched BMs (SLBMs)	656	1,005
Strategic Heavy & Med. Bombers	415	830
Sub-launched Long Range CMs *	0	324
Mobile Intercontinental BMs **	0	300
Mobile Intermediate BMs	0	130
	2,125	4,039

* CRUISE MISSILES
** BALLISTIC MISSILES

STRATEGIC DEFENSIVE WEAPONS COMPARISON

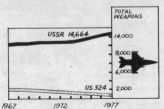

USSR 14,664
US 324

TOTAL WEAPONS
14,000
8,000
6,000
2,000

1967　1972　1977

JAN 1978 BALANCE	US	USSR
Interceptor Aircraft	324	2,600
Surface-to-Air Missiles	0	12,000
Anti-Ballistic Missiles	0	64
	324	14,664

MAJOR SURFACE COMBATANT SHIPS AND SUBMARINES

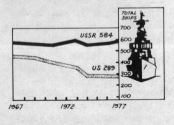

USSR 584
US 289

TOTAL SHIPS
700
600
500
400
300
200
100

1967　1972　1977

MILITARY MANPOWER

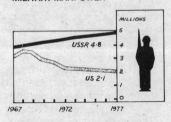

USSR 4·8
US 2·1

MILLIONS
5
4
3
2
1
0

1967　1972　1977

CONVENTIONAL GROUND FORCE WEAPONS

■ USSR ▨ US

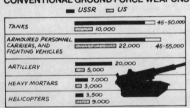

TANKS	10,000	45-50,000
ARMOURED PERSONNEL CARRIERS, AND FIGHTING VEHICLES	22,000	45-55,000
ARTILLERY	5,000	20,000
HEAVY MORTARS	7,000 / 3,000	
HELICOPTERS	3,500 / 9,000	

DEFENCE EXPENDITURES
(EXCLUDES MILITARY ASSISTANCE, PENSIONS AND CIVIL DEFENCE)

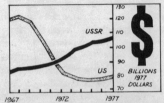

USSR
US

130
120
110
100
90
80
70

BILLIONS 1977 DOLLARS

1967　1972　1977

Information dated October 1979

BASED ON A CHART PUBLISHED IN U.S.A. BY:
THE COALITION FOR PEACE THROUGH STRENGTH

totally different civilization has emerged in Russia during the past sixty years, which as Solzhenitsyn explained to us, has an unstoppable momentum for revolution and war. The Soviet régime, backed by the dreaded KGB – the most sophisticated terror machine in the world – is not restrained from evil by honour, humanity, the Ten Commandments, treaties, the Golden Rule, or the Marquess of Queensberry Rules for a fair fight; it has respect only for force in the attainment of international goals.

The West has precious little breathing space left in which to put its own house in order. Unless we *wake up* in time we shall find that we will no longer have the capacity to put one gun on the Soviets because the Soviets will have two guns on us.

American nuclear umbrella

What does this add up to? It means that in the present conditions of nuclear stalemate, which is now tipped in favour of the Russians, nuclear weapons will, in future, only deter other nuclear weapons. What I am saying is that the United States could, and only would, now use their surviving strategic nuclear force in desperation, that is as a last resort in retaliation for a nuclear attack against the continental United States itself, *and not against the continent of Europe*.

With the balance of terror being as it is, how can one possibly expect America now to get itself involved in a nuclear war 'at the drop of a European hat'. She cannot be expected to commit suicide on behalf of Europe; de Gaulle foresaw this long ago, and that is why France developed its own nuclear force – the *Force de Frappe* – which should more aptly be called a force of dissuasion – that is, an essentially deterrent force.

Because Russia has now overtaken the United States in the nuclear field, NATO can no longer go on sheltering under the American nuclear umbrella, which until now, has been so successful in keeping the peace.

For the sake of economy, the NATO European allies have put all the emphasis on deterrence – sheltering under the American nuclear deterrent – and made little preparation for defence, should deterrence fail.

Conventional forces.

NATO's available conventional forces have been reduced to such razor-edge limits that they are now at their irreducible minimum level, so that if Russia was to attack West Europe *before* the Cruise missiles and Pershing 2 ballistic missiles are deployed on European soil – 3 to 4 years from now – the West would quickly be over-run.

Therefore, it is now *conventional forces* that are needed to deter and defend ourselves against the *conventional forces* of Russia and her

Warsaw Pact satellites. NATO cannot possibly match tank for tank, or soldier for soldier, but what we can do is to standardize our weapons and equipment and use technology to close the numerical gap by increasing our mobility and fire power, with the new range of very accurate conventional missile delivery systems, against tanks, against aircraft and against ships.

Chemical Warfare

Recent Soviet military literature postulates the use of new types of chemical weapons in place of low-yield nuclear weapons since, unseen and unheard, they do not damage buildings or other structures and would not, therefore, slow the momentum of their armoured assault against Western Europe. *Theatre* nuclear weapons and chemical weapons, according to current Soviet military doctrine, have assumed a pre-eminent role in the war-winning strategy of the Warsaw Pact.

General Bernard Rogers, the Supreme Allied Commander of NATO, stated as recently as June this year that in order to *deter,* in our strategy of flexible response, the use of chemical weapons against us, the West must have the capability to *retaliate* with *modern* chemical weapons. He explained that because NATO's chemical weapons are not modern enough, it increases the likelihood of our having to react in a retaliatory, escalatory manner, with theatre nuclear weapons.

Therefore, what the European nations of NATO now need is not merely a meaningful contribution in a modern *theatre* nuclear stockpile and much improved *conventional* forces, but also a modern *offensive* chemical warfare capability. The Western European Union (WEU) stated at their conference in Paris on the 4th June, 1980, that the real danger of chemical warfare was illustrated by the evidence that the Russians have 100,000 fully-trained soldiers capable of mounting a chemical offensive on three or four fronts simultaneously.

It was also stated at the WEU conference that one possible scenario for war would be the use by the Russians of chemical weapons on the Central European front to neutralize opposition and enable Soviet forces to thrust forward to the Channel ports. It is 10 years ago that this precise solution was adopted on a NATO Exercise by the NATO Commander representing the Warsaw Pact Commander-in-Chief. The use of chemical weapons had to be ruled out otherwise the Exercise would have been over before it had even started. Ten years is a long time. We learn very slowly — *far too slowly*.

In fact, chemical warfare could so easily become the 'poor man's' equivalent to the nuclear weapon.

The Most Powerful Battlefield Deterrent

To check a Soviet blitzkrieg assault, there are revolutionary advances in mini-nuclear weapons technology, such as the enhanced radiation warhead more commonly known as the "Neutron Bomb" and shell — a miniature battlefield nuclear warhead — which kills by lethal gamma rays and not by blast and fire. The neutron warhead, about the size of a cricket ball, releases up to 80% of its total power as an intense burst of nuclear particles and gamma rays so penetrating that they are lethal to soldiers even in heavy tanks. But they do minimum damage to buildings and leave so little radioactive fall-out that troops can enter a combat zone within minutes. *(See Appendix E)*

This is the most powerful battlefield *deterrent* today. It would slaughter hundreds of thousands of Soviet troops in the first wave of a blitzkrieg attack without inflicting casualties to civilians and massive destruction to buildings and devastation of the countryside.

In a letter to *The Times*, London, published as long ago as August 1977, I wrote:-

"The brutal truth is that owing to the criminal negligence of politicians and the weak-kneed resistance of service chiefs, our conventional strength has been allowed to fall to such a parlous level that the neutron bomb will be the West's only salvation.

Were the Russians to mount a massive tank attack against Western Europe the 'Neutron Bomb' would be the best known way to stop them, causing the loss of far less lives and destruction than the old fashioned 'dirty' nuclear weapons which have been employed in Europe for the past decade."

But the Soviets craftily launched a propaganda campaign against the neutron weapon. The result was that NATO was intimidated into deploying it and President Carter backed down. Mr. Brezhnev's concern is that neutron weapons could bring the new Soviet T71 tanks to a speedy halt should they attempt to invade Western Germany.

The neutron warhead reinforces deterrence and may be the one weapon that will persuade the Soviet Union that the time has come to engage in meaningful discussions on a reduction of arms in Europe.

The Fallacy That The U.S.S.R. Poses No Threat.

In the 1960s the collective strength of the Western Alliance and the overwhelming superiory of the U.S. and Western strategic nuclear forces assured the security and stability of Europe and the United States.

In the first five years of this decade, however, the position has been dramatically reversed. Soviet penetration of the Middle East, Indian Ocean, Africa, Asia and the Far East has been achieved primarily against the background of an enormous build-up in nuclear and conventional forces at great economic sacrifice, while the West's military capability has steadily declined.

We have been witnessing the growing evidence of Russian militarism and Russian determination towards global expansionism, imperialism and hegemony under the pretext of détente.

The brutal truth must be faced that the Soviet forces have gone from strength to strength while NATO has continued to stagnate. I have never ceased to wonder at the numbers of holders of high office to whom the Soviet Union poses no threat outside the pages of a Fleming novel.

Those who are unable to see this threat, can be likened to *'foolish curs, that run winking into the mouth of a Russian bear, and have their heads crushed like rotten apples!* (Shakespeare 'Henry V')'.

Is the choice between war or surrender?

The arrogance of the Soviet Union at the last SALT II (Strategic Arms Limitation) meeting in Moscow, their total disregard of world opinion condemning their activities in Angola, the Horn of Africa, South Yemen and Afghanistan, and the glorification of the exploits of their lackeys, the Cubans, are manifestations of the growing confidence of the Politburo that they are on the way to achieving the major goals of Marxist-Leninist doctrine without firing a shot or sacrificing a single Soviet soldier (except in Afghanistan).

They now believe that the erosion of political *will* in the West has reached the stage when there is unlikely to be any hostile reaction by the West to further Soviet involvement in countries outside the Warsaw Pact frontiers.

If the erosion of the Western Alliance's military capability, and more important the *will* to use force when other means fail, continue at their present pace, the ultimate fate of the United States and Europe could be the choice between nuclear war or surrender.

The warning by Alexander Solzhenitsyn

Alexander Solzhenitsyn was desperately trying to tell us the truth in the BBC *Panorama* interview on 1st March, 1976, when he made an impassioned appeal for the West to come to its senses before it is too late. In many respects it was an endorsement of Mrs. Thatcher's call to the nation: 'Britain awake'.

Unless we do awake, we shall be ripe for plucking. The Russians themselves have said: "The role of the Red Army is to stand by ready to shake the tree when the rotten fruit is ripe to fall". They should know; so even if we are not prepared to listen to Solzhenitsyn's warning, let us at least heed the warning sounded by the Russians themselves.

As was only to be expected, the reception by the media to Solzhenitsyn's warning varied from ebullience to patronage, to the familiar effete blend of mockery and indifference and to downright ridicule and sickening drivel. As Peter Simple said in *The Daily Telegraph,* London, of 9th March, 1976, this is "a good example of some of the things Solzhenitsyn is warning us against: the refusal of

Western liberals and pseudo-liberals to hear and understand; their obstinate clinging, at all costs, to their own peculiar kind of pseudo-smart mental and moral denseness."

Pro-Russian Diatribe

Such is the bovine apathy and appalling ignorance that exists in the crucial area of defence that a surfeit of vociferous armchair strategists have surfaced, who have been allowed to get away with too much altering and faking of the West's real defence requirements. Offices are piled high with left-over intellectual garbage of gobbledygook peddlers who have succeeded in gaining a living with their ludicrous defence theories. Too much of their fatuous humbug is pro-Russian diatribe geared to serve Russian diplomacy.

Task, forces and threat no longer match up.

The soldier is bound by political decisions, but this must not deter him from continuing to assess the military facts and possibilities and placing his findings clearly before the politicians. If the task given him by the politicians and the forces given him by the politicians and the threat presented by the Warsaw Pact no longer match up, then it is up to the soldier to say so and to point out the dire consequences at stake.

In December 1976 the alarm was sounded and patriotic public opinion alerted after the disclosure that Britain's Chief of the Defence Staff – the late Marshal of the Royal Air Force Sir Andrew Humphrey – and the heads of the three Armed Services had taken the exceptional step of visiting the Prime Minister to register objections to defence cuts.

The politicians must be made to recognize the risks they are incurring, that they are bound to take account of it in their calculations and accept *the responsibility*. The defence of the Realm is the *first priority* of goverment.

What is required is a leader of world class who will restore among the people of the countries of NATO the realization that neither material prosperity, nor welfare, nor social advancement can be theirs unless they can be sure of their safety and their independence.

The Naked Truth

The situation is now far too grave for politicians to have a monopoly when it comes to making public statements on vital defence strategy. Senior serving 'military' men can no longer afford to bow to the principle that they are prevented by formal boundaries from speaking their minds. Political etiquette must take a back seat.

Britain's 1980 Defence White Paper contained the extraordinary statement that: "The NATO aim is to deter attack by possessing nuclear

267

weapons: should deterrence fail and an attack occur which conventional forces alone could not contain, NATO could threaten to use – and if necessary actually use – nuclear weapons to cause the aggressor to abandon his attack." Whoever wrote that naïve description of NATO's aims has obviously never read any Soviet military literature.

Wishful thinking statements by some of the political leaders of the West – even the highest in the land – appear to be designed deliberately to deceive the people by concealing and distorting the truth. If this is not so, then they must be crassly ignorant of the facts of life concerning modern conditions of warfare and nuclear strategy in particular.

The majority of today's leaders have not learned the bitter lessons of history, nor seemingly are they *willing* to learn. Like their predecessors they are busy putting their political careers and political parties first and the security of the West a poor second. Instead of paying their subscriptions in full to NATO, they take refuge under the phoney détente and under the shelter of America's now phoney nuclear umbrella.

One can excuse such people for not being able to understand a great deal of the more complex details of strategic nuclear technicalities, for Ministers of the Crown and Ministers of the State are merely politicians temporarily in office. But a wilful concealment of our now perilous position *cannot* be excused. Such negligence of duty, if disaster strikes, would invoke the condemnation of our descendants for untold generations and, without doubt, if the light of the Christian West is extinguished, *that of the Almighty Himself.*

The 'Iron Lady'.

Fortunately Britain has in Mrs. Thatcher a person who has the moral courage to unveil the sinister aims of the Soviet Union. She first did so on 19th January, 1976, when leader of the Conservative Party in opposition in Parliament. The Soviet journal *Red Star* accorded her the title 'Iron Lady'.

The appalling apathy, lethargy and ignorance of many political leaders of the West is not to be wondered at when one sees the alarming extent to which they are so blinkered by dogma against reality that they have become utterly indifferent to any important development in the defence field.

Mrs. Thatcher showed that she does not indulge in wishful thinking either about the capability or the intention of the Kremlin, which has embarked on a massive armaments build-up without parallel in history. This concentration of military strength far exceeds any conceivable requirement for the Soviets' own defence and can only have the most ominous implications for the West.

The weapons and forces that the Russians are building up have no usefulness except to destroy, blackmail or dominate the United States and Western Europe and spread communist influence throughout the world.

Mrs. Thatcher gave a lead to Western politicians who, according to their political beliefs and standards of integrity, are concealing the present serious situation from their peoples in varying degrees. There is a conflict between acting on the dictates of their conscience and doing what will best please their electorate. This leads most politicians into playing down the threat and the needs of the defence when speaking in the domestic environment, but being much more realistic when they are outside their country talking to an audience of NATO statesmen gathered together at Brussels.

Mrs. Thatcher's speech and Russia's guilty reaction to it did a great service in opening a debate and reviving the public's interest in the security of the home base and the defence of NATO's military front, and at the same time revealing to the man in the street the stark realities of the menace of Russia's ever-increasing military might on land, at sea and in the air.

Six months later, on 31st July, 1976, Mrs. Thatcher made her second major speech of warning against Russia. This occasion marked the eve of the first anniversary from the great Helsinki swindle on European co-operation.

Then on 18th October, 1979, as Britain's Prime Minister, she gave a lead from the very top by making a frank and forceful speech in Luxembourg, in which she said: "Europe enjoys a stability and prosperity which would have seemed unimaginable when NATO was founded. But the threat remains. It is symbolized by the massive armies ranged by the Russians against us in the East, and by the stream of propaganda which they continue to direct against our institutions and aspirations.

"Let me be clear. The Soviet armies in Europe are organized and trained for attack. Their military strength is growing. The Russians do not publish their intentions. So we must judge them by their military capabilities."

Russia can strike America without suffering unacceptable retaliation.

The strategic studies by V. Ye Savkin and A.S. Sidorenko are now available in English translations, so there is no longer any excuse or justification for members of Congress and their Western European counterparts to be misinformed about the threat that we now face.

What are the main lessons to be learned from the writings of Savkin and Sidorenko?

1. Frightening superiority over NATO

There is now not the slightest doubt that the Russians are able to increase their nuclear, chemical, biological and con-

269

ventional capability to a degree that will give them a frightening superiority over the NATO alliance.

2. Attack with tactical nuclear weapons from the word 'Go'.

They are prepared to fight a battle with tactical nuclear weapons from the word 'Go' if necessary, but they genuinely believe that the disintegration of the West will continue, aided and abetted by the subversive activities which are now all too apparent in every European country, until the stage is reached when they will be able to pose such a threat to a fragmented Western World that they will attain their political objectives without firing a shot. (They underestimated the situation in Afghanistan). Time after time in these books, the Russian authors stress that no economic sacrifice will be too great to achieve the ambitions of Marxism-Leninism.

3. Surprise attack.

Savkin emphasized that the advent of "nuclear weapons has considerably increased the role and importance of the *surprise* offensive".

4. 'First Strike', a *sine qua non*.

Sidorenko explained in these words the Soviet firm belief in the doctrine of pre-emptive nuclear strikes: "to refuse the 'first strike' is to be derelict in responsibility to the homeland."

5. A defensive posture is doomed to defeat.

While NATO's doctrine emphasizes *deterrence,* Soviet doctrine states that defensive operations, although sometimes unavoidable, are "a forced and temporary form of combat actions". Soviet military teaching states that "a side which only defends is inevitably doomed to defeat".

6. Deterrent concept of nuclear weapons is derisory.

America's and NATO's military doctrine which disavows the 'first strike' and which emphasizes the defensive, the *deterrent* concept of nuclear weapons, and the selective and controlled use of tactical nuclear weapons for political signalling purposes, is the subject of derision in Soviet doctrine.

7. 'Mutal Assured Destruction'. (MAD)

The Russians do not accept the American strategy of a

'balance of terror', or MAD – the acronym for 'Mutal Assured Destruction'. MAD means that if either superpower, after suffering a surprise attack, can count on retaining enough strategic nuclear weapons to destroy the other, no government could afford to risk war.

By 1982 the Soviets will have the capability of destroying most of America's land based missiles in a surprise attack, together with many of their missile submarines and nuclear bombers. Some experts believe it may be even sooner than 1982. Others believe it will be later when they will be running into such severe domestic difficulties at home that they may be tempted to lash out as a diversion and be at their most dangerous.

In any case, as I have already said elsewhere, the Americans will not be able, in the same time scale, either to strike with sufficient accuracy at the Soviet intercontinental ballistic missile force, or to develop means of protecting their own.

The Soviets will thus have achieved strategic nuclear superiority. Instead of a balance of terror which equally restrains both sides, the terror will be mainly on the part of the United States.

8. Deterrence has failed.

The Kremlin leaders believe they already have enough military superiority, combined with such elaborate civil defence installations and preparations, that they will be able to destroy America's nuclear capability, without suffering unacceptable retaliation.

If this is true, *deterrence* has indeed failed.

9. Is nuclear superiority really usable?

When the appeasers ask their political question, "Is nuclear superiority really usable", let them read the Soviet answer, which is "Yes".

Just because something is unthinkable to us does not mean it it is unthinkable to the Soviets. Good intentions based on humane feelings, but not on accurate information, are a great danger to our security, and are *much more* likely to lead to an unintentional nuclear war than a mistake in calculations.

The Soviets know that no country and no Alliance can attack them today and expect to win. They know that when America had unquestioned nuclear superiority and could have destroyed them at little or no cost to the United States, they did not do so.

10. Population losses in a nuclear war.

The public must not listen to devious politicians telling them that the Soviets do not have a first-strike doctrine when they can read Soviet doctrine stating the firm belief as mentioned in paragraph 4.

Let them read the Soviet civil defence doctrines and become familiar with existing Soviet plans. Let them learn that the Soviets estimate that they could hold their population losses in a nuclear war to the range of 6 to 8 per cent, lower than their World War II casualties and lower than the self-inflicted casualties of Russia's great purge.

11. Soviet Forces and Doctrines Geared to The Offensive.

Unilateral disarmament lobbyists insult one's intelligence when they argue that the Soviet Union is a large land-based defensive power whose huge military forces are necessary to protect her immense land mass and to defend her borders from attack by NATO or China. Neither NATO or China has the offensive structure, capability or mobility to attack the Soviet Union.

Russia's actions in placing herself astride the oil supply line to Western Europe and acquiring African bases have *nothing whatsoever to do with the defence of the Soviet homeland*. To fail to see this additional threat to the effectiveness of NATO is to stick our heads even deeper in the sand.

The build-up of the Soviet strategic missile forces has gone far beyond anything that can be construed as a deterrent, and it is continuing, together with their build-up of mass superiority in conventional forces on the ground, in the air and at sea.

The doctrine, deployment, structure and magnitude of the Soviet Army clearly indicate a military machine which is designed specifically to launch a massive, surprise "blitzkrieg" attack with lightning speed, and maintaining a stunning rate of advance of 70 miles per day; the cutting edge being armoured and motorized formations, with nuclear and chemical weapons playing a decisive role.

In Europe such a speed would bring Soviet forces to the Rhine in less than 48 hours and to the Channel ports within a week. Against China it would mean a lightning penetration in depth and an envelopment of Manchuria before Chinese forces could organize an effective territorial defence.

12. The Soviets military capabilities.

On 12th December, 1979, Marshal of the Royal Air Force, Sir Neil Cameron, Britain's former Chief of the Defence Staff, gave the Fuller-Liddell Hart Memorial Lecture in London, his subject being "Defence and the Changing Scene". The details of the Soviets military capabilities listed below are extracted from his lecture.

The Soviet Army has:

* 174 divisions including 8 airborne divisions.
* A considerable numerical tank superiority over NATO and of high quality. Their tanks and armoured vehicles are equipped to operate in a nuclear environment.
* A rapid build-up in heavily armed and armoured helicopters — 40,000 helicopters altogether.
* A considerable chemical warfare capability.
* A dynamic growth in their strategic mobility forces which gives them the ability with Aeroflot assistance, to move 50,000 troops, i.e. equivalent to a large percentage of British Army of the Rhine (BAOR) — in 24 hours from the Soviet Union to one front or another.
* A strong amphibious force.
* The ability with part of their considerable Hind helicopter force and airborne divisions to get in behind NATO's forward dispositions, with the aim of causing the maximum amount of havoc in conjunction with armoured attack.

The Air Marshal described the Soviet SS20 as a highly mobile missile system with triple warheads, and with a range to reach comfortably all the main targets in Europe and China. Being mobile it is very difficult to target.

In the air the Russians are now producing aircraft and weapons systems with increasing range, weapon load and accuracy, such as:

The Backfire bomber which is virtually a missile system because the missile weapons it carries has a stand-off range of about 400 km. *Backfire can cover all targets in the United Kingdom.*

Foxbat and Flogger C which can reach targets in the Midlands to the south of England flying direct from the Baltic area.

The posture of these three aircraft is now *offensive* in nature.

The Air Marshal emphasized the vulnerability of NATO's reinforcements and resupply across the Atlantic, against Russia's satellite surveillance, long-range acoustics, stand-off weapons, sea-skimming missiles and high-speed nuclear submarines.

He admitted that our own offensive and defensive mining capability had been neglected, whereas the Soviets have both massive stocks of modern and sophisticated mines – about 400,000 – and the ability to lay them, with the result that the approaches to naval bases and large areas of the ocean could be denied to us.

The Air Marshal said that some would argue that although the Warsaw Pact has the capability it lacks the intention to launch an attack. But as the British Prime Minister said in Luxembourg in October 1979, *"We must judge them by their military capabilities."*

Moscow's 'Games'

Appreciation to *Sunday Express*, 15th June, 1980.

As the 1980 Olympic Games approached, British Prime Minister, Mrs. Margaret Thatcher, stated in Parliament: "I sometimes wonder what more the Russians will have to do in Afghanistan by way of atrocities before they convince our Olympic athletes that they should not go to Moscow."

The boycott of the Games was no longer a means of registering repugnance of Russian aggression as such. It was the catalogue of terrible atrocities against humanity being committed by Russia's occupying army that cried out for the most vehement censure. The war in Afghanistan is not a war between rival armies: it is a battle to slaughter and butcher a civilian population – men, women and children – into total submission.

To have gone to Moscow was as if the athletes going to Berlin in 1936, went in the full knowledge that the Jews in Nazi Germany were going to die in the gas chambers.

CHAPTER

23

The Solution for the Survival of the West

A Question of Will

Let us now crystallize our thoughts as to the prime requirements necessary to fire the latent spirit of the West, in order that it might act quickly, co-operatively and effectively in the defence of civilization.

The requirements are:

1. A global outlook and appropriate strategy. The limited NATO boundaries are now outdated at the Tropic of Cancer and in the Middle East, Africa and the Indian Ocean. The countries that might now be considered as possible members or associates are: South Africa, Japan, Spain, Israel, Brazil, Argentina and Australia.

2. A sense of urgency that the "warning time" must now be measured in days rather than in weeks, months or years.

3. The need for extremely timely political decisions.

4. Maintenance of the nuclear deterrent and, in this context, the development of the Cruise missile, the "Neutron Bomb" and an *independent* British nuclear deterrent.

5. Considerable increase in conventional strength by sea, land and air, in order to raise the nuclear threshold and to assure the security of our territory and communications.

6. Immediate readiness at home and abroad.

7. Standardized and inter-operative equipment has been the major Allied requirement for years; obstacles such as national pride, vested commercial interests, differing staff requirements and secrecy regulations need to be overcome.

8. Western response to the Soviet challenge should include economic sanctions.

9. Western preparedness, particularly within Great Britain, to include a viable Home Defence organization and the recruitment and training of a militia along the lines of the Swiss system, covering the whole territory in great depth throughout Europe.

10.   The need for quick response combat forces to deal with military crises, aid to a civil power, peace keeping and disaster relief worldwide.

11.   A massive public relations exercise with an emphasis on truth concerning the present siege of the West.

12.   A reversal of the propaganda war which the West has been losing by default, despite having overwhelming evidence and obvious truth on its side. Soviet military action, and the action of their proxy forces, usually follows conquest by propaganda and subversion. The following should be imprinted upon the minds of every citizen in the Free World:

"EXTERNAL ENCIRCLEMENT, PLUS INTERNAL DEMORALIZATION, PLUS THERMONUCLEAR BLACKMAIL, LEADS TO PROGRESSIVE SURRENDER."

Global Strategy

Because defence is indivisible, NATO cannot shut its eyes to events taking place beyond its present boundaries, which is what it first tried to do during the Arab-Israeli War of 1973. In future, the alliance must be far more outward looking and realize that the defence of the Mediterranean cannot be divorced from the security of the Middle East, Africa and the Indian Ocean. Nor can NATO's southern boundary at sea, end at the Tropic of Cancer.

In spite of the political implications involved, there is an overriding case for NATO's boundary to be extended below the Tropic of Cancer, to include *joint* defence of the Gulf. Inasmuch as 66% of the world oil reserves lie near the Persian Gulf, stability must be safeguarded in that theatre otherwise the continuing access to energy by the U.S. the NATO countries and Japan will be at grave risk. Therefore, there must be joint defence of the Gulf.

If Soviet maritime expansion is to be curbed, Japan must expand its navy and assume a far greater responsibility, jointly with the U.S. navy, in the area of the West Pacific and must protect the sea lanes through China and South-East Asia waters. After all, about 90 per cent of Japan's oil requirements are carried by tankers from the Middle East across the Indian Ocean.

A permanent maritime presence must be established at Diego Garcia, in the form of a joint American, British, French and Dutch naval task force, with amphibious and air components. There must be a continuous naval presence in the Arabian Sea and north-west Indian Ocean.

If Soviet designs are to be thwarted a new military command – located outside the region – should be created with the Commander-in-Chief having at his disposal a quick response combat force ready to be airlifted into the region. This would result in formal and regular joint

277

military consultation, planning and exercises with the countries in the area and a proper use and interpretation of intelligence.

Part of the quick response combat force should consist of a multi-national force similar to NATO's Allied Command Europe (ACE) Mobile Force (AMF). Such an Allied Force would demonstrate the solidarity of the West and their capability to respond immediately to any threat from the Soviet Union to essential oil supplies.

The Allied Force would not be a "Fire Brigade", but rather a "Flag Waving Brigade" to deter a 'fire' from breaking out.

The Russians are aware that grabbing the oil would be like grabbing Europe. Therefore, there must be a new Alliance for the defence of this part of the world, just as there is the Atlantic Alliance – NATO – which is entirely defensive in scope and acts as a deterrent to Soviet aggression.

It is imperative that top priority is given forthwith to the global nature of the Soviet threat and the vulnerability of the lifelines to the West and Japan. This new defence concept should include Japan and Spain in the first instance, with Brazil, Argentina and Australia joining thereafter.

If the Soviet Union's strategy is global, as indeed it is, then the West's strategy must also be global.

Missile Gap.

The United States must close the strategic nuclear missile gap, for nothing in the world can defend freedom against the Soviet nuclear arsenal except the nuclear power of America.

NATO must be equipped with the highly effective enhanced radiation warheads – the so-called "Neutron Bomb" – which can be delivered with such precision against Warsaw Pact armoured forces that they could materially alter the tank/anti-tank equation in favour of the defence – i.e. NATO.

In particular the new generation of cruise missiles could prove a most important technological advance. Therefore, on no account must America forego its ability to develop this weapon. Theatre medium range nuclear missiles, in the form of the Cruise missile and the Pershing 2 ballistic missile, must be deployed in Western Europe to counter the Soviet SS20 which is already deployed in large numbers.

At present Europe has no effective anti-ballistic missile defence nor deterrent against this latest Soviet intermediate-range nuclear missile, the mobile SS20. This is the world's most advanced intermediate range ballistic missile.

Each missile carries three independently targetted nuclear warheads with a range of more than 2,200 miles, which means they can hit any target in Western Europe from Gibraltar to the North Cape. For example, the three pre-targetted warheads of just one missile could hit,

THE RIVAL MISSILES

CHART 6

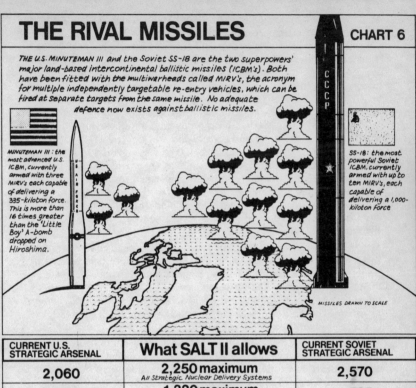

THE U.S. MINUTEMAN III and the Soviet SS-18 are the two superpowers' major land-based intercontinental ballistic missiles (ICBM's). Both have been fitted with the multiwarheads called MIRV's, the acronym for multiple independently targetable re-entry vehicles, which can be fired at separate targets from the same missile. No adequate defence now exists against ballistic missiles.

MINUTEMAN III : the most advanced U.S. ICBM, currently armed with three MIRV's each capable of delivering a 335-kiloton force. This is more than 16 times greater than the 'Little Boy' A-bomb dropped on Hiroshima.

SS-18: the most powerful Soviet ICBM, currently armed with up to ten MIRV's, each capable of delivering a 1,000-kiloton force

MISSILES DRAWN TO SCALE

CURRENT U.S. STRATEGIC ARSENAL	What SALT II allows		CURRENT SOVIET STRATEGIC ARSENAL
2,060	**2,250 maximum** All Strategic Nuclear Delivery Systems		2,570
1,046	**1,320 maximum** All types of MIRVs		795
1,046	**1,200 maximum** MIRVed SLBMs* and ICBMs		725
550	**820 maximum** MIRVed ICBMs		600
0	**Frozen at existing levels** Modern heavy MIRVed ICBMs (Such as SS-18)		308

CURRENT U.S. CONVENTIONAL ARSENAL	What SALT II ignores	CURRENT SOVIET CONVENTIONAL ARSENAL

Uniformed personnel 2,026,345

Tactical aircraft 5,364

Field artillery 5,500

Tanks 12,100

Aircraft carriers 13

Cruisers/ destroyers/ frigates 161

Attack submarines 81

Uniformed personnel 4,400,000

Tactical aircraft 8,000

Field artillery 20,000

Tanks 50,000

Aircraft carriers 2

Cruisers /destroyers/frigates 284

Attack submarines 195

*SLBM = Submarine-launched ballistic missiles

say, Heathrow Airport and the two RAF Stations at Brise Norton near Swindon, and Cottesmore near Oakham.

Or, one missile with its three pre-targetted warheads could destroy London's main electric generators, the communications centre for outgoing messages to military command posts, and the BBC's main transmitters. You will see from the top lefthand diagram of Chart 5 on page 262 that the U.S.S.R. has 130 SS20's – and more than this now – which the Russians have deployed on their extreme western border.

Since 1978, Russia has been producing and deploying the SS20 missile, first at the rate of one a week, *and now it is one every five days.* By the end of 1983 Russia will have 400 of these missiles in place and their overwhelming threat will be such as to provide Russia with a nuclear blackmail. In other words, Russia could issue an ultimatum without having to go to war – *surrender or fry!*

NATO, therefore, must have a matching deterrence in the form of the Cruise missile and the Pershing 2 rocket, although they will not be in place until 1983.

Already in Britain and in the four other European countries where these nuclear weapons are to be deployed, voices are being raised in protest – much to the delight of the Soviet Union, of course. To say, as the protesters do, that "the cruise missiles are a deadly threat to us all" is the exact opposite of the truth. *It is the SS20 which is the deadly threat to us all.* The cruise missiles are designed specifically to render that threat less potent.

The protesters in Britain claim that the deployment of these missiles on British soil will multiply the lethal danger of accident or miscalculation. Nuclear warheads on manned aircraft and missiles, including United States aircraft and missiles, have been deployed in Britain since the early 1950s. There have been no accidents and no miscalculations in the past thirty years.

The NATO council's decision to deploy cruise missiles in Britain and Europe is intended to redress the serious imbalance in theatre nuclear weapons (which favours the Soviet Union) and improve NATO's capability to *deter* war, not make it more likely as the protesters erroneously assume. *Britain has been a target for nuclear attack ever since the Soviet Union acquired nuclear weapons in 1949. It is still, and will remain, a target for nuclear attack whether or not cruise missiles are deployed on her soil.*

The protesters are beseeching the Government to reverse the decision which gave authority for cruise missiles to be deployed in Britain, and if this should fail, they are urging the people of Britain to join their band of brothers in what they describe as "contesting the installation of cruise missiles in Britain".

The vast majority in Britain are people of common sense; they will do nothing of the sort. The people of Britain and indeed of the whole

NATO alliance have no wish to become part of the Soviet communist empire either by war or subversion.

Others are arguing that if Britain were to have no nuclear weapons on their soil there would be no incentive to the Soviets to attack with nuclear weapons if only because they would have a useless devastated land to take over.

Such people have forgotten the experience of Japan. As the Japanese had no nuclear weapons, the United States was able to procure a quick surrender by dropping only two nuclear bombs, and that was only for the purpose of *demonstrating* the existence of such weapons of war. If the United Kingdom had no nuclear weapons, the Soviet Union could do the same and probably without dropping any bombs at all. The mere threat would secure capitulation.

The major deterrent to the Russians from doing to Britain what they have done to the countries of Eastern Europe is the U.K.'s nuclear deterrent, which makes any *invasion* of the United Kingdom by Russia a gamble for them.

Any weapon system on British soil designed to respond to the Soviet SS20 must be under British control because we can no longer expect an American President to authorise the use of American nuclear weapons against the Soviet Union as distinct from Soviet forces advancing into Europe. But we now know that the warheads of the Pershing 2 and the 160 American cruise missiles to be deployed in Britain, will be in sole charge of United States personnel. National approval will be required to release them and the weapons will be subject to Presidential release through the PAL (permissive action link) safeguard, which ensures that even when release is agreed, the warhead cannot become live until PAL is activated electronically by the President. Hence, all the more reason why Britain must have its own independent theatre and strategic nuclear deterrent.

Britain's Independent Strategic and Theatre Nuclear Capability

Britain's diplomacy will avail us little unless we are seen by friends and adversaries alike to maintain and *increase* our own defence capability. Diplomacy and defence must go hand in hand. What should Britain's defence priorities be?

The superiority achieved by the Soviets in strategic nuclear power makes it more essential than ever for Britain to have an independent nuclear deterrent under *independent British control,* even if committed for ordinary purposes to NATO. Britain cannot expect the United States to risk their homeland to protect the U.K. Equally unless we have a deterrent of our own we shall be wide open to Soviet nuclear blackmail.

The 1980 Defence White Paper put the matter thus: "An adversary assessing the consequences of possible aggression in Europe would have to regard a NATO defence containing these powerful independent ele-

281

ments as a harder one to predict, and a more dangerous one to assail, than one in which nuclear retaliatory power rested in United States hands alone." This, in essence, is the indispensable force of the case for an independent British nuclear capability.

The decision announced on 15th July, 1980, for the Trident-1 (C4) missile system for Britain, may truly decide the fate of our peoples for generations to come. If indeed this means the sacrifice of our conventional warfare capability, we will be committed to suicide.

The cost of the Trident submarine strategic nuclear delivery system will be about £7,000 million, *not* £5,000 million, which is the figure that has been bandied about. Its purchase will inevitably mean a cut-back in British army and air force equipment in the 1990s, even to the extent of bringing back the British Army on the Rhine (BOAR). Britain must increase, not decrease, its conventional warfare capability. Trident is too expensive for Britain *unless* the present Conservative Government is prepared to increase defence expenditure by at least 5% annually to pay for it. Furthermore, it is virtually certain that another Labour Government would cancel the whole project, as the first Trident submarine will not *begin* construction until about 1987!

Cruise missiles are the answer for Britain. They are cheaper and, unlike the Trident, have a *dual* capability of posing:

a.   An accurate *theatre* nuclear threat.
b.   A *strategic* nuclear threat to major cities and industrial complexes in the Soviet Union.

Since Britain will have 160 of the American ground-launched version of the Cruise missile by 1983-85, what better policy could we have than an entirely British force of either ground-launched or air-launched cruise missiles, which could have exactly the same warheads but with four times the *accuracy* of submarine-launched missiles and at less than a quarter of the cost.

Tests carried out in the United States with simulated Soviet defence systems (fighter aircraft and surface-to-air-missiles) showed that it is very difficult indeed to find, track and attack a cruise missile. It has a radar cross-section of 0.05 square metres compared to a F111 fighter aircraft with 8 square metres, or put another way – the radar reflectivity of a cruise missile is 1/1,000th that of a B52 bomber aircraft.

To deal with the various opinions, informed and uninformed, it is necessary to spell out the strategic realities in no uncertain terms. If we fail to get it right now, there will be no second chance – if indeed we still have time to make the *first* chance sure?

The unilateral nuclear disarmers should realize that a denuclearised Europe is not likely to survive for long. On the other side of the argument, those who support exclusive NATO control of the European nuclear trigger, have to accept that a political decision to use the deterrent might not be taken in time.

Rather than close off our options, when our present deterrent comes in for renewal in a few years' time, it is vital that Britain should retain the *largest feasible* number of options to deal with the unpredictable. Unless the necessary degree of uncertainty is maintained in Soviet calculations, as to what our response will be, Kremlin imperialists can *afford* to gamble on the belief that a United States Administration would freeze, when the price for defending Europe was a nuclear assault on the North American Continent.

I submit, therefore, that the case for an independent British strategic nuclear capability is unarguable. To take the position of the nuclear disarmer, by saying that in giving up our nuclear capability we will make a contribution to the de-escalation of the build-up of nuclear weapons, as a former Chief of the Defence Staff was reported as saying recently, is like looking into a building through solar control glass – *a one-way vision,* which reflects only the image of the observer.

If indeed we are limited to seeing the image of Soviet Russia – our declared adversary – as that of our own, deception with terrible consequences must ensue. The appalling habit of "mirror-imaging" is one of the West's main weaknesses in all of its discussions on the role of nuclear weapons in a future war.

The question of whose finger should be on the nuclear trigger can be judged from the following points:

1. One Finger on the Trigger

i.e., The President of the United States. NATO's own Journal published what President Carter is reported to have said in the 1976 election campaign:
"I would not, as President, authorise the use of nuclear weapons except when the security and existence of the United States were in danger."

2. Fourteen/Fifteen Fingers on the Trigger – NATO

Impossible for the unanimous political decision to be taken in time.
Crisis management is NATO's weakness at present.

3. Britain's Own Finger on the Trigger.

a.   Deterrent against: (1) Attack (2) Blackmail
b.   Ability to speak to the Russians from a position of strength.
    We do not appear naked at the conference table.
c.   Allow for the unpredictable. The only safe prediction today is that the unexpected must be expected. As the Mideast

283

Yom Kippur War showed – and the Russian invasion of Afghanistan – with spies in the sky you can photograph the enemy's capability, but you cannot photograph what is in his mind – his intention.

d.   If the Cruise missiles on British soil are not under this country's control, there is even greater reason why Britain must have its own independent nuclear deterrent/capability.

e.   Insurance policy. We must ensure against the worst case, i.e., war – just as in our daily lives we insure against accident, theft, sickness and loss of life.

4. Confusion

If retired Service Chiefs of the highest rank and highest appointment (i.e., Chief of the Defence Staff – CDS) are not unanimous, then what is the man in the street to think, let alone the politicians?

Civil Defence.

I come next to air defence against conventional attack. When I was on the headquarters staff of Allied Forces Central Europe in 1965/67, the only threat to the U.K. came from nuclear missiles or nuclear bombs. The only defence against such an attack was retaliation. There was therefore little need for air defence except to prevent intrusion by unfriendly reconnaissance planes. Now all this has changed. The Soviets are deploying bombers like the Backfire which have the capability of launching a *conventional* attack on any point of the British Isles. Therefore the air defence requirement is plain enough if we are to assure our own security and ensure the security of our airfields and ports for reinforcements from the United States.

In a letter published in *The Times,* London, on 12th March, 1980, I wrote:-

"I have followed with interest the articles and letters that have appeared recently in your newspaper on the need for an up-to-date form of Civil Defence. What seems to be overlooked, however, is that it will not take a *nuclear* strike to inflict severe casualties and destruction on this country. A *conventional* strike is now the most likely threat.

The Soviets now have long-range aircraft such as the TU-22 Backfire bomber which are capable of launching air-to-surface stand-off *conventional* missiles of devastating lethality and destruction, and with such pinpoint accuracy and precision that the Home Office, for instance, could be picked out from the Ministry of Defence.

Because of our strategic location *vis-à-vis* the North Sea and Atlantic and the very large numbers of reinforcements of aircraft, men and supplies that will be passing through this country, we are now the Soviets' No. 1 target.

The air defence, maritime defence and civil defence of the Home Base are hopelessly inadequate. As a start we should plan to make use of underground car parks and similar facilities which were not available in such quantity in World War II, and we must resurrect a modern form of Civil Defence. For the modest sum of £20,000 per county we could raise an *all-volunteer* Civil Defence and thus show our resolution and will to defend ourselves. Volunteers would flock to the C.D. colours.

As for a nuclear attack, it would not necessarily be such as to reduce the whole of Britain to ashes. The Russians have acquired small yield weapons and accurate delivery systems which can take out targets such as airfields and dock facilities without destroying the entire countryside surrounding them. Most people in Britain would survive such attacks, but more would be saved by the creation of a civil defence plan to help those in the most likely target areas on the lines that I have suggested."

Britain's Private (Red) Army

With the present state of anarchy and subversion in Britain – which amounts to industrial terrorism – will not take a nuclear strike to neutralize the U.K. A dock strike will do. Britain has now reached the stage where those who want to work are afraid to do so for fear of losing their jobs, such are the strong-arm tactics of the shop stewards who are now in control. The union chiefs lead from the rear. Mrs. Thatcher should now bite the bullet. In a broadcast to the nation she should explain exactly what is happening, who are the villains in the piece and what she intends to do about the deplorable situation.

"The workers of the world are beginning to unite to defeat this Conservative Government." Thus did the secretary of the Wales area Trades Union Congress announce the international Marxist-inspired backing for the steel strike which, whatever its leaders may say, *was* political and aimed at forcing the elected government to adopt socialist policies which the electorate rejected less than a year ago.

While the bulk of the striking workers were neither Marxist nor politically motivated, they were very effectively controlled by the Marxist militants who were to be found in strategic positions throughout the trade union movement, particularly at factory level.

The development of the so-called mass or flying pickets placed in the hands of the Marxists a private army which was effectively used to intimidate and discipline workers who did not toe the line. It was also used to overwhelm the police by physically blockading the factory gates and forcing a closure.

This private army was very effectively used on St. Valentine's Day in February when the workers of a private steel works, who had no dispute with their employers, were forced to join the strike after over one thousand 'pickets' had struggled with police. The workers were told that

"Thanks! You're saving me the trouble of finishing you off myself!"

Appreciation to *Sunday Express,* 13th January, 1980.

there would be twice that number around the works the next day if they did not do as they were told. The Company Chairman said "intimidation and anarchy has won a total victory", and one of the non-communist trade unionists declared: "loss of life has nothing to do with the trade union movement, but after what we have been through today it is obvious lives may be lost".

He went on to criticize the Yorkshire miners' leader, Mr. Arthur Scargill, a dedicated Marxist who pioneered this technique, for "interfering" in a matter which had nothing to do with him. The strike leaders stated that they had not asked him to attend with over three hundred battle-hardened street fighters.

Britain was witnessing a classic Marxist take-over of both the democratic socialist Labour Party and the Trade Union Movement, and it was interesting to see how the democratic socialists reacted.

About the same time there was a nation-wide Labour Party television broadcast. It was led by the Labour Party youth officer, a Marxist who was appointed to his full time post despite opposition from Mr. Callaghan, the former Prime Minister. The programme accused the police of provocation, violence and racial prejudice and called for the disbanding of the Special Patrol Group. The reason for this being that the SPG is an effective weapon against the politically motivated private army which is being trained and perfected with its own logistic and command structure.

This modern development of a political private army, which reminds one uncomfortably of the Brownshirts of the Hitler era, can be traced to the successful closing of the Saltley Coal depot during the coal miners' strike in 1972 under a Heath-led Conservative government. That was organized by Mr. Arthur Scargill, who tried to repeat the success during the Grunwick dispute under a Labour administration. He failed largely because of the skill and determination of the London police, who were ready for him, and the courage of the workers, mainly British Asians, who fully backed their management. But the Labour government criticized the management, who had broken no law, and praised the strikers who had. It did this because the social democrats lacked the political courage to risk their careers by denouncing the Marxist tactics.

Mrs. Thatcher and her government are fully aware of the dangers and are expected by the British people to defend this serious assault upon British democracy. During a very black period in the Second World War, Sir Winston Churchill gave the following wise, important warning:

"Nothing can save England if she will not save herself. If we lose faith in ourselves, in our capacity to work, guide and govern, if we lose our will to live, then indeed, our story is ended."

With the steel strike and other industrial troubles, the above message is most vital and as essential today as it was the day Churchill made this statement.

DARK PARTY—" Ax yer pardon, sir ! But if you was agoing down this dark lane, p'raps you'd allow me and this here young man to go along with yer, 'cos, yer see, there ain't no perlice about, and we're so precious feared o'being garrotted! "

Appreciation to *The Daily Telegraph*, 19th February, 1980.

Home Defence.

If, as I have said above, the U.K. is the Soviets' No. 1 target for neutralization, the main deficiencies for the defence of the Home Base are:
* Defensive mining at sea.
* Home Naval force.
* Air defence aircraft.
* Surface to air guided weapons (SAGW). Our long concrete runways are very vulnerable and could be rendered useless by stand-off *conventional* missiles.
* Anti-tank mines.
* Territorial, naval and air reserves.
* Special constabulary
* Civil Defence.

As the former Defence correspondent of *The Daily Telegraph* has emphasized in some recent letters, the most decisive factor in war is morale. As he rightly points out, to ensure that national morale stands up to the Soviet military build-up and its explicit use to blackmail the West, supported by the anarchists from within the U.K., steps must be taken to protect the population. The order of priority is protection against conventional and chemical attack and to mitigate the worst effects of nuclear attack.

"Not only", says Brigadier Thompson, "is this necessary for the morale of the general population but it is equally necessary for the morale of our forces serving overseas."

Unlike Britain's NATO allies, the U.K. has not been physically invaded in two World Wars which is one reason for its flaccid Home Defence posture. Article 3 of The North Atlantic Treaty stipulates that each country will maintain and develop its individual and collective capability for its own national security.

With the bulk of its Regular Armed Forces serving outside England, Britain has no Home Guard, no Civil Defence, only a hacked, carved up and understrength volunteer Territorial Army. The Armed Forces and the Police are now stretched as tight as a violin string. Unlike the countries of the Warsaw Pact, the neutral countries of Western Europe and most of her major European allies, Britain is now virtually without any properly constituted Home Security and Civil Defence forces in being on the ground.

Successive British Governments, whether Socialist or Conservative, have been dangerously negligent in ignoring the well-proven military axiom that there are two Fronts to defend, the Home Front as well as the Military Front. They are complementary and of equal importance, because between them they form the NATO shield. Britain has failed miserably to pay its NATO subscription in this respect.

Even Norway and Denmark put Britain to shame. The combined total population of these two countries is the same as that of the Greater London area and yet within 20 hours Norway can mobilize about 110,000 reservists, 70,000 armed Home Guard and 150,000 fully equipped and trained Civil Defence; and in 24 hours the figures for Denmark are 88,000 reservists, 69,000 Home Guard and 60,000 Civil Defence.

Maintaining inadequate conventional forces in Europe, whittling away trained reserves and leaving the Home Base wide open to attack, does not add up to a 'deterrent' policy, whether it be with or without a credible nuclear potential. If a country becomes so ill-equipped that it cannot protect itself against attack, or against provocative harassment of its merchant ships and civil aircraft, then that country is extremely vulnerable to military, political and economic blackmail.

By failing to provide the country with adequate trained reserves and Home Defence, Britain is indicating to Russia that she might not have the will to resist, never mind the capacity. In the 1930s, Britain's politicians gambled with the nation's security. Then, at least, the country was given some warning. Next time there will be no such warning.

Britain must recreate a citizen's volunteer reserve for three quite distinct roles; first, duties in aid of the civil power; second, home defence; third, as a framework for expansion in the event of war.

U.K. Ever-ready Mobile Force.

The U.K. must resurrect its ever-ready mobile force of about brigade group size, including a parachute and amphibious capability, and air transport and offensive air support.

Of course, what I am proposing will add to the defence budget, but one cannot underestimate the threat and danger that I have described in this book. It is certain that a 3% increase in the defence budget will not be enough. Something of the order of 4% to 5% will be necessary. There must be cutback in government expenditure elsewhere – whether on the support of "lame-duck", bureaucrats or civil servants and the like. There are more civil servants in the Inland Revenue than there are sailors in the Royal Navy. The number of British soldiers deployed on NATO's central front is less than the number of civilian employees employed by some of the larger County Councils. We are spending more on cosmetics than we are on defence – all the measures I have outlined would help the serious unemployment problem.

Defence spending cannot be maintained at a constant level if that level bears no relation to Russia's relentless determination to achieve military superiority, with more and more *offensive* power and wider options. It is high time that defence was taken out of the political arena and excluded from cuts in public expenditure. What is the use of having a welfare state if a country cannot ensure its own security and survival?

It was the Chancellor of the Exchequer of a British Socialist Government in 1969, who said: "Once we cut defence expenditure to the extent where our defence is imperilled, we have no houses, we have no hospitals, we have no schools. We have a heap of cinders" — the very same man made defence cuts amounting to £10,000 million!

Standardization

There is far too much waste and duplication in NATO. We want much more co-operation in arms purchases. The jargon is called rationalization. In other words, interdependence, and not independence. With far more NATO standardization of weapons, equipment, logistics, training and tactics, we would get twice as good defence at half the present price. What we want is value for money and not "jobs for the boys". There are far too many over-staffed and over-stuffed headquarters.

In contrast to the Warsaw Pact nations, where proliferation of weapons systems is minimal, the arms industries of NATO members have long over-lapped in ever more expensive products. As a result, the alliance uses ten different armoured personnel carriers, four types of main battle tanks, an array of anti-tank weapons and a broad selection of fighter aircraft. A study six years ago put the cost of such redundancy at $2.6 billion lost annually in research and development alone, with another $7 billion wasted in procurement costs. The figures now are believed to be higher.

The Battle for Information.

It was a Norwegian poet who said: "Peace is the most ruthless creature in the world. One must fight for it all the time."

To prevent war, we must wage peace. It is a battle of information. Those already converted will listen to Generals and academic strategists. But this is not nearly enough. The dangers to our security and survival must be identified and explained to the man in the street. Mrs. Margaret Thatcher has already done this, but it requires much more repetition.

From bitter past experience, the political leaders of a Socialist government will never discharge this responsibilty for reasons of political expediency and because of their moral cowardice.

I will say again, it is power, and the will to exercise it, that impresses the Soviets. It is weakness that will encourage them to adventure. Defence is a *national priority*. We must rouse the people and our allies to recognize the dangers ahead. We must call on them to make the sacrifices of money and comfort that will be needed if we are to rearm fast enough. It will not be an easy course; and those who adopt it will be labelled as warmongers by their critics. It was so before the last war.

Surrender or Defeat if We Fail to Re-arm.

I do not underestimate the risks of a turnabout from the present policy of appeasing Soviet imperialist aims to one of resistance. The Soviet leaders are well aware that once the West has decided to resist their advances, our economic potential must restore us to a position of parity with and, if we wish it, superiority over the Warsaw Pact. We must, therefore, expect that the Kremlin imperialists will press for a showdown while they still enjoy military superiority.

But this is a risk we have to run. If we fail to rearm, or if we allow the oil of the Gulf or the minerals of Southern Africa to be lost to the West, *we shall face the choice between surrender and defeat*. But if we stand up *now* to Soviet Imperialism, late though it is, there is a good chance that the uncertainties of nuclear war and the strength we can still deploy in particular threatened areas will give the Soviet leaders pause and lead them to stop short of the brink of war.

In Conclusion – Individual Action Vital

The period 1982-85 which we shall enter less than two years from now, may prove to be the most crucial phase of history yet experienced by the Western World.

To the extent that Marxist rebellion and revolution is in our midst already, we have a measure of 'hell on earth'. However, few can have contemplated the inferno that the Soviets would loose upon a defeated West – or what is more to the point, upon those who attempted to resist their totalitarian rule.

It is no exaggeration to say that what is at stake is not only the whole future of the West, but civilization itself and the Christian West as we know it – whether indeed *your* children and grandchildren will live their lives as free men and women, or face the trauma of a new Dark Age.

If you can do nothing but pray – then pray *now!* But it is certainly true that all can influence *someone* to face the realities of the menacing storm rising from the East.

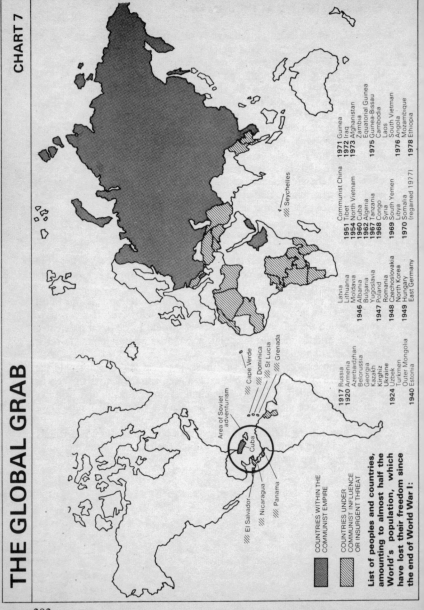

THE GLOBAL GRAB

CHART 7

Area of Soviet adventurism

Cape Verde
Dominica
St Lucia
Grenada

El Salvador
Nicaragua
Panama
Cuba

Seychelles

■ COUNTRIES WITHIN THE
COMMUNIST EMPIRE

▨ COUNTRIES UNDER
COMMUNIST INFLUENCE
OR INSURGENT THREAT

**List of peoples and countries,
amounting to almost half the
World's population, which
have lost their freedom since
the end of World War I:**

1917 Russia
1920 Armenia
       Azerbaidzhan
       Belorussia
       Georgia
       Kazakh
       Kirghiz
       Ukraine
1924 Uzbek
       Turkmen
       Outer Mongolia
1940 Estonia

       Latvia
       Lithuania
       Moldavia
1946 Albania
       Bulgaria
       Yugoslavia
1947 Poland
       Romania
1948 Czechoslovakia
       North Korea
1949 Hungary
       East Germany

       Communist China
1951 Tibet
1954 North Vietnam
1960 Cuba
1962 Algeria
1967 Tanzania
1968 Congo
       Syria
1969 South Yemen
       Libya
1970 Somalia
       (regained 1977)

1971 Guinea
1972 Iraq
1973 Afghanistan
       Zambia
       Equatorial Guinea
1975 Guinea-Bissau
       Cambodia
       Laos
       South Vietnam
1976 Angola
       Mozambique
1978 Ethiopia

South Africa

In the latter half of June 1980, I visited South Africa for the third time in two years and discussed the present situation in the country, and in Southern Africa as a whole, with prominent high-ranking experts whose job it is to "keep their finger on the pulse". What are my conclusions?

It behoves the Soviet Union, the Western World, the Third World, the United Nations, the Organization of African Unity, and indeed the whole world, to realize quite clearly that South Africa, with her great military strength, has no intention whatsoever of succumbing to conventional attack, guerrilla offensives from any country, or internal insurrection and urban terrorism. There can be absolutely no doubt that those States in Africa which provide launching pads for Communist trained armed guerrillas and terrorists will suffer terrible retribution from the swift retaliatory military might of South Africa's Armed Forces. On no account will South Africa commit suicide. Those who are intent on pushing South Africa to the brink must not be surprised if their extremist threat to the very existence of the South African society evokes the ultimate defence as made possible by its *nuclear* capability.

A recent visitor to South Africa was Professor Churba, the Washington strategist and adviser on security matters to Presidential candidate Mr. Ronald Reagan. He advocates that South Africa should develop its own nuclear weapons for dropping from sea-borne helicopters so that it can offer the West a credible domination of the Cape sea route. Professor Churba maintains that "Overt nuclear anti-submarine warfare (ASW) capability is a key to an alliance between South Africa and the United States".

After treating South Africa as a pariah for two decades, the U.S. now admits and accepts that it could not handle any serious military threat in the Persian Gulf region, nerve-centre of the West's oil supplies, without the full co-operation of South Africa. This is the conclusion of the Pentagon's latest 129-page study for the White House on Persian Gulf options. Although the analysts came to this conclusion reluctantly, because of political opposition within their ranks, they decided that the logic of the case was overwhelming – no crises in the Indian Ocean or Persian Gulf areas could be handled by the U.S. without using South African facilities. One important consideration was that the sea routes around the Cape would have to be protected for the West and denied to the Soviet Union, and the necessary anti-submarine warfare could not be mounted without using South African bases.

In South Africa, black nationalist terrorism has spread of late from remote border regions into urban areas. In late January, South Africans were shocked by a daring three-man guerrilla raid on a bank near Pretoria. The South African Police refused to negotiate. A shoot-out left all three dead, plus two of their unfortunate hostages. Minister of Police Louie le Grange warned that any such incidents in the future would be met with the same remorseless response.

Then came the acts of urban terrorism in the form of sabotage of the oil-from-coal plants at Sasol and Secunda.

Prime Minister Pieter Botha, meanwhile, is pushing ahead on his ideas for a new "Constellation of states" in Southern Africa – a hoped for answer to counter demands for radical change. Mr. Botha has outlined plans for constitutional reform to provide for increased representation from the country's Indian and Coloured (those of mixed race) minorities. A plan to provide urban-dwelling Blacks with increased self-government would follow. Mr. Botha has offered to meet in a grand conference with moderate Black leaders, to discuss South Africa's future.

Will a new grand design work? Mr. Botha faces plenty of criticism. Some conservative Afrikaner whites are wary of the proposed changes. And radical nationalist groups, fearing that peaceful changes just might be acceptable to the majority, have vowed to fight harder than ever to "bring down the entire house", and grab the power for themselves before it's too late. One outlawed organization has declared 1980 to be the "year of action".

Sanctions Would Harm All

Peace in Southern Africa as a whole, including Zimbabwe, is impossible without peace in the region's cornerstone nation – South Africa. Enemies of the Free World know this point well.

Pressure is mounting in the United Nations to impose trade sanctions, even a global trade boycott against the Pretoria government. The trigger to effect such drastic action could be a Namibia stalemate, or a step-up of terrorism within South Africa, with corresponding police crackdown.

In either case, emotional cries would fill the halls of the U.N. General Assembly calling for sanctions. Such a demand would play directly into the hands of the Soviets, who have been building a world-girdling offensive naval force with the avowed purpose of cutting the Free World off from its sources of raw materials. South Africa, with its treasure trove of minerals essential to Western industry, is one of Moscow's prime considerations.

Could such a blockade come about? Louis H. Gann and Peter Duignan, in their new book. *South Africa: War, Revolution or Peace?* examine this distinct likelihood especially in view of the fact that South Africa is not likely, because of its military strength, to succumb to either conventional attack or internal insurrection.

"A naval blockade of South Africa might be considered a less bloody way of forcing the country to its knees. Conceivably, the U.N. might... call upon the Soviet Union and its allies to blockade South African ports until South Africa agreed to dismantle its political system. The Soviet Union might even offer to work in collaboration with U.S. naval forces as part of an international campaign against "racism"...

"Such a policy... would, in fact, destabilize the whole of Southern Africa and deny to the West the resources of South Africa at a time when it supplies vital strategic mineral resources to the non-communist world".

The United States, now excessively dependent upon foreign sources of supply, would suffer serious damage in a cut off of vital minerals. Western Europe would be hurt even more so (which might cause Europe to think twice before approving such a plan).

But those who would suffer most of all, say authors Gann and Duignan, "would be backward, vulnerable states like Mozambique, Malawi, Zambia, Lesotho, Botswana and Swaziland that have economic ties with South Africa". And certainly, more advanced but still vulnerable Zimbabwe could be added to that list.

The Worst Handwringers

While I was in South Africa a great fillip was given to the morale of the four million white South Africans by a newspaper article written by a British journalist. People were literally chortling with glee at its pungent remarks urging South Africans to stop their constant apologies to the outside world and the reprinting, after embellishment from overseas, of their *own* destructive political propaganda – the worst form of hand-wringing imaginable.

All is Not Shooting and Violence

White South Africans are as sensitive to and upset over killings and casualties as anyone outside their country. What they object to is the different treatment of such tragic news-stories coming from abroad. I will exemplify this.

In June, a South African police patrol was accosted by a group of rock-throwing and knife-wielding school youngsters. The police eventually felt their lives threatened and used their firearms. Two youths, one 15 and one 20, were tragically killed. The story of "child murder" went round the world with various embellishments. President Carter's spokesman found himself impelled to address a press conference in order to "deplore the use of violence and the loss of life" – which had already been deeply regretted by the South African police, government and media. Shortly before this no fewer than 15 American Blacks had been killed in riots in Miami, several of them by the police. Conditions for Blacks in the U.S. were revealed as often so bad, that the much maligned nation of South Africa would find it hard, if not impossible – and undesirable – to match them. But no sanctimonious statements deploring the use of violence in Miami were heard from South Africa – only regret and sympathy for the loss of life and for those endeavouring to maintain the peace.

Another example of double standards can be applied to the unrest in India where the recent massacre in the north-east region resulted in 200,000 refugees and 1,000 people being butchered followed by a spate of ambushes, burnings, mob violence, shootings and stabbings. As I write this, almost every day new outbursts of savagery, arson, rioting and protest add to the spreading bush fire of trouble. There can be no doubt that if this explosive situation is mishandled the violence will become even bloodier. The blame for this convulsion can be laid at the feet of the Central Government for their neglect of the region – a festering sore of economic deprivation. In Assam three-fifths of families live below the poverty line. In some other states the position is even worse.

Deadly Publicity

By comparison with this state of affairs South Africa is a veritable Mecca. Yet it continues to receive deadly publicity from overseas. Attacks on South Africa have been at a level they have not had to endure since the Biko affair. Critics are demanding that they end *apartheid,* give Blacks economic parity, and advance them politically on a one-man, one-vote basis. It is not just the usual chorus of anti-

Appreciation to *The Daily News,* S.A.

apartheidists and leftist-liberals, but countries that have not customarily applied public pressure on South Africa are joining in.

Condemned

They stand condemned, and are being unjustly singled out for attack. They have no intention of giving in to overseas pressures any more than any other independent, sovereign country would. Much of the criticism and the condemnation, is ill-judged and based on a prejudiced evaluation of the situation, the nature of the problems they face and the efforts being made to resolve them. As the nation demonstrated when it is rallied around former Prime Minister Mr. John Vorster, in 1977, to resist American pressure for one-man, one-vote majority rule, there is no way in which foreign governments or foreign organizations can force South Africa to adopt any policy which is anathema to it. That does not mean that they can maintain the status quo; that they can retreat into a *laager* and fight it out to preserve a system which is no longer tenable from their own standpoint, not that of overseas opinion.

Most thinking South Africans recognize that they have to find solutions themselves to their own problems, solutions that may not follow the Westminster system of government but are peculiarly their own. It is here, through their own relationships, through their own assessments, through their own strivings, that their destiny will be decided.

Unfortunately, the bright hopes that were engendered by Prime Minister Mr. P. W. Botha's adjust-or-die philosophy, his conciliatory visits to Black territories and areas, and his general emphasis on a new deal acceptable to everyone, have been dimmed somewhat. Perhaps it is because of the blocking effect of the conservative backlash in his own party. Or perhaps it is again the case of a Prime Minister putting party unity before the country's need for bold, imaginative new directions.

Whatever the reason, there has been a slowdown in the movement for change though not a halt to it. This is being exploited by the liberal Press there which has cast doubts on Mr. Botha's intentions. Overseas newspapers, as well as governments, are also reflecting similar misgivings. The fact that Mr. Botha is no longer receiving a good Press abroad is affecting the more confident approach to the country shown by overseas investors and opinion-makers.

Dramatic Progress Now Required

This is to their defamed country's detriment. It is a pity Mr. Botha is in danger of losing the favourable image he created initially. The expectations which he aroused cannot now be jettisoned without causing disillusionment and agitation among people of colour. Also, the thrust of his policies have to gather momentum once more if he is to be regarded as the man who will bring South Africa into a new age. One can but hope that Mr. Botha will, therefore, resume his initiative, and build on the vast goodwill which his previous approach demonstrated.

It was in June 1979, that the President of the Chamber of Mines came out in support of the constellation of States, as a "sensible recognition of the interdependence of the peoples of this region". The Government should get on with the project, show dramatic progress and capitalize on the recent meeting of 250 top business leaders.

Although the Prime Minister's 12 point total strategy is regarded as the basis for the new deal, nobody has yet given a broad picture of the country as it will emerge under this plan. It is time the Government did so.

There is the President's Council, which has still to be formed, but which will be a starting point for new constitutional development. It has to be sold as a concept to significant Coloured and Indian leaders, and the Government also has to convince Black moderates that the Council of Blacks is not a second-class body by comparison.

What is required is that Mr. Botha emerges from the present lull with the same vigour and determination which he showed when he launched the country on a road of change. People believe he can do it. But they also believe that he must be seen, with a fair measure of urgency, to be doing it.

It is in the interests of the Western World that South Africa should remain stable. But the West indulges in exaggerated fault-finding and gives support to exiled 'freedom' movements, while the U.N. – that hotbed of Russian puppets – demands various embargoes, sanctions and hostile actions against South Africa.

I foresee that if the West continues to harass South Africa, allows the desire to appease the Marxists to colour their attitude to the Namibian problem, and are quite prepared to let Zimbabwe go the same way as the currently tyrannized and starving Zambia, Tanzania, Angola and Mozambique – and many more further to the north on the African continent – there will be little to prevent escalation into a full scale world conflict, nuclear, conventional, or both. And that could mean final disaster for Western civilization.

The situation in 1938 was not dissimilar, with Germany the threatening power in place of Russia. There was one man, who clearly saw where blind appeasement would lead – Winston Churchill, at that time a highly unpopular and lonely Cassandra of Britain.

Sir Winston Churchill wrote in his history of the Second World War, which conflict he dubbed the unnecessary war, the following comment on the attitude of the Western allies, including the United Kingdom:

"Still, if you will not fight for the right when you can easily win without bloodshed; if you will not fight when your victory will be sure and not too costly; you may come to the moment when you will have to fight with all the odds against you and only a precarious chance of survival. There may even be a worse case. You may have to fight when there is no hope of victory, because it is better to perish than live as slaves".

The Taiwan Relationship

It is not generally known how close the relationship is between Taiwan and South Africa. The Taiwanese Premier Sun Yun-Suang paid an official visit to South Africa in April this year, the occasion concluding with the signing of scientific and technological agreements between the two countries. The two countries established full diplomatic relations on 26th April, 1976, and in the last few years high-ranking government officials of the two countries have exchanged visits. Trade between them grew at an average rate of 37·5% a year between 1973 and 1978, while in 1979 Taiwan's exports to South Africa were worth (U.S.) $77·3 million, and imports $214·4 million.

Conferences are held annually to discuss co-operation in agriculture, industry, trade, science and technology. The first was held in Taipei in March 1977, the second in South Africa in August 1978. The third conference, elevated to ministerial level, was held in South Africa in November 1979 and achieved substantial results.

In January 1979, the Board of Foreign Trade of Taiwan and the South African Maize Board concluded a maize trade agreement under which South Africa will supply 600,000 tons of maize a year. In October 1979, a fisheries agreement was concluded providing the Republic of China with the right to engage in tuna fishing in the maritime economic zone off South Africa.

On 29th May, 1979, the two countries held a conference on science and technology at which they agreed to undertake co-operative projects on a selective and small-scale basis in agriculture, *defence* technology, *atomic* energy, medical science, industrial research and development, engineering techniques, energy research and development and unicellular protein water treatment.

The two countries have also concluded a bilateral air transport agreement to open a service between Taiwan and Johannesburg. Because of the booming trade and tourism between the two countries, the Taiwan and South African governments will be concluding an agreement exempting the two countries from income tax on earnings derived from air transport.

South West Africa (Namibia)

During most of June the South African Defence Forces launched a large, protracted and sustained cross-border operation – "Operation Smokeshell' – against the South West African People's Organization (SWAPO) guerrilla/terrorist concentrations in Angola. The operation was in two phases, during which about 360 SWAPO fighters had been killed. At least 250 tons of military equipment, mostly of Russian make, was captured and another 50 tons destroyed. The equipment ranged from Soviet armoured personnel carriers and SAM-7 heat-seeking missiles to AK-47 automatic rifles.

The operation was in response to an offensive campaign mounted by SWAPO earlier this year, aimed against civilian targets in Namibia. On 10th June the South African Army made a three-pronged attack on SWAPO bases, killing about 200 alleged terrorists with a loss of 16 of its own men.

In the second phase of "Smokeshell", during which South Africans were engaged in mopping-up operations across the border, 162 SWAPO guerrillas died for the loss of one South African. SWAPO's military infrastructure and 40 storage depots were destroyed. The command structure of SWAPO's military wing was dealt such a severe operational and logistical blow that the organization will take months to recover and reorganize. Two years ago there were 8,000 SWAPO guerrillas fighting, but they have suffered such heavy losses this year that they will be unable to make them up through new recruitment – certainly for some time.

It was towards the middle of the year that the South African Defence Force had discovered a major SWAPO build-up in Angola. Accordingly, it was decided to break and pre-empt SWAPO's campaign. The destruction of the main base from which SWAPO mounted its terror campaign across the border in Namibia signals South Africa's determination not to permit a repetition of the Rhodesian debacle in South West Africa. In Rhodesia the Marxist forces were able to achieve through terror a hold on the rural population that proved to be an essential prelude to political victory. In Namibia the Defence Force is

300

doing more than merely "hold the ring" to win time for a political solution – it has thrown SWAPO on the defensive.

The Security Council met and passed a resolution ordering South Africa to pull its troops out of Angola – or "face more effective measures". There was no mention of SWAPO aggression against South West Africa; no mention of the justifiable reasons for their troops crossing the border to put SWAPO bases out of action. They were, in the eyes of the U.N., guilty of aggression, and so had to be threatened, warned and condemned.

It was a hypocritical business, since the U.N. wears blinkers in the case of SWAPO and only takes note of the border war when South Africa is forced to act. All their complaints of double standards and double dealing, all their protestations that the allegations against them were ludicrous, fell on deaf ears. The Director-General for Foreign Affairs and Information, Dr. Brand Fourie, said the Security Council's resolution was a foregone conclusion because "facts do not count with the U.N. South Africa is condemned, but nothing is said of the people who cause all the trouble and nuisance, in other words – SWAPO".

The reason is obvious. The U.N. General Assembly has repeatedly claimed that SWAPO is the sole representative of the people of South West Africa. Therefore, in terms of the policy adopted in matters such as this, SWAPO is regarded as being within its rights to try to "liberate" the people of the territory (even if they don't want SWAPO to "free" them). South Africa has seen this kind of thing in Angola, in Mozambique, in what was Rhodesia, in Uganda and in other African countries. As long as you kill and maim men, women and children in the name of "liberation" you are heroic and acceptable to the world organization. But heaven forbid that you try to maintain law and order against forces seeking to achieve power through the barrel of a gun. Then you are condemned and threatened by the U.N.

SWAPO has had a bad mauling. There is now a leadership crisis in the organization; its losses exceed the number of recruits, and its image in countries that support it has been affected by its military ineffectiveness. Nevertheless, the border war will continue, and pressures for sanctions against South Africa will grow more insistent in ratio to South Africa's military successes, or as the demands for an early ceasefire and implementation of the U.N. plan fail to achieve an unequivocal response. South Africa will, it is obvious, continue to give the South West African people their military protection while they work out their destiny. But whether that destiny will be achieved on the basis of an internal, go-it-alone settlement or a U.N. supervised one remains to be seen.

One way to counteract Angola, SWAPO and U.N. propaganda, to refute the accusations of naked aggression and to inform the public in South Africa, and the Free World, of the truth, would be to allow

"Well, Abdul, these South African hot pursuit operations are getting serious"

Appreciation to *Pretoria News*, S.A.

reputable military correspondents – there must be some impartial, unbrainwashed ones still left – into the operational area at an earlier stage, accompanied by Army public relations officers. This can be done in such a way as to ensure that the success of an operation would not be prejudiced, nor the element of surprise lost.

However, one can appreciate that the bitter lessons of the Americans in Vietnam have not been lost on the South African military hierarchy. As I said in my book *The Bear at the Back Door,* there can be little doubt that newspaper stories and television coverage of the Vietnam war was largely responsible for sapping the moral fibre of the American people to continue the struggle. War is an unpleasant business, and when it is brought into the living room in colour, the ultimate effect on public opinion in an open society is predictable. Blood shows up distinctly and disturbingly on colour television, not that I believe that white public opinion in South Africa would be adversely affected, because in that country "men are men" and made of sterner stuff.

Winning a Low-Intensity Conflict

It was during the time of my visit to South Africa that Mr. Martin

Spring, the publisher of a highly reputable Newsletter, had recently been privileged to visit the Namibian operational area to assess the situation for himself. His findings correspond closely with what I wrote and forecast in my last book. His up-to-date findings are so revealing and valuable that they should reach as wide an audience as possible. It is for this reason that I now include his report in the Epilogue to my book:

"In many ways the clearest example of the progress achieved is the Eastern Caprivi region, a territory the size of Northern Ireland and almost entirely surrounded by potentially hostile countries (see map below).

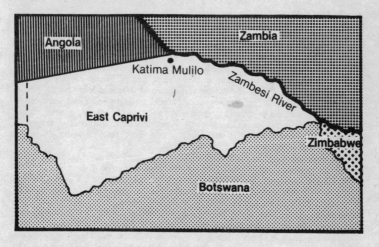

The first terrorist incident in Eastern Caprivi occurred in 1965. After that SWAPO steadily mounted a revolutionary offensive with increasing success. By the mid-1970s the local people were sufficiently hostile to the South African forces and willing to believe SWAPO propaganda and promises of free university education in other countries that more than 500 Caprivians a year were crossing the Zambesi into Zambia (out of a total population of only 25,000 at that time) to join SWAPO. In 1978 the SWAPO forces were sufficiently confident to launch direct attacks against South African bases, killing 10 soldiers and wounding 20 in one hit by artillery rocket.

Today East Caprivi is almost completely peaceful, with only 2 landmine incidents reported so far this year. The population is so disillusioned with SWAPO and impervious to its propaganda that in recent months there has not been a single confirmed case of anyone crossing the border to join SWAPO (there were only 5 confirmed departures the whole of last year). The territory has become a bastion of Mr. Dirk Mudge's pro-SA DTA party, SWAPO's rival for power in the future independent Namibia. The Defence Force is so popular that when it last appealed for recruits, more than 1,000 Caprivians volunteered.

How was this remarkable transformation achieved?

Firstly, by "active defence". When SWAPO units attacked South African bases in 1978, the South African Defence Force struck back hard across the borders in Zambia and Angola, destroying all their bases and killing hundreds of terrorists. To prove to Caprivians who had the upper hand in the military conflict, many bodies of the SWAPO dead were brought back for display to the population. Thanks to excellent intelligence, South Africa has been able to prevent any rebuilding of the terrorist infrastructure. "We will not allow the enemy to get to within striking distance again," said a senior briefing officer. "This will be achieved, if necessary, by selected pre-emptive strikes".

Secondly, by involving Caprivians in their own defence. In 1977 a Caprivian battalion of the South Africa Defence Force was formed, which is now fully operative as a trained fighting unit blooded in combat. As a special gesture to the Caprivians (whose first language is Lozi, shared with the Barotse of neighbouring Zambia, and whose second language is English), it is the only unilingual, English-speaking unit in the Defence Force. There is no racial discrimination of any kind in this unit. White officers and NCOs and Black NCOs share a single "leader group" mess. Pay scales are identical for both races, with trained infantrymen receiving $390 a month in cash, plus usual benefits such as free accommodation and medical care. Camps are of a high standard, with attractive timber dwellings for soldiers' families surrounded by lawns and bougainvillaea. A permanent township is being planned for the families with 450 homes as well as clinics and recreational facilities.

A third important factor has been the civic action campaign. ("Hearts and Minds"). The Defence Force has involved itself deeply in the development and modernization of East Caprivi. National servicemen have offered their civilian skills as teachers, agriculturalists, technicians, doctors, vets, foresters and game wardens. At the request of the local government, servicemen have acted as advisers, instructors and supervisors. The first-ever matric (university entrance level exam) class taught by national servicemen achieved an 86% success rate. Production of maize, the staple cereal, has been raised tenfold in 5 years.

Fourthly, the Defence Force is alert to the requirements of psychological warfare, motivated by Mao's dictum that guerrilla offensives must fail if the sympathy, co-operation and assistance of the civilian population cannot be gained. There is constant contact with the ordinary people so that grievances can be reported and acted on at an early stage. SWAPO has been completely discredited because it is widely realized that its promises turned out to be baseless and its propaganda false. It is the local government and the Defence Force together which are "delivering the goods".

To what extent is South Africa's achievement in East Caprivi relevant to what is happening elsewhere in the low-intensity conflict along Namibia's 1,800 km northern border? One must first take a look at the broader picture.

Until about March 1979, the military were considerably restricted in their activities by political circumstances. For example, it was difficult to set up road blocks to search civilians for arms and explosives at a time when elections were being held and U.N. teams were visiting the territory, as this would have been portrayed as "intimidation". Since then the military have had more freedom of movement and initiative, and this has changed the pattern of the military situation. For example, terrorist losses have increased from about 20 a month to about 80 (apart from the 300 plus destroyed in the most recent raid into Angola).

Nearly all of the activity is in a small but relatively densely populated area of Owambo bordering Angola. Here the number of landmine incidents is increasing and there are about half-a-dozen acts of sabotage each month. But reported incidents of intimidation have declined sharply from 27 in March 1979, to four in May 1980.

Military strategy appears to be based on these principles:

* Destruction of SWAPO terrorists at their bases inside Angola, and prevention of the building of a forward infrastructure for assaults into Namibia;
* Limiting infiltration of raiders across the border through good intelligence and aggressive follow-up of all reported contacts;
* Protection of leading personalities in Owambo, whose assassination has been

one of SWAPO's principle objectives, to rob the population of its natural leaders and frighten it into co-operation;

* Proper identification and control of movement by people within the country.

There are important differences in the war situation among the various sectors. While Owambo is active, Kavango and West Caprivi in the central sector are quiet, partly because UNITA forces in control of large areas of neighbouring Angola are hostile to SWAPO, which is supported by Angola's ruling MPLA.

The lesson of East Caprivi seems to be that Marxist revolution *CAN* be defeated on the battlefield in Southern Africa. But a comprehensive total strategy is required. Essential elements would seem to include deprivation of sanctuaries from which the aggressor can operate, the minimum of political restraints on the military's freedom of action, placing of civil authority in the hands of local Black leaders (not White dominated committees in the distant, liberal cities not exposed to the harsh realities of terror), extensive involvement of troops in providing practical development assistance, and a political dispensation which offers prospects of a brighter future for all races".

The External Build-up Against South Africa

First, there are in Africa about 45,000 Cubans, 2,700 East Germans, 2,000 Russians and between 2,000 and 3,000 Eastern Bloc military personnel, consisting of Bulgarians, Rumanians, Czechs and others. These are located in Angola, Zambia, Tanzania and Mozambique. In addition, Machel of Mozambique is stiffened by large numbers of Tanzanians.

Second, there are the Russian trained and equipped guerrillas and terrorists in Namibia and South Africa's neighbouring states of Botswana, Zimbabwe and Mozambique. Then there are the several thousand ZIPRA forces of Nkomo still in Zambia poised ready to be deployed. I received an eye-witness account of a large number of plane-loads of the very latest Russian equipment landing at Lusaka, Zambia, during June. Obviously a SWAPO political victory in Namibia would increase the pressure on South Africa. Meanwhile, Mugabe and Machel will be unable to resist guerrilla activity from their soil indefinitely. Indeed, Russia will ensure that sooner than later they will be sucked into "the last unfinished business of African independence."

With its modern armaments and a total mobilizable strength, including paramilitary forces, of 404,500, 97% of them white, there is absolutely no doubt that South Africa's military might can crush any conceivable form of external aggression from its neighbours.

Internal Insurgency

General Malan, former Chief of the S.A. Defence Force, now Minister of Defence, takes into account the lessons of Vietnam, Rhodesia and the French performance in Algeria, but also the lessons of political violence in every conflict-ridden society, such as the United States, Italy, Spain, Northern Ireland, Cyprus, the Malayan Emergency and Borneo, the Mau Mau in Kenya and so forth. Internal insurgency in South Africa on a similar scale is bound to come and General Malan realizes only too well that it will be a very different enemy to SWAPO in Namibia.

Well-financed ANC guerrilla units backed by the moral authority of the United Nations and the Organization for African Unity will establish bases and take root amid the depression and squalor of the resettlement areas of the homelands – as they have already done in Botswana and Swaziland. The rate of infiltration of arms will increase; farms, white settlements, key points, police stations and vital installations will have to be protected and defended against sabotage and attack, including bombings, fire-bombings, rockets and missiles, etc. Ways and means must be found of combating this threat which will economize in manpower and obviate the necessity for wider white mobilization, thus preventing a sapping of the economy and discouraging white emigration, but also ensuring that General Malan's "sliding scale" will not slip steadily towards a total war footing.

According to a recent survey in *The Economist,* London, entitled "The Great Evasion", General Malan's view is that South Africa has to be able to "shift back and forth along a sliding scale between a war and a peace economy". Survival depends not just on military strength but on "the continued advancement of the well-being of all South Africans." Echoing the "hearts-and-minds" theories of the British Army he has stressed in newspaper interviews the need to win the "trust and faith" of the blacks. According to *The Economist* article, "by implication he is telling the government it is for politicians, not soldiers, to halt the growth of black alienation. In other words, it is not within the power of the military to "keep South Africa white".

The Economist maintains that:

"These arguments, much discussed between General Malan and Mr. Botha during the latter's term as Minister of Defence, are now central to Mr. Botha's as yet abortive reformist ambitions. He had deliberately retained the defence portfolio, disbanded the BOSS empire of his old *verkrampte* enemy, General van den Bergh, and brought the new security machine (DONS) under the wing of the military. A revamped State Security Council has been brought centre-stage under the cabinet with a "security planning budget" increased tenfold this year from R45,000 to R490,000 (£22,500 to £245,000). General Malan himself has become a major force within the government, involving himself directly in those policies directed at the black population. He has been particularly active over group areas and homeland relations – often to the intense annoyance of the officials and even ministers chiefly concerned.

One has only to look at a map of homeland South Africa to see why. The proliferation throughout "white" South Africa of black-controlled refuges to add to the existing scatter of Botswana, Lesotho, Swaziland and the Transkei would present a near-impossible policing problem, however compliant the black homeland defence forces might be. The new "state" of Bophuthatswana includes territory just half an hour's drive from the centre of Pretoria. And the contiguous Transkei, Ciskei, Kwazula territories on the eastern seaboard, packed with dispossessed black South Africans, are not ideal neighbours for a nervous white government – least of all when the Mantanzima and Sebe régimes in the first two are showing every sign of totalitarian instability."

Botswana – Swaziland

It is obvious that the death of Sir Seretse Khama, the former President of Botswana, and the impending death – at the time of my writing – of the ailing octogenarian King Sobhuza II of Swaziland, will result in pressures being built-up against South Africa.

While Botswana has had no formal diplomatic relations with Pretoria, it has through self-interest been obliged to maintain extensive trade and economic links with South Africa. Because of its vulnerability – sandwiched as it is between the black states of Zimbabwe, Zambia and Angola, on the one side, and South Africa and South West Africa (Namibia) on the other – Botswana has consistently refused to allow South African resistance movements to set up bases on its territory.

Now there are bound to be growing demands for more radical government to provide bases for guerrillas, saboteurs and terrorists to infiltrate South Africa. Dr. Kenneth Koma, leader of the minority opposition Botswana National Front (BNF), espouses Marxist Policies and the party has a considerable following among Botswana youth. This expanding radical opposition will almost certainly call for a severance of all ties with South Africa.

The situation could be much more volatile in Swaziland where there are signs of increasing militancy among the youth of the country. Whoever succeeds King Sobhuza will face a major problem of relations with South Africa, although Swaziland is less dependent than Botswana, having a border with Mozambique and access to the port of Maputo.

Zimbabwe – Rhodesia

Zimbabwe's avowed Marxist Prime Minister, Robert Mugabe – recently elected by the South African Society of Journalists as "Newsmaker of the Year" for his "Statesmanship in helping to bring peace to Southern Africa" – is beginning to show his true colours. Under OAU pressure he has now pledged "political and diplomatic" support for action against South Africa; the preliminary, one presumes, to the granting of terrorist bases to the ANC and PAC.

Mr. Mugabe, no doubt, has certain debts to pay – most notably to Moscow, his chief weapons supplier during the seven-year war against Rhodesia. Nevertheless, faced with a decimated economy, Mr. Mugabe today has certain fundamental choices before him.

He can co-operate with South Africa, best positioned of any nation on earth to assist him and his people on their long road to recovery. Or he can join Zambia, Mozambique, Tanzania and Angola on what is already a proven march to regimented socialist suicide: in which case his new nation's birth pangs will turn almost immediately to death rattles.

An exaggeration? Not if you look at the history of Black Africa, at the long succession of nations which have proved there is only one thing wrong with independence: *you can't eat it.*

Two Crises

Things aren't working out well in Zimbabwe. Reconciliation and hope are being overtaken by recrimination and doubt. Mr. Mugabe, the once-confident one, is showing signs of insecurity, with a plotter behind every thorn tree. South Africa, it seems, is one of the chief villains, being accused of training dissident groups and of allowing, or encouraging, former Rhodesians, based in South Africa, to carry out an abortive plot to disrupt the country's independence celebrations with sophisticated explosives and weapons.

An arms cache, including Russian-made Strela heat-seeking surface-to-air missiles and several explosive devices, was said to have been found in a truck just outside Salisbury. (How South Africa, or Rhodesians based in South Africa, could obtain Russian missiles is not explained). The cache is alleged to have been taken into Zimbabwe by elements who used to live in Rhodesia and were then based in South Africa. The plotters, according to Mr. Mugabe, intended to assassinate the country's new leaders and foreign dignitaries.

308

South Africa's Director-General for Foreign Affairs and Information, Dr. Brand Fourie, has dismissed the allegations as "ridiculous", saying "We have one motto – never to get involved in nonsense." Unless the Zimbabwean Government can produce proof of its allegations they can only be dismissed as contemptuously as Dr. Fourie has done.

Mr. Mugabe's would not be the first African Government to try to divert attention from its many pressing problems by dreaming up plots to overthrow it. Internally the chief Black political antagonists are beginning to look at each other with growing suspicion. The Rev. Ndabaningi Sithole, leader of ZANU, has accused Mr. Mugabe's Government of organizing the recent attempt on his life and of trying to eliminate members of rival political parties. Mr. Sithole has also accused Mr. Mugabe's ruling ZANU (PF) party of being determined to have a one-party State "By hook or by crook."

It would be a "totalitarian State in which the existence of other parties is not to be tolerated and in which the power of the ruling party is to be absolute and placed beyond public control and criticism." He also accused the government and ruling party of keeping the whole country "cowed by fear and intimidation" to pave the way for their one-party State. Taking into account the history of Black African "liberation", this would not suprise one. Most of the former colonies fell into the hands of despots who introduced dictatorships or one-party governments that were far worse, in every respect, than the colonial administrations they replaced.

Mr. Mugabe and his former Patriotic Front partner, Mr. Joshua Nkomo, are also beginning to glower at each other, Mr. Mugabe accusing Mr. Nkomo's ZIPRA men of openly trying to flout his Government's rule. He has told Parliament that this is taking place on instructions from their "local leadership", but that there was no evidence to link it with the hierarchy of Mr. Nkomo's party. Mr. Nkomo, however, has denounced the remarks as a "slap in the face," which "we can't accept." This is the first open confrontation between the two and will seriously strain Mr. Mugabe's government of national unity. Whatever the truth of the matter, Zimbabwean army and police units are hunting down dissidents, mainly ZIPRA men, in the Midlands, and according to Mr. Sithole, there is a "lot of lawlessness" in the eastern districts as well.

Clearly, Zimbabwe is far from peaceful – or being at peace with itself.

Crisis of Confidence

The radio and television are now being used for blatant Marxist and anti-South African propaganda; threats are being made to rewrite the country's history; the tempo of Africanization in the civil service is being increased; ties with South African sport are in the process of being broken; and diplomatic links between the two countries will be severed one of these days.

Besides the White crisis of confidence, Mr. Mugabe has a crisis of expectation among Blacks. But the more he leans over to satisfy Black expectations, the more he will lose the confidence of the Whites. What will happen?

A great number of Whites will simply pack-up and leave, as I show later on. Mr. Mugabe will increasingly seek scapegoats for his problems, both inside and outside Zimbabwe; his troubles with Mr. Nkomo will accentuate, and he will attempt to curb or eliminate opposition to himself and his party. If he succeeds, he will turn Zimbabwe into the Marxist State he always planned to make it. If he does not, there may well be a civil war.

One thing of which we can be certain: The honeymoon between Mr. Mugabe, the Whites and moderate Blacks and even his former PF partners is slowly coming to an end.

Rapidly Deteriorating Agricultural Sector

Mr. Robert Mugabe's once-high hopes of massive American handouts for his reconstruction programme appear to be falling on singularly stony ground. Reportedly under heavy pressure from ultra-liberal, rabidly anti-South African Congressman Steve Solarz, the U.S. House of Representatives is preparing to grant $25-million to Zimbabwe's Marxist government over the new fiscal year, starting 1st October, 1980. Even that amount, according to Salisbury reports, has some fairly tight strings attached to it.

Zimbabwe is the victim of escalating conservative anger about the Carter Administration's overly generous support of Communist governments. This, following $75 million dished out under State Department urging to the new Marxist Sandanista régime in Nicaragua in May. Be that as it may, America's $25 million is not going to go very far in resurrecting Mr. Mugabe's near-ruinous economy, particularly the rapidly deteriorating agricultural sector. Indeed, for a war-torn economy, a paltry $25 million (Mr. Mugabe had earlier said he expected to receive $1,000 million from Washington over the next three years) is perhaps worse than nothing at all.

How will such a sum be spent? Salisbury cynics suggest that, judging by present trends, "it will be just enough to pay for new fleets of Mercedes-Benz limousines for Ministers, for new luxury aircraft and first-class air tickets to the U.N., O.A.U. and various assorted "summits". Or, perhaps, to wipe out Joshua Nkomo's increasingly active dissident forces in the Zambesi Valley."

310

What Zimbabwe needs above all, of course, is tens of millions poured into its ravaged agriculture, particularly ranching. According to reliable information during the last weeks of the Muzorewa government, the national herd at that point had been almost completely decimated. It was estimated that during the seven-year terrorist war a total of 4·2 million cattle, many of them pedigree breeding stock, had been wiped out.

Nor is that disaster yet at an end. Cattle rustling is still at such a peak that the Mugabe Government is now drafting in troops to protect the herds in areas where marauders are particularly prevalent.

White Flight

Next, because the successive Smith-Muzorewa governments had to divert ever-increasing amounts of money into the war effort, dam building and many much-needed irrigation projects went by the board. Such irrigation schemes are essential if Zimbabwe agriculture is to revive – and, again, it will call for a huge investment over a long period.

But finally, Zimbabwe's biggest and most immediate problem is not cash. It is the rapidly escalating White flight. No official estimates on this are available. But, from eminently reliable sources in Salisbury, it appears that 75,000 Whites are now preparing to *"defect to the West"* – to use the current Salisbury phrase – before the end of this year. That is double the April estimate, while the exodus in May reached the figure of 1,500. When Mugabe first came to power, his publicly declared policy of moderation and reconciliation soothed many Whites, persuaded them that it was worth staying, to give it a try.

That attitude is again under radical change. Inflammatory political revolutionary broadcasts by the ZBC have not helped the position. Nor has the soaring crime rate. Nor the progressive interference by "comrades" in industry and commerce. Few Whites really want to leave their homeland. They go very reluctantly. But they are going because they feel they are being forced out by a government which has failed to devise conditions which will ensure their continued stay in the country.

It appears that Zimbabwe's White population, which at its peak stood at around 280,000, has now dipped below the 200,000 mark. With 75,000 leaving by the end of this year, plus an estimated 50,000 in the first half of next year, the White population will be reduced to 80,000. Among those departing are many White farmers; 6,000 strong in 1975, now nearing the 4,000 mark.

Where are they going? The Australians are grabbing as many skilled people as they can. So is the Argentine. Others are going to Chile, Brazil, New Zealand and, of course many are returning to Britain. South Africa? Contrary to what both Britain and the U.S. believe, *the bulk* of Zimbabwe-Rhodesian Whites want to go there. Few would

311

question that these are among the most desirable immigrants the Republic could benefit from.

Many are of South African extraction, or have intimate association with that country. They share the same culture, the same African background. They are people of guts, stubborn determination, skilled, intelligent – as they proved up to the hilt when this tiny band of Whites succeeded in keeping the whole Rhodesian economy afloat under 15 years of vicious U.N., British-inspired sanctions.

They are of the same stubborn stock Boer and Brit, that helped build that country. Yet, curiously, many report that they are having "extreme problems" in gaining work and residence permits enabling them to settle in South Africa. With South Africa's current desperate shortage of skills, few will have any long term trouble in finding employment, but according to reliable reports, it takes them anything from six weeks to eight months to get the necessary stamps enabling them to join the South African community.

The Mugabe government cannot afford the exodus of Whites on this scale. Even if he received one billion dollars in U.S. aid, it would not compensate for the loss of those essential skills, of the farmers and industrialists who have helped hold his country together.

Vote of Confidence in South Africa

But if they are determined to go, can *South Africa* afford to lose them? Are these not ideal immigrants for a nation under pressure? Most important of all, does their wish to go there to settle in the Republic not represent the greatest possible vote of confidence in that nation's continued existence?

Free and Fair Elections?

The following information was given to me by extremely reliable sources.

Intimidation in the countryside was rampant. There was the instance of six girls having burning sticks thrust into their vaginas as a warning to the "assembled multitude" that this was what would happen to those who did not vote for Mugabe. While approaching polling booths Mugabe's agents – out of sight of the supervising teams, security forces and police – gave the cock crow and the symbolic sign of cutting the throat.

Many voted two or three times at different polling booths – transport being laid on to enable them to do so. Voters came in from the neighbouring states of Zambia, Botswana and Mozambique and then returned to their countries of residence.

Ballot boxes were opened at Salisbury instead of at the nearest major town. During the journey, there was time for the ballot boxes to be opened. Perfidious Albion was not above suspicion and stinks in the nostrils of those who allege that these incidents took place. They were adamant that they have cast iron proof of their veracity. All I can do is to repeat these accusations in the sure knowledge that in the end the truth will come to light.

Other allegations are that the Central Intelligence Organization (CIO) was long ago penetrated by Britain's MI5. I was told that during the war the National Resistance Movement of Mozambique had a broadcasting station in Rhodesia and their guerrillas received logistic support from Rhodesia in their struggle against Comrade Machel. Some time after the Election that brought Mugabe to power, the CIO are alleged to have passed on to Machel the locations of all the camps and bases of the National Resistance Movement with the result that they were attacked and wiped out.

Speaking in a exclusive television interview for BBC *Panorama* on 11th August, 1980, Lieutenant-General Peter Walls, Zimbabwe's former Supreme Military Commander, claimed that Prime Minister Mrs. Margaret Thatcher, ignored his plea to declare the pre-independence elections null and void. "I won't forgive her for that", he said. "I would like at least to have had the courtesy of a reply".

General Walls said that Mr. Mugabe's victory had been the result of intimidation – a practice common among African leaders, through their followers. He also spoke of how close he came to leading a white *coup* against Mr. Mugabe and the "distinct possibility" of civil war. As a direct result of the *Panorama* interview, Premier Mugabe said while on an American visit in late August, that General Walls "cannot be one of us, and we must assist him to leave the country".

To What End?

On 25th August, 1980, Zimbabwe became the *153rd* member of the United Nations. Just nine days later, on 3rd September, this latest member of the world organization severed diplomatic ties with South Africa, despite the almost total dependence of Zimbabwe on South African transport routes and the close economic ties between the two countries.

With the foundation of White leadership so recently removed, where now, in the breakdown of co-ordination in this vital strategic area, is the glory of the 'peace' and – thinking only a year or two ahead – where lies the future defence of the West in the southern hemisphere?

Zambia

After 16 years in power, time seems to be running out for one of the darlings of Western liberals; Zambia's Kenneth Kaunda. Faced with an economy which is a total disaster area (the national debt now stands at more than R2,000 million – £1,000 million), senior army officers are today openly stating that it is time for Kaunda to go.

Although he himself vigorously denies this, there are well-founded reports that there was an attempted *coup* and attempts to assassinate Kaunda earlier this year, resulting in a number of officers being detained. The rumbles are everywhere, as demonstrated by Mr. Elias Chipimo, former Zambian High Commissioner in London and until very recently chairman of the local board of the Standard and Chartered Bank. Speaking in Lusaka, Mr. Chipimo pointedly suggested that the message of the recent Liberian *coup* was that one-party States were perhaps not a good idea "for it so often means that the Head of State can only be removed at gunpoint".

Kaunda immediately branded Chipimo "an enemy of the State". So great were the resulting dictatorial tantrums that the bank's head office hurriedly disassociated itself from Mr. Chipimo and his remarks. He resigned 48 hours later. That did not quell the storm. Zambia's economic and educated élite are totally disillusioned with Kaunda's ideas of "humanistic socialism", plus his wholesale nationalization of all the main industries and their consequent abysmal performance.

Even the London *Observer,* long one of Kaunda's most loyal admirers, has turned against him. "For Kaunda . . . . . the removal of the Rhodesian external threat has meant that, for the first time since his country won independence in 1964, the ineptitude of his régime is coming under public criticism".

Ironically, Kaunda himself commissioned the report which could destroy him. This comes from the world-famous French agronomist Professor Rene Dumont. His report presents a stunning indictment of incredible, crippling incompetence and all the excuses are ripped away. The monstrous waste of millions upon millions of Western gift dollars is brutally exposed. Once Kaunda realized the politically explosive nature

314

of the Dumont Report, he immediately did his best to suppress it. But, thanks to various Ministerial leaks, its contents are probably the chief topic of conversation in Lusaka today.

Dumont, now retired, knows Zambia well. In 1977 he spent three weeks touring the country's rural areas. In preparing his report, he warned that he was going to be "very blunt". His first recommendation was that the Kaunda régime "should stop practising *apartheid* in Zambia and treat the peasant of this country as an equal". He warned that widespread poverty in rural areas was getting worse all the time, stating, "there will be serious famine if corrective measures are not taken soon".

Spectre of Starvation In a Most Fertile Land

That report was ignored. The latest is even more blunt. At the seat of Zambia's problems, he says, are the disastrous agricultural policies "which have left one of Africa's most fertile countries starving to death; Zambian agriculture has been totally ruined". He then details the appalling plight of the average Zambian, contending that "a rich man's pigs have a better diet than the average citizen".

The country is importing maize by the trainload: a total of R55 million (£27·5 million) worth from South Africa alone in the current season. For many of the 5·5 million population the trains are arriving too late. The report estimated that 30% of the children suffer from malnutrition and 70% are underweight. More than eight out of 20 die before the age of five.

Dumont questions the value of rural reconstruction centres established by the Government to boost food production. "They have spent millions of kwachas on these centres since 1975 and not one of them is self-supporting. Most produce less than 10 bags of maize per person per year. Every year since 1976, production was diminished. Zambia's main food producers remain the White farmers, the people Kaunda threatened to kick out in 1978.

Kaunda's socialist policies, continues Dumont, have done little to create wealth or distribute it evenly, but have done much to encourage laziness and dishonesty. "Egalitarian promises have resulted in an urban élite of party officials cruising the roads in chauffeur-driven Mercedes, and peasants working two days to be able to afford a bag of salt".

"In clinics, you find large posters reading: 'In case of cholera, wash with soap'. But there is no soap. When children have diarrhoea, one is supposed to give them salt and sugar. But there is none to be found. There are no longer any shops in the bush. People are forced into a subsistence economy which has been mutilated. They are incapable of producing".

Half the country's tractors are out of order through lack of maintenance. Half the country's bicycles (in many areas the only means of transportation) are inoperable because of lack of tyres, tubes and pumps. More than 22,000 classrooms have been built, but more than half have no exercise books, pencils or written books – and no pupils.

Dumont argues for basic rural development. "Zambia has forgotten the meaning of self-reliance. It needs to invent an economic system which uses the country's own resources; animal draught instead of tractors; manure instead of chemical fertilizers; carts instead of oil-propelled engines, as well as a better distribution of the resources produced to satisfy the basic needs of all the population, not just providing luxuries for a privileged few".

In a recommendation which should endear him to hard-pressed Western tax payers who have forked out millions to prop up the chaos, Professor Dumont says he feels the time has come to call a halt to the cash pouring into a country "fast qualifying for the title of the world's greatest sponger".

For years, most of Zambia's ills have been blamed in one way or another on the war next door. Now the war has ended but the problems have not.

Tanzania

The *Wall Street Journal* recently commented that most writings on Tanzania's President Julius Nyerere "border on hagiography" – the study of saints. "His policies are revered in London and Washington; his words have moulded the opinions of a generation of officials in the U.S. State Department and the British Foreign Office".

But what is Nyerere's own record? What miracles has he achieved for his own people? Let us examine the man behind the myths.

MYTH: Internationally, Nyerere is acclaimed as Africa's leading crusader against racism, notably South African racism.

FACT: Nyerere (the name commemorates a plague of army worms at the time of his father's birth) himself quite possibly qualifies as Africa's greatest racist. He is irrevocably pledged to "the eradication of the White presence in Africa". On 29th June, 1972, Tanzanian Whites were told: "There is no future for Europeans in socialist Tanzania. In the long run, this is no country for you".

Promises

Earlier, under the 1967 Arusha Declaration, he had precipitated the first great White flight from Tanzania by arbitrarily nationalizing hundreds of farms, with promises (so far unfulfilled) of compensation to be paid over a period of anything from 10 to 25 years. Today 13 years later, Tanzania – as with so many African States which have expelled their White farmers – Nyerere's country is in total agricultural collapse, with millions of his people facing outright starvation. It was Nyerere who persuaded the British that the Marxist Robert Mugabe was the best bet to lead an independent Zimbabwe. Privately, he now predicts that within two years all the Whites will be gone from Zimbabwe. With Rhodesia gone, Nyrerere says his first priority is to "liberate South Africa from White minority rule".

MYTH: Nyerere claims that he remains a practising Roman Catholic; denies that he is a Marxist; contends that internationally he is "non-aligned".

317

FACT: He has literally brought Tanzania to its knees by instituting a system he describes as "scientific socialism" – Lenin's term for communism. It was Nyerere who initially opened up Africa to the Russians.

Violence

More than any other leader, he is responsible for the solid loop of Marxist States now stretching coast-to-coast across Central Africa. And, for a non-Marxist, he is remarkably fond of quoting from Karl Marx's *Das Kapital*.

MYTH: Nyerere insists that he is "a man of peace".

FACT: Nyerere is not a peaceful man. In March 1963, his TANU party mouth-piece printed the slogan: "Violence Pays, Peace Does Not Pay". That remains Nyerere's slogan to this day. In complete violation of the OAU's sacrosanct principle of territorial integrity, Nyerere has helped topple three Black African régimes: the Comatros in 1975, the Seychelles in 1977 and Uganda in 1979.

He, as an independent Black leader, forcibly deposed neighbouring Black rulers. Nyerere's passionate support of the terrorist onslaught against Mozambique, Rhodesia and South Africa is too well known to need comment.

MYTH: The halls of the OAU and the U.N. ring repeatedly with Nyerere's denunciation of the "human rights" position in South Africa.

FACT: For Nyerere himself, human rights begin at the water's edge. Tanzania has been accused by Amnesty International of holding more political prisoners (accompanied by the use of torture) than South Africa.

MYTH: In addresses in Europe and the U.S., Nyerere uses high-flown rhetoric in praise of "freedom".

FACT: In Tanzania itself, no dissent is tolerated by Nyerere. The newspapers and radio were long ago brought under tight Government control. In a one-party State, all avenues of opposition and free expression are closed.

More Aid

MYTH: Nyerere claims that his system of "scientific socialism" is designed to make Tanzania self-reliant.

FACT: Though he preaches self-reliance, Nyerere in fact accepts more foreign aid than any other Black African leader. Donors, led by the U.S., the World Bank, Scandinavia, Canada, West Germany and Holland, have poured billions into Tanzania over the past 19 years. The U.S. alone has given more than R1,000 million (£500 million). It has rarely been thanked for it. On the contrary, Nyerere spearheads the U.N. drive to "rid Puerto Rico of American colonialism".

Nyerere and Tanzania are what White liberals think Africa is all about; poor and idealistic. Poor it certainly is.

Low Income

At independence in 1962, Tanzania was classified by various U.N. agencies as among the 25 poorest nations on earth. The position has not improved. It is now one of the 15 poorest nations on earth. Only 474,000 of its 16 million people are wage-earners. In real terms, per capita income (R147/£73·5) is lower than it was in 1962.

Most African States are little more than kleptocracies. Tanzania is no different. When things began getting tough in 1967, Nyerere nationalized a wide spread of foreign business holdings. Apparently not having heard of the failure of such schemes in other, more sophisticated countries, he tried to compensate for the resulting loss of foreign investment with his *ujaama* concept – family villages, or collectivized farming.

Not everybody was entranced by the idea. By 1973, only 2 million farmers had signed up. In 1974–75 the "man of peace" ordered the forcible resettlement of the rest, sometimes at gunpoint, sometimes by burning down or ploughing the traditional villages under, or by other measures which he today delicately calls "certain excesses". Some 93% of Tanzania's population has today been herded into the *ujaamas*. The promised health clinics, schools and farm aid that were to follow have largely not materialized.

Reports are being received of increasing soil exhaustion around the 8,000-odd main collectivized villages. Says one U.N. report: "The soil is over-grazed, over-worked and under-fertilized".

Nyerere says his sytem of "scientific socialism" is designed for "the meeting of people's needs, not the making of profits".

Desperate

Of the 330 Government organizations set up to run nationalized businesses, ranging from clothing manufacture to clove distribution, 155 have already collapsed. Of those still functioning, more than a third operate at heavy loss, despite holding a monopoly on the market.

Desperate at the economic and agricultural devastation around him, Nyerere has recently begun calling for renewed Western investment. It remains notable by its absence. Millions of Tanzanians will this year taste the bitter fruit of their leader's brand of socialism, of the long years in which he has sacrificed the interests of his people (hungry not for glory but for food) to his own personal vanity.

319

Addressing a party congress after the 1975 elections, Nyerere undertook to retire in 1980. Exactly as with his colleague, Kenneth Kaunda of Zambia, many of his own people will agree that it is time for him to go.

So much for the collapse of a country and the myths and facts of Nyerere.

Black Africa

A great deal has happened in Black Africa in the past 22 years since 1958, when Ghana became the first to lead the "liberation" parade. How great were the dreams of those years, the giddy optimism about "Africa, the Continent of the Future". And today? Already, in less than a generation, Africa has become the continent of faded dreams, the once-high hopes meshing almost nowhere with the melancholy reality.

As those in Southern Africa know all too well, Black Africans were told they were being exploited, that the White-run countries were police States practising racism, discrimination, repression. But now, with the "exploiters" gone, Black economies almost everywhere have declined drastically or have collapsed. Africa today is the poorest continent on earth – and the most unstable.

Trinidadian writer Shiva Naipaul recently toured Africa. In his book *North of South: An African Journey,* he argues that the continent has returned to the 18th century. "Hopeless, doomed continent! Africa was swaddled in lies . . . lies of liberation. Nothing but lies".

Less bitter but hardly less pessimistic about the future is the ultra-liberal London journalist Colin Legum, for decades one of the most ardent campaigners for Black African independence: "Africa's post-colonial conditions of political instability will, if anything, be greater in the 1980s than in the previous two decades".

Let us examine some of the hard facts about Africa in 1980. According to various United Nations reports:

* The life expectancy in 21 Black African states is less now than it was 40 years ago.

* Black Africa's per capita income is the world's lowest, its infant mortality rate (137 per 1,000 births) the world's highest.

* Almost 90% of Africans live in countries where food production is declining. U.N. indices for agricultural development show that in 31 Black States food production has failed to keep pace with population increase, while in 11 countries food production has actually declined 15% or more.

321

* One in four Black Africans is "severely malnourished". The calorie consumption in 31 countries is below the "bare minimum" requirements as laid down by the Food and Agriculture Organization (FAO).
* Kwashiorkor has recently become widespread in large areas of East, West and Central Africa and it is thought that some 2·5 million children are suffering from one form or another of this disease.
* According to the World Food Council, there are at present some 42 million people in Black Africa suffering from some form of delibilitating deficiency disease "and the figure appears to be on the increase".
* According to UNESCO estimates, more than 80% of the Black African population was illiterate in 1966; 74% was still illiterate three years ago.
* In 12 Black States the GNP declined between 1970 and 1975, despite massive injections of international aid. Black Africa contains 22 countries with a per capita income ranging between R87/£43·5 and R260/£130 a year; 14 countries had a per capita GNP of under R87/£43·5.
* According to a study made by the International Labour Organization (ILO), unemployment and under-employment affect an average of 45% of the active populations in Black States.
* According to ILO criteria, 69% of Black Africa was living in "conditions of extreme poverty in 1973", with conditions showing a steady deterioration. Between 1963 and 1972, the number of people living "in extreme poverty" increased by 10·8% in Africa, as against 0·8% in Latin America and 10·7% in Asia.
* Various U.N. reports declare that parts of Black Africa are "undeveloping". Twelve states had a GNP lower in 1975 than in 1970.
* Black Africa is among the least-developed areas on earth. According to Unido, a country is industrialized when the share of its manufacturing sector in the overall GNP reaches at least 30%. It is semi-industrialized when that percentage is between 10 and 20, and it is not industrialized at all when the share of manufacturing in the GNP is less than 10%.

"The current share of Black Africa in the total world industrial output is around 0·9%. According to current OAU 'Programmes of Action' it is hoped to lift this to 2% by the year 2000 – still miserably and dangerously low.

That is the merest glimpse of a vast human tragedy of the most profound kind. Against that background, Premier Mugabe will be doing his people no favour by leading them into the same morass that now engulfs most of his Black African mentors.

Too Many Mouths and Too Little to Feed Them

It was America, determined to break the economic power of the old colonial empires, which was primarily responsible for forcing premature independence on Black Africa. Clear warning of Washington's intentions came in 1957 when Vice-President Richard Nixon (as he then was) reported to the Senate Foreign Relations Committee after his African tour:

"American interests in the future are so great as to justify us in not hesitating even to assist the departure of the colonial powers from Africa. If we can win native opinion in this process, the future of America in Africa will be assured".

The "decolonization" of Africa is now complete. What has it achieved? The Americans have not won "native opinion" – the Kremlin has been far more successful there. And for most Black States, independence has brought very little relief indeed from disease, famine, poverty, corruption, war and illiteracy.

Many and various are the disasters that have brought Black Africa to its knees. The real problem is easy to define, but far less easy to solve. And that is: *Black Africa is facing a major agricultural disaster*, largely because its population growth is rapidly exceeding the ability of the soil to support such growth.

In 1900 Africa's total population was estimated at 120 million; in 1920, 141 million; in 1940, 176 million; in 1950, 206 million. Present population is estimated at 420 million. The current all-Africa birth rate is so high that by the year 2000, it is expected that the 1980 population will have doubled to 800 million.

Population growth jumped from about 2% in 1960 to 2·8% in the early 1970s. U.S. estimates are that the annual increase will be 2·9% by the late 1980s. The World Population Conference in Bucharest in 1974 disclosed that about 64 million people in Black Africa had no access to birth control services. It also stated that family planning had met with considerable resistance.

In almost all of Black Africa food sufficiency is dropping all the time. It is estimated to be 80% food-sufficient. If present trends continue, that figure will drop to a suicidal 60% by the year 2000. Self-sufficiency is so much on the decline that between 1960 and 1970, Black Africa's cereal imports alone increased by 38%. On a per capita basis Africa – once a major food exporter – now imports more grain on average than either India or China.

According to a study based on U.N. statistics, no Black African country gave priority to agricultural investment during the decade 1960–70. "With the exception of three countries – Egypt, Sudan and Tunisia – agricultural investment represented only a tiny fraction of the total". There has, says the report, been little change in the position since. Output per hectare in Black Africa is only one-third as high as in other developing areas. Worse, in Black Africa only 1·2% of the total cropland is fertilized.

The seriousness of Africa's food situations, say experts, needs to be emphasized in view of the relationship existing between quality of nutrition on the one side, and quality of health and level of productivity of population on the other. Childhood malnutrition, they point out, results in stunted physical growth, mental damage and vision impairment that affects learning and behaviour.

The starvation level of millions of Blacks, resulting in anaemia, kwashiorkor (Africa's most serious nutritional disease) and TB, accounts for much of the overall listlessness of Black Africa's work force. To this must be added VD, now reaching epidemic proportions as tribal traditions break down and prostitution becomes a major industry. And the parasitical diseases – yellow fever, malaria, hookworm, sleeping sickness, bilharzia and river blindness – are rapidly regaining their sinister title as "the real rulers of Africa" because of lack of spraying.

Ironically, some of the most highly publicized aid programmes have added to the problem. Highly endemic bilharzia has accompanied such famous irrigation schemes as the Gezira in the Sudan, the Volta Dam development in Ghana, as well as smaller projects in Nigeria, Tanzania and Angola. As things stand today, the basic human ingredients for drive and success are just not there. Nor are they likely to emerge as long as present attitudes in much of Black Africa persist.

There may be hardly any money for food. But there is, apparently, *lots of money available for bombs!* Let many of the Black leaders wrestle with the choice between maize or guns, and often the choice is guns. Today, largely (but not entirely) under Russian influence, African countries are increasing the diversion of insane amounts of their scarce resources towards armaments for mutual destruction, instead of strengthening unity and focussing attention on the priority areas of social and economic development.

Commenting on the fatal order of priorities, the Society for International Development (SID) says: "Of the 83 developing countries which imported arms in 1978, more than one-fifth were among the very poorest in the world, with an average income of under $200 (about R173). In short, these are the very same nations that belong to the Food and Agriculture Organization's category of "vulnerable and most seriously affected groups" in terms of food shortages.

"The poverty is so stark and on so vast a scale that no statistic could illustrate the inhuman degradation suffered by the vast majority of

324

the citizens of the Third World. Malnutrition saps their energy, stunts their bodies and shortens their lives.

"Illiteracy darkens their minds and forecloses their future.

Simple, preventable diseases maim and kill their children.

Squalor and ugliness pollute and poison their surroundings.

Even the miraculous gift of life itself, and all its intrinsic potential, is eroded and reduced to a desperate effort to survive."

That is the grim truth about conditions in much of Black Africa today. But where are the churchmen, the foreign correspondents, who will tell the world this story?

They will not tell it because it is not fashionable to tell it – and it is not fashionable because, like Vietnam, the disaster of Black Africa is a disaster for the liberals who helped bring it about.

South Africa Possesses a Weapon more Powerful than the Atom Bomb – Food

Daily now, the long grain trains roll into Black Africa from the silos of South Africa. The trains carry South African maize into Zambia, Zaire, Zimbabwe, Mozambique, Malawi, Lesotho, Swaziland, Botswana. And that is not all. From the quaysides of Durban and East London, the grain ships are loading South African maize and wheat for Kenya, Angola, the Ivory Coast and many other States of Black Africa.

All told, 200,000 tons of grain will be shipped to Zambia over the next few months, 120,000 tons to Mozambique. Zimbabwe has already received 20,000 tons. Salisbury sources predict more will be needed once the present pitifully poor harvests are brought in. In short, it is South African maize which will in the next few months rescue millions of starving Black Africans.

That is a relatively new situation; so new that neither South Africa, nor Black Africa itself, has yet had time to assess the full, long-term impact of these huge grain shipments. But one thing is certain:

If it has the courage to use it, South Africa – far and away the largest food supplier in Africa and fifth largest in the world – today possesses a weapon more powerful than the atom bomb.

Few Black African leaders are interested in statistics. But statistics tell the story.

Explosion

To cope with the explosion of new mouths to feed, Black Africa needs to increase its food output by at least 4% a year. This is not happening. Food production is actually *declining* by 1·3% a year.

According to the U.N. Economic Commission for Africa, food sufficiency dropped from around 90% in 1955 to 80% in 1970. If the

325

present trend is not reversed, it will drop to a projected 60% in the year 2000.

For years the doomsday prophets of Worldwatch, the Club of Rome and the FAO have warned of the mass devastation that could result from a vast "population surplus, food deficit" situation. Black Africa is now rapidly moving into that situation.

The Situation is Catastrophic

On present projections, the 1980s will almost certainly be the decade when hunger statistics become corpses in the streets. There is argument about precisely how bad the current crop failures, aggravated by the worst drought in 15 years, are in Central, East and West Africa. There can be no arguing about the empty shelves, the long food queues, the cracked earth, the dry river beds, the emaciated and dying cattle.

A Worldwatch expert who recently visited Tanzania and Central Africa describes the position as "catastrophic". The lid, he said, was just about to blow off. "Very soon what we are going to need here is a massive famine-relief programme."

The tragedy is that most of these are man-made famines; much of Africa's present suffering is entirely of its own making. Technically, there is no reason why anybody in Africa should go hungry. Pre-independence, most Black African states were to a greater or lesser degree food exporters.

In 1934–38, Black Africa exported one million tons of grain annually. By 1950, grain exports had risen to an annual total of around five million tons. But by 1960, the position had turned round completely and, it seems, irrevocably. In that year, Black Africa imported two million tons of grain. In 1970, it imported five million tons; in 1976 10 million tons. This year, according to one U.N. estimate, it could require upwards of *18 million tons*.

Of Africa's 49 Black States, all but a handful are now food importers. What went wrong? Drought gets much of the blame for collapse of this seasons's crops, but that is only part of the story. Overall, the continent's farming lands are hopelessly mismanaged. Pests diminish the harvests; proliferating rate populations destroy much of the stored grain. There has been no accompanying heavy inputs of fertilizers, water, technology and social engineering.

Grim Picture

Add to this the wholesale destruction of once-viable agricultural economies in countries like Tanzania, Mozambique, Angola and Zambia by half-baked Marxist and socialist theories, and you approach the real trouble. The most devastating factor of all, however, is the refusal of many African leaders to accept the need for birth control. As a result, the continent today is unable to cope with continued population growth of such proportions.

Says Lester Brown of Worldwatch: "The old equilibrium (between births and deaths) has been destroyed, but a new equilibrium has not yet been developed. That the current disequilibrium cannot continue indefinitely is certain".

"Unless a way is soon found to control the problem of the African population explosion, massive starvation will take over as a partial solution to that problem. In other words, famine will provide a sort of barrier to an uncontrolled birth explosion . . ."

That, then, is the grim picture. That is why so many African leaders, without a good word for South Africa and only too anxious to achieve its destruction, still want to nail down contracts for South African maize. There are good reasons why they want it.

First, its quality is among the best in the world. Second, because of the interlocking railway systems, it can get to the famine-threatened countries quickly and efficiency. If landlocked Zambia had to depend on emergency supplies coming through the congestion of Dar es Salaam, the people would starve before they ever saw one kernel of South African maize.

Food Lever

The South African attitude is that it will sell maize to whoever has the money to pay for it. But were the position reversed, would these Black States succour South Africa? More and more observers sympathetic to that country's problems are expressing the opinion that South Africa should apply its agricultural capacity as a lever on Black States to adopt less militant policies. These observers also see South African grain as a tool which could at least loosen links with the U.S.S.R. Or to stop them harbouring and supporting anti-South African terrorists.

The Making of Africa's New Dark Age

Economically, politically, agriculturally, socially, medically – Black Africa is today a crisis-ridden continent marching steadily towards a catastrophe.

Why is this so little understood? Largely because so many in the West – the United Nations, the World Bank, the U.S. State Department, the British Foreign Office, the liberal media, the WCC – all those who have helped to create the disaster are fearful of the facts.

Yet the evidence is indisputable. Country after country – Zambia, Zaire, Tanzania, Ghana, Liberia, Angola, Mozambique, Ethiopia, Chad,

327

Uganda, the Central African Republic – has been pushed to the brink of economic collapse by fiscal mismanagement, government corruption and official thievery, by towers of international debt, by nationalization, confiscation, by premature "Africanization" of the job markets, by destroyed agricultural systems, by the return of the great plagues like malaria, tsetse fly, locusts, by civil and tribal wars.

A Comparison of The Records of Two Men

As evidence, one need examine the records of only two men: Tanzania's Julius Nyerere and the Ivory Coast's Felix Houphouet-Boigny.

* As I have already revealed, Tanzania, in worse shape than most African States, has adopted many of the worst features of the totalitarian régimes its leader admires. Millions of people have been marched off, often at gunpoint, to Nyerere's calamitous collective villages.

   It is a chilling picture of people being uprooted, their lifestyles turned upside-down, their country reduced to beggary, to suit the whims of one man. It is alleged that much of this was done on the advice of a former London Transport House official and graduate of the London School of Economics.

* The Ivory Coast, on the other hand, is the French-speaking Kenya of Africa. Pro-Western and capitalistic it is prosperous and with no time for the "liberation" of South Africa which pre-occupies poverty-stricken Zambia, Tanzania, Mozambique, Botswana and the rest.

What Should Be The Strategy?

Abidjan, not so many years ago a sleepy little West African town with a population of no more than 20,000, is now a modern city of 500,000. As U.S. writer David Lamb recently pointed out, the Ivory Coast devotes 20% of its budget to education, holds no political prisoners and is growing faster than any non-oil-producing nation in Black Africa.

This, too, is the work of one man. Just as Nyerere has imposed his dream of "scientific socialism" on Tanzania, so President Houphouet-Boigny has made his vision of prosperity a reality on the Ivory Coast. Yet it is Nyerere whom many in the radical belt of Southern-Central Africa have been persuaded to take as their model.

How can the strategy of Black Africa be put right? Clearly, this will require profound wisdom and creative thought of a type as yet hardly discernible on most of the continent. First, Africa will have to learn that one cannot forever get something for nothing. Only Africans can drastically reduce the increasing number of mouths to feed; only Africans can reform economic structures and radically increase food production.

It was on 1st May, 1980, that Mr. Robert Mugabe said he expected U.S. assistance to Zimbabwe to total "as much as a billion dollars spread over the next three to four years". He is not going to get that much. With Western economies now taking their worst post-war beating, foreign-aid allocations everywhere are being trimmed back. In any event, inflation has diminished economic aid by the industrialized nations by 40% in real terms over the last five years.

Next, Mr. Mugabe and other Third World mendicants should question the philanthropy of American and other benefactors. Although this is not shouted from the rooftops, the U.S. ties most of its aid to "Buy America" purchases. The average, quoting U.N. documents, for all countries is 60%.

Aid a Misnomer

Such "tied" aid raises the price of goods that could have been obtained cheaper from more competitive sources. Only competitive bidding gives poor countries fair value for their money. Without this, aid becomes a misnomer – not a genuine subsidy to manufacturers in the export business.

Domestically, there is much that African States can do for themselves:
* The first requirement is to limit population growth. The poor countries must recognize that they are, to quote U.S. economist Rawl Farle, "in an anxious race between demography and development".
* They must introduce extensive land reform, with a return to Africa's traditional identification with agriculture.
* They must strive to improve their own human calibre. "What holds back many poor countries is the people who live there," says P. T. Bauer, referring to widespread torpor, lassitude, fatalism and a preference for the inactive, contemplative life.

Prime Essentials

Here one of the prime essentials is to reform education. School curricula should stress vocational training. Many poor African States have plenty of lawyers and graduates in literature, but woefully few technicians, engineers and mechanics.
* They must reject prestige projects; learn that health care comes before national airlines, agriculture before huge sports stadiums, education before vast conference halls.

329

* They must encourage foreign investment, foreign entrepreneurs. Many Black African States are hostile to business and take a dim view of profits. Today they are paying the penalty.
* They must learn to live in peace with one another. At present there are 35 or so foreign-supported African "liberation" movements pledged to bring down the following countries: South Africa, South West Africa, Zaire, Mozambique, Angola, Djibouti, Guinea, Guinea-Bissau, the Congo, Malawi, Kenya, Benin, the former Spanish Sahara, Reunion, Mauritius and the Canary Islands.

Are any or all of these objectives realistic?

They had better be made so, for if they are not a new Dark Age is likely to lie ahead for the teeming millions of this turbulent, tumultuous continent.

The Overall Situation

From what I have described it must be clear beyond doubt that Black Africa is becoming a desperately hungry continent and the general outlook over the next ten years is grim indeed. The enormous number of refugees, the critical unemployment problem, the increase in population, the total disarray of agriculture, the decrease of foreign aid, the collapse of infrastructure due to insufficient skilled and trained personnel; all these factors will confront Black African leaders with so many disasters in every direction that they will be unable to cope without massive aid from the Republic of South Africa and the West.

Apart from the Aswan Dam, the Russian Bloc has never instituted, or been capable of instituting any real infrastructures in the territories over which they have gained control. The Russians have in no way contributed material aid or given large-scale agricultural assistance. All they have done is to draft in surrogate forces and weapons. No other colonial power has ever been so unpopular in Africa as are the Russians – not with the élite, but with the masses. Angola is providing a very costly investment for Moscow, and is increasingly embarrassing for Fidel Castro, with all his own problems at home.

In the event of a major conflagration elsewhere, it is likely that sometime after 1985, we shall see a Russian rollback in Africa. Experience has shown that African territories with strong Russian links tire of these after 15 to 20 years. That period will start around 1985. The Republic of South Africa must be able to hold the ring until then, *if necessary by itself.*

Most people believe that one section in particular in the Republic of South Africa has been at the receiving end of adverse propaganda ever since the National Party electoral victory of 1948. This is not the case. The Afrikaners have been the target of anti-propaganda for the past 80 years, the more virulent and successful onslaught coming from its own Press.

More than 90% of the hostile publicity fed to the outside world about the Republic of South Africa emanates from within the country

331

itself. Not only has this had a serious cumulative effect on world opinion but has also gone far towards polarising Black-White relations. The South African press has been far more effective than any Russian radio programme has ever been and will live to rue the day.

Western style democracy will not work for the Republic of South Africa any more than it is now working in the United Kingdom itself, where the Trade Union Movement is intent on usurping the power of Government, the Labour Party's militant left-wing is intent on changing the whole social structure and system of society, where law and order is breaking down and vandalism and hooliganism is rife, and where defence of the Realm is not accorded the national priority to which it is entitled at a time when the West is moving fast into a period of high-risk.

Fortunately, South Africa has an abundance of men of character and resolve. They will fight to the last man against the enemy from within and from without. While I am in no position to judge the calibre of their politicians I am, however, qualified to judge the quality of leadership in the higher echelons of their Armed Forces and the Army in particular. I doubt if such strong men, high leadership and sheer professionalism can be matched by any other country in the world today.

How does Russia intend to organize The Battle for South Africa?

The Soviet domination of Angola and the sell-out of Rhodesia to an avowed Marxist and terrorist leader are merely skirmishes, preliminary to a final assault on the vast mineral base and power-base that is South Africa.

The Soviet design is to turn that rich, strategic land area from its Western orientation, then dominate the West's vital oil route and halt the tanker traffic at will. If the Soviets were to succeed in this objective, they would control the Indian Ocean and the bulk of Western Europe's most important raw materials and food. Western Europe would then be thrown back on the submarine-infested North Atlantic for the final struggle – *or surrender*.

The first fundamental element to grasp is that the Kremlin is absolutely convinced that the West simply dare not support any White government in South Africa, because to do so would be to stand accused of siding against legitimate Black nationalist liberation movements. Therefore the Soviet planners now have the tremendous strategic advantage of knowing that they can count on the West supporting a Black Marxist-revolutionary government in South Africa rather than a pro-Western Black régime not supported by Moscow.

This being so, the second essential to grasp is that it is now the Kremlin's firm resolve to instigate and exploit a White-Black power-struggle in South Africa, which they are convinced they can ensure the Blacks will win.

332

Once they have achieved this aim, the Soviets will employ the common technique of Communist advance through further revolutionary subversion, namely by exploiting the conflicting interests between the Black parties, encourage the differences to widen through propaganda and violent actions, then start to control the different groups – by now fighting each other – and finally take over the group which becomes dominant.

This would create the power vacuum necessary to enable Moscow to seize control of the mineral wealth of South Africa and dominate the Cape sea route – the oil and strategic materials jugular vein of Western Europe. Almost 70% of Western Europe's crude oil imports, compared to 30% of America's, are transported by sea around the Cape of Good Hope. So are 70% of Western Europe's imports of strategic raw materials and 20% of its food imports.

The Soviets brutal occupation, subjugation and annexation of Afghanistan imposes a threat to the security not only of Pakistan but also of the entire South Asian peninsula. Another and more important threat to the West's oil and jugular vein is the Soviets' possession of Afghan air bases, which will enhance their ability to block or even sever the vein in the Persian Gulf itself. If Russia were to follow up its annexation of Afghanistan by advancing into Pakistan or Iran, gain the warmwater ports in the Gulf and Arabian Sea, so achieving a grip on the vital oil – this could trigger off the Third World War.

What should The West do to thwart Moscow's Designs?

* As I said in the first page of this Epilogue, the U.S. cannot handle any serious military threat in the Indian Ocean and Persian Gulf areas without the full co-operation of South Africa.
* The sea routes around the Cape must be protected for the West and denied to the Soviet Union.
* The necessary anti-submarine warfare could not be mounted without using South African bases.
* Therefore the Simonstown Agreement, peremptorily abrogated by a British Socialist Government in 1975, must be re-activated. Its ending was a frightening victory for Soviet maritime strategy as well as for left-wing agitation in Britain. For the latter reason it was not merely strategic folly, but highly suspect.
* As I stated in Chapter 23:
  1. NATO's maritime boundary must be extended below the Tropic of Cancer, to include *joint* defence of the Gulf.
  2. There must be a continuous naval presence in the Arabian Sea and north-west Indian Ocean.

333

    3. There must be a new Alliance for the defence of this part of the world – at sea, on land and in the air – just as there is the NATO Atlantic Alliance.

    4. If the Soviet Union's strategy is global, as indeed it is, then the West's strategy must also be global.

* Any economic blockade or further embargoes on South Africa will not only rebound on the perpetrators and bring terrible suffering on the blacks of the whole of Africa, but also play straight into the hands of the Soviets by helping them to achieve their aims.

* The West must stop being pushed around by the new and unrepresentative cockpit of the UN – an element indulging in anti-colonial postures at the behest of their Soviet tutors, who are blatantly encouraging what is euphemistically called "armed liberation struggles". This, in plain language, means the use of the gun as the sole weapon for resolving disputes.

* Much of the highly organized shouting about South Africa is not really concerned with *apartheid* at all. *Apartheid* is being used as a convenient smoke screen, a diversion, to ensure that South Africa falls like a ripe plum into the lap of the Soviets.

* For the President of the United States, a country which has so much Black unrest and poverty and so many Indian reservations, to go into a dither about *apartheid* is a glaring example of self-righteous piety and blatant hypocrisy.

Lest I be smeared as a racist, let me remind the reader that I have had the good fortune to spend the major part of life serving, working and living with black and coloured peoples, including staying in their homes, eating their food, speaking their languages and respecting their religion and customs.

If I were at the head of affairs in South Africa I would implement *apartheid* as racial *differentiation* – not discrimination.

How should South Africa fight its Own Battle for Survival?

I have touched on this problem at the beginning of this Epilogue and also under the three headings "Winning a Low-Intensity Conflict"; "The External Build-up Against South Africa"; and "Internal Insurgency".

On the African continent, South Africa – and I include South West Africa – is now the only remaining bulwark against Russian expansionism, and they know it. They also realize that the most dangerous threat facing South Africa is insurgency, terrorism, urban guerrilla warfare and racial violence.

Subversive warfare is Russia's long, hard way of achieving by vicious stealth and cunning guile what conventional war would produce more quickly, though at greater risk. Therefore, the gravity of South Africa's future internal situation cannot begin to be appreciated unless it is seen in the context of the pernicious threat of Russia's subtle and insidious strategy of subversive warfare. It is the technique and process of softening up and rotting a country from within.

Throughout the world it is the Russian hands which are manipulating the strings of anarchy, industrial unrest, racial disharmony, violence, revolution and internal insurgency. The Soviets will fight the war for South Africa, not by outright aggression with their own troops, as in Afghanistan, but by remote control, in other words revolutionary war by proxy.

Externally they will use their hatchetmen from Cuba and Warsaw Pact countries to train and arm guerrillas and terrorists from Black Africa to enable them to operate in tightly knit teams, each well-armed with a high degree of violent technological sabotage skills, capable of triggering car bombs, explosives, land mines, booby traps and incendiaries by remote control. There will be teams armed with Soviet-made SAM-7 ground-to-air missiles and stand-off anti-tank missiles, the latter being capable of inflicting severe damage not merely against armour, but on vital installations.

Externally, also, will be the SWAPO and the well armed and trained Zimbabwe guerrilla armies and terrorists launched from Angola, Botswana, Zimbabwe and Mozambique, supported in depth by sanctuaries in Zambia and Tanzania. I have already mentioned how those States who give launching pads to these guerrillas and terrorists will suffer terrible retribution from South Africa's swift retaliatory military might. It may well be necessary to carry the war into the countries concerned, but certainly hot pursuit and pre-emptive strikes will have to be the order of the day if the enemy is to be kept beyond striking distance and their infrastructures destroyed.

Even so, with such a long border to dominate day and night, week in and week out, plus an enormous coast line, every modern technical device will be required if infiltration tactics on a large scale are to be kept within manageable limits. But there will be no front line as such in the accepted sense. Infiltration by sea and from the air – in the latter case parachute landings – will also be well within the military capability of Russia and Warsaw Pact trained, *and led,* terrorists and guerrillas.

I am not suggesting that the borders can be sealed in the form of a barrier similar to that along the 870 mile border between East and West Germany, with its network of wire, automatic firing devices, minefields, watch-towers, bunkers, patrol roads and surveillance equipment. But what I am suggesting is that there must be a series of such 'porcupines' and that vulnerable points, key areas and installations throughout the country will have to be 'scientifically' protected with the most modern forms of surveillance, detection and lethal devices. Otherwise a disproportionate number of security forces will be tied down in purely static defence, at a time when every available able-bodied man will be required in a mobile, offensive role.

So much for the enemy from without.

The Communists and the two Marxist movements, the African National Congress, and the Pan-African Congress, do not want agreement. They are willing to sacrifice the blood and the lives of Africans to achieve their political policies. They rapidly turn otherwise peaceful demonstrations into violent riots. The enemy from within are being organized to stir up industrial unrest, foment strikes, incite racial hatred, boycott classes, close universities, carry out arson, bombings, sabotage, rob banks, commit selective assassinations – all this culminating in nation-wide bloody riots and revolution.

South Africa faces total onslaught by urban guerrilla and subversive warfare both from within and without. To prevent and defeat this will require a total strategy involving nothing less than placing the country on an operational footing, and there is no time to lose. The flabby, velvet glove, low profile conduct of operations as practised in Northern Ireland would be futile, so would the American policy in Vietnam of "Search and Destroy". The technique must be "Clear, Hold and Dominate". The threat must be eliminated, not contained. There is no doubt in my mind that the South African Security Forces, including the police, have the expertise, equipment and strength to crush any form of aggression from within and without.

I have already explained that South Africa, as the largest food supplier in Africa, possesses a weapon more powerful than the nuclear weapon. Another weapon, to compete with industrial unrest and strikes, is the manpower available from Taiwan. Taiwan is greatly over-populated and would be willing to provide a work force of at least one million anti-communist Chinese to work in key industries and establishments, particularly the vital and massive oil-from-coal plants.

South Africa's conventional capability is so superior that its conventional military deterrent is more than equal both in a regional and continental context. In terms of conventional warfare it would be a tremendous undertaking even for a superpower such as the U.S. or U.S.S.R. to invade South Africa.

If, however, the build-up against her were to become more than she could compete with by conventional means, then she must have the capacity not only to use tactical nuclear weapons against troop concentrations, communication centres and other military targets, but also possess the ability to threaten the home territories of the attacking powers. Furthermore, with the greater part of the world aligned against her she cannot afford to send her envoys naked into the council chambers.

Lastly, just as it has been possible to win the hearts and minds of many of the people in the operational area in South West Africa, so should it be possible to win the hearts and minds of a high proportion of the people of South Africa. But it will require a highly organized political, psychological and propaganda warfare strategy, combined with the advancement of the well-being of all South Africans. The people will support a cause if they are told the truth, and the truth is that Communist Russia is on the rampage like Nazi Germany in the 1930s. South Africa is the prey they aim to devour – by more subtle means than outright aggression.

How the Soviet Union exploited détente

U.S.-Soviet détente began with the first visit by an American President – Richard Nixon – to Moscow in May, 1972. Russia has managed to exploit the relationship to its advantage in four key areas.

Global Competition

In 1972, Russia and America agreed to refrain from "efforts to obtain unilateral advantage at the expense of the other." In 1973, they signed an Agreement on Prevention of Nuclear War in which both agreed "to avoid military confrontation," to "refrain from the threat or use of force" and to consult each other in any war-threatening emergency.

Result: Russia repeatedly has intervened in the affairs of other countries to expand its power.

1973. Moscow, aware of an imminent Arab attack on Israel, failed to consult the U.S. and obstructed American cease-fire efforts.

1975-1976. Soviets intervened in Angola's civil war, transporting and supplying a proxy army of Cubans. Outcome: A Communist Angola.

1977-1978. Russia intervened in Ethiopia with Cuban forces.

1978. Russia delivered vast arms supplies to Vietnam, setting the stage for an invasion of Cambodia.

1979. Soviet military advisers and Soviet-sponsored Cuban forces trained and supported South Yemeni troops who invaded North Yemen.

1972-1979. Russia built up its military power in Cuba by sending in nuclear-capable MiG-23 warplanes, by developing a possible nuclear-submarine base there and by installing a Red Army combat unit.

1979. Soviet troops invaded Afghanistan and set up a puppet government there in an unprecedented use of Russian forces outside Moscow's satellite empire.

The Arms Race

The centrepiece of détente has been the strategic-arms-limitation agreement – SALT I – signed and ratified in 1972. That pact, freezing the number of Soviet and American nuclear missiles and limiting antimissile-defence sites, was supposed to curb the arms race.

Result: The arms race has continued to escalate, with Russia gaining steadily and substantially on the United States.

Nuclear weapons. Russia with a massive build-up has overtaken the U.S. and threatens to gain overall nuclear superiority.

Armed forces. In conventional strength, the Soviets have increased their advantage. While the U.S. has reduced its forces by 1.4 million to a level of 2 million in 10 years, Russia has expanded its forces by 400,000 to a total of 3.7 million.

Sea power. The Russian Navy lagged far behind the U.S. in size and capability just a decade ago. Today it can challenge the U.S. in any ocean. The submarine fleet outnumbers that of the U.S.

Soviet-American Trade

In 1972, the U.S. and Russia agreed "to promote the development of mutually beneficial commercial relations" and to negotiate a trade agreement. American businessmen looked to a big new market.

Result: Trade has grown slowly, totalling in 1978 only 2.7 billion dollars — less than that with Switzerland.

Grain. The bulk of U.S. sales to Russia consists of grain, which accounted for 1.7 billion dollars of the 2.7 billion total in 1978.

Industrial trade. Moscow blames the U.S. for disappointing gains in trade of its own industrial goods, charging that Washington has failed to honour a commitment to grant most-favoured-nation treatment for Soviet exports to America. Congress has withheld such treatment until Moscow guarantees more-liberal emigration policies for Jews.

Technology

Russia and America signed a 1972 agreement to co-operate in the fields of science and technology.

Result: The exchange has been largely a one-way affair, with Russia importing U.S. technology but providing little in return.

A highlight of the promised co-operation was the joint Soyuz-Apollo space flight in 1975.

The Soviets complain that they are denied much of the advanced American technology they require, due to U.S. restrictions. Americans charge the Soviets have diverted to military uses much of the equipment acquired ostensibly for civilian purposes.

Example: Trucks built with American technology were used in the military invasion of Afghanistan.

Reprinted from *U.S. News & World Report*, 14th January, 1980. Copyright (1980) U.S. News & World Report, Inc.

The Rebellious Tribe in Russia's Path

Now that Russia has taken over Afghanistan, the remote region of Baluchistan is a prime candidate for future Soviet trouble-making.

Moscow views the rugged lands of the independence-minded Baluchi tribesmen — an area about twice the size of Arizona that ranges across parts of Iran, Pakistan and Afghanistan — as an inviting path to achieve a long-held ambition: Control of a warmwater port on the Arabian Sea.

Few Western experts believe that a Soviet military invasion is an immediate threat. More likely are Russians attempts to exploit the intense nationalism of the Baluchis with the aim of creating a new Asian entity under Moscow's thumb.

Soviet control over a "Greater Baluchistan" would put Russia in a position to cut the West's sea-lanes to Persian Gulf oil.

Objectives of a Soviet move south would be the existing port of Gwadar in western Pakistan or an uncompleted facility that the deposed Shah started to build at Chahbahar in eastern Iran. Either one could enable Russian warships to control access to the gulf through the narrow Strait of Hormuz.

Discord triggered by the Baluchis' drive for self-rule makes their homeland a logical Soviet target.

In south-eastern Iran, about 500,000 Baluchis seethe with resentment over what they regard as oppressive rule from Teheran. As Sunni Moslems in a Shi'ite-dominated nation, they regard themselves as outsiders, linked by custom, language and allegiance to the tribe, not to the central government.

Demands for self-rule often led to fighting with the Shah's forces. Now, violence has erupted against the régime of Ayatollah Khomeini in the isolated town of Zahedan.

Defiance and discontent also dominate actions of 2.5 million Baluchis in Pakistan, the bulk of whom live in the poor western-most province of Baluchistan. The tribe has a long record of revolt against national authorities and tied down a large part of Pakistan's armed forces in a 1973-77 uprising.

Baluchistan now is relatively quiet under martial law that was imposed by Islamabad in mid-1977. But young Baluchis, unhappy and restive, could spark a new outbreak of violence at any time.

A third — and far smaller — group of Baluchis lives in the southern

February – March 1965

India moves two infantry brigades into disputed Rann of Kutch area (3,500 square miles) together with air and naval deployment close to Pakistan's borders, 7th April, 1965. Pakistan Army went into action and ejected Indian forces from disputed area, informing Security Council. India threatened to extend the conflict to other areas.

Ceasefire agreed to with effect 1st July, 1965, and dispute referred to a Tribunal, who awarded disputed area to Pakistan in October 1967.

April 1965 – August 1965

India builds up military strength in State of Jammu and Kashmir in violation of U.N. resolution after the Rann of Kutch reverses mentioned earlier. Pakistan launches "Operation Gibraltar" (Freedom Fighters into Kashmir State) to neutralize Indian threat and build-up, followed by "Operation Grand Slam", with regular Forces, capturing Dewa, Chamb, Jaurian 6 miles inside disputed Kashmir State. 6 Indian Air Force (IAF) aircraft go into action to stop advance. Pakistan Air Force (PAF) shoots down four Vampires. On 6th September Indian Army and Air Force attacked Pakistan, crossing the International Border in and around Lahore Sector. Indian attack repulsed with heavy casualties.

8th September 1965

Indian Army launches main effort with four infantry divisions and one armoured division against elements of one infantry division and an armoured Brigade group in Chawinda (East of Sia̶l̶ ... ... brought to a halt with heavy casualties. Pakistani Fo̶ ... ... Karan, 6 miles inside Indian territory, and large tracts in ... India suggests ceasefire; accepted by Pakistan on 23rd September, 1̶ ...

Tashkent Agreement of 1966 restores captured territory to both sides. Kashmir dispute remains unresolved and India refuses to implement U.N. Resolution on plebiscite in Kashmir.

January – March 1971

Political unrest in East Pakistan inspired by Indian infiltrators.

25th March 1971

Pakistan Army goes to the aid of the civil power in East Pakistan and restores the situation by July 1971, ejecting Indian infiltrators and Indian para-military forces operating inside East Pakistan.

343

November 1971

By November 1971 India had concentrated three Corps, comprising 8 infantry/mountain divisions, a parachute brigade, a regiment of T-55 Russian tanks, and three regiments of PT-76 Russian Amphibious tanks around East Pakistan, and built-up a superiority of almost 3 to 1 in ground forces, 4 to 1 in air forces and 6 to 1 in naval forces.

On 21st November, Indian attacks commenced against East Pakistan from the north, north-west, west and east, without a formal declaration of war, as in 1965. By 3rd December, 1971 when Indian intentions were clear, Pakistan retaliated with an air attack from West Pakistan on 3rd December, and all out war commenced in West Pakistan also.

India launched its main effort with elements of four infantry divisions and three armoured brigades in West Pakistan against a one-divisional front east of Sialkot. On the East Pakistan front, having achieved strategic superiority, India launched multi-dimentional thrusts from four main directions against Pakistani forces, together with 5th Column forces operating inside East Pakistan which had been harassing the Pakistan Army, Navy and Air Force for the past 8 months. Whereas in West Pakistan the main effort was beaten to a halt with heavy casualties, and only tightly held areas were over-run by Indian Forces, in East Pakistan after inflicting heavy casualties on the Indians, and putting up stiff resistance, with little or no air support, no reserves and limited logistic support, the Governor of East Pakistan agreed to a ceasefire and a surrender through U.N.O. intervention, on 16th December, 1971.

The State of Jammu and Kashmir, the cause of three conflicts in 24 years, remains a disputed territory in spite of U.N. resolution for a plebiscite.

America's Abortive Operation in Iran

While I would not attempt to compare the brilliantly executed operation of the Special Air Service (SAS) at the Iranian Embassy on *home territory* in London, with the long distance operation by the U.S. Commando force, there *are* some distinct lessons to be drawn from the success and failure of each operation.

Of one thing I am certain – the SAS operating in Iran would have achieved success. Although the logistical problems were formidable, with proper attention given to the 'rules of the game', outlined below, the resultant *débâcle* would have been avoided.

In terms of the *politico-military* judgments that have to be made in these situations, I would comment as follows:

If the seeds of failure are sown by the political high command – as undoubtedly happened in the U.S. operation – then the meticulous planning and the leaving of nothing to chance, which I would have laid down as being the essential ingredients of success, would have acted as the counter-poise; producing either the release of the hostages or, by drawing attention to the inadequate political directive, the elimination of the causes of failure.

One of the most crucial aspects of the failed mission was basically a case of the action being too little too late. 'Strike while the iron is hot' is a good military axiom. Israeli planners and our own SAS throughly understand the meaning of this expression. President Carter seemingly does not, for the operation was launched almost six months from when the hostages were taken. Contingency plans must have existed – if not, why not? Was it lack of resolve, fear of adverse reaction on the part of the Soviet Union, or worse – a case of moral cowardice?

We might also reflect – in terms of the high quality of intelligence that is required to mount any successful operation and/or the effecting of changed circumstances – that had not the CIA been publicly castigated and virtually destroyed over the past few years, there could have been a far different basis upon which to mount operations in Iran.

The Reasons Why the U.S. Operation Failed

1. **Reserves:**
    In the case of helicopters the reserves must be at least 100%, i.e. 1 for 1, at normal operational range. Increase the

345

range then the percentage of reserves must also be increased. Why? Because:

a. The helicopter is a sensitive and vulnerable piece of machinery.

b. In this case the helicopters were operating at extreme range.

c. Sandstorms must be expected in desert terrain with the danger of damage to delicate engine components.

In the case of personnel in such a complicated rescue operation, there must be a replacement for every member of the team, whether combatant or technical.

This cardinal principle of sufficient logistical and combat back-up was broken.

2. **Planning for the Worst Case:**

Every Commander must plan for the worst case, for the unexpected and be ready to deal with any eventuality. This requires split-second flexibility.

What are the eventualities?

a. *Accident in the air or on the ground*

This occurred and because the principle in 1 above was broken, the whole rescue operation was an abject failure.

b. *Weather*

Soldiers must pay as much attention to the weather as do sailors. In this case there was a sandstorm – a most likely occurrence in such desert terrain, and yet it was not planned for.

c. *Sickness*

One sick man can abort such a delicate operation unless his replacement is immediate and his evacuation pre-planned.

d. *Casualties*

Must be expected and planned for. For each team member in the first 'string' there must be back-up members in the second and third strings. Treatment and evacuation of casualties is a *sine qua non* if morale is to be maintained. To leave behind casualties in such an operation is unheard of and would not have occurred with expert planning.

e. *Timings*

Rendezvous with clandestine agents and transport already in place can go wrong. Planning must take this into consideration.

f. *Surprise*

The element of surprise is essential. In this case the sudden arrival of a bus-load of civilians should never have occurred had clandestine agents been doing their job properly.

All or some of these can go wrong and contingency plans made accordingly. Every type of eventuality, including equipment failures, must be injected into the constant rehearsals for such sophisticated operations. In this case, the lack of planning included a failure to hold a full dress rehearsal in the desert of the American west.

3. **Achievement of mission:**
   This is the over-riding dominant factor. When you fight, *you fight to win!* But if disaster strikes, on-scene commanders should ensure that all classified material is destroyed. In this case, they did not do so.

4. **Lessons:**
   The lessons learned elsewhere were ignored. In my own cross-border operations, known as Operation 'Claret', in the Borneo confrontation with Indonesia, I laid down my Golden Rules, described by Tom Pocock:
   Not one man was lost.
   Not a wounded man was left behind.
   We always achieved maximum surprise and success.
   Training for the unexpected was unceasing. Every conceivable spanner was thrown into the works during the training and rehearsals for each and every operation.
   Above all our operational intelligence on the enemy's latest movements in and near the target area was extremely accurate and right up to the minute.

SAS

The successful raid on the Iranian embassy in London, on 5th May, 1980, which was conducted in such an exemplary manner by the Special Air Service (SAS) Regiment was, when all is said and done, only what the world has been led to expect of them. Instead of the quiet, self-effacing acknowledgment of praise for a job well done, which used to be a familiar characteristic of the British, the country seemed to go berserk and indulged in a positive orgy of mutual backslapping, self-congratulation and own-trumpet blowing. The reason for this, I suppose, was that the public had become so subjected by television and radio to a ceaseless torrent of gloom, despondency and bad news that the feat by the SAS, which was televised live for all to see, acted as a tremendous tonic, expecially when the ever-boastful Americans had so recently bitten the dust. If anyone could put back the word *Great* in Britain once again it would certainly be the Armed Forces of the Crown, despite the worst endeavours of militant Left-Wing politicians and Trade Union leaders to carve them down to the bone, and despite the lack of dynamic leadership and inspiration in the country as a whole.

The 'Neutron Bomb'

Opposition to the "Neutron Bomb" has been intense both in the United States and in Europe, while the news media have not provided the information needed for the ordinary citizen to understand the issue at stake.

In very elementary language the facts are as follows:

The "Neutron Bomb" actually is not a *bomb*. It is a battlefield weapon, a projectile that is fired in the same manner as a "standard" atomic battlefield weapon, with which it should be compared. It is properly called an Enhanced Radiation Reduced Blast Weapon or an ERRB Weapon. Its special characteristics can be more readily understood after reading a brief description of a "standard" atomic weapon.

All atomic weapons have three major effects upon explosion; radiation, air blast and heat. All effects diminish with distance from the point of explosion.

Fig. 1 is based on the explosion of a 10 kiloton "standard" weapon at the centre of a three mile square area. The circles correspond to the following effects:

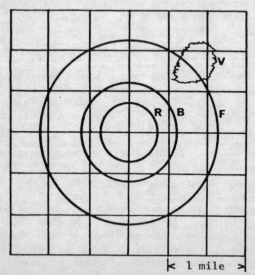

Fig. 1 – The Three Effects Of The Explosion Of a Standard Battlefield Atomic Weapon.

R represents the circle within which the radiation (mainly gamma rays and neutrons) is sufficiently strong to kill men inside tanks or in other armoured vehicles.

Within circle B, ordinary buildings will be demolished by the outrushing blast of air.

Within F, the heat from the explosion will be so great as to set fire to combustible materials.

Village V is likely to suffer considerable damage from fire.

Radiation is the product of explosion that puts tanks out of action. It does so by killing the crews. Tanks, themselves, are not damaged much by radiation, nor for that matter, by blast or fire unless close to the point of detonation.

Obviously, the use of atomic (nuclear) weapons to stop invading enemy forces in tanks or armoured vehicles will also cause severe damage to the people and buildings of the invaded country. Elimination or reduction of this damage is the characteristic that makes the ERRB Weapon so desirable.

As its name implies, the Enhanced Radiation weapon puts out much more radiation in proportion to blast and heat than the standard atomic weapon does. In fact a 1 kilton ERRB weapon has about the same radiation pattern as the 10 kiloton standard weapon of Fig. 1. However, blast and heat are much less. Consequently, the circles corresponding to B and F in Fig. 1 are inside circle R shown in Fig. 2, which illustrates the explosion of a mere 1 kilton ERRB Weapon.

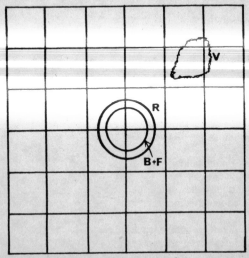

Fig. 2 – Radiation, Blast and Fire Resulting from Explosion of a 1 Kilton ERRB Weapon.

The Fox's Prophecy

The following selected verses, to which the very apposite title of "The Fox's Prophecy" has been given, were found among the papers of the late Mr D. W. Nash; and were probably written by him about the Winter of 1870-71. At that time the writer was, no doubt, much impressed by the brilliant military triumphs which Prussia and the Federated German States had during the preceding autumn against France, and possibly his mind was full of forebodings as to what the rise of a great new and ambitious power like Prussia (Germany) might mean to England. However that may be, they have an extraordinary relation to the circumstances of the present time.

Huntsman 1865-68

Tom Hill was in the saddle,
    One brighter November morn,
The echoing glades of Guiting Wood
    Were ringing with his horn.

The diamonds of the hoar-frost
    Were sparkling in the sun,
Upon the fallen leaves the drops
    Were shining one by one.

The hare lay on the fallow,
    The robin carolled free;
The linnet and the yellow finch
    Twittered from tree to tree.

High in his stirrups raised he stood,
    And long he gazed around;
And breathlessly and anxiously,
    He listened for a sound

But nought he heard save the song of bird,
    Or jay's discordant cry;
Or when among the tree tops,
    The wind went murmuring by.

No voice of hound, or sound of horn,
    The woods around were mute,
As though the earth had swallowed up,
    His comrades — man and brute.

He thought, 'I must essay to find,
    My hounds at any cost;
A huntsman who has lost his hounds
    Is but a huntsman lost.'

Then round he turned his horse's head,
    And shook his bridle free,
When he was struck by an aged fox,
    That sat beneath a tree.

He raised his eyes in glad surprise,
    That huntsman keen and bold;
But there was in that fox's look
    That made his blood run cold.

He raised his hand to touch his horn,
    And shout a "Tally-Ho!"
But, mastered by that fox's eye,
    His lips refused to blow.

For he was grim and gaunt of limb,
    With age all silvered o'er;
He might have been an Arctic Fox,
    Escaped from Greenland's shore.

But age his vigour had not tamed,
    Nor dimm'd his sparkling eye,
Which shone with an unearthly fire —
    A fire could never die.

And thus the huntsman he addressed,
    In tones distinct and clear,
Who heard as they who in a dream,
    The fairies' must hear.

351

"Huntsman," he said — a sudden thrill,
    Through all the listener ran,
To hear a creature of the wood,
    Speak like a Christian man —

"Last of my race, to me 'tis given,
    The future to unfold,
To speak the words which never yet,
    Spake fox of mortal mould.

"Then print my words upon your heart,
    And stamp them on your brain,
That you to others may impart
    My prophecy again.

"Strong life is yours in manhood's prime,
    Your cheek with heat is red,
Time has not laid his finger yet
    In earnest on your head.

"But ere your limbs are bent with age,
    And ere your locks are grey,
The sport that you have loved so well
    Shall long have passed away.

"Then think not that I speak in fear,
    Or prophesy in hate;
Too well I know the doom reserved
    For all my tribe by fate.

"Too well I know, by wisdom taught,
    The existence of my race
O'er all wide England's green domain,
    Is bound up with the Chase.

"Better in early youth and strength
    The race for life to run,
Than poisoned like the noxious rat,
    Or slain by felon gun.

"Better by wily slight and turn
    The eager hound to foil,
Than slaughtered by each baser churl,
    Who yet shall till the soil.

"For not these hills alone,
      The doom of sport shall fall;
O'er the broad face of England creeps,
      The shadow on the wall.

"The years roll on: old manners change,
      Old customs lose their sway;
New fashions rule; the grandsire's garb
      Moves ridicule today.

"The woodlands where my race has bred,
      Unto the axe shall yield;
Hedgerow and copse shall cease to shade
      The ever-widening field.

"The manly sports of England
      Shall vanish one by one;
The manly blood of England
      In weaker veins shall run.

"The furzy down, the moorland heath,
      The steam plough shall invade;
Nor park nor manor shall escape –
      Common, nor forest glade.

"Degenerate sons of manlier sires
      To lower joys shall fall;
The faithless lore of Germany,
      The gilded vice of Gaul.

"The sports of their forefathers
      To baser tastes shall yield;
The vices of the town displace,
      The pleasure of the field.

"For swiftly o'er the level shore
      The waves of progress ride;
The ancient landmarks one by one
      Shall sink beneath the tide.

"Time honoured creeds and ancient faith,
      The Altar and the Crown,
Lordship's hereditary right,
      Before that tide go down.

THE NEXT DOMINO?

"Base churls shall mock the mighty names,
  Writ on the roll of time;
Religion shall be held a jest,
  And loyalty a crime.

"No word of prayer, no hymn of praise
  Sound in the village school;
The people's education
  Utilitarian rule.

"In England's ancient pulpits
  Lay orators shall preach
New creeds, and free religions
  Self-made apostles teach.

"The peasants to their daily tasks
  In surly silence fall;
No kindly hospitalities
  In farmhouse or in hall.

"Nor harvest feast nor Christmastide
  Shall farm or manor hold:
Science alone can plenty give,
  The only god is Gold.

"The homes where love and peace should dwell
  Fierce politics shall vex,
And unsexed woman strive to prove
  Herself the coarser sex.

"Mechanics in their workshops
  Affairs of State decide;
Honour and truth – old-fashioned words –
  The noisy mob deride.

"The statesmen that should rule the realm
  Coarse demagogues displace;
The glory of a thousand years
  Shall end in foul disgrace.

"The honour of old England
  Cotton shall buy and sell,
And hardware manufacturers
  Cry 'Peace! – lo! all is well.'

"Trade shall be held the only good,
    And gain the sole device;
The stateman's maxim shall be peace,
    And peace at any price.

"Her army and her navy
    Britain shall cast aside;
Soldiers and ships are costly things,
    Defence an empty pride.

"The German and the Muscovite
    Shall rule the narrow seas;
Old England's flag shall cease to float
    In triumph on the breeze.

"The footsteps of the invader
    Then England's shore shall know,
While home-bred traitors give the hand
    To England's every foe.

"Disarmed before the foreigner,
    The knee shall humbly bend,
And yield the treasures that she lacked
    The wisdom to defend.

"But not for aye — yet once again,
    When purged by fire and sword,
The land her freedom shall regain
    To manlier thoughts restored.

"Taught wisdom by disaster,
    England shall learn to know
That trade is not the only gain
    Heaven gives to man below.

"The greed for gold departed,
    The golden calf cast down
Old England's sons again shall raise
    The Altar and the Crown."

355

Abadan, 31
Abbotabad, 73; Walker visits, 78
Abu Dhabi, 138
Aden, S. Yemen; bases, Russian,
  17; 154, 155; British to blame
  for destabilizing, 16, 29, 139–40;
  Gulf of, 11; compensated by US
  floating bases, 34; strategic
  importance, 1, 8, 9, 11, 16
Adriatic Sea, 174, 175, 186
Aegean Sea, oil, 13
Afghanistan; 43-67; airfields, 57;
  army, 48, defections from, 237;
  coup 1978, 12, 24; deportation
  of tribes possible, 239; invasion
  of, 1979, 2, 8, 9, 12, 15, 17, 266,
  reactions to, Iran, 124, US, 31-3,
  159-60, Yugoslavia, 171;
  neutralization plan, 64-5;
  Olympic boycott and, 67, 275;
  roads, 56; refugees from, 47-8,
  67, 99-100, 165-6; strategic
  repercussions, 333; Soviet
  difficulties in, 66, 270; workers
  in Iran, 11
Africa; agricultural decline, 321-6,
  329-30; British objectives in, 8;
  Horn of, 2, 126, 248-9, 266;
  liberation movements, 330;
  Russian objectives in, 68-9, 161-
  2, 181, 318, 335; Southern, 8, 9,
  293; US push into premature
  decolonization, 323

Agha Shahi, 104-5
AK-47, Russian rifles, 300
Alaska, 41
Albania, 174-5, 179
Alexander, Andrew, 195-6
Algeria, 16, 66, 247
Alireza, Ali Abdallah, Saudi
  ambassador the US, 20
Allied Mobile Force (Land) AMF
  (L), 217-8, 278
Alport, Lord, on need for Indo-Pak
  reconciliation, 71
African National Congress (ANC),
  161, 162, 214, 306, 308, 336
Amery, Julian, 25-6; on Moscow
  influence on Mugabe, 196
Amin, Hafizullah, Soviet-backed
  Afghan leader, Sept-Dec 1979;
  44, 53-5, 124, 165, 168; rump of
  followers in Cabinet executed, 67
ANC, see "African National
  Congress"
Angola; DMZ with Namibia
  negotiations, 202; economic
  chaos, 298, 325, 326; South
  Africa and, grain from, 325,
  "Operation Smokeshell", 300,
  301, 303-4, terrorism threat to,
  335; Soviet ambitions, Cuban
  involvement, 2, 8, 9, 21, 27, 29,
  162, 191, 247, 266; UNITA's
  success in south, 211, 230-4
"Anorak Express" NATO exercise,
  Norway, 1980, 217-8

appeasement, Anglo-American, 2,
  8-9, 53, 64, 207, 298
ARA, Free Iranian Liberation
  Army, 235
Arabia, the Gulf and the West, 140
Arabian Sea, 11, 12, 186; defence
  of, 277, 333
Arafat, Yassir, Chair, PLO, 98,
  251, 252
arc of crisis, 19-26, 163
Argentina, and defence of West,
  278
Arktika, Soviet icebreaker, 224
Arusha Declaration, 1967, 317
ASEAN; and Afghan crisis, 185;
  and Cambodia, 259
Asian Collective Security System,
  53
Assad, President of Syria,
  insecurity, 253
Athabaska, US, tar sands of, 41
Atlantic, Soviet threat, 220, 222,
  332
Australia, and defence of West, 278
Austria, Afghan neutrality plan
  analogy, 64-5
Awami League, Pakistan, 73
Ayet, Dr Seyed Hassan, Islamic
  Republican Party, predicts
  revolution in Pakistan, 89
Azerbaijan, 46, 123, 126, 237
Azores, 34

B52, 34, 282
Baader-Meinhof gang, 121, 131
Bab el Mandeb, 11, 17; Strait of,
  131
Backfire Bomber (TU 22), Soviet,
  39, 222, 249, 256; threat to
  Britain, 273, 284
Bacteriological weapons, 7, see
  "chemical warfare"
Bahrein, 15, 17, 34
Bakaric, Dr Vladimir, on Tito's
  attitude to Russia, 172
Bakhtiar, Dr Shahpour, 119, 126
Baltic Fleet, Soviet, 221, 225
Baltic Sea, 218, 221
Baltic Straits, 227
Baluchistan, 46, 98-9; United,
  Soviet promotion of, 63, 90, 98-
  9, 126, 167
Bandar Abas, Russian visit, 16
Bangladesh (East Pakistan),
  formation of, 12, 19, 73-4
Bani-Sadr, Abolhassan, former
  Pres. of Iran, 127
BAOR, Trident's purchase would
  forfeit, 282
Barents Sea, 222-4
Barron, John, 89
Basra, Iraq, 16
Bauer, P.T., on human
  underdevelopment, 329
Bazargan, Dr, 119

Bear at the Back Door, The,
  Walker, 81, 182, 189, 190, 193,
  214, 302
"Bear" TU 95 (20) Soviet aircraft,
  69
Beheshti, Ayatollah Mohammed,
  late Sec.-Gen, Revolutionary
  Council, Iran, 127
Benin, 330
Berbera, US naval base plan, 254
Bhutto regime, Pakistan; army
  hatred of, 72, 82; Baluchistan
  administration suppression, 99;
  conspiracy theory, Bangladesh
  split, 73-4; Commonwealth
  withdrawal, 71; India war and,
  70-6; nuclear reprocessing
  controversy and, 111-2, 117
Biko, Steve, affair of, 296
BMD (APC) Russian tank, 61
BMP, 61
BNF, 307
Borneo; lessons of, 305, Walker in,
  255
Bornholm, island of, test for
  NATO, 229
Botha, Pieter, Prime Minister,
  South Africa; reforms, 206, 294,
  306; on Zimbabwe election, 201
Botha, R.F., South African
  Minister of Foreign Affairs, on
  Muzorewa government, 194
Botswana, ANC in, 306; BNF in,
  307; dependence on South
  Africa, 295, 325; threat, 335
Brazil, and defence of the West,
  278
Brezhnev, Leonid; cartoons, 103,
  177; Cuban base firmness, 28;
  détente humbug, 245; promise of
  support for Afghan régime, 50
Brezhnev Doctrine, 171-2, 236
Britain, Great; Aden's
  abandonment, 16, 22, 129;
  Afghanistan and, 43; African
  policies, 8; air defence, 282-3;
  AMF (L) 218; anti-nuclear
  lobby in, 280, 282-3; Anglo-
  American alliance, 10; civil
  defence, 284-5, 276, 288-9;
  defence cuts, 220, 267, 289;
  ever-ready mobile force, 289;
  Far East objectives, 8; Icelandic
  cod war, strategic importance of,
  settlement, 219; independent
  nuclear weapon and, 281-3;
  MI5, Rhodesia, 313, Middle
  East objectives, 8; NATO and,
  7; oil, Norwegian shelf and, 225;
  Oman, support, 129-33;
  Pakistan and need to bring back
  into Commonwealth, 170;
  reinforcement of, US,
  Mediterranean, 33; Soviet threat
  to, 274, 280; Zimbabwe,
  responsibility for, 194-5, 203,
  207-8, 211

INDEX

Brown, H., former US Defence Sec.; 36, 38, 184, 256
Brown, Lester, on impending African disaster, 327
Brzezinski, Z., former US National Security Adviser; arc of crisis, 19; *Between Two Ages* (1970), 29-30; offers aid in Pakistan, 92, 96; refuses to see Savimbi, 231
Bulgaria; 13, 27; arms for Iranian secessionists, 123; Macedonian unrest encouragement, 172-3; Soviet task force in, 131
Burki, Jamshed, 50-1, 65
Burma, Walker served in, 78

Callaghan, James, 8, 286
Cam Ranh Bay, Soviet use, 155-6, 163
Cameron, Sir Neil, Marshal of RAF, on Soviet capability, 273-4
Camp David, 26, 95
Cambodia (Kampuchea). 9, 17, 27, 29; model for spy trials in Iran, 123; ports for USSR, 155; Vietnamese invasion of and refugees into Thailand, 182, 191, 259
Canada, 112, 218
Canary Islands, 330
Cape route, 1, 2, 153; defence of, 8, 163, 293-4; Soviet threat to, 9, 17-8, 22, 153, 192, 197, 198, 213; volume of oil through, 5, 160, 153
Caprivi, Eastern, Namibia, reversal of guerrilla infiltration, 303-5
Caribbean, 2, 19, 26
Carrington, Lord, British Foreign Sec.; defence budget cuts, 194; failure in Zimbabwe. 194-5, 203; 207, 208; PLO not a terrorist organization statement. 251, 252; promises British presence East of Suez. 160
Carter Jimmy, former US President; Afghan crisis reaction, 10; assessment of, 181; Cuba climbdown, 27, 28; defence budget 1980, 230; Indian Ocean demilitarization and, 152; Iran hostages crisis and, 20-1, 27, 121, 122, 240, rescue attempt 124; Nicaragua, failure to aid Somoza, 26; Pakistan aid cutting and, 111; South African schoolchildren killings and, 295; speech, Notre Dame University, 20, 29; statement, Yugoslavia, 173-4
Carter Doctrine, 33, 37
Caspian Sea, 118
Castro, Fidel, 231, 247
Cattara, Gulf of, 174
Chad, chaos, 327

Ceausescu and Romanian defiance of Soviet pressure 175
Cejna, Maj.-Gen., on Soviet invasion plans for Yugoslavia, 174
CENTO, Bhutto demands stronger, 112
Chamberlain, Neville, appeasement and, 8
Chaudhary, and execution of Bhutto, 72
chemical warfare, 7, 57, 58, 264
Chile, removal of Allende, 240
China, 180-8; Afghanistan arms, 61; Albania, friendship, 174; Angola, FNLA support, 233; Cambodia and, 259; India and, 165, 169; Karakorum highway and, 24; Libya and, 115; Pakistan friendship, 24, 63, 84-5, 92, 96; rearmament of, 8, 184, 187; Rhodesia, arms for, 207; US consult over Afghanistan, 83-4; USSR and, 3, 8, 85, 182, 185, 187, 272; Vietnam, punitive expedition, 8, 182; warning to West, 83-5
Chipimo, Elias, criticism of Kaunda, 314
Christianity; and Communism. Poland, 244; threat of extinction, 268, 292
Churba, Prof., and change in US South African policy, 293
Churchill, Winston; Iron Curtain metaphor, 244; on England's need to save herself, 287; on necessity of eventually fighting, 298-9; on Soviet contempt for weakness, 245
CIA, Central Intelligence Agency; KGB, contrast with, 236; Iran, failure, 20, 121, 127; Pakistan accusation, 84; predicts energy crisis in USSR. 242-3; weakness of, 239-40
CIO. Central Intelligence Organization, Rhodesia, and betrayal of National Resistance Movement, Mozambique, 313
Cold War, German fear of return to, 41
Comatos, *coup* by Nyerere, 318
Commercial Farmers' Union, Zimbabwe, cautious optimism of, 199
Commonwealth, British; monitoring group, 212; Pakistan's withdrawal, 71, 170;
Commonwealth, Socialist, and Brezhnev Doctrine, 171
Congo, Cubans in, 247, 330
Constellation, US carrier, 156, 158-9
Crossman, Richard, diaries, on Carrington, 208-9
Cruise missile, 34, 227, 262, 282

Cuba, 2, 247-50; Carter climbdown over, 27, 28, 247, 249; Cuban missile crisis, 1962, 28; Jack Jones visits, 192; proxies for Soviets in revolutionary wars. 2, 8, 21, 22, 68–9, 130, 131, 230–3, 266, 247, 305; UNITA success against, 230–3
Cyprus; Greek-Turkish feud, 13; lessons of, 305; Turkish invasion, 141; US ambassador killed, 28
Czechoslovakia, 27; analogy of 1968 invasion, 29, 54, 55, 56, 61, 64, 84, 179, 237; Soviet tank divisions in, 1976; troops in Africa, 305

Dabengwa, Dumiso, ZIPRA, 209
Daily Telegraph, The,; Peter Simple column March 1976 on pseudo-liberal deafness, 266-7; Rhodesia letter, March 1980, 200; Walker letters to, 25-6, 82, 1973 defence cuts protest, 194, October 1977 "Red Shadow Over Rhodesia", 191-2; Wall letter to, on nationalism exploitation, 206
Daoud, President, Afghanistan, 12, 24, 44
Da Nang, Russian port facilities, 155, 163
Dadoo, Yusef, Nat. Chair., CP of South Africa, 161
Dahlak archipelago, Ethiopia, Soviet bases, 155, 163
decolonization, US responsibility for premature, 323
Delta, Soviet nuclear warheaded submarines, 220-1, 225
Demirel, Süleyman. deposed Prime Minister, Turkey, 144
Deng Xiaoping, former Deputy Prime Minister, China, visit to USA, 184
Denmark, 216, 29; bases policy. 219, 20; defence cuts. 227; good home defence, 289
Desai, Morarji, denial of Indian plan to repeat 1974 nuclear explosion, 114
détente, as appeasement, 2, 64, 95, 245, 263, 267; West German commitment to, 40-1. See also "SALT"
Dhofar region, rebellion, 132
Diego Garcia; expansion of base at, 17, 34, 157-8, 159, 160, 163, 166, 254; need for joint presence, 277
Djibouti, French Foreign Legion in, 11, 15
disarmament, Western, Russian aim, 2
Downes, US carrier, 156
DTA party, Namibia, 303
Dubai, 15

357

Dubs, Adolph, US Ambassador, Kabul, assassinated 1979, 52
Dumont, René, 314
Dumont Report, on Zambia, 314-6
Durand Line; definition, 1894, 43; Soviet threat and, 9-10, 12, 45, 55; Walker visits, July 1979, 50, 51
Durozzo, Albania, 175

Ecevit, Bulent, deposed Opposition Leader, Turkey, 142-4
Economist, The, on South African reforms, 306
EEC; Afghanistan and, 57, 64; near-recognition of PLO, 252; supplies to USSR, 64; Turkey and, 147; Yugoslavia and, 173
Egypt; agricultural investment, 324; Amery on, 26; Fatah plan to oust Sadat, 253; foreign workers in Saudi Arabia, 135; return of territory to, 252; war, 1973, 6, 61-2; West and, 34, 64; USSR and, 16
8 Days—Middle East International on Pakistan bomb plot, 104
Eisenhower Doctrine, 90
El Salvador; Cuban involvement, 247; Nicaraguan troops in, 26
electronic warfare, 6
Ellenborough, 25
embargo, arms to South Africa, British, 8; arms to Turkey, US Congress, 13
Epishev, Gen. Alexei, 231
Ergashev, Maj.-Gen. Kudrat, MVD, 237
Eritrean resistance to Cuban attack, 8
Estonia, 27
Ethiopia; chaos in, 327; protests at Diego Garcia US base, 159; Cuban involvement in, 8, 9, 11, 15, 21, 27, 29, 126, 247
Europe, Western; Afghan invasion and, 10; need to emerge from phoney US umbrella, 263, 267, 281-3; South Africa vital to, 295, 332, 333; Soviet threat to, 3, 17-18, 30, 96, 221, 228, 265, 272; Turkey as cornerstone of, 147; vulnerability to disruption of oil supply, 13-15, 118, 126, 129-33
Evren Gen. Kenan, Head of State, Turkey, warning of takeover, 144, 145, 150

F 15 fighters, for Japan, 256
F 111 and cruise missile, 282
Fahd, Crown Prince, Saudi Arabia, 131
FAO, Food and Agricultural Organization, 324, 326

Farle, Rawle, US economist, on African population growth, 329
Fatah, Al, 252, 253
Fawaz, Emir, former Gov. of Mecca, 137
Finnmark, Soviet plans for, 220, 228
FNLA, Angola, National Front for the Liberation of Angola, 230-3
Fourie, Dr Brand, South African Dir. Gen. for Foreign Affairs and Information, 301, 309
Fighting General, Walker biography, 216
Flogger C, 273
Foxbat, 273
Framework for Regional Co-operation, 34
France; Afghanistan invasion reaction, 7, 36, 40, 160, 168; NATO withdrawal, 13; nuclear deterrent, 263; Pakistan attempt to buy nuclear reprocessing plant from, 108, 112, 113, 116, 117
Frelimo in Zanla, 207

Gabon, possible base for FNLA, 233
Gaddafi, Col., Islamic Marxism of, 134
Gandhi, Mrs. I., conspiracy theory over 1971 war, 73; pro-Soviet stance on Afghanistan, 164, 168
gas, natural, Iranian pipeline to USSR; Kara Sea, Russian exploitation, 225; Pakistani reliance on, 111
Gaulle, de, C., late President, France, anticipation of need for European nuclear independence, 263
Gensher, Hans D., West German Foreign Minister, 40
Germany, East; Baltic exercises, 225; Iron Curtain reality, 244-5; proxies for revolutionary wars, 2, 27, 58, 130, 249, 250, 305
Germany, West; division from East, 244-5, 335; HQ of AMF (L), 217; rearmament of, 257
Ghana; Cuban involvement, 1961, 247; disappointment of independence hopes, 321, 324, 327
Gilmour, Sir Ian, former Lord Privy Seal, 196, 197
Glagolev, Dr Igor S.; on Soviet aims, 160-2; on Mugabe's Zimbabwe election victory, 197
Glistrup, Mogens, suggestion of European surrender, 227
Golden Arrow Division (7th), Walker served in, 50, 78
Golf, Soviet nuclear armed submarine, in Baltic, 225

Golienewski, Col. Michael, on Khomeini's Moscow involvement, 122
Gorshkov, Admiral S., *Sea Power of the State,* navy as global instrument, 69, 153, 154, 181
grain to Black Africa from South Africa, 325, 331; to USSR from US cut, 33
Grand Design, Soviet, 1-2
Grange, Louie le, South African Minister of Police, on urban terrorism, 294
"Great Game", the, prevention of Russian advance to warmwater ports, 25; and Indian "Little Game", 53, 76
Greece; AMF (L) and, 218; feud over Cyprus, 13; next domino after Yugoslavia, 13; NATO and, 13
Griffith, William, and Islamic proportion of USSR, 235
Gromyko, threat to Pakistan, 99; visit to India, 1980, 166
GRU, 11, 88-9
Guam, US facilities, 163
Guatemala, 26, 247
Guinea, Guinea-Bissau, 330
Gulf; of Aden, 11, 15; of Cattara, 174; of Oman, 15, 46, 63; Persian, defence of, 277, 293-4, 333, oil, majority of world's reserves near, 2, 5, 7, 15, 126, 277, 292, Soviet threat to, 9, 11, 15, 46, 63, 126, 157, 186, 234
gunboat diplomacy, Soviet, 3
Gwadar, target for USSR, 63, 79

Haiphong, Soviet facilities, 155, 163
Haishenwei, 17
Hamid, Gen. Shahid, Minister for Information and Broadcasting, Pakistan; on danger to Moscow from Islam, 235-6; on desire for civilian government, 72; Walker meets, 82-3
Haq, Lt.-Gen. Fazale, Governor of NWFP, 50, 78-9, 99
Harriman, Gov. Averell, advice to Carter on Yugoslav posture, 173-4
Hassan, King of Morocco, target, 16
Hawkins, Air Vice-Marshal H., invites Walker to Rhodesia, October 1977, 189-90
Hayward, US Admiral T., 162
HCK, proposed US troop transporter, 34
Helms, Jesse, US Republican Senator, on Marxist Nicaraguan troops in Central America, 26
Herat, 44, 50, 55, 66
Hind helicopters, 273

high-risk period for West, 6, 35, 263, 291, 331-2
Hilton, Prof. Ronald, 120
Ho Chi Minh city, 163
Hodeida, Soviet facilities, 154
Hollingworth, Clare, on threat to Japanese oil supply, 254-6
Honduras, 247
Hong Kong, refugee problem, 183
Hormuz, Strait of; defence of, 33, 129, 130, 133; threat to, 12, 13, 17, 22, 31, 63, 249
Horn of Africa; Soviet airlift to, 248-9; strategic importance, 8, 126, 266
hostages, US, in Iran, 20-1, 27, 30, 31, 87-8, 91, 121, 122, 233-4; rescue attempt, 124, 345-7
Houphouet-Boigny, Felix, and Western model of, 329
Hoxha, Enver, and Albanian anti-Russian stance, 174
Hua Guofeng, former Prime Minister, China, visits England, 1979, 183
Huang Hua, Chinese Foreign Minister, on Malacca Strait as crux of Soviet foreign policy, 259; three nation tour Mar., 1980, 185
Humphrey, Sir Andrew, late RAF Marshal, protests at 1976 defence cuts, 267
Humphrey, Gordon J., US Senator, on arc of crisis, 163, on Gulf defence, 157
Hungary, 27, 175; minority in Yugoslavia, 172; 1956 uprising, 28-9, 56, 61, 237
Husain, Brig. Noor, Dir. Gen. of Pakistan Institute of Strategic Studies, on Indian covert role, 53, 73-6, 106
Hussain, Pres. Saddam, Iraq, 253-4
Hussain, Maj.-Gen. Saghir, conspirator in anti-Zia *coup* attempt, 1980, 102

IAEA, and supervision of research reactor, Pakistan, 107
Iceland, strategic importance, 218, 219
IMF and rescue of Turkish economy, 148
Incirlik, Turkey, US base at, 146
India; 164-70; Afghan invasion 165; Bhutto-Gandhi conspiracy, 70; China and, 169; Kashmir invasion danger, 167; "Little Game", 52-3; Nicobar Islands secret base, 159, nuclear programme, 108-117; Pakistan and, 71, 91, 97, 161, 165; Soviet arms for, 91, 97, 168-9; tank preponderance, 169; violence in, 296; Walker experience, NWF, 59-60; see also Appendix C for Pakistan conflicts

Indian Ocean, 151-163; Afghan buffer loss and Soviet outlet to, 12, 16, 17, 68, 90, 95, 118, 122; defence of, 277, 293-4, 332; Soviet fleet in, 7, 10, 152, 153, 163; UN resolution on, 1971, 151-2
Institute of Africa, USSR, 161
Institute for Policy analysis, Washington, 157
International Summary, Walker newsletter, 1976, 181
Iqbal, Mohammed, Maj.-Gen., 80
IRA, 121, 131. 251, 259-60
Iraq, 9, 13, 21, 114, 122, 143, 159, 234-5, 247, 253
Iran, 2, 9, 118-24; counter-revolution, 235; Kurds in, 143; rebuilding relations with West, 37; Russian threat, 9, 13, 24, 56, 63, 333; Shah's patrol of Strait of Hormuz, 129; trials in, 49; Western loss of influence in, 11, 122; see also "hostages", "Shah"
Ireland, Northern, 259-60, 305
Iron Curtain, 244
Islam; Alamite sect, 142; Alliance, Islamic need for, 64; Communism and, 128, 235-6, 239; guerrilla resistance and, 46-7, 49, 100, 166; Pakistan political changes and, 74, 86, 89, 166; Shia sect, Bahrain, 138, Iraq 253-4, Saudi Arabia 136, USSR, 237; Sufi sect orders, 238; Sunni sect, Bahrain, 138, Iraq, 253, Turkey 142; in USSR, 235-9
Islamabad; Soviet fomented dissidence in, 63; US embassy stormed, 27, 87-8
Islamic Alliance for the Liberation of Afghanistan, 94
Israel; Amery on. 26; analogy with Afghanistan, 61-2; loss of Iran and. 12; nuclear activity, 107, 114; offers facilities to the West, 64; Palestine mini state and danger to; 250; Saudi Arabian instability and, 136; survival of, importance, 7
Italy; Communist pressure in, 175; contribution to AMF(L)
Ivan Rogov, Soviet amphibious assault ship, 154
Ivory Coast; food aid, 325; model, 329

Jacobs, Dr Everett M., on Arafat, 1980, 252
Jalalabad, 50, 55, 66
Jamaica, Cuban advisers, 247
Jane's Fighting Ships, 160
Japan, 254-6; dependence on oil imports, 6, 7, 15, 18, 19, 118, 126, 133, 249, 277; naval expansion need, 277; US support for, 28, 30

Jenkins, Clive, 192
Jones, Gen. David, Chairman, American Joint Chiefs of Staff, pleads defence spending needs to Senate, 35
Jones, Jack, 192
Jumu, *casus belli,* 106
Jutland and Danish defences, 227, 228

Kabul, 43, 48-9, 56; massacre in, 64, fortified, 66
Kahota, alleged Pakistani nuclear enrichment plant, 113, 116
Kampuchea, See "Cambodia"
Kangai, Kumbirai, Minister of Labour and Social Welfare, Zimbabwe, 210
Kara Sea, natural gas deposits, 225
Karakorum Highway, 24, 73, 106, 184; Walker visits, 73
Kardeli, Edvard, Yugoslav, 172
Kandahar, fortified by USSR, 66
Karmal, Babrak, Afghan leader, 1979, 54, 55, 66-7, 124
Kaunda, Kenneth, President, Zambia; disastrous policies, 314-5; support for Nkomo, 201
Kashmir; *casus belli,* India/Pakistan, 71, 75, 106; danger of India/Soviet invasion, 167
Keflavik, Iceland, US monitoring from, 219
Kelly, J.B., *Arabia, the Gulf and the West,* 140
Kennedy, Pres. J.F., and Cuban crisis, 37
Kenya, 151, 254, 330; facilities for US, 162, 166; food aid, South Africa, 325; Mau Mau lessons, 305
Kenyatta, false analogy with Mugabe, 210
KGB, 192; anti-Islamic work, 239, 263; in Africa, 214, 231; in armed forces, 122 3; in Iran, 11, 120; J. Barron, 89; Pakistan, 88 9, 101; use of terror, 236-7
Khalqi party, Afghanistan, 49-50, 52, 66
Khalid, King of Saudi Arabia, 134
Khalilzad, Zalmay, on Pakistan nuclear reprocessing, 111-3
Khama, Sir Seretse, late Pres. Botswana, 307
Khan, Air Marshal Asghar, 75
Khan, Ayub, former President, Pakistan, 75-6, 112
Khan, Iqbal, Gen., 81
Khan, Brig. Mohammed Jafar, 80
Khan, Munir Ahmad, PAEC Chair., 104
Khan, Lt. Gen. Sawar, Governor of Punjab, 82
Khan, Gen. Tika, 83
Khan, Yahya, late Pres., Pakistan, 75, 99

Kharbarovsk, Soviet HQ on Pacific, 256

Khattack, Lt. Col, Ali Kuli Khan, 80

Khmer Rouge, and Cambodian refugee problem, 258

Khojak pass, Baluchistan, 80-1

Khomeini, Ayatollah; cartoon, 32; exile in France, 119, 125; pawn in Russian plan, 115-6, 118, 120, 122, 124; role in future, 128, 235; Schlesinger on, 32

Khormaksar, S. Yemen, Soviet build-up, 130

Khuzestan, 46, 126, 143, 234, 235

Khyber Pass, 10, 36, 45, 48, 90; vulnerability of, 53, 99, 101, 184

Kiev, Soviet carrier, 154

Kissinger, Henry; alleged threat to Bhutto, 112-3; on danger to Pakistan, 166-7; on weakness of US policies in Africa, 21, Iran, 27, 30

Kitson, Alec, praise of USSR, 192-3

Kitty Hawk, US carrier, 159, 234-5

Koma, Dr Kenneth, and opposition BNF in Botswana, 307

Kompong Som, probable Soviet facilities, 155

Korea 3, 28, 29; Chinese terrorists in, 185; danger from North, 256-7; DMZ, sensitive frontier, 256-7; war, history of, 257

Kosygin, Alexei, guarantee to Kabul regime, 1979, 50

Khruschev, Nikita, and Cuban missile crisis, 1962, 28; Iran, 120

Kremlin Plan, 69, 118, 154

Kurdistan, 124, 126, 142-3, 145-6

Kurds; damage to Iranian army, 235; Fatah training for, 142; mass executions of, 234

Kurile Islands, Japan, disputed with USSR, 256

Kutch, Rann of, conflict 1965, 75

Kuwait; expels Iranians, 138; Soviet ambitions, 15

Lancaster House Conference, London, 1979, 194-5, 199, 210, 213, 231

Landi Kotal; and defence of NWFP, 101; Walker visits, 1979, 51

Laos, 9, 27, 29

Latvia, 27

Lavrov, Ivan, warns Pakistan of US-Chinese conspiracy, 83-4

Lebanon, 9; Kurds in, 143; PLO train in, 142; Syrian invasion of, 162

Legum, Colin, on African instability, 321

Lenin, Soviet nuclear powered icebreaker, northern link for warships, 224

Leningrad, Soviet repair base, 224

Lesotho, 295, 325

Liberia, chaos, 327

Libya, 2, 9, 16; analogy with Iran, 124; Cuban advisers in, 247; feud with PLO, 234; finance for Pakistan nuclear technology allegation, 115, 117; international terrorism and, 121; support for S. Yemen, 29, 114

Long Beach, US missile cruiser, 159

Loram, Vice-Admiral Sir David, on Soviet naval threat, 163

Lusaka, Commonwealth Conference, 1979, 196; Non-Aligned Summit, 1970, 151

MacArthur, General Douglas, on need for victory in Korea, 28, 256

Macedonia, potential flashpoint, 174-5

Machel, Samora, President, Mozambique, 196, 207, 305

MAD, Mutual Assured Destruction, 270-1

Madagascar, 16, 151, 155

Madani, Admiral, likely leader of Iranian counter-revolution, 235

Malacca, Straits of, 17, 156; key to Soviet Far East Policy, 259

Malan, Gen. Magnus, Minister of Defence, SA; on West's danger, 162; policies against internal insurgency, 305-6

Malawi, 295, 320, 325

Malaysia; Chinese terrorists in, 185; Walker's experience in, 190

Malik, Maj.-Gen. (retd.) Tajmal Husain, plot against Zia, 102

Malik, Maj.-Gen., and "Operation Gibralter" in 1965, 75

Manekshaw, Field Marshal Sam, Walker visits, 76-7

Maputo, Soviet-controlled port, 155

Marks, John, former Chair, CP of South Africa, 161

Mashad, Iran, 56

Masira island, off Oman, as Western base, 64, 133

Massawa, Ethiopia, Soviet-held port, 155

Matine Daftary (National Democratic Front) Iran, and hope for pro-Western change, 126

Matthöfer, Hans, W. German Finance Minister, and rescue of Turkish economy, 148

Mauritius, 330

Mecca, mosque attack, 124, 134, 136, 139, 234

Medina, attempted attack on mosque, 136-7

Mediterranean; British reinforcement in, 33; "southern tier" strategy and, 8; Soviet ambitions in, 1, 2, 7

Melmukov, Gen. Levon N., KGB official in Uzbekistan, 237

Mexico, 26

MI-24 Soviet helicopter gunships, 66

MiG-17, Cuban aircraft, 130

MI-18 Soviet transport helicopters, 66

MiG-21 Soviet aircraft, 66, 130

MiG-23 new Soviet aircraft, 130, 249

Midway, US carrier, 156, 159, 234

Minsk, Soviet carrier, 154, 155, 156

Minuteman, 34

Mogharabbi, Deputy Army Chief Maj. Gen. Ahamad, KGB agent, 123

Montgomery, late Field Marshal, 208

Morocco, Soviet target, 16

Moslem Brotherhood, subversion in Saudi Arabia, 135

Moss, Robert, 142, 144

Mossadegh, Mohammed, Iranian Prime Minister, toppled 1953, 127

Mozambique; Cuban advisers, 247; chaos, 298, 301; Marxist dictatorship of, 191; grain from South Africa, 325, 326; threat to South Africa, 335; Zimbabwe and, 196

MPLA, 231-2, 305

Msika, Joseph, ZAPU, 209

Muchachi, Clement, ZAPU, 209

Mudge, Dirk, DTA party, 303

Mugabe, Robert, 194, 196, 210-11; election appeal, 196, 202, 204-5; future policies, 197-9, 201, 322-3; South Africa and, 305, 308; tribal split and, 196, 207, 209, 214; US aid expectations, 329

mujahideen, Afghan warriors, 58-9, 61, 66

Mundo, El, Venezuela, Arafat interview, 252

Munich Agreement appeasement pattern, 2, 8, 207, 298

Murmansk, ice-free Soviet naval base, 217, 219, 222-4

MVD, 237, 239

Muzorewa, Bishop, 195, 196, 207-8, 210

MX, US nuclear missile, 34

Naipaul, V.S., on African regression, 321

Namibia, 161, 162, 202, 206, 211, 230, 294, 300-6. See also "South West Africa", "SWAPO" napalm, in Afghanistan, 60

National Resistance Movement, Mozambique, betrayal of, 313

NATO; Afghanistan and, 10; "Anorak Express" exercise and, 217; British contribution to trimmed, 1973, 194; Carter doctrine, need to support, 37; China and, 180-1, 183; conventional defences, need for, 263-4; expansion of, 276, 278, 333; failures of, 267; Greek-Turkish feud and, 13; home defence part of, 288; independent nuclear weapons need, 278-84; Japan and, 256; oil dependence of, 15, 133; Soviet blitzkrieg plans and, 216-29; standardization of, 290; Turkey and, 141, 147; Walker's experience in, 59-60, 89

Nawaz, Shah, Foreign Sec., Pakistan, talks with India, 165

neutralization plan, for Afghanistan, 64

Nicaragua, 26, 30; Cuban involvement, 247; troops in El Salvador and Guatemala, 26, US aid, 310

Netherlands, and Pakistan nuclear programme, 111, 116

Neto, Dr Agostinho, late Pres., Angola, 231

"Neutron Bomb", 10, 265, 278, Appendix E

Nicholson, Brig.-Gen. J.N. memorial, 79-80

Nicobar islands, Indian naval base, 159

Niger. uranium for Pakistan allegation, 117; Nigeria; Carrington anxious to preserve good relations. 195; potential invading force against South Africa. 161-2

Nimitz US nuclear powered carrier. 33

Nixon, Richard, former US Pres.; Peking visit, 180; premature decolonization pressure, 323; refusal to allow Soviets into Cienfuegos; use of CIA in Chile, 240

Nkala, Enos, Zimbabwe Finance Minister, 213

Nkomo, Joshua, 194, 199, 208, 210, 213, 214, 230, 309, 310

North of South, 321

North-West Frontier, 12, 46; dependence on tribal protection, 100-1; India fears Pakistan from, 65; Kissinger on danger to, 167; Walker's experience, 59-60, visits, 50, 77-9; Zia vists, 99-101

Norway, 216-29; Home Guard 221, 289; oil 224-5

NOW! analysis of Carrington in Zimbabwe, 195-6, 207-8

nuclear weapons; China and, 187; India and, 108-10; Israel and, 107, 109; Japan and, 256-7; "Neutron Bomb", NATO and, 10, 278-84; Pakistan nuclear programme and, 92-3, 98, 102, 104-17; South Africa and, 107, 109; Soviet aim of pre-emptive first-strike superiority in, 3, 39, 269-71; SS20 against Japan, 256; submarines, 220, 222, 225; US desire for non-proliferation, 108-9; nuclear stockpiles in Norway accusation, 218

Nujoma, Sam, 211

Nyerere; assessment of, 317-20, 328; and Zimbabwe election result, 201

OAU, 293

O Kuh-yol, N. Korean Chief of Staff, and reunification of Korea prediction, 257-8

Observer, disillusionment with Kaunda, 314

OECD and Turkish rescue, 148

Okita, Saburo, Foreign Minister, Japan, and US pressure to increase defences, 256

Olympics, Summer 1980, boycott attempt, 33, 36, 64 , 67, 217, 275

Oman, Gulf of, Soviet aims, 63

Oman, Sultanate of, 13-15, 129-33; facilities for US, 34, 162, 166; poor relations with Arab neighbours, 133

"Operation Gibraltar" 1965, 75

"Operation Polarka" for invasion of Yugoslavia. 174

"Operation Smokeshell" South African cross-border operation. 300

Orion P.3 NATO anti-sub. aircraft. 256

Oveissi, General, former martial law supervisor, Teheran, and Kurdish rebels, 235

Owen, David, British-American proposals for Zimbabwe, 192

Oxus, river, 46, map, 55

PAC Pan-African Congress, 310, 336

PAEC Pakistan Atomic Energy Commission, 104

Pakhtoonistan source of friction, 12

Pakistan, 70-103, 164-5; Afghan refugee problem, 47-8, 67, 165; China supports, 24, 63, 84-5, 92, 96; Commonwealth withdrawal, 71, 170; Durand Line and, 43, 45; Iran's loss and, 12, 333; Khyber Pass, 36, 45, 48, 53, 90,

99, 101, 110, 184; Soviet nuclear venture, 92-3, 98, 102, 104-17; "hot pursuit" into, 66, 84, intelligence in, 88-9, 101, threat to, 9-10, 21, 45, 56, 63, 186; US offers military aid to, 33, 63, 90-1; World Bank aid, 67; Walker visits, 50, 68, 70-7, 80-3

PAL, system of Presidential control over US nuclear weapons abroad, 280

Parcham movement, Afghanistan, 66

Pasni, 63

Pathans; Durand Line and, 43; Pushtoonistan and, 63; Walker's experience of, 12

Patriotic Front, Zimbabwe, 161, 162, 192, 201, 202, 207

Pavlovsky, Gen., C-in-C of Soviet ground forces, 54

Penkovsky papers and evidence of Soviet plan for surprise attack, 261

Perim Island, 131

Pershing missile, 227, 278, 280

Persian Gulf, see "Gulf"

Peshawar; visit by Walker, July 1979, 50, 78-9; Zia visits, 100

Petropavlovsk, Soviet naval base, 163

Philippines, 20

PINSTECH, Pakistan Inst. of Nuclear Science and Technology, 105

Pirincilik, Turkey, US base, 146

PLO, Palestine Liberation Organization, 11, 98, 131-2, 142-3, 234, 250-3

Pocock, Tom, *Fighting General,* 216

Podgorny, implementation of plan to isolate S. Africa, 161

Poland, 27, 175, 225, 241, 243–4, cartoon 246

Pope John-Paul II. 244

Portugal, Azores airstrips. 34

PPP, Pakistan People's Party, not admitted in election, 85-6

Pravda warning to Norway Feb. 1980, 216

Press; role in appeasement, 53; British television, 83; Islamic bomb accusations by, 106, 109-10, 112 115-7; PLO Lebanon broadcasts; South Africa handwringing by, 295, 331-2, 297-8; Turkey, Soviet broadcasts into, 139-40; Vietnam war role, sapping US morale fibre, USSR use of to bolster morale, 62

psychiatry as punishment, USSR, 241

psychological war, need for Western use of, 230, 232, 239, 336-7

Pushtoonistan, Soviet promotion of, 63

Qatar, Soviet ambitions, 15
Quetta, Walker visits, 80-1

race; in South Africa, 296, 334, 335; in US, 123, 296, 335; in USSR, 235-7
Rapid Deployment Force, US, 34, 35
Rashid, Sheik bin Said al Muktum, Prime Minister of UAE, 139
Reader's Digest, 235
Reagan, Ronald, foreign policy on South Africa proposals, 293
Red Army, Japan, 121, 131
Red Brigades, Italy, training in South Yemen, 131
Red Sea; "southern tier" strategy and, 8; USSR and, 11, 15, 17, 29
Red Star, christening of "Iron Lady", 268
refugees; Afghan, into Pakistan, 67, 81, 99-100, 107, 166; Cambodian, into Thailand, 258; Chinese, into Hong Kong, 183
Reunion, 330
Rhodesia, see "Zimbabwe"
Roberto, Holden, 232-3
Rogers, Gen. Bernard, Supreme NATO Commander, Europe, 227, on need for chemical weapons, 264
Rumania, 13, 27, 56

Sadat, President Anwar, Egypt, and national sensitivity, 64
Sahara, Spanish, 330
Said, Sultan Qaboos bin, ruler of Oman, 132
SALT II, 30, 33, 36, 40, 64, 95, 141, 161, 183, 244, 245, 254, 263
SAM-7 anti-aircraft missiles; for mujahideen, 66; in SWAPO, 300, 335
Sandinistas, Nicaragua, 26, 30, 310
Santos, Jose Eduardo, dos, President Angola, 231
Sathe, Ramehandra Daltatrya, Foreign Sec., India, 165, on Chinese threat, 167
Saudi Arabia; 2,15, 134-7, 151; army of, 135, 136; foreign workers, 134-5; oil supplies, 15; royal family of, decline in prestige, 124, 134, 136, 139; Soviet threat perception, 135, US ally, but critical, 15, 20, 21, 130
SAVAK, Iranian secret police, UN commissioners led on tour of prison, 127-8
Savimbi, Jonas, UNITA leader, 211, 231-3

Savkin, V. Ye, and Sidorenko, A.S., on Soviet strategic superiority, 269-71
Scargill, Arthur, Yorkshire miners' leader, 286-7
Schlesinger, James, former US Energy Sec., 173; on need for firm action in Gulf, 19-20
Schreiner, US ambassador, Seoul, 257
Selous scouts, Walker observes, 191, 193
Senegal, possible base for FNLA, 233
Seoul, vulnerability, 257
Severomorsk, 222
Seycheiles, presence of Russian Navy, 16, 155; Nyerere helps topple government, 318
Shepilov, Alexei, Chief Commissar, visits Afghanistan 1979, 54
Shah, of Iran; "crimes" UN investigation, 127-8; gendarme role, 118; overthrow, 11, 125, 126, 130, Western culpability in, 16, 28, 30, 119-20, 122, 125, 126, 139
Shelepin, visit to Britain, 192
Sherwell, Christopher, journalist, and trespass accusations, Islamic bomb story, 110
Shrimsley, Anthony, on Carrington's failure, 207
Sibenik, Yugoslavia, 174
Sibir, Soviet nuclear-powered icebreaker, 224
Sihanouk, Prince, 259
Silundika, George, ZAPU, 209
Simferopol, USSR, 238
Simonstown agreement, for base in South Africa, abrogated 8, 22, 160; need to reactivate, 333
Sinop, Turkey, US listening station, 146
Sithole, Rev. Ndabaningi, ZANU, accuses Mugabe of organising assassination attempt, 309
Soames, Lord, 199, and Commonwealth Monitoring Group, Zimbabwe, 212
Society for International Development, SID, on arms spending by poor nations, 324
Smith, Ian, Rhodesian former leader, 190, 195, 199, 208; on British betrayal, 200
Socotra, Soviet naval facilities, 154, 155
Solzhenitsyn, Alexander, on West's blindness, 244, 263, 266
Somalia, 8, 11, 34, 155, 166, 254
Somoza, President, Nicaragua, fall of, 26, 30
South Africa, 293-9; ANC in, 306; arms embargo, 8; defences, 215, 293, 303, 332; democracy and, 332; grain to Black Africa, lever, 325, 331; homelands 306;

Mozambique and, 196, 325; nuclear capacity, 293, 336; oil, minerals, routes for, vital to West, 1-2, 7, 162, 181, 197, 292; Press handwringing, 295, 331-2; reforms, 206, 294, 297-8; Simonstown agreement, 8, 22, 160; Soviet-inspired terrorist threat to, 211, 214, 230, 332-6, 317; Taiwan ally, 299, 326; UN sanctions threat, 124, 181, 294, 298; uranium enrichment, 107; US relations change, 293-4, 333; Zimbabwe whites' refuge preference, 311-2; see also "South-West Africa"
South Africa; War, Revolution or Peace?, 295
South China Sea, 17, 163
South-West Africa (Namibia), 206, 211, 300-6; Angolan training camps for, 230; DMZ negotiations, 202; danger of UN sanctions following stalemate, 294
"southern tier" strategy, Middle East, 8
space, Soviet aims in, 3
Spain, need to involve in West's defence, 278
Special Air Service, SAS, Iranian embassy siege rescue, 260
SPG, Special Patrol Group, vilification campaign, 286
Spitsbergen, Soviet coal mines, 224
Split, 174
Spring, Martin, on East Caprivi success, 303-5
SR-71s, US surveillance planes, 249
SS20, Soviet missile, 39-40, 256, 273, 278-9
Steinlaub, US General, dismissed for opposing US rundown in Korea, 257
Stoltenberg, Thorvald, Minister of Defence, Norway, 217
Subic Bay, Philippines, US base, 156, 158
Sudan, 16, 34; agricultural investment, 324
Suez Canal, 7
Sunday Telegraph, 240
supertankers; Japan and, 277; unable to dock in US, 26
surveillance; US, 7, 13, 141, 146, 219, 220; Soviet "trawler" fleets, 153
SWAPO 161, 162, 211, 300-6; threat to South Africa, 335
Switzerland, home defences, 276
Swaziland; ANC in, 306; impending death of King Sobhuza, 307; relations with South Africa, 295, 307, 325
Symington Amendment, USA, freezing arms sales and aid to Pakistan, 1979, 91, 97

Syria; invasion of Lebanon, 162; Israeli nuclear threat, 114; Kurds in, 143; Soviet influence, 9, 21, 253; training of Turkish guerrillas, 142; union with Libya 10 Sep. 1980, 253; violence, 253

T-54, Soviet tank, 46
T-62, Soviet tank, 46, 256
T-71, Soviet tank, 265
Tadzhiks in USSR, 237
Taiwan, trade, defence, technology relations with South Africa, 299, 336
Tanzania, 199; socialist chaos in, 298, 317-20, 326, 327, 328, 335
Tarakki, Nur Mohammad, Afghan, Soviet protegé, coup April 1978, 12, 44, 46, 47-51, 52, execution 124
Tartars, Crimean national rights demands, 238-9
Tass, Soviet news agency, wrong expectations in Zimbabwe elections, 206
Tehran, US embassy hostages from, 27, 31, 121
Tekere, Edgar, former Minister of Manpower Planning and Development, Zimbabwe, threat to white representation and Constitution, 213
Termez, port of Oxus river, preparations 1967 for Afghan invasion, 46
terrorism; black nationalist, South Africa, 230, 293, 294, 335-6; international, 121; Ireland, 251, 259-60; training for, South Yemen, 131
Thailand, 258-9
Thatcher, Mrs Margaret, Prime Minister, 203; "Iron Lady" christening, 268-9; Ireland and, 260; Olympic games boycott 275; Rhodesia policy and use of Carrington, 194, 208, 313; speeches; 19 Jan. 1976, "Iron Lady", 268; 31 July 1976, "second warning", 269; 18 Oct. 1979, Luxembourg, 269, 274; trades union militancy and campaign against, 285, 287
Thompson, Brigadier, on need for home defence, 288
Three Mile Island, plant accident, and anti-nuclear lobby, 111
Tibet, 167, 185
Times, The, letters to; Iran and Nazi criminals, 120; Jacobs, March 1980 on Yassir Arafat, 252; Walker letters: June 1977, on Rhodesian cross-border raid, 193, August 1977, on "Neutron Bomb", 263, March 1980, on Backfire bomber, 283

Ting Wen-pin, Counsellor, Chinese Embassy, London; Walker meetings with, 12 Feb. 1976, 24 March 1976, 8 June 1977, 17 April 1978, 180-2
Tinsulanonda, Gen. Prem, Prime Minister of Thailand, 259
Tito, Josef Broz, late Pres. of Yugoslavia, 171-4, 176-7, 179
Tor Kham, visit by Walker, 1979, 50-1
Trident, US nuclear-armed sub., 221, 282
Truman Doctrine, and Turkey, 147
Tsushima Straits, Soviet warning flotilla through, 256
TU-16, Soviet bomber, 154
TU-22, see "Backfire"
Tudeh, Iranian CP, 11, 122, 124
Tunisia, 16, 324
Turkestan, Eastern, Soviet ambitions for, 186
Turkey, 141-50; Aegean oil and, 13; AMF(L) in, 218; non-aligned tendency, 13; facilities offer to West, 64; Soviet threat to, 2, 9, 12, 13, 21

U-2 reconnaissance over Turkey, 141
Umm Qasr, 16, 17, 154, 158, 254
university of revolution, Western, need for, 250
unemployment, W. Europe, solution by arms production, 6
UNITA, anti-Marxist guerrillas, southern Angola, 211, 231-3, 305
Uganda, 191, 301, 328; Nyerere and, 318
ujaamas, Tanzania, and failure of African socialism, 319, 328
United Arab Emirates, UAE, 15, 138-40; Islamic bomb scandal and, 106; PLO in, 132
United Nations, UN; Afghan invasion and, 33, 317-9, 99-100; Angolan recognition, 233; Cuban proxy wars, need to debate issue in, 249-50; India bitterness over, in Kashmir, 168; Indian Ocean and, 151-2; Iranian hostages debate 123, sanctions call 31, 124; Namibia DMZ and, 202, 206;Pakistan help for Afghan refugees protest, 99-100, 329; Soviet domination of, 298; SWAPO raids into Angola and, 300; Tartars appeal to, 238; South African sanctions call, 124, 181, 294, 296, 298
United States; aid, 310, 323, 329; arc of crisis perception, 19; blocks Pakistan's nuclear reprocessing purchases, 108; CIA weakness, 239-40;

decolonization, pressure for, 323; defence capability overtaken, 37-9, 262; Iran, failure to support Shah, 20, 30, 139, hostage crisis, 27, 30; Kurdish involvement ends, 146; Nicaraguan failure, 26, 30; Norwegian weapons stockpile accusation, 217; nuclear blackmail and, 228-9, 283; race in, 123; South Africa and, 293-4, 297; Vietnam watershed, 22; see also "Carter", "Nixon", "Kissinger", "Schlesinger".
USSR; Africa, Soviet troops in, 305; capability for destruction by 1982, 271; Cape stranglehold plan, 9, 16, 22, 197, 213, 293-4, 332; economic weakness of, 241-4, energy crisis in, 242-3; European blitzkrieg plan, 221-2, 226, 265, 272; Islamic minorities in, 235-8; Master Plan, 11-18; merchant fleet, 152-3; military capabilities, 273; naval build-up, 131, 163, navy 218-222; nuclear predominance, 3, 38, 39, 257; proxies in revolutionary wars, 2, 21, 68-9, 247, 266, 333; tactical beliefs, 269-71; warmwater port, ambitions for, 13, 63, 118, 122, 132, 186, 333, 335; see also entries under individual countries for threat to, and map, 292
Uzbekistan, USSR, 237

Vance, Cyrus, former Sec. of State, USA; admits knowledge of nuclear-associated building in Cuba, 28; and Pakistan's nuclear programme, 108-9
Venezuela, 26
Vietnam, 2, 9; analogy with Afghanistan, 62, Rhodesia, 195; Chinese punitive invasion of, 1979, 8, 182; expansionism of, 8; Soviet aid, Cuban advisers for, 17, 182, 247; Soviet facilities in, 155; US humiliation in, 22, 29, 98, 182, 233-4, 302
Virgin Islands, 26
Visakapatnam, 154
Vladivostok, base for Pacific fleet, threat to Western sea routes, 156
Vorster, John, former Prime Minister, South Africa, and resistance to US pressure for universal suffrage, 297

Wall, Patrick, 206
Walker, Sir Walter; addresses Commons meeting, 192; Bear at the Back Door, 81, 182, 189, 190, 193, 214, 302, 357; Burma experience, 78; letters to Daily Telegraph, 25-6, 82; Times, June

1977, on Rhodesian cross-border raids, 193, August 1977 on "Neutron Bomb", 263, March 1980 on Backfire bomber, 283; meets Gen. Shahid Hamid, 82, 83, Gen. Zia ul-Haq, 82-3, Maj. Gen. Mohammed Iqbal, 80-1; Gen. Iqbal Khan, 81, Brig. Mohammad Jafar Khan, 80, Lt.-Gen. Sawar Khan, 82, Gen. Shahid Hamid, 82, 83, Ting Wen-pin, 180–2, Walls, Gen. Peter, 110; *Fighting General* biog. of., 216; NATO experience, 59-60, 89; 216; newsletter 1976, 181; Pathan campaigns, NWF, 12; visits Baluchistan, 80, Karakorum Highway, 78, India, 76-7, NWFP, 50, 70-6, 77-80; Peshawar, 50, 78-9, South Africa, June 1978, 293, 302, Zimbabwe-Rhodesia, Oct. 1977, 189-90, May 1978, 192;

Walls, Lieut. Gen. Peter, former C-in-C. Rhodesian forces; stays on to integrate guerrillas into Rhodesian forces, 205, 211; protests at election conduct, predicts civil war, 314; Walker visits, 190

Walton, Sir Cussack, and Khyber railway, 51

warmwater port, and Soviet ambitions in Arabian Sea, 186, 333, Iran, 118, 122, 132, 335, Pakistan, 12, 63, 333

Warsaw Pact, ground forces concentrations, 6; see also individual members

Weisner, Admiral Maurice, on Soviet naval threat, 163

Wellington, Duke of, and the "Great Game", 25

WEU, Western European Union, and Soviet chemical warfare capability, 264

White Sea, USSR, 224

Whitelaw, William, Home Sec., and refusal to tolerate terrorism, 260

Will, George F., on US decline, 28

Windward and Leeward Islands, 26

World Bank; aid to Pakistan, 66 Turkey, 148

Worldwatch and predictions of African catastrophe, 326, 327

Worsthorne, Peregrine, on lack of subtlety in Carter's handling of hostage crisis, 240

Wynne, Greville and Penkovsky papers, 261

XM-1, US main battle tank, 35

Yemen, South; anti-Islamic policies, 238; Cubans in, 232; protests at Diego Garcia base, 159; Soviet influence in, 2, 9, 11, 12, 15, 27, 29, 129-30

Yemen, North; invasion of, Feb. 1979, 130; Soviet threat to, 15, 129-30

Yom Kippur war, 61, 284

Young, Andrew, 208

Yugoslavia, 171-9; defences, 175-6; economy, 173, 177; non-alignment, 179; regionalism, 177; Soviet threat to, 6, 56, 171

Yuzbasyov, Maj. Gen. Marius A., KGB, Azerbaijan, 237

Zaid bin Sultan al Nahyan, Sheik, of Abu Dhabi, Pres. of UAE, 139

Zaire, 16, 230, 233, 325

Zambia 295, 298, 303-4, 305, 314-16, 325, 326, threat to South Africa, 335

Zanla, 204, 207

Zanu, 196, 199, 204, 309; Zanu(PF), 310

Zanzibar, 16

Zapu, 201; Cabinet posts, Zimbabwe, 209; friction with Zanu, 209-10

Zeeland, 228

Zhang Wenjin, Chinese, Deputy Foreign Minister, visits US, 184

Zia ul-Haq, Gen., President, Pakistan, 95-8; Afghan Foreign Minister, meets 1979, 52; Afghan refugee problem, exploitation of, 166; Bhutto, refuses to pardon, 72; Commonwealth, desire to re-join, 71; *coup* attempt, March 1980, 102; Islamic codes, reinstates, 86; Islamic bomb denial, June 1979, 104; PPP, refuses access to elections, 85-6, press censorship and, 86-7; US aid, difficulties in accepting, 90-4, 116; US embassy Islamabad storming, slow response to 87-8; warning to West, 53

Zimbabwe-Rhodesia, 308-13; agriculture, 310-11; aid, 310, 325, 335; British betrayal, whites' feeling, 251, 199-200, 208; constitution, new, 200-1; forces, 191; election, 203-5, 312-3; South Africa and, 295, 305; strategic springboard, 192, 308; tensions, 213, 308-12; US and, 161, 191-2, 310; war in, 2, 27, 204; white flight, 311-2

Zipra, 209, 305

Zvogobo, Eddison, 209